MW00527024

The Conciliarist Tradition

The Conciliarist Tradition

*Constitutionalism in the
Catholic Church 1300–1870*

FRANCIS OAKLEY

OXFORD
UNIVERSITY PRESS

OXFORD
UNIVERSITY PRESS

Great Clarendon Street, Oxford OX2 6DP

Oxford University Press is a department of the University of Oxford.
It furthers the University's objective of excellence in research, scholarship,
and education by publishing worldwide in

Oxford New York

Auckland Bangkok Buenos Aires Cape Town Chennai
Dar es Salaam Delhi Hong Kong Istanbul Karachi Kolkata
Kuala Lumpur Madrid Melbourne Mexico City Mumbai Nairobi
São Paulo Shanghai Taipei Tokyo Toronto

Oxford is a registered trade mark of Oxford University Press
in the UK and in certain other countries

Published in the United States
by Oxford University Press Inc., New York

British Library Cataloguing in Publication Data
Data available

Library of Congress Cataloging in Publication Data
Data available

ISBN 978-0-19-926528-2 (Hbk.)   978-0-19-954124-9 (Pbk.)

1 3 5 7 9 10 8 6 4 2

Typeset by Laserwords Private Limited, Chennai, India.
Printed in Great Britain
by
Biddles Ltd.,
King's Lynn, Nafolk

To

LOL *and* SUZANNE

Preface

IN THIS BOOK, which comes inadvertently to press at a moment of deepening crisis in the authority structures of the Western, Latin, or Roman Catholic Church, it is my purpose to draw out from the historiographic shadows and return to the bright lights of centre stage the robust if persistently underacknowledged tradition of constitutionalist thinking and aspiration which for long centuries tugged uneasily at the adamantly monarchical consciousness of that ancient and hallowed institution. By the last years of the nineteenth century, when it was finally consigned to oblivion by the First Vatican Council's twin definitions of papal jurisdictional primacy and doctrinal infallibility, that tradition had endured already for more than half a millennium. And there still remain fugitive straws in the wind suggesting that not even the subsequent century and more of official disapprobation and theological disregard has succeeded entirely in negating the long preceding centuries of stubborn (though largely forgotten) affirmation.

If the deepest roots of this Catholic constitutionalist tradition were engaged in patristic soil, in the communitarian nature of the ancient Church and its essentially conciliar mode of governance, it was to draw its legal clothing and the lineaments of its constitutional precision from the commentaries of the medieval canon lawyers. And it was to encounter its shaping moment in the great institutional crisis which the disputed papal election of 1378 and the subsequent persistence of rival lines of claimants to the papal office eventually engendered. Crystallized now in the form of what came later to be known as the conciliar theory, it gave powerful voice to the essentially constitutionalist conviction that side by side with the institution of papal monarchy (and in intimate connection with it) it was necessary to give the Church's communal and corporate dimension more prominent and more regular institutional expression. Stipulating that the ultimate focus of authority resided in the universal Church itself rather than its papal head, it insisted that under certain circumstances the general council representing that church—acting even apart from or in opposition to the pope—could exercise a governmental authority superior to his. By so doing, it could impose constitutional limits on the exercise of his prerogatives, stand, if need be, in judgement over his actions and, at last resort, even move to depose him.

It was by acting on such principles, by deposing the rival papal claimants and electing a new pope whose legitimacy came to be universally accepted, that the Council of Constance (1414–18) succeeded in putting an end to the schism. But that whole conciliarist episode it has been customary to portray, at least since Vatican I, as nothing more than an unfortunate and revolutionary moment in the ongoing life of the Church, a turn of events radical in its origins and rapid in its demise. And that (mounting historical evidence to the contrary) has served to conceal from us the prominence, tenacity, wide geographical spread, and essential continuity of the tradition of conciliarist constitutionalism which, having found historic expression at Constance, contrived for centuries to come to compete stubbornly for the allegiance of Catholics with the high papalist or ultramontane vision of things entrenched so powerfully in Italy and especially so at Rome. If the latter is so much more familiar to us today, it is because it was destined after 1870 to become identified with Roman Catholic orthodoxy itself. And it is only, one cannot help suspecting, our very familiarity with that high papalist outcome that has contrived to persuade us of the necessity of the process.

My own engagement with the conciliarist tradition is itself of long standing. The earlier part of the book builds upon my previous work on the subject; the latter part extends it forward into the more recent past. It would, then, make lengthy and (I fear) tedious reading if I were to try to acknowledge individually all the multiple obligations I have incurred in the course of pursuing that work. But some debts are outstanding. For the sabbatical support and research awards and appointments that afforded me the opportunity to spend much-needed time in a whole series of European and American research libraries, I must thank the President and Trustees of Williams College, the American Council of Learned Societies, the National Endowment for the Humanities, the Institute for Advanced Study, Princeton, The National Humanities Center, North Carolina, the Woodrow Wilson International Center for Scholars and the Folger Shakespeare Library, both in Washington DC. For their careful reading of the manuscript and generous extension of help, criticism, and advice, I must thank my friends Brian Tierney of Cornell University and James Heft of the University of Dayton, as well as the anonymous readers for the Oxford University Press. For their characteristically prompt and efficient work in preparing the manuscript for the press, I must once again thank

Donna Chenail and her staff in the faculty secretarial office at Williams College. For permission to incorporate with minor changes into Chapter 3 some material drawn from my 'Constance, Basel, and the Two Pisas: the Conciliarist Legacy in Sixteenth and Seventeenth Century England', *Annuarium Historiae Conciliorum*, 26/1 (1994), 1–32, I must thank Verlag Ferdinand Schöningh, Paderborn.

For similar permission to incorporate in Chapter 6, again with minor changes, material drawn from my '"Anxieties of Influence": Skinner, Figgis, Conciliarism and Early Modern Constitutionalism', *Past and Present: A Journey of Historical Studies*, 151 (May, 1996), 60–110, I must thank The Past and Present Society, Oxford, holder of the World Copyright of that article. For the kindly prompting that led me to return to work on the conciliarist tradition at a moment when other interests were tugging me in a different direction, I must thank the late Heiko Oberman, to whom late medieval and early modern studies owe so very much. Again, I must thank the Vice Chancellor of Oxford University and the other members of the Berlin selection committee for the invitation to return to Oxford in the Michaelmas Term of 1999 as the Sir Isaiah Berlin Visiting Professor in the History of Ideas. And I must similarly thank Sir Keith Thomas and his colleagues at Corpus Christi College for inviting me into their midst as a Visiting Fellow, as well as those other colleagues and friends at Oxford who extended themselves to make me welcome. In revised and extended form, the Berlin Lectures which I delivered during that term constitute the core of the book. Its overall format and specific texture, then, have in many ways been determined by its genesis in the lecture mode. The footnotes I have striven (though with uneven success) to limit in both number and length. With the exception of works printed in collective volumes, the citations in those footnotes are given in abbreviated form. Full titles and locations may be found in the Bibliography.

Finally, as is fitting for a work that engages so long-lived a phenomenon as conciliarist constitutionalism, I wish with this book to honour the oldest, most enduring, and most cherished of my friendships, one rooted so deeply in school and college days as to have survived unscathed the separation of continents and the hostility of time.

F.O.

Williamstown, Massachusetts
December 2002

Contents

Prologue: Memory, Authority, and Oblivion

> But what is forgetfulness but a privation of memory? How then is that present for me to remember, which when it is so, I cannot remember?
>
> (St Augustine[1])

> Collective memory . . . is a current of continuous thought whose continuity is not at all artificial, for it retains from the past what still lives or is capable of living in the consciousness of groups keeping the memory alive. By definition it does not exceed the boundaries of the group.
>
> (Maurice Halbwachs[2])

> The mirror is a poor metaphor of the public memory. . . . When we look closely at the construction of past time, we find the process has very little to do with the past at all and everything to do with the present. Institutions create shadowed places in which nothing can be seen and no questions asked. They make other areas show finely discriminating detail, which is closely scrutinized and ordered.
>
> (Mary Douglas[3])

> The past as it was experienced, not just the past as it has subsequently been used, is a moment of memory we should strive to recover.
>
> (Patrick J. Hutton[4])

A millennium and more after St Augustine's celebrated musings on the topic, my concern in this book is very much with the matter of remembering and forgetting. In particular, it is with what I have come to regard,

---

[1] St Augustine, *Confessiones* 10.16.2, 116–17.

[2] M. Halbwachs, *The Collective Memory*, tr. F. J. Ditter, jun., and V. Y. Ditter (New York: Harper & Row, 1980), 80.

[3] M. Douglas, *How Institutions Think* (Syracuse, NY: Syracuse University Press, 1986), 69–70.

[4] P. H. Hutton, *History as an Art of Memory* (Hanover: University Press of New England, 1993).

over the years, as a quite startling instance of institutional (and institutionally sponsored) forgetting. Such things have long since attracted the attention of social scientists, and, of recent years, adamantly atheoretical though historians can often be, they themselves have not hesitated to turn to the social sciences for useful insights apt to help them in their own effort to chart the rocks and shoals that conspire to render the transit from present to past so persistently challenging and frequently so very treacherous.

For those concerned with the ways in which institutional histories come to be shaped, with the complex processes whereby some areas come persistently to be highlighted and others, as Mary Douglas notes, consigned to the shadows, one or two of those insights have proved to be particularly pertinent. The sober recognition, for example, of the degree to which the collective historical remembering of great events and heroes past is as much a work of construction, driven by present preoccupations and needs, as it is one of simple retrieval.[5] Or the further recognition of the fact that, socially shaped as it is, and if it is indeed to endure, 'collective memory' requires 'the support of a group delimited in space and time'.[6] The perception also that for its effective construction the collective memory presupposes, not simply remembering, but a measure also of socially or institutionally sponsored forgetting.[7] All such essentially 'constructivist' intuitions need somehow to be disciplined, of course, by the historian's instinctive but countervailing sense that collective memory must be something more than a work of presentist construction, that it must necessarily convey elements of persistence and continuity stubbornly enduring from a past that is in some measure resistant to later efforts at proleptic reshaping.[8]

---

[5] One telling and highly pertinent illustration of this is the role played in the medieval centuries of what have since come to be known as the False or Pseudo-Isidorean Decretals. Produced in 9th-cent. France, they were intended at their inception to 'make use of the acknowleged authority of Rome in order to break the much closer and more dangerous authority of the [recently restored] metropolitans' over the bishops. In subsequent centuries, however, they came to be used to provide a forceful and seemingly historical warrant for the more vigorous extension of papal jurisdictional authority over the universal Church. See Klaus Schatz, *Papal Primacy*, tr. J. A. Otto and L. M. Maloney (Collegeville, Minn., Liturgical Press, 1996), 68–71.

[6] Halbwachs, *Collective Memory*, 84.

[7] Forgetting amounting at times to nothing less than 'structural amnesia'. Thus Douglas, *Institutions*, 70.

[8] Lewis A. Coser, 'Introduction: Maurice Halbwachs 1877–1945 ', in Halbwachs, *Collective Memory*, 26–7. This appears to be what Hutton also has in mind when he speaks (*History*, p. xvi) of 'the power of influence the past possesses in its own right, apart from our conscious efforts to reconstruct it'.

While much of the initial concern of historians with such issues focused on the historiography of the nation state,[9] it has since begun to encompass other and broader horizons, among them those afforded by the medieval centuries.[10] And it is from those centuries that I propose to take my own start, focusing on the Western, Latin, or (in the modern era) *Roman* Catholic Church, an institution which has exemplified in quintessential fashion the twofold process of refashioning while preserving the past. My concern will be with matters ecclesiological, with that Church's systematic reflection on its own nature and structures, and, more particularly, with an arresting case of ecclesiological forgetting, the creation of a 'shadowed place in which nothing can be seen'.[11] Just how arresting a case of forgetting it will be easier to assess if we set it against a related case of institutional remembering. It is with that contrasting case of remembering, then, that I should properly begin.

ANCIENT MEMORIES: POPES, BISHOPS, AND 'THE BOND
OF MUTUAL CONCORD'

However important its foundations in earlier centuries (and they were, confessedly, *very* important), we should acknowledge the fact that the papacy as we know it today, an essentially monarchical power possessed of sovereign authority over the entire Roman Catholic Church worldwide, is very much the product of the second thousand years of Christian history. Indeed, in the degree to which, via effectively centralized governmental agencies, mechanisms, procedures, and instrumentalities of communication, it is actually able on a day-to-day basis to impose its sovereign will on the provincial Churches of Roman Catholic Christendom, the papacy is the achievement, more precisely, of the past two hundred years at most, and may be said to have reached the peak of its prestige and the apex of its effective power within the Church probably no earlier than the pontificate of Pius XII (1939–58).[12]

[9] Here the works of Philippe Ariès, Maurice Agullion, François Furet, and Pierre Nora come especially to mind. See Hutton, *History*, 1–22, 91–105, 143–53.
[10] Thus, e.g. J. Coleman, *Ancient and Medieval Memories* (Cambridge: CUP, 1992); G. M. Spiegel, *Romancing the Past* (Berkeley: University of California Press, 1993); P. J. Geary, *Phantoms of Remembrance* (Princeton: Princeton University Press, 1994).
[11] Douglas, *Institutions*, 69–70.
[12] Given the tight and more or less universal control the papacy has come to exercise over episcopal appointments, it is well to be reminded that '[u]ntil roughly 1800, Rome's intervention in the appointment of bishops in dioceses outside the Papal States was rare',

The primacy of jurisdiction to which popes laid intermittent claims during the early Middle Ages and which, from the thirteenth century onwards they were to succeed in vindicating within the orbit, at least, of Latin Christendom, is not, then, to be read back into the primacy of honour accorded to them among the several patriarchates of Christian antiquity. Still less is it to be confused with the coordinating role that the Roman see appears to have played as a 'unifying center of communion' (*Einheitszentrum der Communio*)[13] in a universal Church conceived, above all, as a family of local episcopal Churches, participants alike in a sacramentally based community of faith uniting believers with their bishop in given local Churches and, beyond that, uniting all the local Churches of the Christian world one with another. The characteristic institutional expression of those bonds of communion was that complex pattern of collaborative episcopal governance and synodal activity which stands out as so marked a feature of the Church's earliest centuries. And that essentially conciliar mode of governance was to find its culmination at the level of the universal Church in the great succession of ecumenical councils stretching from Nicaea I (325) to Nicaea II (787). Only in the second half of the eleventh century, indeed, with their vigorous leadership first of the Gregorian reform and, later, of the crusading movement, did the popes begin to undertake a more than intermittent exercise of judicial authority and of truly governmental power over the entire universal Church. Only in the thirteenth century, with the rapid expansion of that governmental role, did they come to be viewed as credible claimants to the *plenitudo potestatis*, the fullness of jurisdictional authority over that Church. And only with that development did they begin to emerge in no small measure as sacral monarchs, true medieval successors of the erstwhile Roman emperors, claiming many of the attributes of those emperors and using some of their titles, surrounded by their ceremonies, wearing their regalia, exploiting their laws, and eventually showing little hesitation about invoking the most secular of sanctions against those powers that seemed seriously to threaten their imperial position.[14]

---

accounting for no more than approximately 4–5% of the total episcopate in the Latin Church—thus John R. Quinn, in P. Zagano and T. W. Tilley, eds., *The Exercise of the Primacy* (New York: Crossroad, 1998), 21. Cf. Quinn, *The Reform of the Papacy* (New York: Crossroad, 1999), 117–39.

[13] This is the formula deployed by Stephen Otto Horn, 'Das Verhältnis von Primat und Episkopat in ersten Jahrtausend: Eine Geschichtlich-Theologische Synthese', in *Il primato del successore di Pietro* (Vatican City: Libreria Editrice Vaticana, 1998), 193–213 (at 205).

[14] For an extreme though not unprecedented list of papal prerogatives drawn up by an anonymous papalist author in the pamphlet known as the *Determinatio compendiosa* (1342),

later MA → claims on temporal jurisdictional authority

By the later Middle Ages, however forcefully reiterated in theory they might still be, papal claims to any essentially *temporal* jurisdictional authority superior to that of emperors and kings were already teetering in practice on the brink of bankruptcy. Far more significant for the long haul—and certainly for developments in the twentieth and twenty-first centuries—were papal claims to a jurisdictional superiority in relation specifically to the internal governance of the universal Church itself. By that time, that Church had come to be distinguished from the secular states within the boundaries of which it functioned as a separate entity, juridically self-sufficient and governmentally autonomous, a 'perfect society' to which the terms 'Christian commonwealth', 'ecclesiastical commonwealth', 'ecclesiastical polity', 'ecclesiastical kingdom', had come to be applied. All of that witnessed eloquently to the fact that, over the course of the centuries preceding, a profound change had taken place in the typical understanding of the notion of ecclesiastical office itself. By the twelfth century, the New Testament understanding of that office as ministerial and grounded in love of others had long since been nudged to one side, or at least transformed, by a very different mode of understanding which found expression in an essentially political vocabulary drawn from the Roman law and connoting the type of relationship prevailing in the world at large between rulers and those ruled. Already by the seventh century the word *jurisdictio* had been taken into canonistic usage from the civil law, and over the following centuries it had been used intermittently to denote the general administrative activity of ecclesiastical government. By the twelfth century, with the immense growth of papal governmental activity and the flowering of legal studies both civil and canonistic, the process of juridification had become so marked as to evoke from St Bernard of Clairvaux his famous admonition to Pope Eugenius III (1145–53) to the effect that the pope should properly be the successor of Peter, not of Constantine, and that at Rome the laws of Christ should not be supplanted by 'the laws of Justinian'.[15] By the following century, nonetheless, with the process of juridification having if anything accelerated, the canonists had subjected ecclesiastical power to a probing legal

claims on jurisdiction over internal governance

see R. Scholz, ed., *Unbekannte kirchenpolitschen Streitschriften aus der Zeit Ludwigs des Bayern* (Rome: Loescher, 1914), ii. 544. It applies to the pope language and sentiments used by Roman lawyers of the emperor. Thus, e.g. 'living law' (*lex viva*), 'not bound by the laws' (*solutus est legibus*), 'that which pleases him has the force of law' (*ei quod placet, legis vigorem habet*). For a translation and a brief commentary underlining what the list excluded and what it did *not* mean, see F. Oakley, *The Western Church in the Later Middle Ages* (Ithaca, NY, and London: Cornell University Press, 1979), 164–8.

[15] St Bernard, *De consideratione*, l. 4, 4.3, in *PL* 182: 732, 776.

analysis and had come in the process to deploy a crucial distinction that was destined to play a central role in the delineation and understanding of the papal primacy all the way down to the Second Vatican Council when, for the first time in nearly eight centuries, it began finally to lose ground.[16]

The distinction in question was that between the power of ecclesiastical jurisdiction or government (*potestas jurisdictionis*) and that sacramental power or power of order (*potestas ordinis*) which priests and bishops possessed by virtue of having received the sacrament of holy orders. Within the power of jurisdiction, in turn, it had become customary to distinguish a double modality, one pertaining to the internal and the other to the external forum. The former (*potestas jurisdictionis in foro interiori*) concerned the domain of the individual conscience. It was a power exercised quintessentially through the sacrament of penance, it was exercised only over those who voluntarily submitted themselves to its sway, and it was directed to the private good. This was not the case, however, with the power of jurisdiction in the public sphere (*potestas jurisdictionis in foro exteriori*), which was a coercive power pertaining to a public authority, exercised even over the unwilling and directed to the common good of the faithful. Unlike the powers wielded by ecclesiastical bodies, whether today or in the pre-Constantinian era (in both cases powers wielded over essentially private societies whose membership is no less voluntary than is that, say, of modern universities or trade unions), it was a truly governmental power akin to that wielded today by what we call the state. This was the power the canonists had in mind when they ascribed to the papal monarch reigning over the ecclesiastical kingdom the fullness of jurisdictional power (*plenitudo potestatis*). And this was the power, accordingly, 'the full power of nourishing, ruling and governing the universal Church', that the Council of Florence had in mind when it concluded *Laetentur coeli* (6 July 1439), the decree of union with the Greek Orthodox Church, with what was the first conciliar definition of the Roman primacy and one that was

[16] As also, it seems, did the very word *jurisdictio* itself, which in the voluminous texts of Vatican II puts in an appearance only nine times—see William Henn, 'Historical–Theological Synthesis of the Relation between Primacy and Episcopacy during the Second Millennium', in *Il primato del successore di Pietro*, 222–73 (at 267–8). Having noted (235) that 'the distinction between the two powers of order and jurisdiction is of fundamental importance for the way in which primacy and episcopacy came to be related in the West', he adds, speaking now (267) of Vatican II and the 1983 Code of Canon Law, that 'the framing of the relation between primacy and episcopacy in terms of the distinction between order and jurisdiction seems to have been, to some extent, superseded'. For the distinction itself, its history and pertinent literature, see *Dictionnaire de droit canonique* (Paris: Letouzey & Ané, 1935–65), vii. 98–100, s.v. 'Pouvoirs de l'église'.

to serve as the model for the more extended definition which the First Vatican Council was later to promulgate in its dogmatic constitution, *Pastor aeternus* (18 July 1870).[17]

Absent, however, from both definitions was a particular claim concerning papal power whose presence the logical development of high papalist claims from the thirteenth century onwards might as well have led one to expect: namely, the sweeping claim that the pope was himself the direct source of all jurisdiction in the Church. And what accounted for that absence would appear to be nothing other than a striking instance of institutional remembering, the survival, in effect, from the conditions prevailing in the Church during much of its first millennium of what, in the context of the high papalist tradition, may properly be viewed as something of a stubborn 'counter memory'.

After all, if the high-papalist doctrine had made no special claim for the pope in relation to sacerdotal or sacramental powers (with respect to the power of order he was but a bishop among bishops), it had asserted that the power of jurisdiction in the external forum Christ had bestowed in superior and unique measure upon the Apostle Peter. Moreover, from the time of Innocent III (1198–1216) onwards until the fully fledged doctrine reached completion in Juan de Torquemada's great *Summa de ecclesia* (1453), it was claimed with increasing frequency and growing elaboration that the pope, by now monopolizing the old episcopal title of Vicar of Christ, was not only superior in jurisdiction to other bishops but also the *source* of the jurisdictional powers wielded by all those lesser prelates. As the theologian Augustinus Triumphus argued in 1315 and with reference to Matthew 16: 19:

When Christ, therefore, granted the power of jurisdiction, he spoke not in the plural but the singular, saying to Peter alone 'To thee I shall give the keys of the kingdom of heaven,' as if clearly to say: although I have given the power of order to all the apostles, I give thus to you alone the power of jurisdiction, to be dispersed and distributed through you to all the others.

Hence, it is not Christ but the pope as successor of Peter who 'confers the power of jurisdiction on the other prelates of the Church' and who can, similarly, 'take it away from them'.[18]

[17] G. Alberigo and N. P. Tanner, eds., *Decrees of the Ecumenical Councils* (London and Washington, DC: Sheed & Ward and Georgetown University Press, 1990), i. 523–8; ii. 813–15.

[18] Augustinus Triumphus, *Tractatus brevis*; in R. Scholz, *Die Publizistik zur Zeit Philipps des Schönen und Bonifaz VIII* (Stuttgart: F. Enke, 1903), 492. Cf. M. J. Wilks, *The Problem of Sovereignty in the Later Middle Ages* (Cambridge: CUP, 1963).

From this point of view, the bishops were no longer seen to possess (as in the past) any sort of indissoluble bond with their local Churches; nor were their jurisdictional powers over those Churches seen to be grounded in their sacramental consecration. Instead, they were viewed in effect as papal functionaries playing an assigned and delegated role in the government of the universal Church, susceptible, therefore, of appointment, removal, or translation from see to see at the will of their papal master. And this essentially high-papalist understanding of the way in which jurisdictional power was distributed among the ranks of the hierarchy, espoused influentially by Torquemada in the fifteenth century, by Thomas de Vio, Cardinal Cajetan, in the sixteenth, and by Francisco Suarez and Robert, Cardinal Bellarmine, in the seventeenth,[19] was destined to endure right down into the mid-twentieth century, at which point it was precluded in theory (though not dislodged from the established routines of curial practice) by the Second Vatican Council's teaching on episcopal collegiality. And if it failed thus eventually to carry the day, it was only because of the remarkable survival into the medieval and modern centuries as a proud counter memory of a very different understanding of the episcopal status. That understanding was not only different but also much more ancient. It dated back to an era when every bishop was viewed as a successor of the apostle Peter, 'joined' with all his fellow bishops, as Cyprian put it, 'by the bond of mutual concord and the chain of unity',[20] and with them responsible, in collegial solidarity and via the practice of vital synodal cooperation, for the well-being of the entire Christian Church.

Symptomatic, perhaps, of the strength of that memory—though it has not attracted a great deal of attention from historians—is a move made by the bishops assembled at the Fifth Lateran Council (1512–17) in an attempt to put a stop to the damage being done to the coherence of their jurisdictional authority by the papal privileges and exemptions extended to the members of the great international mendicant orders of friars. With that end in view they proposed the establishment of an episcopal 'sodality' or 'confraternity' (*episcopalis societas, confraternitas, sodalicium*), and, beyond that, petitioned the pope that they be allowed a common chancellor and a common treasury, and also permitted to hold meetings when it was necessary to do so in order to consult the needs and protect the interests of the episcopate as a whole. Both the pope and the cardinals reacted very coolly to this initiative and imposed on the whole idea a 'perpetual silence'.

---

[19] See Henn, 'Historical–Theological Synthesis', 237, 247–8, 251–2.
[20] Cyprian, *Ep.* 68, in *CSEL* iii. 2. 746, lines 3–5.

So the move failed.[21] But when one recalls the extent to which the council was composed of (and dominated by) Italian prelates, and when one recalls, too, their (and its) well-deserved reputation for docility in relation to pope and curia,[22] the striking thing about this proposal is the fact that it was advanced at all. And though their later footdragging in response to the urgings of contemporary proponents of high-papalist views took a different form, the bishops assembled in mid-century at Trent (in the end a much more internationally representative group than their predecessors at the Lateran Council had been) were so robust in their insistence on the divine (not papal) derivation of their own jurisdictional power as to derail papal plans for the proclamation of a decree defining the relationship of pope to episcopate.[23] In the absence of any such definition, then, 'episcopalist' views of one sort or another were able during the seventeenth and eighteenth centuries not only to thrive in France,[24] Germany, and the Austrian territories,[25] but also, during that same era, and perhaps more surprisingly, to find a strong resonance in English Catholic recusant circles and even in the newly founded United States of America.[26]

Much was to change in the wake of the French Revolution, with the subsequent rise to prominence in the Church of ultramontane sentiment and its eventual triumph at the First Vatican Council.[27] But even as that council went about solemnly defining the infallibility and jurisdictional primacy of the Roman pontiff, it still refrained from attributing the jurisdictional powers of bishops to papal delegation. In response, moreover, to episcopal concerns expressed during the drafting process, it explicitly affirmed that 'bishops . . . succeeded to the place of the apostles by appointment of the Holy Spirit'.[28] Echoing that precise affirmation in 1875,

---

[21] The pertinent documents (with arguments for and against the proposal) are printed in C. Baronius *et al., Annales ecclesiastici*, xxxi, anno 1516, nos. 1–4 (citing Paris de Grassis); also in C. J. Hefele and J. Hergenröther, *Conciliengeschichte* (Freiburg im Br.: Herder, 1855–90), viii, app. H and J, 845–53. These documents are not reprinted in C. J. Hefele, *Histoire des conciles d'après les documents originaux*, tr. and ed. H. Leclercq (Paris: Letouzey & Ané, 1907–51), though the affair is discussed (viii. 517–24). See also the discussion in Oakley, 'Conciliarism at the Fifth Lateran Council', *Church History*, 41 (1972), 456–7. There is no more than a passing allusion to the proposal in O. de la Brosse *et al., Latran V et Trente* (Paris: Éditions de l'Orante, 1975), 78, where it is referred to as 'lointaine ébauche, et moins pure de la collegialité.'

[22] Ignaz von Döllinger, in *Kleinere Schriften*, ed. F. H. Reusch (Stuttgart, 1890), 419, described the council as Leo X's 'italienisches Taschenkonzil, das sogenannte fünfte lateranische'.

[23] For which, see below, Chs. 1 and 2.   [24] For which, see below, Ch. 4.

[25] For which, see below, Ch. 5.   [26] For which, see below, Ch. 4.

[27] For which, see below, Ch. 5.

[28] Thus *Pastor aeternus*, cap. 3, in Alberigo and Tanner, *Decrees*, ii. 814.

in a joint declaration responding to a statement circulated by Otto van Bismarck, the German chancellor, the German bishops insisted that 'it is by virtue of the same divine institution upon which the papacy rests that the episcopacy also exists'. Further—and it should be noted that their stance won the approval of the redoubtable Pius IX himself—that 'it is a complete misunderstanding of the Vatican decrees to believe that because of them "episcopal" jurisdiction has been absorbed into the papal'. Writing, admittedly, in the aftermath of Vatican II (and moved, perhaps, to mould for themselves a past congruent with their own contemporary aspirations), some theologians have been led accordingly to conclude that while

> Vatican I may be said to have brought an end, so far as acceptable Catholic teaching is concerned, to several episcopalist doctrines current in the Church's second millennium, by explicitly acknowledging the divine institution of the episcopacy and by affirming that the primacy in no way detracted from the authority of bishops, Vatican I may equally be said to have brought to an end the more absolutist theories of papal primacy [current in the past] and paved the way [accordingly] for Vatican II.[29]

Whether or not that was quite the case, it is certainly true that the return to scriptural, patristic, and historical sources that was to characterize so much of Catholic theologizing in the twentieth century did promote a resulting recognition of the centrality to the Church's governance in its earliest centuries of episcopal colleagueship and conciliar activity. And that, in turn, sponsored a recuperation of what has come to be called 'the ecclesiology of *communio*'.[30] In mid-century, then, while reaffirming Vatican I's teaching on the papal primacy, the Second Vatican Council, in *Lumen gentium*, its constitution on the Church, sought also to complement it with the doctrine of episcopal collegiality. Affirming that bishops, by virtue of their episcopal consecration, possess the offices (*munera*) of 'sanctifying', 'teaching', and 'governing', *Lumen gentium* went on to emphasize the collective or 'collegial' responsibility of bishops worldwide (by 'divine institution' successors to the original 'apostolic college') for

---

[29] Henn, 'Historical–Theological Synthesis', 260–1. Cf. K. Rahner and J. Ratzinger, *Episkopat und Primat* (Freiburg: Herder, 1961), 38–45; J. M. R. Tillard, *The Bishop of Rome*, tr. J. de Satgé (Wilmington, Del.: Michael Glazier, 1983), 25–34. For the text of the German episcopal declaration, see H. Denzinger and A. Schönmetzer, *Euchiridion definitionum* (Rome: Herder, 1965), 3112–17.

[30] For which see e.g. J. M. R. Tillard, *Church of Churches*, tr. C. De Peaux (Collegeville, Minn.: Liturgical Press, 1992); M. M. Garijo-Guembe, *Communion of the Saints*, tr. P. Madigan (Collegeville, Minn.: Liturgical Press, 1994); and the issue of *The Jurist*, 36/1–2 (1976), devoted *in toto* to that ecclesiology.

the mission and well-being of the universal Church. 'United with its head, the Roman pontiff, and never without its head,' it declared, 'the order of bishops is also the subject [i.e. bearer] of supreme and full power' over that universal Church, and that 'supreme power is . . . solemnly exercised in an ecumenical council'.[31]

But if the divine institution and sacramentally based collegial responsibility of the episcopate is clearly affirmed, it is also made insistently clear, both in the text of *Lumen gentium* itself and in the Prefatory Note (*Nota explicativa praevia*) which the Theological Commission communicated to the council fathers at a critical moment on 'higher [presumably papal] authority' and as an authentic norm of interpretation, that the 'solicitude' which the bishops are called upon to exercise for the whole Church is a *pastoral* solicitude, not one 'exercised by any act of jurisdiction'.[32] At every point, indeed, the jurisdictional or juridical power appears to be assigned to the episcopal college's papal head alone. Only in 'hierarchical communion with the head of the college and its members' can bishops exercise their various offices, governance included. Only through papal convocation and confirmation can a council be ecumenical. Only with papal approbation can conciliar acts become valid. Further than that, as head of the college, the pope 'alone can perform certain acts which are in no way within the competence of the bishops', can proceed, taking 'into consideration the good of the Church' and 'according to his own discretion' in 'setting up, encouraging and approving collegial activity', and, 'as supreme pastor of the church, can exercise his power at all times as *he thinks best* (*suam potestatem omni tempore ad placitum exercere potest*)'.[33]

As a result of these manifestly uneasy formulations concerning the ultimate locus of authority in the Church (absent, it should be noted, from the 1963 draft of the constitution but firmly embedded in the 1964 final version and well-buttressed by the papal *nota explicativa praevia*), the Latin Church would now appear to possess not one but two agencies endowed with supreme ecclesiastical authority: the supreme pontiff acting alone, and the college of bishops united with its papal head. The ecclesiology of *jurisdictio*, or rather that of Vatican I, and the still older and now

---

[31] *Lumen gentium*, cap. 3, §§ 21–2, in Alberigo and Tanner, *Decrees*, ii. 865–7.

[32] *Lumen gentium*, cap. 3, § 23, in Alberigo and Tanner, *Decrees*, ii. 867. The *Nota explicativa praevia* is printed here after the text of the decree and commences with the injunction that 'The doctrine set forth in this third chapter [of *Lumen gentium*] must be understood and explained in accordance with the mind and the statement of this note'—Alberigo and Tanner, *Decrees*, ii. 899.

[33] *Lumen gentium*, cap. 3, § 22, in Alberigo and Tanner, *Decrees*, ii. 866–7 (italics mine); cf. *Nota explicativa praevia*, ibid. 899–900.

rediscovered ecclesiology of *communio* are placed side by side but remain unconnected.'[34] Further than that, 'this lack of connection is more serious in Church practice than in theology'.[35] The latter claim, certainly, would appear to be very much on target. The novel and somewhat opaque phrase 'hierarchical communion' may be more ingratiating and less hard-edged than the more traditional 'jurisdiction', but the emphasis in post-conciliar practice has persistently been placed on 'hierarchical' rather than 'communion'. And, again in practice, the meaning of the phrase has become more or less synonymous with the more robust 'hierarchical subjection' and 'true obedience' bluntly alluded to in Vatican I's *Pastor aeternus*.[36] Touted though it was, both in advance and in retrospect, as a practical manifestation of collegiality, the first Bishops' Synod which Paul VI called into being in 1967 fell well short of that goal. Its successors have done no better. Being a merely advisory body, with 'its potential deliberative (decision-making) function' deriving not 'from God through the episcopal consecration of its members, but from the pope', commentators understandably asserted even at the time that it did not really fulfil all the requirements of 'a truly collegial act', as that is defined in the provisions of *Lumen gentium*.[37] And with the subsequent shift at Rome into a posture of Thermidorian reaction, some have come to see 'the very notion of collegiality' as imperilled by a 'return to a monarchical exercise of Church authority' or, at least, transformed into 'a sleeping princess' consigned to a state of 'suspended animation'.[38]

What is missing, clearly (at least in terms of actual day-to-day practice), is some structural or constitutional adaptation capable of mediating between the sacramentally grounded responsibilities of the college of

[34] Schatz, *Papal Primacy*, 170. And this was to pose a real problem for those charged with revising after the council the 1917 *Code of Canon Law*. Grumbling that 'from a juridical standpoint, the texts of Vatican II are full of problems and inconsistencies', one commentator has noted that 'the incorporation of the principle of collegiality was the greatest difficulty in drafting the 1983 code'—thus Knut Wolf in J. P. Beal *et al.*, *New Commentary on the Code of Canon Law* (New York: Paulist Press, 2000), 425 and 428–9. The successive drafts of *Lumen gentium*, cap. 3, § 22, may be found in G. Alberigo and F. Magistretti, eds., *Constitutionis Dogmaticae Lumen Gentium Synopsis Historica* (Bologna: Instituto per le scienze religiose, 1975), 102–11.

[35] Ibid.

[36] *Pastor aeternus*, cap. 3: 'officio hierarchicae subordinationis, veraeque obedientiae obstringuntur', in Alberigo and Tanner, *Decrees*, ii. 814.

[37] That was the view expressed in 1967 by the distinguished scholar, Giuseppe Alberigo, cited in F. X. Murphy and G. MacEoin, *Synod of '67* (Milwaukee, Wis.: Bruce, 1968), 18–19.

[38] Thus P. Granfield, *The Limits of the Papacy* (New York: Crossroad, 1987), 81 (citing Gabriel Daly, 'Faith and Theology: The Ultramontane Influence', *The Tablet* (18–25 April 1981), 381).

bishops and the (essentially political) jurisdictional prerogatives attaching to the papal primacy as it has developed over the past thousand years. Or, put more bluntly, some firmly institutionalized control function, some in-built governmental mechanism capable of imposing practical constitutional restraints on the freewheeling exercise of that primatial authority.[39] And it is precisely at this point that the case of institutional or ecclesiological forgetting on which in this book I propose to focus now enters the picture.

CONCILIARIST CONSTITUTIONALISM AND THE POLITICS OF
OBLIVION

One way of looking at Vatican II's placement of a 'sacramental, ontological ecclesiology of *communio*' side by side with a 'juristic unity' or papalist ecclesiology of jurisdiction is to see it as an awkward juxtaposition of two very different understandings of the nature of the Church.[40] The former, an essentially patristic and (in at least some meanings of that word) 'episcopalist' understanding of the Church dating back to its earliest centuries; the latter, a vastly different and essentially *political* understanding that had risen to prominence only much later in the intensely juristic and corporatist climate of the Middle Ages, and had reached its maturity in the early modern period when absolute monarchy had become the most universally admired form of polity. About that juxtaposition there is something oddly asymmetrical. Something, one cannot help thinking, some mediating form perhaps, is missing. And something, indeed, *is* missing.

What appears largely to have faded from the collective memory is the fact that if, in the wake of the great twelfth-century revival of Roman law, the medieval canonists had come to conceive of the papal leadership of the

[39] If I read him correctly, that is the direction in which Archbishop John R. Quinn was heading in his 1996 Oxford lecture, 'The Exercise of the Primacy and the Costly Call to Unity' (in Zagano and Tilley, *Exercise of Primacy*, 16–18) where, invoking the Constance decree *Frequens* (on which, see below), he lamented the failure of the pope to observe its stipulation that general councils be assembled at regular and designated intervals. Similarly, Archbishop Maxim Hermonink's proposal at the 1985 Bishops Synod—for which, see Granfield, *The Limits of the Papacy*, 95–6.

[40] Thus Kasper, *Theology and Church*, 158: '*Communio hierarchica* is . . . a typical compromise formulation which points to a juxtaposition of a sacramental *communio* ecclesiology and juristic unity ecclesiology. It has consequently been said that the Vatican II texts contain two ecclesiologies' synthesized only in a 'highly superficial fashion'. Cf. Schatz, *Papal Primacy*, 169–70; Tillard, *Bishop of Rome*, 34–50; William Henn, 'Historical–Theological Synthesis of the Relation between Primacy and Episcopacy during the Second Millennium', in *Il Primato del successore di Pietro*, 262–73.

Church 'in terms of the Roman law of sovereignty; they also explained the
collegial structure of the Church in terms of the Roman law of corporations'.[41] And in terms, at least, of one type of canonistic understanding of
corporations (itself based largely on the model ready at hand in the classic
relationship between a bishop and the canons of his cathedral chapter),
power was divided between the head of a corporation and its members,
with the power of the head not deriving from but being limited none the
less by the power inherent in the members. 'Applied to large-scale government,' and the universal Church was certainly such, 'this model of a corporation would yield, not a simple republicanism, but a complex doctrine
of mixed or limited government—or, put differently, a doctrine of divided
sovereignty.'[42]

During the Middle Ages, then, the doctrine of papal sovereignty, with
its understanding of ecclesiastical unity as pivoting on, or deriving from,
its papal head, was not alone. Side by side with it existed another understanding of that ecclesiastical sovereignty and that unity. No less juris-
tically shaped, that rival understanding was much more responsive,
however, to the age-old collegial and conciliar pattern of governance in
the Church and bore with it potent memories of the ecclesiology of
communio that we have seen to have been central to the patristic Church's
self-understanding. That alternative approach 'stressed the corporate
association of the members of a Church', whether at the local or the universal level, 'as the true principle of ecclesiastical unity'.[43] Had it not been
consigned to institutional oblivion, it could well have served, by virtue of
its conflation of communitarian and juridical features, to mediate in
practical fashion between the sacramentally based and explicitly non-
juridical[44] doctrine of episcopal collegiality and Vatican I's (and, for that
matter, Vatican II's) adamantly juridical doctrine of the papal primacy.
For it gave rise to the conviction that, side by side with the institution of
papal monarchy (and in intimate connection with it) it was necessary to
give the Church's communal and corporate dimension more prominent
and regular institutional expression. And that was to be effected most notably by the assembly of general councils representing the entire community

[41] Tierney, *Religion, Law, and the Growth of Constitutional Thought*, 19.   [42] Ibid. 27.
[43] And 'which envisaged an exercise of corporate authority by the members of a Church
even in the absence of an effective head'—Tierney, *Foundations*, 240.
[44] Thus *Lumen gentium*, c. 3, § 23, in Alberigo and Tanner, ii. 867, speaking of the fact that
'as members of the episcopal college and legitimate successors of the apostles, the individual
bishops, through the institution and command of Christ, are bound to be concerned about
the whole Church', is careful to add that 'this solicitude is not exercised by any act of jurisdiction'. Cf. Granfield, *Limits of the Papacy*, 82–4.

of the faithful and not necessarily limited in their voting membership, therefore, to the ranks of the episcopate alone. Stipulating that the ultimate locus of authority resided in the universal Church itself rather than in its papal head, it insisted that under certain circumstances the general council representing that Church—acting even apart from or in opposition to the pope—could exercise a jurisdictional or governmental authority superior to his, and, by so doing, impose constitutional limits on the exercise of his prerogatives or serve as a control function to prevent their abuse. This conciliar and essentially constitutionalist pattern of thinking rose to prominence during the late fourteenth and early fifteenth centuries in the context of the Great Schism of the West and, via the deposition of the rival claimants to the papal office and the subsequent election of a new pope whose legitimacy came to be universally accepted, made possible its termination at the Council of Constance (1414–18).

About all of this, however pertinent it might well seem to be to current ecclesiastical discontents, one finds surprisingly little in contemporary ecclesiological treatises.[45] Nor does it figure prominently in general ecclesiastical histories, and that despite the fact that, for the past half-century, it has been the focus among historians at least of an enormous amount of attention.[46] Even more surprisingly, it has found no significant presence in

---

[45] Thus it has no part e.g. in Tillard's exploration of the ecclesiology of communion is his *Church of Churches* and gets only the most glancing of references (and then via the final report of the Anglican-Roman Catholic International Commission) in Garijo-Guembe, *Communion*, 223 (cf. 190, 227). Similarly, in the issue of *The Jurist*, 36/1–2 (1976) devoted to 'The Church as Communio', as also in *Pouvoirs: Revue française d'études constitutionelles et politiques*, 17 (1981)—the whole issue devoted to 'Le Pouvoir dans l'Église'. P. Granfield, *Papacy in Transition* (Garden City, NY: Doubleday, 1980), 78–85, 166–74, and idem, *The Limits of the Papacy* (New York: Crossroad, 1987), 55–6, is somewhat more helpful, as also is L. M. Bermejo, *Infallibility on Trial* (Westminster, Md.: Christian Classics, 1992), 365, who, having discussed the particular case of Constance in the contest of the process of 'reception', observes that it 'seems to have landed us into a labyrinth of options and disturbing alternatives which we rarely face, but which . . . should be taken seriously'. Similarly, E. C. Bianchi and R. R. Reuther, eds., *A Democratic Catholic Church* (New York: Crossroad, 1992), with its general insistence (8) that 'Renewal-minded Catholics . . . must begin to ask the hard question about the relationship between historical realities and theological and ethical norms'. E. C. Bianchi, 'A Democratic Church: Task for the Twenty-First Century', ibid. 54–7, citing *Haec sancta* and the significance of the conciliar movement (at 42–4), concludes that 'the collapse of these conciliar reforms proved disastrous for the Church in the sixteenth century'. John Beals, 'Toward a Democratic Church: The Canonistic Heritage', ibid. 52–73, shares the same emphasis and concludes (59) that after 'conciliarism self-destructed in the babble of Basle . . . [and] . . . ecclesiology became hierarchology, constitutional thought about the divine right of the ecclesial community atrophied'.

[46] Thus A. Frenken, 'Die Erforschung des Konstanzer Konzils (1414–1418) in den letzten 100 Jahren', *Annuarium Historiae Conciliorum*, 25 (1993), 1–509, lists in excess of 1,500 items, the bulk of them produced over the course of the past fifty years.

the burgeoning literature of complaint and reformist hand-wringing stimulated of late by the vigorous reassertion of papal sovereignty over the worldwide Church, as well as the stubborn vindication of curial control and the concomitant evisceration of episcopal collegiality in practice, even while it is being celebrated in theory.[47] And its absence is hard to explain as anything other than a highly successful instance of institutionally sponsored forgetting.

The fact is that it has long been customary to portray the whole conciliar episode as nothing more than a stutter, hiccup, or interruption in the long history of the Latin Catholic Church, an unfortunate and revolutionary episode, radical in its origins and rapid in its demise. In this book, however, it will be my purpose to claim to the contrary that the roots of the conciliarist tradition were thrust deep into earlier (and unimpeachably orthodox) ecclesiological soil, and that that tradition was by no means destined to lapse into desuetude with the ending of the schism and the papacy's later defeat of its conciliarist opponents at the Council of Basel (1431–49).[48] That we should ever have been inclined to think that it did so is explicable only, I believe, by the onset in 1870, in the wake of the First Vatican Council's historic definitions of papal primacy and infallibility, of what for want of a better term may be called an ecclesiastical politics of oblivion. What ensued was the rise to hegemony among Church historians (and not only Roman Catholic Church historians) of what amounted, in fact, to a high-papalist constitutive narrative, one that has minimized where it has not ignored the persistence of conciliarist views across northern Europe in the sixteenth century,[49] their reinvigoration in France, England, and Venice in the seventeenth,[50] as well as their spread into Germany and the Austrian territories in the eighteenth.[51]

Admittedly, it has been usual to concede that tattered remnants of that conciliar ecclesiology were to be found caught up in those provincial, obscurely subversive, and usually statist ideologies that have gone down in history as Gallicanism, Richerism, Febronianism, and Josephinism. But those disparate, occluding, and (usually) nineteenth-century labels have themselves served, in fact, to conceal from us the prominence, tenacity,

---

[47] Or, in Tillard's gentler formulation (*Bishop of Rome*, 44), there has proved to be 'a basic incompatibility between the ways of monarchy, which the title Roman pontiff suggests, and the wishes of a synodal assembly . . . Recent Roman synods have done no more than set the customs of a monarchy alongside the procedures of an assembly without being able to coordinate them.' Cf. the comparable remarks of Quinn, in Zagano and Tilley, *Exercise of the Primacy*, 13–24, and idem, *Reform of the Papacy*, 110–16.

[48] For which see below, Ch. 1.   [49] For which see below, Ch. 3.
[50] For which see below, Ch. 4.   [51] For which see below, Ch. 5.

wide geographic spread, and essential continuity of that age-old tradition of conciliarist constitutionalism which, for long centuries, competed stubbornly for the allegiance of Catholics with the high-papalist or ultramontane vision of things so powerfully entrenched in Italy and at Rome. If the latter is so much more familiar to us today, it is so because it was destined after 1870 to become identified with Roman Catholic orthodoxy itself. And it is only, one cannot help suspecting, our very familiarity with that papalist outcome that has contrived to persuade us of the necessity of the process.

In the past, historians concerned with the conciliar movement clearly felt obliged to explain how it could be that the seeds of such a constitutionalist ecclesiology could have contrived to germinate in the stonily monarchical soil of the Latin Catholic Church. But in thus framing the issue, or so I will be suggesting, they were picking up the conceptual stick at the wrong end. Given the depth of its roots in the ecclesiological consciousness of Latin Christendom and the strength with which it endured on into the modern era and right across northern Europe, the real question for the *historian* at least may rather be how and why that constitutionalist ecclesiology perished and, in so doing, left so very little trace on our historical consciousness. For perish it certainly did. When in his *View of the State of Europe during the Middle Ages* (1818) the English historian, Henry Hallam, came to write about the ending of the Great Schism at the Council of Constance by the deposition of the rival claimants, he spoke of 'the Whig principles of the Catholic Church' embodied in the decrees *Haec sancta* (asserting the jurisdictional superiority under certain circumstances of council to pope), and described that decree as one of 'the great pillars of that moderate theory with respect to papal authority which . . . is embraced by almost all laymen and the major part of ecclesiastics on this side of the Alps'.[52] By the end of the century, however, in the wake of the ecclesiastical and theological developments that had culminated in 1870 in the First Vatican Council, what Hallam, writing in 1816, had seen as a live and commonplace ecclesiological option for the Catholics of his day had become a matter of interest only to the archaeologists of defunct ideologies. Vatican I's definitions of papal primacy and infallibility had seemed to leave Catholic historians with little choice but to treat the conciliar movement as nothing more than a revolutionary moment in the life of the Church, and Catholic theologians with no alternative but to regard the conciliar theory as a dead issue, an ecclesiological fossil, something lodged deep in the lower carboniferous of the dogmatic geology.

[52] H. Hallam, *View of the State of Europe in the Middle Ages* (London, 1901), iii. 243–5.

So much, indeed, was this the case that in 1908 the editors of even so learned a compilation as *The Catholic Encyclopedia* did not deem it necessary to include in that work an article on conciliarism. The subject was given some attention under the heading of 'Gallicanism', but the author of that article did not hesitate to make the prevailing sentiment of his day abundantly clear. 'Stricken to death, as a free opinion, by the Council of the Vatican,' he said, '[Theological] Gallicanism could survive only as a heresy; the Old Catholics[53] have endeavoured to keep it alive under this form. Judged by the paucity of the adherents whom they have recruited—daily becoming fewer—in Germany and Switzerland, it seems very evident that the historical evolution of these ideas has reached its completion.'[54]

The absence of any appeal to the conciliarist position in the debates generated by the modernist crisis, which came to a peak at about the same time, would appear to confirm the rectitude of that judgement,[55] and ecclesiological developments in the decades ensuing have not done much to shake it. During the 1960s, it is true, in the context of the intense ecclesiological debates stimulated both by Vatican II and by the dramatic events punctuating that council's immediate (and polarizing) aftermath, a few attempts were made to draw attention to the relevance of the conciliarist position and to its appeal as a viable (or, at least, currently pertinent) ecclesiological option.[56] But those attempts met with no success, and the tradition of conciliarist constitutionalism receded once more to its established status as a fragile counter-memory lingering on the very margins of theological concern, or, at most, as a minor perturbation in the outermost orbit of the ecclesiological consciousness.[57] Theologians of

---

[53] The reference is to the schismatic 'Old Catholic' Church, a loose grouping of independent ecclesial communities, partly stimulated by rejection of the Vatican I definition of papal primacy and infallibility and drawn together in the 1889 Union of Utrecht.

[54] A. Degart in *The Catholic Encyclopedia* (New York: Robert Appleton Co., 1907–14), vi. 355, s.v. 'Gallicanism'.

[55] See below, Epilogue.   [56] See below, Epilogue.

[57] Reflecting, perhaps, the sense prevalent even among historians that the claims advanced by Hans Küng and Paul de Vooght (for which see below, Epilogue) to the effect that the Constance decree *Haec sancta* constituted a valid dogmatic definition had been forcefully and successfully contradicted and consigned already by the late 1970s to no more than a 'marginal position'. Thus E. Meuthen, 'Das Basler Konzil in römisch-katholischer Sicht', *Theologische Zeitschrift*, 38 (1982), 277–8 n. 8. Antony Black in 1979, however, entered what amounted to a brief but robust dissent from that point of view, arguing (somewhat optimistically, I would judge) that 'We may speak [today] of a general conciliar renaissance'—see his *Council and Commune* (London: Burns & Oates, 1979), 210–22. Similarly, and more recently, N. P. Tanner, *The Councils of the Church* (New York: Crossroad, 1999), 70–1, and P. Collins, *Papal Power* (London: Fount, 1997), though the author notes (p. ix) that his 'purpose in this book is not primarily historical'.

non-historical bent may doubtless be content to explain why this had necessarily to be so. Historians on the other hand, may be forgiven for wanting to rescue from the shadows and return to the bright lights of centre stage the memory of a tradition of thought powerful enough, after all, to have endured in the Catholic consciousness for half a millennium and more. Whatever the case, that, certainly, is the task I have set myself in the pages that follow.

1

Christendom's Crisis: The Great Schism, the Conciliar Movement, and the Era of Councils from Pisa to Trent

On Friday, St George's Eve, there was another session. In this session, our Holy Father, Pope Martin, gave to all who were present at the Council of Constance permission to leave and likewise absolution. Afterward, he gave the people his blessing in the upper court. Our Lord King stood beside him, dressed as an evangelist, wearing his imperial crown and holding the orb in his hand while a man held a naked sword before him. Cardinal Conti proclaimed to the people in Latin the indulgence of seven years for mortal sins and seven Lents. Master Peter repeated it in German, and everyone was given permission to go home.[1]

In the passage above, Ulrich Richental describes the closing session of the Council of Constance, which took place on 22 April 1418, almost six centuries ago now, and at a moment when the newly elected pope, Martin V (1417–31), with plague moving in on the city, was anxious to speed the council fathers on their way and to prepare for his own departure.

Constance may not be exactly a household word—not, certainly, to historians of representative assemblies or even to contemporary ecclesiologists. For the past forty years, admittedly, it has been the focus of intense interest among specialists of historical bent.[2] But it deserves more

---

[1] Tr. L. R. Loomis from Ulrich Richental, *Chronik des Constanzer Concils*, ed. M. R. Buck (Tübingen, 1882), in J. H. Mundy and K. M. Woody, eds., *The Council of Constance and the Unification of the Church*, tr. L. R. Loomis (New York and London: Columbia University Press, 1961), 182.

[2] Thus, of the more than 1,500 pertinent publications which Frenken lists as having appeared over the course of the past century, most date to the past half-century. This great

widespread attention than that. It numbered among its participants humanists of the calibre of Pier Paolo Vergerio, Leonardo Bruni, and Poggio Bracciolini, and, by affording an occasion for learned colleagues from Italy and Germany to meet, it played, along with its successor council at Basel, a role of some significance in the diffusion of humanist ideas.[3] It also attracted into its magnetic field not only the papal but also the imperial chancery, as well as the official representatives of a host of other European countries and became for a while the international crossroads at which much of Europe's diplomatic business was conducted. In effect, as has well been said, it was 'as close as the Middle Ages came to the Congress of Vienna or the United Nations'.[4] In size alone, it was one of the most imposing of medieval gatherings. Richental, a citizen of Constance who had to help find quarters for the city's flood of distinguished (and not so distinguished) visitors and a man who seems to have had a precocious taste for statistics, listed—in addition to Martin V and John XXIII, the pope who convoked the council, and a host of other officials, temporal and spiritual—some 5 patriarchs, 33 cardinals, 47 archbishops, 145 bishops, 93 suffragan bishops, 132 abbots, 155 priors, 217 doctors of theology, 361 doctors of both laws, 5,300 'simple priests and scholars', 3,000 and more merchants, shopkeepers, craftsmen, musicians, and players, and over 700 'harlots in brothels . . . who hired their own houses'—these last to be distinguished, he hastens to add, from 'some who lay in stables and wherever they could, besides the private ones whom I could not count'.[5]

Nor was it size alone that distinguished the council. It was the greatest and certainly the most memorable of the general councils held by the Latin Church, one called upon not only to address the threat posed at both ends of Europe by the Wycliffite and Hussite heresies, but also to respond to the pent-up demand for reform 'in head and members' that had been mounting in urgency for at least a century and a half. It assembled, moreover, at a moment of supreme crisis in the life of the Church, and one that was recognized as such by contemporaries. It was a moment, after all, when 'the

scholarly effort has reached something of a culmination in Walter Brandmüller's massive, 2-vol. *Das Konzil von Konstanz* (Paderborn: F. Schöningh, 1991–9).

[3] P. Lehmann, 'Konstanz und Basel als Buchermarkt', in Lehmann, *Erforschung des Mittelalters* (Leipzig: Hiersemann, 1959), i. 1253–80. Morimichi Watanabe, 'Humanism in the Tirol: Aeneas Sylvius, Duke Sigismund and Gregor Heimburg', in Watanabe, *Concord and Reform* (Aldershot: Ashgate/Variorum, 2001), 241–6.

[4] C. M. D. Crowder, *Unity, Heresy and Reform* (New York: St Martin's Press, 1977), 24; P. H. Stump, *The Reforms of the Council of Constance* (Leiden: E. J. Brill, 1994), 26.

[5] Richental, *Chronik*, 189–90.

great and terrible schism'[6] which came later to be known as the Great
Schism of the West had endured already for almost forty years since the
disputed papal election of 1378. A moment also when the attempt of the
Council of Pisa (1409) to heal the division of allegiances which that election had spawned had resulted only in the addition of a third (or Pisan)
line of claimants to a papal title already scandalously contested by two
rival lines of popes based, respectively, at Avignon and Rome. Constance
was to meet that crisis and resolve that dilemma. Wrangles, compromises,
and failures notwithstanding, it was also to make a more effective response
to the demand for church-wide reform than historians in the past were
usually willing to concede.[7] But in order to comprehend the formidable
nature of the challenges the council was to confront, it is necessary to bring
to the task some sense at least of the fundamental and long-term disabilities under which the medieval Church had persistently laboured, as well
as a grasp of the immediate, near-term circumstances precipitating the
crisis which finally overtook it in the late fourteenth century. For the roots
of the Great Schism and of the fifteenth-century constitutional crisis that
stemmed from it were not simply engaged in the unsolved problems and
unhappy contingencies of the mid-fourteenth century ecclesiastical
world. Beyond that, they were thrust deep into the life of the medieval
Church as it had unfolded during the centuries preceding.

LONG-TERM DISABILITIES; NEAR-TERM PRESSURES

Of the in-built weaknesses characteristic of the medieval Church, two
enduring and intersecting disabilities stand out as being of truly fundamental importance: the first, the politicization of the Church's self-
understanding; the second, the transformation of the very idea of
ecclesiastical office itself. Their importance is evident because they established the mental categories in terms of which even the most intelligent and
spiritually minded of people did their thinking on matters ecclesiastical;

---

[6] The words (*magnum et horrendum scisma*) are those of Cardinal Fillastre in his *Diary of
the Council of Constance*, in Mundy and Woody, *Council of Constance*, 200; tr. from *Fillastres
Gesta concilii Constanciensis*, in H. Finke, *Acta Concilii Constanciensis* (Münster: Regensbergschen Buchhandlung, 1896–1928), ii. 13–170 (at 13).

[7] Thus Stump, *Reforms*, building on and extending the earlier work of B. Hübler, *Die Constanzer Reformation und die Concordate von 1418* (Leipzig: B. Tauchnitz, 1867), makes a
powerful case in support of this view. For an earlier (1946) straw in the wind signalling this
impending interpretative shift, see K. A. Fink, 'Papsttum und Kirchenreform nach dem
Grossen Schisma', *Theologische Quartalschrift*, 126: 110–22.

it is evident, too, because they set the limits within which even the most dedicated of Church leaders and zealous of Church reformers were destined of necessity to manœuvre.

To the first of these disabilities we have already had occasion to allude,[8] for it reflected the post-Constantinian juridification of the Church and of the categories of its structural self-understanding. With it came the concomitant subordination of the scriptural understanding of office as essentially ministerial, involving above all service to others, to the less demanding, more familiar, and administratively manageable *political* mode of thought. Here, what the Gregorian reformers of the eleventh century actually succeeded in achieving did much to set the pattern of development for the centuries succeeding. Anyone prone to minimizing the essential continuity of late medieval papal history with that of the earlier period would find it a sobering experience to glance at the twenty-seven blunt propositions of the *Dictatus papae*, the celebrated document that, in March 1075, was inserted in the papal register. Those propositions not only reflect the thinking of Gregory VII (1073–85) himself, but also provide the key to the principal directions of papal policy right down to the fourteenth century. In some of them—the claim, for example, that the pope could depose bishops or reinstate them or translate them from see to see[9]—one can see adumbrated that drive to exercise the fullness of papal jurisdictional power over the provincial churches of Christendom that was to be pushed so vigorously by Alexander III in the twelfth century and by Innocent III and Innocent IV in the thirteenth, but was to reach its peak only in the fourteenth after the papal court had been settled at Avignon.

At the same time, the silences of the *Dictatus papae* can also be revealing. For what Gregory and his followers left undone goes a long way to explaining the fundamental and enduring weakness of the medieval Church and the difficulties with which would-be reformers at the Councils of Vienne (1311), Pisa (1409), Constance (1414–18), Basel–Ferrara–Florence (1431–49), Lateran V (1512–17), and Trent (1547–63) were destined again and again to grapple. Herein lies the second major disability under which the medieval Church was condemned to labour.

Whatever the success of the Gregorians in reducing the degree of direct royal and imperial control over episcopal appointments (and they could not eliminate it), they did little to undercut the whole system of noble proprietary control over churches. Under the influence of barbarian custom

[8] See above, Prologue.
[9] *Dictatus papae*, arts. 3, 5, 13, 25; in S. Z. Ehler and J. B. Morrall, eds., *Church and State through the Centuries* (London: Burns & Oates, 1954), 43–4.

and feudal institutions, that system had grown up during the early medieval centuries and had spread throughout Western Europe until it embraced most of the parish churches and a goodly proportion of the monasteries, too. The long-term significance of this particular failure lies less in the further measure of lay control it left standing—for churches had come to be *owned* directly by bishops and monasteries as well as by kings and nobles[10]—than in the fact that it permitted a further transformation in the notion of ecclesiastical office itself, a blurring of the crucial distinction that the Romans had made and that we ourselves make between the holding of office and the ownership of property. This mingling paralleled a comparable development in secular political life, and it is reflected in the medieval employment of a single word (*dominium*) to denote both proprietary right and governmental authority,[11] and in the adoption of a feudal term 'benefice' (that is, fief—itself involving a conflation of governmental authority and proprietary right) to denote ecclesiastical office. It is reflected, also in the fact that when, in the twelfth century, the canonists came to classify according to the categories of the revived Roman law the accumulated body of rules concerning the disposition of ecclesiastical benefices, they treated them as belonging not to public law but to private[12]—not, that is, to the branch of law concerned with the public welfare and enforced in the interest of the common good, but to that branch pertaining to the protection of private proprietary right. It is reflected again in the persistent, almost instinctive, tendency of medieval clergy and laity alike to regard ecclesiastical office less as a focus of duty than as a source of income or a matter of proprietary concern. It is reflected further in that it was to the ecclesiastical benefice, accordingly, that underfinanced kings, princes, and popes alike felt free to turn when, burdened with increasingly onerous and expensive governmental tasks and persistently denied the right to raise tax revenues adequate to those needs,

[10] There has been a good deal of disagreement among historians about the origins of the 'proprietary church'. Despite its overemphasis on Germanic origins, the best introduction to the subject is still the inaugural address delivered at Basel by Ulrich Stutz, *Die Eigenkirche als Element des mittelalterlich-germanischen Kirchenrechtes* (Berlin: H. W. Müller, 1895). For an English translation of this classic statement, see G. Barraclough, ed., *Mediaeval Germany* (Oxford: Basil Blackwell, 1948), ii. 35–70.

[11] Whereas Roman lawyers used the word solely to denote proprietary right and we ourselves use its somewhat archaic derivative 'dominion' to denote authority of a governmental nature. Similarly, the word 'benefice', drawn from the vocabulary of feudalism, and possessed of proprietary connotations, was used to denote a spiritual office.

[12] In this connection see G. Barraclough, *Papal Provisions* (Oxford: Basil Blackwell, 1935), 83, who stresses the importance of Alexander III's decretal, X. 2. 13, c. 7; in E. Friedberg, ed., *Corpus juris canonici* (Leipzig: B. Tauchnitz, 1879–81), i. 282–3.

they had to find the wherewithal to remunerate and reward the growing bureaucracies upon whose diligent service their administrations depended. It is reflected finally, and therefore, in the development and systematic extension of that whole system of 'papal provision' whereby the pope intervened to set aside the right of existing patrons and came eventually to 'provide' candidates to all the major benefices in the Church and to a large proportion of the minor benefices that were in the gift of clerical patrons.[13] All of which represented an immense and systematic intensification in the exercise of the pope's jurisdictional power. And while this whole system was perfectly legal and could scarcely have operated without widespread clerical support, the disadvantages attaching to it clearly outweighed the advantages. Presupposing as it did the material conception of the benefice, it nourished accordingly the stubborn abuses of pluralism (accumulation of several benefices in the hands of one man) and nonresidence against which generations of reformers were destined to rail in vain.

Without some minimal recognition of the presence of these two enduring disabilities and of the complex ways in which they interacted, it would be hard indeed to make sense of the path that led from the great papal successes of the eleventh, twelfth, and early thirteenth centuries to the more questionable achievements of the Avignonese papacy and, thence, to the onset of the Great Schism, to the subsequent demand of church reformers for 'reform in head and members', and to the conviction in particular of the reformers whom we know as 'conciliarists' that the achievement and enduring effectiveness of such reform would be guaranteed only if significant changes were made in the very constitution of the universal Church. As early as 1245, during the first Council of Lyons, disturbing signs of trouble to come had appeared.[14] Like its great predecessor, the Fourth Lateran Council of 1215, that council did bear witness to the pope's supreme legislative authority, and it did so in striking fashion. But distressing signs of jurisdictional turbulence pointed in a gloomier direction. The Council of Lyons met during a six-year exile of pope and curia not simply from Rome but also from Italy; it was forced to hear a formal appeal from the sentence of deposition it had handed down in the case of the Emperor Frederick II to the judgement of a future pope and a future general council; and it was the recipient of a protest of a group of English noblemen against the papal

---

[13] Barraclough, *Papal Provisions.*

[14] Signs evident in the interesting account given by Matthew Paris in his *Chronica Majora*; ed. Luard (London: Longman & Co., 1872–83), iv. 430–73 (440–4 for the English complaint to the pope against the extortions of the curia).

grant of English benefices to Italians. That particular protest, moreover, was not an isolated one. It came in the company of other grievous complaints from such unimpeachable sources as the saintly Louis IX of France and the great philosopher-bishop of Lincoln, Robert Grosseteste, concerning the burdens that increasing papal taxation and provision of candidates to benefices were placing on the provincial churches of Christendom. Complaints were being voiced, indeed, about the mounting disorder in the whole traditional system of episcopal government caused by the increasing centralization of ecclesiastical administration in Rome.

It was by virtue of the vigorous leadership it had exerted as sponsor of the crusading movement and as initiator and implementer of ecclesiastical reform that the papacy from the time of Gregory VII had risen to greater and greater eminence. Accordingly, once it began to show signs of faltering in that leadership, it was threatened by a fall from very high estate. And, as the thirteenth century wore on, falter of course it did. Rather than being disposed of, the problems evident already at the time of the First Council of Lyons were allowed to fester and they were to grow in seriousness during the decades leading up to the Council of Vienne (1311–12). Prior to that council, Clement V (1305–14) had requested that memoranda be submitted detailing the state of affairs in the Church and recommending appropriate reforms. Surviving memoranda generated by that exercise suggest quite ominously that the papacy itself, with its centralizing encroachment on the traditional pattern of episcopal government and its lavish heaping of privileges on the international orders of mendicant friars whose activities transcended diocesan and national boundaries, was now coming to be seen as a crucial part of the problem.[15] A legislative response, of course, was made at Vienne. But it fell short of the sweeping demands for reform 'in head as well as members' that the bishops William Lemaire of Angers and William Durand of Mende had submitted. In his *Tractatus maior*, as part of his attempt to restore and defend the integrity of episcopal authority, Durand had sought to transfer 'the responsibility for the law of the Church from the papacy to general councils, which would meet at ten-year intervals', intruding on the central budgetary process, enjoying a control function over the granting of dispensations from old laws, playing an indispensable role in the creation of new, and, in general, imposing unprecedented restrictions on the exercise of the papal plenitude of power.[16]

[15] J. Lecler, *Vienne* (Paris: Éditions de l'Orante, 1964).
[16] C. Fasolt, *Councils and Hierarchy* (Cambridge: CUP, 1991), 1–2.

Prophetic as it was of the reforming efforts pursued a century later at the Council of Constance, in the teeth of stern papal displeasure this radical programme got nowhere in Vienne. While the council was still in session, Durand deemed it wise to backtrack on his earlier proposals, submitting now a *Tractatus minor* which, while urging many of the same reforms, prudently forbore from ascribing any reforming role to general councils.[17] The change of mood, however, was still palpable. For well over a century, the clergy of the local churches had by and large welcomed the extension of papal power into the affairs of the ecclesiastical provinces, and by their own petitions for privileges, provisions, preferments, and exemptions had done much to stimulate and accelerate that intensification of curial control. Nor did they necessarily cease to do so now. But from this time onwards evidence of clerical opposition to papal policy begins to increase—evidence, even, of bodies of clergy so disgruntled as to be willing, in moments of critical tension, to side with their secular rulers against the pope, or, at least, to acquiesce in policies directed by their rulers against him.

Already at the start of the century that shift in mood had been made brutally clear during the great clash between Boniface VIII (1294–1303) and the French king, Philip IV (1267/8–1314). At that time something of a dangerous coalition had emerged between two disaffected cardinals whom Boniface had excommunicated and deprived of their rank and the counsellors of a king already locked in combat with the pope on the issue of royal taxation of the French clergy. During that conflict, which was to eventuate in the prolonged residence of the papacy at Avignon, the call had gone out to the rulers of Christendom to assemble a general council to sit in judgement on the pope. That call was to be repeated a few years later during the last great medieval struggle between pope and emperor, when the dissident Franciscans Michael of Cesena (d. 1342) and William of Ockham (d. 1349) took refuge at the court of Lewis of Bavaria, and, along with their fellow refugee, the radical Italian antipapalist, Marsiglio of Padua (d. *c.*1343), mounted against pope and papacy a formidable campaign of propaganda. In so doing, they not only revived (and gave additional currency to) the old anti-papal gambits of Philip IV's publicists, but also ventured into much more radical territory. Focusing on and responding to

---

[17] By a salutory clarification which goes a long way to explaining why historians have found Durand's work so confusing and, as a result, have accorded his ideas less attention than they warrant, Fasolt (ibid. 10–11) points out that 'all the printed editions obliterate the distinction between the *Tractatus Maior* and the *Tractatus Minor* [works very different in tone]: they seem to contain a single book with the spurious title *Tractatus de modo generalis concilii celebrandi*'.

the great and ever-widening gulf between the simplicity of the apostolic Church, as they intuited it, and the triumphantly rationalized and increasingly bureaucratized structure of central government in the Church of their own day, they were to leave behind a veritable minefield of arguments directed against what the papacy and the ecclesiastical establishment had come to be in the Avignonese era and would continue to be until the era of Catholic Reformation.

By attaching the term 'Babylonian Captivity' to the Avignonese period of papal exile from Rome contemporary critics implied thereby a tragic exile of the papacy from its proper home and its scandalous subordination to the exigencies of French royal policy.[18] Much support for that point of view is to be found in the contemporary literary sources, especially in the English, German, and, above all, Italian chronicles. Until the voluminous materials preserved in the Vatican archives were made accessible to scholars at the end of the nineteenth century, it was customary for historians to base their views uncritically on 'the malevolent accounts of contemporary chronicles, and the tendentious writings of Petrarch, St Catherine of Siena and St Bridget of Sweden'. As a result, they were led to portray an Avignonese papacy—morally corrupt, financially extravagant, administratively tyrannical—as 'the source of the greatest evils for the Church, and, in the last analysis, the chief cause of the great schism of the West'.[19] Not many historians, I suspect, would be disposed to deny that the very existence of a well-established alternative capital at Avignon (with half the papal curia still, indeed, in residence there) was to help make schism practically feasible. That said, however, the work of the revisionists over the better part of the past century has done much to modify the traditionally negative press enjoyed by the Avignonese papacy. And it has done so most successfully in relation to two of the three features of that papacy customarily depicted in the darkest of hues, namely, the matter of the French affiliation and the personal moral character of the pontiffs themselves, less successfully with reference to the third, the growing centralization and absolutism of ecclesiastical government.

[18] B. Guillemain, 'Punti di vista sul Papato avignonese', *Archivio storico italiano*, III (1953), 181–206, gives a helpful account of the changes which have overtaken the way in which the nature of the Avignonese papacy has been interpreted by historians. Mollat and Guillemain himself have made the most important contributions to these interpretative shifts. See esp. G. Mollat's classic *The Popes at Avignon* (New York: Harper Torchbooks, 1963), and Guillemain's *La Cour pontificale d'Avignon* (Paris: Éditions E. de Boccard, 1962). Renouard, *The Avignonese Papacy* (Hamden, Conn.: Archon Books, 1970), gives a good synoptic account. For a shorter account of the period and the subsequent conciliar epoch (though one fuller than that given here), see Oakley, *Western Church*, 38–79, on which I have drawn for the main outlines of what follows.

[19] Mollat, *Popes*, pp. xiii, 343.

In the first place, it is clear that any attempt to portray the schism as simply the outcome of the francophilia of the Avignonese popes is to be rejected. Had that been the case, the King of France in 1378 would hardly have hesitated, as we know he did, to lend his support to the cardinals after they had disavowed their earlier election of an Italian pontiff and proceeded to the election of a French pope who was later to take up his residence at Avignon.[20] But, then, Mollat established that 'French' though they and the vast majority of their cardinals and curialists undoubtedly were,[21] the Avignonese popes were by no means consistently or even persistently pro-French in their policies and were certainly not so abjectly submissive to French royal pressure as Italian, English, and German contemporaries alleged or as propagandists and historians were later to assume. If national hostilities and traditional diplomatic alignments undoubtedly helped protract the schism, they cannot simply be said to have started it.

In the second place, the corruptions and extravagances of the papal court at Avignon, however real, were neither as extensive nor as dramatic as later publicists and propagandists would have us believe. To some degree at least, it seems that what they were doing was reading back into the Avignonese era the administrative confusion, corruption, and disastrous financial expedients that characterized the badly shaken papal administration of the later years of schism. Clement V (1305–14) admittedly was wildly extravagant and the magnificence of style and easy-going generosity of Clement VI (1342–52) is summed up well in the celebrated reply he was allegedly prone to giving to those who reproached them for it: 'My predecessors did not know how to be pope.'[22] But John XXII (1316–34), a distinguished canonist, was of simple and unostentatious life; so, too, was Benedict XII (1334–42). And the frugality of Urban V's (1362–70) life went far beyond that imposed upon all of Clement VI's Avignonese successors by the burden of debt they inherited from his excesses, exacerbated by the

<hr/>

[20] See below, pp. 34–6.

[21] 'French' because all seven Avignonese popes, 96 of the 112 French cardinals they created, and almost half of the curialists whose native dioceses we know came from Languedoc (see Guillemain, *Cour pontificale*, 401–80 and 700–2). That is to say, they hailed from a region that had long enjoyed a distinct cultural identity and were not Frenchmen at all in any modern sense of the term. It turns out, indeed, that 'John XXII could not read, without the help of a translator, the letters which Charles IV sent to him and which were written in the language used at Paris.' Guillemain, 'Punti di vista', 187; cf. G. Mollat, 'Jean XXII et le parler de *l'Isle de France*', *Annales de St. Louis des Français*, 8 (1903), 89–91.

[22] S. Baluzius, *Vitae Paparum Avenionensium*, ed. Mollat (Paris: Letourzey & Ané, 1914–27), i. 298.

grinding fiscal demands spawned by incessant military campaigns to re-
conquer and pacify the papal states in Italy. As we now know, it is, in effect,
in the pontificate of Clement VI alone that one can discern of the papal
court truly convincing evidence of the profligacy, dissipation, and luxury
of life that was for long associated with the Avignonese papacy taken as a
whole.

If it is not, then, in the moral stature or personal characteristics of these
popes that an explanation must be sought for the enormous freight of contemporary criticism heaped upon the Avignonese papacy, still less is it in
the overwhelmingly 'French' complexion of that papacy. However pertinent to English, German, or Italian complaints, such an explanation
would shed little light on the multiplicity of charges emanating from
France itself. And keeping that last matter in mind (for the revenues that
the Avignonese popes extracted from France exceeded those drawn from
any other country in Latin Christendom[23]), it may be suggested that the
underlying reason must be sought, rather, in what these popes actually
did, and especially in their systematic extension of that whole structure of
administrative centralization and financial exploitation pursued so re-
lentlessly throughout this period, involving a doubling in the size of the
papal curia and its transformation in many respects into nothing less than
a great fiscal machine.

Given the severe decrease in revenue consequent upon loss of control
over the papal states in Italy, as well as the enormous expenses generated
by successive military campaigns to recover and pacify them—thereby fa-
cilitating the eventual return of the papacy to Rome[24]—one can well understand the pressures inducing these Avignonese popes to resort to
exploitative financial expedients. Most notable among those expedients
was a truly massive extension in the system of 'papal provision' referred to
earlier. That system involved the papal preferment to vacant benefices all
over Europe of candidates selected at Rome, as well as the papal creation
on behalf of other selected candidates of 'expectancies' for benefices not
yet vacant. With that, of course, went an almost inevitable extension in the
concomitant abuses of puralism and non-residence. Many leading clerics,
for example, required by their official duties to reside at Rome, amassed in
their hands in lieu of the direct salaries the pope could not pay whole series
of benefices scattered across Europe which they would rarely if ever visit.

[23] Renouard, *Avignonese Papacy*, 73, 104, where be notes that by 1328 the French kingdom
had become the source of half the papacy's total revenue.

[24] Mollat, *Popes at Avignon*, 319–44.

And prominent among those leading ecclesiastics were the cardinals of the Roman curia and their numerous protégés.

All of this, both reflecting and enhancing the papal claim to possess the plenitude of jurisdictional power in the universal Church, represented an immense and systematic intensification in the exercise of that power.[25] Over the years, however, it had redounded to the benefit, not only of the popes themselves, but also of their most intimate collaborators and advisers, the Roman cardinals. Their involvement in the central government of the Church had been deepening ever since the eleventh century, when the election of popes had become their exclusive prerogative. Already in 1289 Pope Nicholas IV had granted them no less than half of the revenues possessed by the Roman church at that time.[26] By the beginning of the fourteenth century their independent power was formidable, their financial strength impressive, the perquisites attaching to their position multitudinous. The state of affairs at Avignon prompted them to insist increasingly on what they considered to be their rightful share in the spoils accruing from the extension of the system of papal provision; it also strengthened their determination to guarantee and routinize their fluctuating involvement in the framing of papal policy, perhaps even to transform it into a constitutional right. In 1352 they expressed that determination with great force when they drew up and swore to what appears to have been the first electoral capitulation affirming both the fiscal and governmental rights of the Sacred College. Unquestionably monarchic though the papal conception of the shape of ecclesiastical government may have been, theirs betrayed increasingly oligarchic leanings. Tensions mounted accordingly—the more so in that many of the cardinals served as the paid lobbyists of secular rulers, pleading at the papal curia on behalf of the policies of their patrons. 'So long as policy, aims and interests of popes and cardinals were identical,' Walter Ullmann has said, 'there was no reason for resistance on the part of the latter.'[27] Should they diverge, however, at least on matters of real seriousness, then trouble no less serious was clearly to be expected.

---

[25] Guillemain's careful calculations for the eight years of Benedict XII's pontificate (1334–42) reveal a total of 4,002 provisions and expectancies (i.e. provisions to benefices not yet vacant) issued—by any standards a massive intervention in the realm of collation to benefices, and one that was to be intensified under his papal successor. See his *La Politique bénéficiale du pope Benoît XII* (Paris: H. Champion, 1952), 129–41.

[26] W. E. Lunt, *Papal Revenues in the Middle Ages* (New York: Columbia University Press, 1934), i. 26–7.

[27] W. Ullmann, *The Origins of the Great Schism* (London: Burns, Oates & Washbourne, 1948), 7.

FROM THE OUTBREAK OF THE SCHISM TO THE
COUNCILS OF PISA (1409), CONSTANCE (1414–1418),
BASEL–FERRARA–FLORENCE (1431–1449)

Diverge those interests eventually did—in 1378, in the wake of the first
papal election after the return of the papacy from Avignon to Rome, a
move concerning the wisdom of which many of the cardinals had themselves expressed reservations. The trouble that ensued was indeed serious.
Nothing less, in effect, than the onset of what has since come to be known
as the Great Schism of the West.

About the immediate events leading up to the outbreak of schism we
are, historically speaking, comparatively well informed. But over the interpretation of those events (as of so much else to do with the conciliar
epoch) subsequent theological disputes have cast so long a shadow that
the availability of historical evidence has not sufficed to secure harmony
of interpretation.[28] Gregory XI's decision in 1377 to return the papacy to
Rome had been a highly conflicted one, taken in the teeth of opposition
from some of his cardinals and threats to his own life posed by the hostility of the Roman nobles. By the time of his death in March 1378, he had
come, it seems, to regret that decision and to plan the papacy's return,
once more, to Avignon.

In the wake of his demise the Roman populace clearly feared that such
a move might still take place, and the conditions under which the papal
election had to be conducted accordingly left much to be desired. A considerable part of the curial apparatus was still functioning off-site at Avignon, and six cardinals had remained there to supervise it. Only sixteen
were in Rome, then, for the election, eleven of them 'French' (though
divided along regional lines), four of them Italian, and one Spanish. Moreover, when the election took place in April, it was marked by suspicion and
dissension within the conclave, accompanied by rioting without, and
punctuated by a moment of chaos when the mob actually broke in. If it

---

[28] On the history of the schism and its conciliar aftermath there are well-informed and judicious accounts by K. A. Fink in H.-G. Beck *et al.*, *From the High Middle Ages to the Eve of the
Reformation* (Freiburg and Montreal: Herder & Palm, 1970), iv. 401–25, 448–87, by Alberigo
in his *Chiesa conciliare* (Brescia: Pardeia Editrice, 1981; the most recent overall account), and
in E. Delaruelle *et al.*, *L'Église au temps du Grand Schisme* (Paris: Bloud & Gay, 1962–4; a fuller
but more dated account). For the outbreak of the schism, M. Seidlmayer, *Die Anfänge des
grossen abendländischen Schismas* (Münster: Aschendorff, 1940), O. Přerovský, *L'elezione di
Urbano VI* (Rome: Pressa la Società alla Biblioteca Vallicelliana, 1960), and W. Ullmann, *The
Origins of the Great Schism* (London: Burns, Oates, & Washbourne, 1948), are indispensable.
K. A. Fink, 'Zur Beurteilung des grossen abendländischen Schismas', *Zeitschrift für
Kirchengeschichte*, 73 (1962), 335–43, though very brief, is excellent.

was concluded with dispatch, that conclusion was marred by scenes of considerable confusion which were to lend credence to the doubts which quickly surfaced concerning its validity. The Roman mob had clamoured menacingly for the election of a Roman. The cardinals, divided among themselves but unwilling to cave in to that demand, and also (they were later to claim) in fear for their very lives, were led to look beyond their own ranks and, further than that, to choose for the first time in over half a century a non-French pope. Their choice was the archibishop of Bari, a compromise candidate who took the title of Urban VI and was to reign from 1378 to 1389. Though no Roman, he did enjoy the advantages of being, at the same time, an Italian, a subject of the Angevin ruler of Naples, and a curial official who had served faithfully and long at Avignon. If his nationality served to appease the Romans, his career to date certainly suggested the likelihood of his being appropriately responsive to the wishes of the cardinals.

His subsequent behaviour, however, rapidly disabused them of such expectations, and his treatment of the cardinals—erratic, abusive, menacing, violent, extending to recourse to judicial torture and suggestive even of insanity—led very rapidly to something of a breakdown of relations with them. In May and June 1378 all the cardinals except the four Italians left Rome for Anagni. They did so with papal permission but, once there, they were beyond papal control, and in August they moved publicly to repudiate Urban's election as having been made under duress and, therefore, invalid. The three surviving Italian cardinals had abandoned him the previous month, and on 20 September they joined their fellow cardinals in conclave.[29] The latter elected in Urban's place one of themselves—Robert of Geneva—who assumed the title of Clement VII (1378–94). Having failed in an attempt to seize Rome by military force, he abandoned Italy in May–June 1379, and took up residence at Avignon.

Subsequent military and diplomatic efforts, notwithstanding, neither claimant proved able to displace the other or to win the allegiance of all Christian nations. As a result, the protracted schism which ensued was a far more serious affair than any of its numerous predecessors and, despite repeated attempts to end it, it was to endure for almost forty years. Both claimants stubbornly refused, either individually or concurrently, to withdraw; both went on damagingly to appoint new flights of cardinals. Loyalties rapidly hardened and, as the years went by, and despite urgent

---

[29] Though (each 'believing that he was the future pope') they all apparently abstained from actually voting. The fourth Italian, Tebaldeschi, had died on 7 Sept., but not before affirming the legitimacy of Urban's election. See Ullmann, *Origins*, 62–3.

pleas to desist, their rival curias understandably strove to perpetuate their claims to office. As a result, opportunities to put an end to the crisis were repeatedly ignored. Benedict XIII was elected in 1394 to succeed Clement VII; Boniface IX, Innocent VII, and, finally, Gregory XII were elected in 1389, 1404, and 1406 respectively, to succeed Urban VI and to perpetuate the Roman line. The result? The development within the Church of widespread administrative disorder, deepening spiritual malaise, and, in the end, grave constitutional crisis.

There is much, doubtless, to be said in support of the traditional tendency to place much of the blame for this sorry state of affairs upon the mounting ambitions and pretensions of the cardinals as well as upon the national and dynastic animosities then prevailing in Europe. The resentment of the cardinals at Urban's startling, precipitate, and ill-tempered assaults upon their dignity, their privileges, and their opulent style of life is not in doubt. Nor is it easy to ignore the fact that the ultimate territorial composition of the two 'obediences', Roman and Avignonese, was in large part predictable on the basis of previous political and diplomatic alignments.[30] Over the past half-century, however, renewed investigations of the disputed election and the contextual factors surrounding it have converged on the conclusion that the doubts later expressed about the validity of Urban's election cannot simply be put down to retroactive resentment but have to be taken more seriously than once was customary.[31] Even at the time, the violence outside the conclave and the fear within had given rise to an admitted measure of uncertainty about the whole proceeding and had induced the Italian Cardinal Orsini to abstain from casting a vote. Within two days of the election, moreover, its validity was being questioned in Rome itself.[32] It was not, indeed, on the facts of the election itself that those who argued, then and later, for the legitimacy of Urban's title chose to base their case. They did so, instead, and revealingly, on the subsequent behaviour of the cardinals (Orsini himself included)—their participation in Urban's coronation, the homage they

---

[30] Thus England and much of the empire sided with Urban, while France, Scotland, and Castile aligned themselves with Clement.

[31] See esp. Seidlmayer, *Anfänge*, Přerovský, *L'elezione*, Fink, 'Zur Beurteilung', and A. Franzen, 'Zur Vorgeschichte des Konstanzer Konzils', in A. Franzen and W. Müller, eds., *Das Konzil von Konstanz* (Freiburg: Herder, 1964), 3–35 (at 3–7). Ullmann's *Origins*, the most recent account in English, though it, too, accords serious consideration to the objections of the cardinals, marks something of an exception to this trend and emphasizes that it was their later judgement about Urban's incapacity that led them to try to invalidate his title. There is also a careful and nuanced account by E. R. Labande in Delaruelle *et al.*, *L'Église*, i. 3–44.

[32] Přerovský, *L'elezione*, 42; Seidlmayer, *Anfänge*, 8–18; Fink in Beck *et al.*, *From the High Middle Ages*, 404.

performed to him, their compromising delay in challenging the validity of his election. Přerovský in particular, however, has emphasized their fearful and anguished doubts about the sanity of the new pope and the extent to which such doubts would appear to have been warranted.[33] 'History still looks at him,' it has been said, 'as more or less mentally deranged.'[34] Emphasized, too, has been the degree to which the cardinals' behaviour at Rome in the fortnight following the election was the outcome of coercion and of fear in face of what had emerged as a 'pathological personality' and fell short, as a result, of constituting any genuine form of 'tacit consent'.

With the official letters about Urban's election which the cardinals sent to the rulers of Europe (the wording of which had sometimes to be approved by the redoubtable pontiff himself), it turns out that they also sent secret messages undercutting the position they were officially affirming.[35] Already in April 1378 Cardinal Pedro de Luna (the future Benedict XIII, pope of the Avignonese line) is reported to have said that 'if the pope or other Romans found out that I or some other members of the Sacred College had doubts about his election, none of us would escape'.[36]

However compelling the other motives traditionally imputed to them, the cardinals, then, unquestionably had some perfectly valid grounds for raising troubling questions about the legitimacy of Urban's claim to be pope. At the same time, and as a result, however convenient such questioning may have been to their own political and diplomatic interests, those rulers who chose eventually to align themselves with Clement VII were able to do so with reasonably good conscience, though sometimes only after considerable hesitation. Only after extensive hearings at both Avignon and Rome and as the outcome of a lengthy judicial process did the Kingdom of Castile declare for Clement. Nor did Charles V of France rush to align himself with Avignon. The old claim that he had already come to an understanding with the dissident cardinals at the time of the second election appears to be groundless.

People at the time, then, and prominent among them those intimately involved in the whole sorry chain of events we have described, appear to

---

[33] Přerovský, *L'elezione*, 65–9, 182–90.

[34] A. Franzen, 'The Council of Constance: Present State of the Problem', *Concilium*, 7 (1965), 37. Later on, the cardinals of his own creation were so convinced of Urban's incapacity as to toy with the idea of subjecting him to a council of guardianship, an idea for which several of them were to pay dearly when Urban discovered the 'plot' against him and had those responsible imprisoned and tortured. See Ullmann, *Origins*, 167–8.

[35] Seidlmayer, *Anfänge*, 243, 288, 332; Fink, 'Zur Beurteilung', 338.

[36] 'Nam si ipse vel alii Romani scirent quod ego vel aliquis ex dominis meis dubitaremus de sua electione, nullus nostrum evaderet' (Baluzius, *Vitae*, ed. Mollet, ii. 701).

have been in a state of 'invincible ignorance' about the matter. Nor are historians today in any better position. The best we can probably do is to recognize that after 8 April 1378, there was one man with a questionable claim to the papal title and after 20 September of that year there were two. The *historical* evidence, certainly, does not permit one simply to insist on the exclusive legitimacy of Urban's title to the papacy (and, therefore, the legitimacy of his successors in the Roman line). If that claim has often been advanced, and it is enshrined, after all, in the current official listing of popes, it should be recognized that it has been advanced on theological or canonistic rather than historical grounds.[37] For centuries, it was certainly not part of the standard case put forward even by papal apologists. Instead, it came to the fore only with the dramatic rise to prominence of ultramontanism in the nineteenth century.[38]

The thirty years subsequent to the unhappy events of 1378 were punctuated by repeated attempts to bring the schism to an end. Apart from efforts by the rival pontiffs themselves to settle the issue by force of arms (the so-called *via facti*), hope centred initially on the possibility of some successful arbitration between the two claimants (the *via compromissi*) and, still more, on the possibility of assembling a general council representing the entire Church to render judgement on the validity of the contested election. This latter view (the *via concilii*), sponsored originally by the Italian cardinals (and especially Orsini) during the months immediately following upon Urban's election,[39] drew support at Paris in 1379–81 from the German theologians Conrad of Gelnhausen (d. 1390) and Henry of Langenstein (d. 1397), as well as from their younger French colleague, Pierre d'Ailly (d. 1420). In a sense, then, the 'conciliar movement' was something of a reality right from the beginning of the schism, although the pressure that the French king exerted on the University of Paris in order to nudge it into alignment with Clement quickly led to a (somewhat) uneasy bracketing there of the conciliarist viewpoint. With the passage of time, however, members of both obediences came to view the Roman and Avignonese claimants as sharing equally the responsibility for protracting the schism. Support shifted accordingly to the *via cessionis*, a plan that envisaged the renunciation of their respective claims by both of the rival pontiffs and the

---

[37] See below, Epilogue.

[38] Thus Juan de Torquemada, Thomas de Vio, Cardinal Cajetan, and Robert, Cardinal Bellarmine all subscribed to the view that no one was the undoubted pope at the time of Constance. See T. M. Izbicki, 'Papalist Reaction to the Council of Constance', *Church History*, 55 (1986), 15.

[39] Seidlmayer, *Anfänge*, 179–80.

subsequent combination of the two colleges of cardinals with the purpose of electing a new and universally accepted pope.

On behalf of the *via cessionis* the German rulers exerted pressure on the Roman pope, as did the French king on his Avignonese rival.[40] But, like the *via compromissi* before it, this approach also failed. The years of seemingly barren diplomacy, however, finally bore unexpected fruit towards the end of 1408 when new life was breathed into the old *via concilii*. With the collapse of a final round of half-hearted negotiations between the Roman and Avignonese popes, the French clergy renewed their earlier withdrawal of obedience from Avignon.[41] At the same time, disgruntled cardinals from both colleges were moved in frustration to forswear allegiance to their respective pontiffs, and to summon a general council of the entire church to meet in Italy. That move attracted widespread sympathy. In an effort to forestall the trouble they could see looming, the rival pontiffs desperately tried to assemble their own competing councils. But neither of these assemblies succeeded in attracting a convincing number of participants; neither could boast of the impressively ecumenical character of the general council that opened at Pisa on 28 March 1409.

Better attended than its predecessor councils at Lyons and Vienne had been, Pisa enjoyed the support of by far the greater part of Latin Christendom.[42] When the Roman and Avignonese popes refused to cooperate with it, and having declared itself to be canonically constituted and a legitimate general council, Pisa embarked upon a careful legal process which culminated on 5 June 1409, in the formal deposition of the two popes as notorious schismatics and obdurate heretics. And no fewer than twenty-four cardinals signed that sentence.[43] In proceeding in this fashion, the fathers

---

[40] The latter going so far in his attempts to coerce Benedict XIII into abdication as to embark in 1398 (with the support of the French clergy assembled at the Third Paris Council) on a unilateral national withdrawal of obedience from the pope. See H. Kaminsky, 'The Politics of France's Subtraction of Obedience from Pope Benedict XIII', *Proceedings of the American Philosophical Society*, 115/5 (1971), 366–97.

[41] A move of no little importance in the incipient vindication of the 'Gallican Liberties'. See Stump, *Reforms*, 6, 10–12; V. Martin, *Les Origines du Gallicanisme* (Paris: Bloud & Gay, 1939), i. 29 n. 2.

[42] Numbered among the participants were 4 patriarchs, 24 cardinals, more than 80 archbishops and bishops (with more than another 100 represented by proxies), more than 100 abbots (nearly 200 more sent their proctors), the generals of the mendicant orders and of most other religious orders, several hundred theologians and canonists, and representatives of many universities, of many cathedral chapters, and of most European princes (the kings of the Spanish peninsula and the German King Rupert were notable exceptions). See Fink, in Beck et al., *From the High Middle Ages*, 418.

[43] Ibid. 422. Cf. the collection of pertinent documents translated in C. M. D. Crowder, *Unity, Heresy and Reform* (New York: St Martin's Press, 1977), 41–64.

[handwritten marginalia: Canonistic teaching ... devout, criminal popes are liable to ... deposition — not by cardinals but by a general council]

assembled at Pisa were following the generally accepted canonistic teaching of the day to the effect that a pope who deviated from the true faith or
who was guilty of notorious crimes that scandalized the Church and were,
therefore, tantamount to heresy was liable to judgement by the Church
and, if need be, to deposition. In so doing, they were also following a well-
established canonistic opinion to the effect that, while in such a legal
process the cardinals properly had certain powers of initiative, the body
competent to proceed to judgement was, not the college of cardinals, but
the general council. Presumably because of that, the greater part of Latin
Christendom appears to have recognized not only the legitimacy of the
Council of Pisa itself, but also the validity of the actions it had taken, including the unanimous election by the cardinals of both obediences of a
new pope, Alexander V (1409–10), whose legitimacy Alexander VI, by his
own choice of title, was still to recognize a century later. Indeed, the survival of the Roman and Avignonese pontiffs in their drastically reduced
obediences may have been assured only by Alexander V's death and by the
fact that his successor, John XXIII (1410–15), was by the most generous of
estimates a man of less than praiseworthy life. As Vincke, the scholar who
edited the conciliar *Acta* of Pisa concluded, it was John XXIII who 'ruined'
the reputation of 'the papal succession of Pisa'.[44]

Survive, however, the Roman and Avignonese popes certainly did, so
that what eventually emerged from the Council of Pisa was the addition of
a third or 'Pisan' line of claimants to the two already existing. The stage
was set thereby for the central role the emperor-elect Sigismund was to
play both before and during the subsequent Council of Constance
(1414–18) as churchmen and secular rulers alike struggled to put an end to
what had now become a wholly intolerable situation. Under pressure
from Sigismund, John XXIII himself was prevailed upon to convoke that
council. He did so with considerable reluctance and with the hope of being
able to control and direct its proceedings by exploiting the numerical preponderance which the multitudinous Italian bishops inevitably enjoyed.
That hope was dashed when the council moved to neutralize that (pre-
dictably) pro-papal preponderance by choosing to follow the example
of Pisa and to organize itself into conciliar 'nations', each casting a
single vote in the general sessions without regard to the number of its

---

[44] Thus Johannes Vincke in *Lex für Theologie und Kirche* (2nd edn.), viii. 521. Cf. Vincke,
'Acta Concilii Pisani', *Römische Quartalschrift*, 46 (1938), 87–330. Fink, in Beck *et al.*, *From the
High Middle Ages*, 452–4. The focus was on John XXIII's unworthiness rather than on any
questioning of his legitimacy. Indeed, 'the legitimacy of the Council of Pisa and of the election of John XXIII was recognized almost unanimously'.

members.[45] It then went on to address the three main issues confronting it: matters pertaining to the faith; the cause of reform; the ending of the schism. It is the last that must concern us here. Together with the widespread recognition of the centrality of general councils to the achievement of reform, it was the task that was to open the way for a historic attempt to impose ongoing constitutional restraints on the pope's exercise of his power.[46]

Concerned about intimations that his misdeeds, real or alleged, warranted public investigation, John XXIII played for time by spreading the word that in the interest of unity he would indeed be willing to relinquish his office. While so doing, however, he himself determined that he would be well-advised to flee the council and thus to disrupt its activities. His flight to Schaffhausen on 20 March 1415, caused great alarm and confusion at Constance and almost achieved that end. In the absence of the pope who had convoked it and the legitimacy of whose title most of the council fathers regarded as unquestionable, the assembly was threatened with disintegration. That might well have come about had not Sigismund moved decisively to bolster its confidence, and had not Jean Gerson (1363–1429), chancellor of the University of Paris and a widely respected theologian of moderate disposition, rallied it on 23 March with his stirring sermon *Ambulate dum lucem habetis*.[47]

In that celebrated address, insisting that 'the Church, or a general council representing it', can limit the pope's use of his plenitude of power 'by known rules and laws for the edification of the Church', Gerson went on to affirm a belief widespread already among the council fathers and certainly central to conciliarist thinking, namely, that the Church or general council 'is so regulated by the direction of the Holy Spirit under authority from Christ that everyone of whatever rank, even the papal, is obliged to hearken and obey it'. With the firm adoption of that stance and the

---

[45] The five were the French, the Italian, the German, the Spanish, and the English. These 'nations', like the nations of the medieval universities, were in fact combinations of nationalities, e.g. the 'German' including the Scandinavians, Czechs, and Poles.

[46] Fink, in Beck *et al.*, *From the High Middle Ages*, 463, notes that in the *De modis uniendi et reformandi ecclesiam in concilio universali* of the curialist Dietrich of Niem, 'which summarized all of reform proposals, there occurs in several places the statement, short and to the point: *concilium ergo generali . . . limitet ac terminet potestatem coactivam et usurpatam papalem*'. See *Dietrich von Niem: Dialog*, ed. H. Heimpel (Leipzig and Berlin: Teubner, 1933), 43, 46–7.

[47] So titled from the opening words drawn from the Gospel according to St John 12: 35: 'Walk while ye have the light, lest darkness come across you.' The text of the sermon is printed in Jean Gerson, *Œuvres complètes*, ed. P. Glorieux (Paris: Desdeé, 1960–73), v. 39–50; English translation in Crowder, *Unity*, 76–82. The words cited below are from ibid. 81–2.

dawning realization that John was unlikely to return or to honour his
promise to resign, the sentiments of the council fathers became increasingly conciliarist. Their hearts hardened, they determined accordingly to
proceed, even in his absence. The outcome was the formal promulgation
at the fifth general session on 6 April 1415, of the famous superiority decree
Haec sancta synodus which declared that the Council of Constance was a
legitimate general council, that it derived its authority immediately from
Christ, and that all Christians including the pope himself were bound, on
pain of punishment, to obey it and all future general councils in matters
pertaining to the faith, the ending of the schism, and the reform of the
Church.[48]

About this historic decree, at least from the mid-fifteenth century onwards, controversy was persistently to swirl. But there can be little doubt
that the subsequent activity of the Council of Constance (and much of
what was later to be undertaken by the Council of Basel) was to be
grounded, implicitly or explicitly, on the claims it advanced. John XXIII,
having been taken prisoner on 17 May 1415, was deposed less than two
weeks later—not, it should be noted, because of doubts about the legitimacy of his title or because he was thought by lapsing into heresy to have
forfeited that title, but, rather, because the council, having tried him, had
found him guilty of perjury, simony, and other forms of scandalous mis-
conduct.[49] That sentence he was to refrain from challenging. Within two
months Gregory XII, the Roman claimant deposed already at Pisa, having
been accorded the courtesy of being permitted to convoke the council
himself (thus legitimating its activities in the eyes of his own followers at
least, if only from that moment forward), proceeded to resign. Of course,
having been permitted so to act, he could also claim to have received from
the council at least tacit confirmation of the legitimacy of the Roman line
of popes. Since the nineteenth century at least, though not earlier, much
has been made of that fact. The members of the council themselves had

---

[48] 'Ecclesia vel generale concilium eam repraesentans est regula a Spiritu Sancto directa,
tradita a Christo, ut *quilibet cujuscumque status etiam papalis existat*, eam audire ac eidem
obedire teneatur; alioquin habendus est ut ethnicus et publicanus. Patet ex immutabili lege
divina Math. xviii promulgata'—Gerson, *Œuvres complètes*, ed. Glorieux, v. 44 (italics
mine). The very words italicized were to reappear not only in the documents preparatory to
Haec sancta (see H. Schneider, *Das Konziliarismus* (Berlin and New York: de Gruyter, 1976),
Beilage I) but also in the text of the decree itself. For the precise wording of that decree and
the various ways in which it has been interpreted, see below, Ch. 2.

[49] A point which Jean Gerson was careful to stress just three years later when, speaking of
the judicial process pursued in John's case, he said: 'in toto processu usque post sententiam
definitivam suae depositionis, reputatus est ab eodem concilio verus papa'. *An liceat in causis fidei a papa appellare* (1418); in *Œuvres complètes*, ed. Glorieux, vi. 286.

not been unaware of that possibility; but their overriding objective was unity, they had John's promise to depart the scene, and they were even less disposed to fuss about a formality that very few of them took seriously than they had been the previous year when they had treated the ambassadors of both Gregory XII and Benedict XIII as official papal delegates rather than merely as private Christians—or, for that matter, later on when, in an attempt to win Benedict XIII over and to finish the business at hand, they extended to him the same privilege of convocation. And that despite the fact that they themselves had endorsed the sentence of Pisa and had recognized John XXIII as sole legitimate pope.[50]

On 4 July 1415, accordingly, Gregory's bull of convocation was read in general conciliar session and his resignation accepted. Despite the extension to him of various diplomatic carrots, Benedict XIII did not prove to be so accommodating. Having finally in December 1415 lost the support of the Spanish kingdoms, and surrounded henceforth only by a tiny coterie of adamant supporters, he was to persist in his claim to be the one true pope right up to his death in 1423. But by then events had transformed him into a redundant curiosity. In July 1417, long after the members of his obedience had declared their own adherence to Constance, he had been judged *in absentia*, found guilty of 'perjury, heresy, and schism', and declared deposed. Several months later, after a protracted and politically charged wrangle on the issue of which should take precedence, reform or the election of a new pope, the latter course of action had won out. A body of papal electors enlarged by the inclusion of deputies from each conciliar nation as well as by the presence of the cardinals from all three of the former obediences, had gone into conclave to choose a new pope and had emerged in triumphant agreement. With the election on 11 November 1417 of one of the cardinals of the Roman obedience who had, however, switched his allegiance to the Pisan pontiffs and who now took the title of Martin V (1417–31), the long agony was over. The church had at last a pope

---

[50] Franzen, 'Council of Constance', 44–5, where he adds that 'the legitimacy of the popes of both Rome and Avignon had been clearly rejected . . . by the canonical deposition of 1409. Those who took part in the Council of Constance did not dream of recognizing either of them again.' It is pertinent in this connection to note that Nicholas V later on, presumably on grounds similarly diplomatic and pragmatic rather than theological or canonistic, permitted the rump-council of Basel the redundant formality of electing him pope as well as the privilege of decreeing its own dissolution. Similarly, Basel's somewhat improbable anti-pope, Felix V, was not only permitted to resign but also to continue exercising papal rights in the territories that had previously constituted his 'obedience'. See Fink in Beck *et al., From the High Middle Ages*, 485. There was absolutely nothing singular about the courtesy extended to Gregory XII and the grounds for making much of it are certainly not to be found in the historical record itself.

whose claim to office was universally recognized to be legitimate and the Great Schism was at an end.

But if the schism was now a thing of the past, the 'conciliar movement' was not. A divided Christendom had indeed been reunited but only because a general council, acting in the absence of its papal head, had formally claimed on certain crucial issues to be the legitimate repository of supreme power in the Church, had been able to vindicate that claim, and had been willing to do so even to the point of trying and deposing popes. In the month prior to the papal election and as part of the reform package to which all the conciliar nations had already given their approval, it had also gone on to set up constitutional machinery designed to prevent in the future any reversion to papal absolutism. In the decree *Frequens* it decreed that general councils were to be assembled, the first in five years' time, the second in seven, and thereafter at regular ten-year intervals. In this decree, complemented by the companion piece of legislation *Si vero*, the fathers at Constance were careful to ensure that, even if the pope chose not to convoke them, general councils would assemble automatically at nothing less than ten-yearly intervals and, in the unhappy event of renewed schism, within no more than a year of its outbreak. As Stump correctly insists, 'the decree was very tightly drawn indeed', stipulating as it did that 'the council will always be ruling (*vigeat*) or will be awaited because of the [previously] set date [for its assembly]'.[51]

In the long haul, this constitutional machinery was to prove less effective than doubtless they had hoped, but clearly not as ineffective as Martin V may conceivably have wished it to be or as his successors persistently sought to render it. As the unhappy events at the Council of Basel were later to prove, the constitutional aspirations reflected in *Frequens/Si vero* were buttressed by the fundamental conciliarist commitment that had found historic expression in the earlier decree *Haec sancta*.[52] So, too, as Martin V himself discovered, was the claim to be able legitimately to appeal from the judgement of a pope to that of a future general council. He made that discovery when his unwillingness to condemn the Teutonic knight, John of Falkenberg, for the advocacy of tyrannicide led the Polish delegates at Constance to appeal from his judgement to that of the next

---

[51] Stump, *Reform*, esp. 105–9 (and 317–18, 382–4), for the drafts produced by the first and second reform committees. Cf. Brandmüller, *Konzil von Konstanz*, ii. 335–58. For the full text, see Alberigo and Tanner, *Decrees*, i. 438–42.

[52] Though not explicitly grounded in the decree. Brandmüller, *Konzil von Konstanz*, ii. 351, properly insists 'dass in *Frequens* jegliche Auspielung auf *Haec sancta* fehlt'. Cf. Alberigo, *Chiesa conciliare*, 229.

general council. Though the surviving evidence is scanty and imprecise, it does appear that the pope, by way of reaction to that move, had had read in consistory on 18 March 1418 the sketch of a proposed bull denying the legitimacy, not simply of that particular appeal, but in principle of *any* such appeal. In the event, Martin (who had implicitly approved *Haec sancta*) refrained from promulgating the putative bull.[53] But the very possibility of its promulgation served to elicit from Jean Gerson an energetic defence of the right of appeal, one that grounded it not only in divine and natural law but also in *Haec sancta*, and did not forbear from noting that if *that* decree were invalid, so too were the actions that the council had based upon it, not excluding the trial and deposition of the rival pontiffs and therefore, the subsequent election of Martin V himself.[54]

Such uncertainties notwithstanding, and in faithful observance of the provisions of *Frequens*, Martin did issue the pertinent summons for the next council to meet in 1423 at Pavia. Having assembled there (attendance was quite sparse), it was soon transferred to Siena and had to go about its business under very difficult political circumstances. Its organization in accordance with the Pisan and Constance model into five conciliar 'nations' facilitated the intrusion of competing political interests and troubling diplomatic pressures into its deliberations. So, too, did the opening up within the ranks of the council fathers of an overt split between those of staunchly conciliarist and those of re-emergent papalist sympathies.[55] Alarmed, it may be, by the threat of collusion between the conciliarist faction and his enemy, Alfonso V, king of Aragon, Martin moved quickly in 1424 to dissolve the assembly. He did so without prior consultation with the

[53] Remigius Bäumer, 'Das Verbot der Konzilsappellation Martins V, in Konstanz', in Franzen and Müller, *Konzil von Konstanz*, 187–213, gives a careful and detailed analysis of the incident, stressing the paucity of the direct historical evidence pertaining to it, but making the case that the prohibition was intended to be valid universally, not directed simply at the Polish action. See also Alberigo, *Chiesa conciliare*, 234–7, and P. de Vooght, *Les Pouvoirs du concile* (Paris: Éditions du Cerf, 1965), 73–6. For Martin V's approval of all things about matters of faith done in the council in a conciliar way (i.e. as opposed to those things done only by the individual conciliar nations), see Alberigo and Tanner, *Decrees*, i. 450–1 n. 4.

[54] This case Gerson made in his tract *An liceat in causis fidei a Papa appellare*, in *Œuvres complètes*, ed. Glorieux, vi. 283–90. Cf. his *Resolutio circa materiam excommunicationum et irregularitatem* (1418), consid. 8, ibid. 294–6 (at 295), and *Dialogus apologeticus*, ibid. 296–304 (at 302–3).

[55] Well reflected in two of the sermons preached at the council, the first by the conciliarist John of Ragusa, who sings the praises of Constance 'in all its acts', the other by his more 'papalist' colleague, Girolamo of Florence, who argued for following 'the old paths' prevailing prior to Constance and the tradition of holding general councils but infrequently. For which, see W. Brandmüller, *Das Konzil von Pavia–Siena* (Münster: Aschendorff, 1968–74), ii. 157–201. Crowder, *Unity*, 140–5, makes sections of these sermons conveniently available in English.

members of the council and before it had really succeeded in getting its teeth into the task of reform. As a result, and as Brandmüller has insisted, its significance 'lies . . . less in dogmatic or disciplinary decrees than in its concrete historical course' which, ominously for the future, had made painfully clear 'the underlying difficulty of cooperation between pope and council'.[56]

Seven years later, again in accordance with the provisions of *Frequens* but this time under palpable pressure, Martin convoked another council to meet at Basel, at the same time appointing Cardinal Giuliano Cesarini (d. 1444) to serve as its president and delegating to him the power to dissolve it. Shortly thereafter he died.[57] In his great task of restoring a stable, functioning, and adequately financed papal administration, Martin had had to confront enormous difficulties, both political and fiscal. The latter were so challenging that when the reforming concordats he had concluded with the several nations reached their five-year term he had had little choice but to modify earlier commitments. While respecting the overall reform provisions of Constance and deferring to the wishes of the countries concerned, he had reverted with relief to the older (and troubling) pattern of provisions and expectations. As a result, while he left behind him on his death a reorganized curia in control of the resources of a pacified papal state, he also bequeathed to his papal successor some very serious problems. The college of cardinals had begun to react negatively to the authoritarian nature of his administration, and when the Council of Basel opened on 23 July 1431, it did so burdened by an enormous freight of reforming expectations. That burden was all the heavier because demands for reform and for the faithful observance of the Constance decrees had been included in the electoral capitulations which the cardinals had drawn up after Martin's death and imposed upon his successor. The new council was burdened also by having as that successor Eugenius IV (1431–47), a much less capable and decisive man who shared all of Martin's fear of conciliar reform but little of the judgement and ability that had enabled the latter to cope with it.[58]

[56] Brandmüller, *Konzil von Pavia–Siena*, ii. 1.

[57] For Basel see esp. Fink's account in Beck *et al., From the High Middle Ages*, 473–87, and J. W. Stieber, *Pope Eugenius IV* (Leiden: E. J. Brill, 1978). Stieber (5 n., 331–3, and 396–7) characterizes Paul Ourliac's account of the Council of Basel (in Delaruelle *et al., L'Église*, ii. 227–92) as high papalist in inspiration, as making 'no attempt to present or explain the council's standpoint', and as presenting, therefore, a 'distorted picture'. He also claims that a similarly 'apologetic' concern 'to vindicate absolute papal monarchy at all costs' mars J. Gill, *The Council of Florence* (Cambridge: CUP, 1959) and his *Constance et Bâle-Florence* (Paris: Éditions de l'Orante, 1965).

[58] It should be noted that in the early months of the council Eugenius was stricken with a stroke, that left him for some time with his right arm and eye paralysed. See G. Christianson,

Reform, then, was destined to be the overriding concern at Basel. But the course of the council was to be shaped (and distorted) by four other factors—two of them internal, two external. The internal factors were its novel form of organization and the growing prominence in its deliberations of the great constitutional question of the relationship of papal to conciliar authority. The external factors were the Hussite wars in Bohemia and the quest for reunion with the Greek Orthodox Church. So far as the internal factors went, and in part because of the uneven pattern of national attendance, for the organization by conciliar 'nations' adopted at Pisa, Constance, and Pavia–Siena was substituted a pattern of organization into four deputations or commissions each roughly representative of the several nations in attendance and of all ecclesiastical ranks. The members were all incorporated individually into the council, and among them there prevailed an atmosphere of greater equality than that characteristic of previous councils. The members of the ecclesiastical hierarchy found it much harder to dominate their clerical subordinates and, in the absence of organized conciliar 'nations', secular rulers now lacked the leverage they had possessed at Constance and had used to marshal support for their policies among the delegates (lay well as clerical) who hailed from their own territories. At Basel, accordingly, the lower clergy in general and the university masters in particular came to play a role more influential than heretofore and one much less subject to hierarchical guidance or (at least in the beginning) to princely manipulation.[59]

This may help explain the tendency of the council fathers to interpret reform in head and members in a rather one-sided fashion, looking primarily to the elimination of what by now had come to be viewed as abuses in the exercise of papal power, both judicial and fiscal. The jurisdiction of the courts of Rome, for example, was restricted in favour of the ordinary courts in the provincial churches. In relation to papal provisions and to annates, and except in manifestly unusual circumstances, all general reservations to bishoprics and abbacies were prohibited; similarly, and this time without exception, all payments connected with the filling of benefices. Such reforming decrees, moreover, most of them approved

Cesarini (St Ottilien: EOS-Verlag, 1979), 28; J. Gill, *Eugenius IV* (Westminster, Md.: Newman Press, 1961), 42.

[59] This state of affairs was to be exacerbated in the later stages of the council when, because the proceedings had dragged on for so long at the expense of pressing responsibilities in their own dioceses or monastic houses, the number of prelates remaining in attendance was not impressive. H. Jedin, *Ecumenical Councils of the Catholic Church* (London and New York: Herder & Herder, 1960), 129, notes that 'in a vote taken on December 5, 1436, . . . the bishops . . . formed much less than a tenth of the participants'.

only after extensive deliberation and during the council's first four years, reflected not only the wishes of the deputation for reform at Basel itself but also the unfulfilled aspirations of successive reform commissions at Constance and, in some cases, the persistent concerns of reformers all the way back to William Durand at the Council of Vienne and beyond. That those measures should have included the renewal of the Constance decrees *Haec sancta* and *Frequens* and the stern reaffirmation of the constitutionalist aspirations embedded in those decrees reflected more specifically the response of the council fathers to the ill-judged hostility Eugenius IV betrayed towards the council.[60] That hostility was to distort the whole course of Basel, leading to bitter disagreement and renewed schism, blunting the drive for reform, and precipitating a lengthy conflict concerning the ultimate locus of supreme authority in the Church.[61] On the theoretical level or level of principle that conflict was not to be settled at Basel. And if it was ultimately to be settled in practice, it was less by dint of ecclesiological argument or the force of theological persuasion than by skilful papal diplomacy, by the intrusion of temporal power, and, after no less than eighteen years of conciliar *sturm und drang*, by the onset of widespread exhaustion.[62]

Because Martin V had reached an agreement with the Greeks to hold a council of reunion on Italian soil, and because he himself had had some reservations about the Council of Basel right from the start, Eugenius had been anxious not to prolong its life. It was he, as a result, who was led to precipitate the first great crisis at the council. Misled, it may be, by the initially poor attendance but in the teeth, none the less, of opposition from some of his cardinals, he moved in December 1431, and less than six months after its assembly, the dissolution of Basel and the convocation of

[60] On which, see Christianson, *Cesarini, passim*.

[61] Already in Jan. 1432, Cardinal Cesarini had written to Eugenius, enclosing a copy of the text of the Constance decree *Haec sancta*, reporting that the council fathers had begun to recur to it, and reminding him that 'the pope must obey the council in those things pertaining to reformation'. Later on, in June of the same year, he did not refrain from recurring to the argument Gerson had used (see above), pointing out to Eugenius that if Constance, its decree *Haec sancta*, and (therefore) the deposition of John XXIII were invalid, so, too, would be the election of Martin V and, accordingly, that of his successor. See Christianson, *Cesarini*, 45, 57–8.

[62] See the useful collection of translated documents relating to the council in Crowder, *Unity*, 146–81. Its endurance led the English envoys at the Frankfurt Diet (1442) to point out sardonically that 'Constance had determined that a council was to be celebrated every ten years, and not for ten years'—cited in Johann Helmroth, 'Basel, the Permanent Synod?' in G. Christianson and T. M. Izbicki, eds., *Nicholas of Cusa on Christ and the Church* (Leiden: E. J. Brill, 1996), 35–56 (at 43). Helmroth adds (35) that its sheer duration was 'perhaps the most amazing characteristic of the Council of Basel.'

another council at Bologna. In so doing, Eugenius badly misjudged the mood of council fathers and cardinals alike, and a startling fifteen of the latter, out of a total of twenty-one, chose to side with Basel. Even more damagingly, he also misjudged the priorities and moral fibre of Cardinal Cesarini, the legate whom he and Martin V before him had appointed to preside over the council.[63] In the wake of an anti-Hussite crusade in Bohemia that had ended only three months earlier in disastrous defeat, Cesarini had committed the Council of Basel to vital negotiations with the moderate wing of the victorious party. He now saw those negotiations imperilled by an ill-judged papal bull of dissolution. When it arrived, then, he did not hesitate to join the council fathers in refusing to obey the pope. Deadlock ensued and, as men of the stature of Nicholas of Cusa (1401–64) joined Cesarini in rallying to the side of the council, that body was understandably led to reaffirm its conciliarist principles in robust and forthright fashion and to go on to act in terms of those principles.

An agreement with the Hussites was to be promulgated in 1436 as the *Compactata* of Prague and ratified by the council (though not by the papal curia) in 1437. But negotiations to that end had begun already in 1433 and the very prospect of an agreement, having been greeted with enormous relief in Germany and eastern Europe, had served to enhance the council's prestige and to render the pope's opposition to its activities well-nigh unsustainable. On 15 December 1433, then, having manœuvred for position with increasing desperation, Eugenius was forced to capitulate. In the final version of the bull *Dudum sacrum*[64] he was led to declare his earlier dissolution of the council to have been invalid and to acknowledge that what the council had done since its inception in 1431 (including, therefore, the repromulgation of *Haec sancta*) had been legitimate throughout.

Dudum sacrum, however, proved in the event to constitute a truce rather than a final settlement. Powerless to overturn reforms that constrained his revenues and curtailed him in the exercise of his prerogatives, and unable to prevent the passage of further reforms inspired by a similar intent, Eugenius sought to ameliorate his plight by simply ignoring in practice the restrictions imposed in theory by those reforms. So much so, indeed, that in January 1436 the council deemed it necessary formally to enjoin him to respect its decrees on the crucial matters of reservations and annates. Moreover, although in the negotiations with the Greeks the bulk

---

[63] For Cesarini and the importance of his leadership during the first years of the council, see the judicious appraisal by Christianson, *Cesarini*.

[64] For the various drafts of *Dudum sacrum* and Cesarini's efforts to bring Eugenius to unequivocal submission, see Christianson, *Cesarini*, 99–112.

of the council's membership insisted that the proposed council of reunion be held either at Basel or Avignon or in Savoy, Eugenius himself persisted in siding with the Greeks and holding out for the translation of the assembly to Italian soil. Already in 1435 Ambrogio Traversari, the Camaldolese superior general and one of the pope's staunchest supporters and representatives at Basel, had begun to argue that Eugenius would do well to transfer the council to Italy, to limit voting membership to bishops (the Italians thus predominating), and then to get that reconstituted assembly to abrogate not only *Haec sancta* but also *Frequens*.[65] And in 1437 Eugenius in effect committed himself to that course of action.

That he was able to get away with so radical a manœuvre reflects the degree to which the council fathers at Basel had come by that time to forfeit some of their earlier credibility. Internal dissension, alarming talk about initiating against Eugenius a judicial process for contumacy (thus evoking the spectre of renewed schism), the arrogation to themselves of some of the functions traditionally discharged by the Roman curia—none of these things had played well to the world at large and they had begun to worry the leadership of the council itself. When at the twenty-fifth general session (May 1437) the majority of the fathers once more rejected his demand that the council remove itself to an Italian city, Eugenius quickly sided with the dissenting minority—later dubbing it, if not the *major* certainly the *sanior pars* of the assembly. In September, then, he proceeded to transfer the council to Ferrara and later in January 1439, alleging the threat of plague, moved it again, this time to Florence.

With this Council of Ferrara–Florence most of the Italians and some luminaries of the stature of Nicholas of Cusa and Cesarini chose now to align themselves. But the majority elected to remain at Basel and the new papal council was destined, as a result, to be poorly attended. While the English and Burgundian rulers did move to recognize it, England sent no delegation and Charles VII of France went so far as to forbid his clergy to attend. Apart from the three Burgundian bishops, then, the only non-Italian bishops in attendance were officials from the papal curia. Because of this it has been noted that the reunion agreement reached with the Greek representatives on 6 July 1439 and proclaimed in the decree *Laetentur coeli* was basically an agreement between Eugenius and the Byzantine emperor (both of them beleaguered souls) as well as between small coteries of dependent clerics on both sides. The speed with which the agreement was to be rejected by the clergy and people of the Byzantine empire (including

[65] Steiber, *Eugenius IV*, 43–4.

even some of those who had helped negotiate it) suggest the accuracy of that appraisal. In the long haul its most significant feature may well have been the fact that it included the first conciliar definition of the Roman primacy, a definition which Hubert Jedin has described as nothing less than 'the Magna Carta of the papal restoration',[66] and which was to serve as the model in 1870 for the First Vatican Council's own solemn definition of the pope's primacy of jurisdiction.

It must be confessed that the Council of Ferrara–Florence achieved little else. In September 1439 Eugenius secured from it an endorsement of his bull *Moyses vir Dei*, which proscribed as heretical and schismatic Basel's recent declaration that the superiority of council to pope as defined in *Haec sancta* was an undeniable article of the Catholic faith.[67] But he appears to have had little further use for the council. Thereafter it faded rapidly from view. No date is recorded for its termination and the general acknowledgement of its status as a legitimate ecumenical council was by no means a foregone conclusion. Over a century later, the French at Trent were still refusing to recognize it as such.[68]

Things were otherwise at Basel which continued to command a goodly measure of (admittedly conflicted) loyalty and a good deal of attention. There the stubborn majority which had stood fast with the council had gone on to declare the superiority of council to pope to be an article of faith, to mount a judicial process against Eugenius leading first to his suspension from office and then to his deposition, and finally to elect in his place Duke Amadeus of Savoy, who took the name of Felix V (1439–49). But it was a blunder on the part of the council thus to have precipitated a new schism within the Latin Church, especially when the papal Council of Ferrara–Florence, only four months earlier, had apparently succeeded in ending the ancient schism between Greeks and Latins. And the attitude

[66] H. Jedin, *A History of the Council of Trent*, tr. E. Graf (London: Thomas Nelson & Sons, 1952–61), i. 19–20, where he adds that 'this definition was the answer to Basel's attempt to erect the Conciliar theory into a dogma', a remark which prejudges, of course, the much controverted question of the dogmatic status of *Haec sancta*. For which, see below, Ch. 2.

[67] That he followed up in 1441 with the bull *Etsi non dubitemus*, in which he went on to impugn the validity of the original Constance decree *Haec sancta* on the grounds that it had been promulgated, not by a true general council, but merely by the followers of John XXIII's obedience. Though Juan de Torquemada had already adumbrated this position privately, *Etsi non dubitemus*, issued a quarter of a century after the solemn promulgation of *Haec sancta*, may well have been the first public ventilation of that viewpoint. See Vooght, *Les Pouvoirs du concile*, 146–51; T. M. Izbicki, *Protector of the Faith* (Washington, DC: Catholic University Press, 1981), 95–106; Stieber, *Eugenius IV*, 43 n. 62, 147 n. 28, 192–3 n. 28; Remigius Bäumer, 'Die Stellungnahme Eugens IV', in Franzen and Müller, *Konzil von Konstanz*, 337–56.

[68] See below, Ch. 3.

now adopted by the secular powers was to make that painfully clear. If few had rallied to Ferrara–Florence, few, equally, rushed to recognize Felix V. France and the German empire set the tone by adopting a neutral stance in which they were to persist uneasily for the better part of a decade.

Those years were to be punctuated by a vigorous diplomatic and propagandistic effort on the part of the Eugenians which was designed to propagate the alarming notion that the 'democratic' ideas of the conciliarists posed a dire threat to every form of monarchical authority, secular no less than papal, and to nudge rulers into allying themselves with Rome in order to fend off this allegedly radical onslaught.[69] It is not clear that that papal campaign met with any marked degree of success,[70] and it is important to recognize that the neutrality to which France and the empire had committed themselves was rather qualified in its nature. While that posture of neutrality certainly reflected an unwillingness to recognize the deposition of Eugenius IV, a move which would have rendered the breach between pope and council irreparable, it did not necessarily signify any rejection of the council's reforming programme or of the conciliarist constitutionalist vision so closely connected with it. Indeed, in the stipulations of the Pragmatic Sanction of Bourges (1438), and with the support of the French clergy, Charles VIII adopted in modified form the bulk of the reforms legislated at Basel in the years preceding. In 1439, the German imperial electors did something similar via the provisions of the *Acceptatio* of Mainz. And if, over the years, political and diplomatic exigencies were to determine the degree to which all such provisions were implemented in practice, the Pragmatic Sanction and the *Acceptatio* both included a clear and influential reaffirmation of the principles which Constance had laid down in *Haec sancta* and *Frequens*.

Although it was to involve, then, a long-drawn-out effort to mediate the dispute between Eugenius and Basel, the new posture of neutrality attempted to do so on the basis of a stance much closer to the conciliarist position of Basel than to that of the pope. It was only after Felix V failed to enlarge the area of his support, and after the fathers at Basel refused to respond to mediation on terms very favourable to them, that Eugenius's persistent diplomacy and his willingness to make exceedingly generous practical concessions in return for princely support began to have the desired effect. The critical shift occurred finally in the February of 1447 when

---

[69] See below, Ch. 2.

[70] Though it did stimulate by way of response from such conciliarists as Andrew of Escobar, Thomas Strempinski, and John of Segovia a historically significant shift in the precise way in which they framed their conciliar theories. For which, see below, Ch. 2.

the Emperor Frederick III, acting rather on the basis of dynastic self-interest than on anything abstract or ideological, broke ranks with the imperial electors and, without insisting on extensive preconditions, initiated the move to recognize the Eugenian claim. That same month Eugenius himself died and, under his successor, Nicholas V (1447–55), the general mood shifted and the atmosphere became a good deal less charged. On 7 April 1449, with France now following the example of Germany in renouncing its neutrality and rallying to the Roman pontiff, Felix V himself resigned. On 25 April the Council of Basel, transferred earlier to Lausanne and having been conceded the formality of itself proceeding to the election of Nicholas V, now went on to decree its own dissolution. And with that event, it has long been customary to claim that the conciliar movement had come to an end and that a new era of papal restoration had dawned.

THE RESTORATION PAPACY AND THE COUNCILS OF PISA (1511–1512), LATERAN V (1512–1517), AND TRENT (1545–1547, 1552–1553, 1562–1563)

It is only the benefit of historical hindsight that permits one, however, the luxury of so exceedingly confident an appraisal. Not much more than a quarter of a century ago Paul Ourliac could speak grandly of the year 1440 as being a great ideological and ecclesiological hinge or turning point, after which theologians, canonists, and humanists alike turned eagerly to the 'constructive' task of engineering 'the triumph of the papal monarchy'.[71] He was able to do so, however, only by dint of relying a little too one-sidedly on the witness of Italian and Spanish clerics (many of them pursuing careers at the papal curia), overlooking how widespread north of the Alps was the post-conciliar disillusionment with the papacy, and ignoring 'how strongly the principal clergy in the Empire, in France, and in Poland were committed to the supreme authority of general councils in the church' as well as to their centrality in the realization of ongoing hopes for reform.[72] He was likewise able to do so only by slighting the price the papacy had been forced to pay in order to triumph over Basel. That price was unquestionably a very considerable one, that of accepting—helping sponsor even—what amounted to a constitutional change of a type very different from that for which the conciliarists had struggled, and one that was to be

[71] Paul Ourliac and Henri Gilles, 'La Problématique de l'époque: Les Sources', in G. Le Bras (ed.), *Histoire du droit et des institutions de l'église en Occident* (Paris: Sirey, 1956–84), 13. 1. 51; cf. Ourliac in Delaruelle *et al.*, *L'Église*, i. 285.

[72] Stieber, *Eugenius IV*, 331–47 (the words quoted appear at 331).

determinative for the history of the papacy in particular and the Church in general all the way down to the nineteenth century.

Long before the outbreak of the Great Schism some secular rulers had embarked on the process of asserting in an increasingly forthright fashion their claim to sovereign jurisdiction over the provincial churches functioning within their territorial boundaries. In so doing, they were in effect reversing a tide that had been flowing in the opposite direction ever since the late eleventh century when the Gregorian reformers had launched their ambitious campaign to liberate the provincial churches from imperial or royal control. By the mid-fourteenth century that process of reversal was particularly well-advanced in England, where kings had become adept at marshalling national anti-papal feeling in order to pressure the papacy into conceding to them an ever larger share of the ecclesiastical spoils (collations to English benefices and taxes levied on the English church).[73] But it was the widespread dissatisfaction engendered by the prolonged years of schism that gave so many rulers the opportunity to move in a similar direction—not least among them the French, who gained mightily from the 1398 and 1406 withdrawals of obedience from the papacy.[74] The disarray and confusion in Church government engendered by the schism constituted a critical phase, then, in the disintegration of what had become under papal leadership and government a genuinely international Church into a congeries of what were, *de facto* if not *de jure*, national and territorial churches dominated by kings, princes, and the rulers of such proud city-states as Florence and Venice. And that process of disintegration was in some measure to be progressive. The fifteenth century was to witness a further parcelling out among the secular rulers of Europe of the pope's sovereign authority over the universal Church or, better, a frequently renegotiated division of that authority between popes and rulers, and one that reflected differences in the shifting balance of power between the pope and the particular rulers concerned. Given the prehistory of the process, none of this is particularly surprising. What is surprising, however, is the degree to which Eugenius IV himself proved willing to participate in

---

[73] See M. McKisack, *The Fourteenth Century* (Oxford: OUP, 1959), 272 ff.; W. A. Pantin, *The English Church in the Fourteenth Century* (Cambridge: CUP, 1955), 84; W. E. Lunt, *Financial Relations of the Papacy with England* (Cambridge, Mass.: Mediaeval Academy of America, 1939–62), i. 366–418.

[74] The second of which, Kaminsky has argued, involved nothing less than 'a major constitutional action', one that placed the king at the head of the Gallican church and left it, at the end of the five years of subtraction, 'fully integrated into the French realm'. See his 'Politics of Subtraction', 368, 396–7. In this he follows in the footsteps of Haller rather than Hübler. For a helpful analysis, see Stump, *Reform*, 3–14.

this whole process of establishing secular rulers as masters of their respective churches so long as those rulers were willing to withdraw their support for the conciliar idea and for the threat of reform in head and members that went with it. Loss of control and concomitant loss of revenues notwithstanding, possession of the actual substance of power over the provincial churches of Christendom mattered less, it seems, than the retention of a theoretically supreme authority over the universal Church. Its almost inevitable corollary, however, the revenues flowing in to Rome from the Church at large having been grievously diminished, was the pressing need for the popes of the Restoration era to turn inward and to focus their attention on the government of the papal states upon which they had now come to depend for a full half of their overall revenues.[75] In effect, however grandiose their theoretical powers as supreme pontiffs and however much people continued to pay lip service to that position, they themselves had to concentrate a good deal of their day-to-day effort on their role as Italian princes,[76] involving themselves in the complex diplomacy and ever-shifting coalitions required by the need to protect their Italian principality, to maintain, accordingly, the balance of power in Italy, to stave off the recurrent threat of French and Spanish intervention in the politics of the peninsula, and when such efforts failed, to control and diminish the extent of that intervention.

Of course, the role and preoccupations of an Italian prince were hardly such as to sustain and promote in the late fifteenth-century popes any active concern with Church reform. Moreover, as the repeated electoral capitulations drawn up by the cardinals reveal, discussion of reform seemed inevitably (and embarrassingly) to focus attention on their own failure to adhere to the solemn provisions of *Frequens*. It tended to call once more to mind gloomy memories of the desperate struggle for survival Eugenius IV had had to wage against the Council of Basel. Despite the outcome of that struggle (politically after all rather than ideologically determined), the idea of the council was by no means dead. Just how alive it was, indeed, the historical scholarship of the past half-century has made unambiguously clear.[77] North of the Alps the sentiment of the clerical leadership (and especially that of the monastic clergy) remained

---

[75] P. Partner, *The Papal State under Martin V* (London: British School at Rome, 1958), 153–4; idem, 'The "Budget" of the Roman Church', in E. F. Jacob, ed., *Italian Renaissance Studies* (London: Faber & Faber, 1960), 256–74.

[76] It is significant that it was during the pontificate of Sixtus IV (1471–84) that Italian superseded Latin as the language of the papal curia.

[77] See below, Ch. 3.

overwhelmingly conciliarist. During the late fifteenth and early sixteenth centuries, accordingly, appeals from the judgement of the pope to that of a future general council were frequent. In our standard general histories of the period, the importance customarily attached to Pius II's bull *Execrabilis* (1460), which prohibited such appeals as nothing less than 'an execrable abuse',[78] has been very much an exaggerated one. In its own day, the bull was viewed less as some sort of binding or definitive judgement than as simply the understandable reaction of a single faction, one that witnessed less to the marginal or heterodox nature of the alleged abuse than to its very currency. Certainly, the half-century and more between the ending of Basel and the onset of the Protestant Reformation was punctuated by such appeals to the judgement of a future general council. The canonists themselves defended the procedure, and against it not only Pius II (1458–64) but also Sixtus IV (1471–81) and Julius II (1503–13) railed in vain.[79]

The understandable proclivity of their royal and princely rivals to use the appeals procedure as a diplomatic stick with which to beat the pope illustrates the type of danger the latter could confront when the currency of conciliarist ideas among clergy disillusioned by what they took to be Rome's abandonment of the cause of reform intersected with the policies, ambitions, or diplomatic needs of their rulers. At such moments, the threat that a general council might actually assemble and renew the decrees of Constance and Basel became suddenly quite palpable. Such a moment occurred in the 1460s when George von Podiebrad, king of Bohemia, negotiated with the king of France and others in the hope of assembling a council.[80] Such was the situation again in the 1520s and 1530s during the pontificate of Clement VII (1523–34) when, first, the Emperor Charles V[81] and later Henry VIII of England[82] both mounted to that end conciliar

---

[78] A translation of the bull is conveniently available in Crowder, *Unity*, 179–82.

[79] G. Picotti, 'La pubblicazione ei primi effetti della "Execrabilis" di Pio II', *Archivio della R. Societa Romana di Storia Patria*, 37 (1914), 33 ff., lists and discusses the various appeals to a general council after Pius II's prohibition. Jedin, *History*, i. 67 n. 4, cites some further instances but notes that Picotti 'does not adequately distinguish between the appeal to the Council as a legal procedure and the demand for a Council and its convocation'. Jedin also notes (ibid. 66–8) that even Pius II's papal successors do not appear to have regarded *Execrabilis* as authoritative and that it was not widely disseminated.

[80] J. Macek, 'Le mouvement conciliaire', *Historica*, 15 (1967), 5–63, and idem, 'Das Konziliarismus in der böhmischen Reformation', *Zeitschrift fur Kirchengeschichte*, 80 (1969), 312–30.

[81] See Jedin, *History*, i. 220–44, and, for the role of his chancellor Mercurio de Gattinara in that particular campaign, J. Headley, *The Emperor and his Chancellor* (Cambridge: CUP, 1983), 86–113.

[82] For which, see below, Ch. 3.

(and, in some ways, conciliarist) campaigns. And still vivid in the memory of Christendom during those latter episodes was the sudden transformation in 1511 of what it would be easy in retrospect to dismiss as a piece of blunted diplomatic weaponry into a potent political and ecclesiological threat. Nothing less, in fact, than the actual convocation by five dissident cardinals (one Italian, two Spanish, two French) of the would-be general council that has gone down in history as the *conciliabulum* of Pisa (1511–12).[83]

In so acting, those cardinals of the opposition did not fail to appeal to the provisions of *Frequens*. But it was no abstract legalism that steeled their courage and moved them to take so radical a step. They were moved, rather, by their own individual disgruntlement with Julius II, and, indeed, with his predecessor, too. They were moved also by the persistence into the age of papal restoration of the old curialist 'oligarchic' tradition, and by memories of the veritable struggle for power that had raged between pope and cardinals during the latter years of the fifteenth century. In that struggle the efforts of the cardinals had been somewhat less than successful and, had the French king withheld his support, it is as hard to imagine their risking the convocation of the council as it is to imagine its successful assembly. But Louis XII did not withhold his support, though his own wish to promote such a council stemmed from very different reasons than theirs—his political ambitions in Italy and his need to respond to Julius II's attempts to thwart them. Early in 1510, in an abrupt reversal of his earlier policy, Julius had thrown in his lot with the opponents of the French presence in Italy. Louis now sought, with the complaisance of the Emperor Maximilian I and the help of the cardinals of the opposition, to encompass his ruin.

Under such circumstances, it is not surprising that the council turned out to be a small and almost entirely French affair. It did little more than reissue the Constance superiority decree *Haec sancta* and pronounce Pope Julius to be suspended from office. Its major achievement, indeed, was ironically that of provoking the pope into an attempt to take the wind out of its sails by himself convoking the Fifth Lateran Council. In that attempt

[83] For Pisa and the subsequent Fifth Lateran Council, see Jedin, *History*, i. 101–38; Brosse et al., *Latran V et Trente*, 14–94; idem, *Le Pape et le Concile*; Oakley, 'Conciliarism and the Fifth Lateran Council?'; N. H. Minnich, 'Concepts of Reform Proposed at the Fifth Lateran Council', *Archivium Historiae Pontificiae*, 7 (1969), 163–251; idem, 'The Healing of the Pisan Schism (1511–13)', *Annuarium Historiae Conciliorum*, 13 (1981), 59–192; Franco Todescan, 'Fermenti Gallicani e dottrina anti-conciliariste al Lateranense V', in L. L. Vallauri and G. Dilcher, eds., *Cristianesimo, secolarizzazione, e diritto moderno* (Baden-Baden and Milan: Nomos, Giuffre, 1981), i. 567–609.

he was wholly successful—so much so, indeed, that Louis XII quickly changed tactics and, after Julius's death in 1513, abandoned the Pisan assembly and indicated his willingness to come to some sort of mutually satisfactory accommodation with Julius's successor, Leo X (1513–21). As for the Lateran Council itself, it was very much a papal council in its organization and procedures and was poorly attended by all except the multitudinous Italian bishops. For long, its decrees were poorly known in Germany and England and its ecumenicity was not recognized in France.[84] Summoned to counteract the effect of the French exploitation of conciliar theory, its proceedings (not surprisingly) were punctuated by anxious attempts to contain that theory. Even in convoking it, Julius II had clearly felt the need to pre-empt any misunderstanding of his action by insisting that the decree *Frequens* had long since lapsed into desuetude and had nothing to do with the action he was taking. Again, and as we have already seen,[85] presumably scenting a dangerous whiff of 'episcopalism' about it, Leo X rejected outright the modest proposal of the bishops assembled at the council to establish an episcopal 'sodality' or 'confraternity' to protect and advance their common interests. Even more tellingly, Leo and his successor moved to destroy the particular alliance that had always threatened to give teeth to the conciliar idea and had just succeeded in so doing, namely, the alliance between the Parisian Faculty of Theology—the most vigorous proponent of conciliarism—and the French king, the ruler most frequently tempted to exploit that theory. And they destroyed it in the fashion that had long since become classic. That is, they set out to reassure the king that he had more to gain by aligning himself with the pope and turning his back on the conciliar idea than by trying to use it as a diplomatic weapon. The Concordat of Bologna, concluded in 1516 while the Lateran Council was still in session, was the outcome of that effort.

Bitterly opposed by both the University of Paris and the Parlement of Paris on the ground that it permitted the resumption of appeals to Rome, restored annates, and came close to affirming the superiority of the pope's authority to that of a general council,[86] it conceded to the French king the right to nominate to nearly all of the bishoprics, abbacies, and major benefices in his kingdom. In return, Leo secured the abrogation of the Pragmatic Sanction of Bourges, the base from which for so long the French conciliarists had been able to operate with impunity. That same year, then, in the bull *Pastor aeternus*, the Lateran Council was moved to

---

[84] Schneider, *Konziliarismus*, 48–9.   [85] See above, Prologue.
[86] R. J. Knecht, 'The Concordat of 1516', *Birmingham University Historical Journal*, 9 (1963), 22–9.

Pragmatic Sanction null and void, and will and void, and decrees of Basel [handwritten marginalia]

declare the Pragmatic Sanction null and void, and, with it, the decrees of the Council of Basel which it had affirmed. Those decrees, it said, dating as they did to the period after Eugenius IV had translated the council to Ferrara, were thus the product of a 'quasi-council' or 'conventicle' since it is the Roman pontiff alone, inasmuch as he has 'authority over all councils', who possesses 'full right and power to convoke, transfer, and dissolve councils'.[87]

Over the years, in an anxious attempt to ground in it a formal conciliar repudiation of the conciliar theory, much has been made of this glancing and oblique formulation. 'To the papal prohibition of appeal to a Council,' Jedin has said, 'the assembly now added a condemnation of the theory itself.'[88] But the bull is in fact concerned with the conciliar question only at one remove. It addresses itself explicitly to no more than the papal right of convoking, transferring, and dissolving councils. It does not spurn the superiority decree which Basel had solemnly reaffirmed at its eighteenth general session[89]—three years, that is, *before* Eugenius had transferred the council to Ferrara. Nor is there any mention of Constance or any rejection of *Haec sancta*. Even at this late date, as Jedin himself concedes, 'it is clear that the curia did not feel equal to a formal declaration of the nullity of the superiority decree of Constance and Basle' even though that had been forthrightly 'suggested in Ferdinand the Catholic's instructions to his envoys at the Council'.[90] The Gallican theologians, certainly, discerned no such intent in the bull. For them, on matters conciliarist, it was to be business as usual and, nearly two centuries later, Bishop Bossuet was at pains to brush aside attempts to construe as anything so formal as a prohibition the few fugitive phrases involved.[91]

Closer to the event, the Faculty of Theology at Paris, by way of protest against the Concordat, did not hesitate to follow the traditional route and

---

[87] Alberigo and Tanner, *Decrees*, i. 642.

[88] Jedin, *History*, i. 133. For a rejection of that claim, see Oakley, 'Conciliarism at the Fifth Lateran Council?', 461–2. Note that Schneider grumbles (*Konziliarismus*, 48 n. 187) that 'eine sehr restriktive Deutung dieser Stelle gibt Oakley'.

[89] i.e., on 26 June 1434, when it once more reaffirmed *Haec sancta*.

[90] Jedin, *History*, i. 133; cf. J. M. Doussinague, *Fernando el Católico* (Madrid: Espasa–Calpe, 1946), app. 50, 539. It is worthy of note, however, that not even Ferdinand thought that the pope's superiority to the council extended to the case of a heretical pope or of a pope whose title to office was in doubt: 'proporneys ante Su Santidad en el conçilio que aquellos dos decretos se revoquen expressamente y se haga nuevo decreto que declare que el Papa es sobre el concilio *excepto en el caso de la eregia como dize el canon Si Papa XL dis y en el caso que dos o tres son elegidos en çisma por Sumos Pontifices que solo en estos dos casos el Conçilio pueda conosçer y sea juez de la causa del Papa y no en mas*' (italics mine).

[91] See above, n. 88.

to appeal to a future general council. By that time, of course, the Lateran Council had itself been dissolved and, with it, the hopes for the long-awaited reforms that its opening sessions had helped excite. By that time, too, Martin Luther had framed his ninety-five theses. In November 1518, in anticipation of the papal sentence, and again in 1520, Luther himself appealed from the judgement of the pope to that of a future general council. In his appeals, ironically enough, he drew the legal sections from the text of the earlier appeal launched by the theologians of Paris.[92] For the pope, it may be, that was worrying enough in itself, but probably less worrying than those later calls, emanating from Catholic as well as Lutheran circles, for the assembly of a 'general, free Christian council in German lands'. But, for one reason or another, worry did not prove enough to precipitate any sort of action that was truly timely, decisive, and effective. In that respect, two particularly surprising things may be noted about the response of the popes to the Protestant challenge. First, their failure for the better part of a quarter-century to convoke the general council for which so many Christian leaders called and upon the determinations of which so many anxious and conflicted spirits reposed their hopes. Second, when finally it did assemble, and despite the challenge laid down by the novel Protestant ecclesiologies of the day, the failure of that long-awaited council to promulgate any dogmatic decree on the nature of the Christian Church—and that despite its readiness to address so many other controverted issues.

Absent the survival into the sixteenth century of a robust tradition of conciliarist thinking, neither of these failures would be fully comprehensible. Luther himself, it should be noted, attributed the reluctance at Rome to summon a council to dismal memories there of the threat that Constance and Basel had posed to papal power.[93] And when Trent finally assembled in 1545, the unfolding of events at the council was such as to make it clear that the apprehension such memories nourished was far from being groundless. If, during the bitter disputes of the council's final phase the papal legates proved able in the end to sideline the hotly disputed issue of the nature and reach of papal power, they well knew that their diplomatic success was predicated on a damaging failure to face up to the most pressing ecclesiological question of the day. Wrapping up their work when the council was at an end, and in sombrely prophetic

---

[92] The two appeals are compared in J. Thomas, *Le Concordat de 1516* (Paris: A. Picard, 1919), iii. 72–4.

[93] For the lead-in to Trent and the marked ecclesiological tensions at that council, see below, Ch. 3.

mood, they were at pains to convey to the pope their own worried sense that peace in the Church would continue to prove elusive and recurring divisions inevitable so long as that neuralgic question was left undecided.[94] Subsequent events were to vindicate the accuracy of that gloomy appraisal.

[94] H. Jedin, *Geschichte des Konzils von Trient* (Freiburg: Herder, 1948–78), iv/2. 57.

2

Gerson's Hope: Fifteenth-Century Conciliarism and its Roots

[It is necessary to distinguish] between 'conciliarism' and 'conciliar.' 'Conciliarism' usually means that the council is in principle above the pope; its most extreme form was developed by Marsilio of Padua and William of Ockham. One cannot say that this teaching was already universally advocated during the Great Schism ... The basic mistake of older scholars ... was to dub all 'conciliar' ideas as 'conciliarist' when they were concerned with the place of the council and with granting the council a controlling function over the person, but not the office, of the pope in some well-known exceptional cases. ... The ambivalent notion of 'conciliarism' has misled many, and still hampers us today in the understanding of the Constance decrees.

(August Franzen[1])

[C]onciliarism was not really a complete and organized doctrine that anyone could have applied with greater or lesser intransigence to the Western Schism, but a movement that was gradually formed, drawing on the traditional doctrinal patrimony with the object of responding to the state of crisis and necessity that had developed in the very heart of Christianity.

(Giuseppe Alberigo[2])

Meanwhile, it has become a commonplace that in the sense of a coherent system there never was such a thing as 'conciliarism.' Rather it should be allowed that there were almost as many conciliarisms as there were contemporary authors writing on the matter. ... With this express proviso, I use, therefore, the simple, undifferen-

---

[1] Franzen, 'Council of Constance', 46.   [2] Alberigo, *Chiesa conciliare*, 345.

tiated concept 'conciliarism'; in the particular case its meaning will
have to be gathered from the historical context.

(Walter Brandmüller[3])

To put it bluntly, there can be no history of conciliar theory, and
therefore no foundations of the conciliar theory, because no such
thing as the conciliar theory was ever a historical reality—except, as
Giuseppe Alberigo has pointed out, as a polemical device designed to
taint defenders of conciliar theory with heresy.

(Constantin Fasolt[4])

Over the years, the anxious attempts of historians to come to terms with
the daunting complexities of conciliar thinking have oscillated between
two polar extremes. Those oscillations are clearly reflected in these
quotations. Seeking, on the one hand, to rescue cosmos from chaos and to
impose the clarity of order where confusion could so easily reign, some
(e.g. Franzen, Bäumer, Andresen) have sought to promote the cause of
understanding by distinguishing between 'extreme' or radical and
'moderate' versions of the conciliarist viewpoint, attempting the while, via
an exercise in legislative definition, to reserve for the former the term 'conciliarist', while advocating the use of the term 'conciliar' to denote the
latter.[5] Or, in more elaborate and developmental fashion (thus Andresen),
by distinguishing successive phases in which an earlier 'curialist conciliarism' modulated at Constance into a predominantly 'ecclesiological
conciliarism', only to be nudged to one side during the Basel years by a
'democratic conciliarism'.[6] Meanwhile, at the opposite end of the
spectrum others (e.g. Alberigo, Brandmüller, Fasolt), while continuing
admittedly to speak about 'conciliarism' and 'conciliar theory', have
fretted with varying degrees of agitation about the propriety of so doing.
They have emphasized, accordingly, the interpretative dangers attendant
upon the imposition of 'extrinsic and improper classifications' on the
past, and have expressed worry about the intrusion into the past of
ideologically driven distinctions. All such moves impede, after all, the
historian's necessary engagement with ideas in their concrete specificity,

---

[3] Brandmüller, *Konzil von Pavia–Siena*, i, Vorwort.

[4] Fasolt, *Councils and Hierarchy*, 318.

[5] Franzen, 'Council of Constance', 46; R. Bäumer, *Nachwirkungen des konziliaren Gedankens in der Theologie und Kanonistik des frühen 16. Jahrhunderts* (Münster: Aschendorff, 1971), 14–15.

[6] Carl Andresen, 'History of the Medieval Councils of the West', in H. J. Margull, ed., *The Councils of the Church*, tr. W. F. Bense (Philadelphia: Fortress Press, 1966), 177–226.

immersed as those ideas necessarily are in the flow of time and shaped, therefore, by the unique particularities of circumstance.[7]

Neither extreme is simply to be dismissed. But neither emerges from scrutiny unscathed. If the former is distorted by the illegitimate intrusion into the historical endeavour of presuppositions that are clearly of theological or canonistic provenance,[8] the latter resonates a little too directly, in some at least of its frequencies, to the strain of 'epistemological hypochondria' that became during the last quarter of the twentieth century so marked a feature of interpretative debate in the humanities.[9] However fashionable it grew to be in its moment of celebrity, the casual dismissal of the very possibility of writing the history of a doctrine or tradition of thought has yet to be grounded in any argument that has as its target anything more substantial than a dialectical straw man.[10] That being so, and it being my purpose in this book to trace the half-millennial history of a tradition of thinking that I believe can properly be identified as 'conciliarist',[11] it behooves me in what follows to find a path that falls somewhere between the two extremes described above, erecting cairns along the way to mark the trail being blazed. And my point of

---

[7] Alberigo, *Chiesa conciliare*, 344–5; Brandmüller, *Konzil von Pavia–Siena*, i, Vorwort; Fasolt, *Councils and Hierarchy*, 318–19.

[8] As Alberigo, *Chiesa conciliare*, 345, correctly observes. 'Mi sembra sempre più chiaro che le distinzioni tra un conciliarismo moderato, uno equilibrato e uno estremista ubbediscono più al tentativo ideologico di salvare almeno qualcosa dall'accusa globale di estremismo formulata dalla polemica curiale, che non a differenziazioni dottrinali effetive.' Similarly, for a case of overreliance on that classification, see Bäumer, *Nachwirkungen*, 15, 265–6. Cf. F. Oakley, 'Conciliarism in the Sixteenth Century', *Archiv für Reformationsgeschichte*, 68 (1977), 129–32; U. Bubenheimer, Review in *Zeitschrift der Savigny-Stiftung für Rechtsgeschichte*, 90 (1973), Kanonistische Abt. 59, 455–65; H. Oberman, 'Et tibi dabo claves, regni coelorum', *Nederlands Theologisch Tijdschrift*, 39 (1975), 97–118. For the intersection of these classifications with the question of the origins of conciliar theory, see below.

[9] See esp. Fasolt, *Councils and Hierarchy*, 318–19, where he evokes with approval 'Quentin Skinner's judgment that it is fundamentally misguided to write intellectual history in terms of the history of doctrines'.

[10] For my own response to the rather hard-edged case Skinner made originally in 'Meaning and Understanding', see F. Oakley, *Omnipotence, Covenant, and Order* (Ithaca, NY, and London: Cornell University Press, 1984), 15–40. For a more recent appraisal of the more carefully modulated point of view to which Skinner now adheres, along with a defence of a 'history of traditions of thought' approach to the history of ideas, see Oakley, *Politics and Eternity* (Leiden: E. J. Brill, 1999), 1–24, 333–41.

[11] Sympathizing here with Brian Tierney's characteristically sensible judgement to the effect that while 'in strict accuracy . . . one should speak of a collection of conciliar proposals rather than of the "Conciliar Theory"', it remains true that 'there was sufficient unity of thought among the various writers to render the latter expression significant and useful.' *Foundations of the Conciliar Theory* (Cambridge: CUP, 1955; rev. edn., 1998), 3.

departure for this *longue durée* will be the pattern of conciliarist thinking that rose to prominence during the roughly three-quarters of a century stretching from the onset of schism in 1378 to the dissolution of the Council of Basel in 1449—during, that is, the era punctuated by the successive Councils of Pisa, Constance, Pavia–Siena, and Basel–Ferrara–Florence that I have become accustomed to calling 'the classical age of conciliar theory'.

THE CONCILIARISM OF THE CLASSICAL ERA

Historians have sometimes been moved to characterize the thirteenth century as belonging still to 'the *prehistory* of ecclesiology', and James of Viterbo's *De regimine christiano* (1301–2) has been called, not without justice, 'the oldest treatise on the Church'.[12] In his *Liber sententiarum*, destined to become the standard textbook on which for the better part of five centuries students of theology cut their dialectical teeth, Peter Lombard (d. 1160) had devoted no separate section to the topic *De ecclesia*. A century and more later, the same was to be true of Aquinas' theological writings. Only in the fourteenth and fifteenth centuries did ecclesiology become a focus of intense concern among theologians. It did so then because of the trials and tribulations that the ecclesiastical institution was forced during those centuries to endure, and because of the flood of publicistic literature those upheavals helped engender. Among those successive crises, three in particular are worthy of note. First, there were the great conflicts concerning the proper relationship between the temporal and spiritual authorities that broke out in the first quarter of the fourteenth century—that between Boniface VIII and Philip IV of France, then, a little later, that between John XXII and Lewis of Bavaria. Second, there was the long-drawn-out dispute over the Franciscan doctrine of apostolic poverty which was to intersect with that latter conflict but which had surfaced already in the 1250s during the conflict between the secular and mendicant masters at the University of Paris and was to grind on, racking both the Franciscan order itself and the Church at large for the better part of the century ensuing. Third, there was the schism that broke out in 1378 and endured for almost forty years.

[12] G. de Lagarde, *La Naissance de l'esprit laïque au déclin du moyen âge* (Paris and Louvain: Éditions E. Nauwelaerts, 1956–70), v. 4; H. X. Arquillière, *Le Plus Ancien Traité de l'église* (Paris: G. Beauchesne, 1926).

For our purposes, the importance of the first of these three disastrous trials is that it spawned the first group of treatises devoted specifically to the Church and to the nature and dimensions of its power: the *De regimine christiano* of James of Viterbo, Aegidius Romanus's *De ecclesiastica potestate* (1302), John of Paris's *De potestate regia et papali* (1301–2), and then, a little later and as a result of the papal–imperial struggle, the *Defensor pacis* (1324) of Marsiglio of Padua, along with a whole series of publicistic writings produced by the great English philosopher and theologian, William of Ockham, most notable among them his enormous *Dialogus* (completed *c.*1334). These works already manifest the anxious scrutiny of Church structures and far-reaching speculation concerning the nature and location of ecclesiastical authority that were also to characterize the publicistic and theological writings generated in connection with the two other great outbursts of controversy concerning the nature of the Church's traditional order. Of these the second, at least at its moment of initiation during the secular-mendicant controversy at Paris in the 1250s, served to generate a bitter debate concerning the proper relationship between pope, bishops, and ordinary parish clergy. In relation to the much-resented privileges conferred by the pope on those belonging to the mendicant orders of friars, some of the latter argued that the bishops were hardly in a position to challenge them, given the fact that the same pope was the source in its entirety of their own jurisdictional power. To which the secular vindicators of the independent jurisdiction of the bishops responded that the supreme position which the popes properly enjoyed by divine ordination as successors of St Peter involved no monopoly of jurisdiction but was in fact *complemented* by the jurisdictional power which Christ had himself conferred independently on the other apostles and, therefore, on the bishops as successors of those apostles. Similarly, though in lesser degree, on the lower clergy as successors of the seventy-two disciples.

The debate this engendered was to resurface again at the University of Paris in 1408 when the great conciliarist, Jean Gerson, was chancellor. And it led him not only to restate the essentially episcopalist position hammered out in response to mendicant claims a century and a half earlier but also to incorporate that position in the greatest of his conciliarist writings.[13] It helped inform, then, the third great outburst of ecclesiological

---

[13] See B. Tierney, *Religon, Law and the Growth of Constitutional Thought* (Cambridge: CUP, 1982), 60–4; and for the pertinent texts in Gerson, L. B. Pascoe, *Jean Gerson's Principles of Church Reform* (Leiden: E. J. Brill, 1973), 146–64. For the deeper background, Y. Congar,

and constitutional debate that the outbreak and stubborn persistence of the schism was to engender. Taken as a whole, along with the canonistic commentaries on which they so often drew, the writings spawned by all three crises confront us, in effect, with a body of thought on matters ecclesiological at once more extensive, more varied, more developed, and more systematic than anything emerging from the centuries preceding.

Of the four marks of the Church designated in the Nicene Creed—one, holy, Catholic, apostolic—the mark of holiness had appeared earlier and more frequently in the various creeds than had the other three. And it was also the characteristic that had given rise to some of the earliest ecclesiological controversies.[14] But in the great late medieval tide of debate concerning the nature of the Church that was to crest during the conciliar epoch, it was less the mark of holiness than that of *unity* that lay at the very heart of disagreement. If, for adherents to the more prominent highpapalist position, the key to that unity lay in the firm subordination of all the members of the Christian community to a single papal head, for others the key lay, rather, in the corporate association of those members. It was from the latter group that the conciliarists of the late fourteenth and fifteenth centuries took their cue. Committed to the belief that the papal headship of the Church was indeed of divine foundation, but moved also, it seems, by memories of what today would be called the ecclesiology of *communio* and by the scriptural and patristic vision of the community of Christians as forming a single body with Christ, its 'primary' or ultimate head, the proponents of conciliarist views sought to combine those two convictions. That is to say, and as J. H. Burns has rightly insisted,[15] their argument with the high papalists was not an argument 'for or against [papal] monarchy as such', but an argument about the *nature* of that papal monarchy. For they sought to harmonize their twin convictions by insisting that side by side with the institution of papal monarchy it was necessary to give the Church's communitarian or corporate dimension more prominent and routine institutional expression, most notably by the regular assembly of general councils representing the entire community of the faithful.

As they went about that task, they were led to advance a complex of ideas susceptible of many more variations than it once was common to

'Aspects ecclésiologiques de la querelle entre mendiants et séculiers', *Archives d'histoire doctrinale et littéraire du moyen âge*, 28 (1961), 35–151, and for the legacy of the dispute in the 17th cent., F. Oakley, 'Bronze-Age Conciliarism', *History of Political Thought*, 20 (1999), 70–2.

[14] Oakley, *Western Church*, 159–62.

[15] J. H. Burns, *Lordship, Kingship, and Empire* (Oxford: OUP, 1992), 127.

assume—too many, certainly, to capture by invoking the simple slogan of the superiority of council to pope, and too elusive and responsive to shifting circumstance to trap within the classificatory schemata developed by such modern commentators as Franzen, Bäumer, and Andresen. Over the years, nevertheless, I have come to conclude that it is possible to discern within the complex fabric of conciliarist thinking as it emerged during its classical age of greatest prominence three broad strands, distinct in their origins and (in some measure) in their subsequent careers, but during this period woven momentarily and fatefully into a coherent, meaningful, and historic pattern. I believe, too, that one's understanding of that overall pattern can be advanced if one teases those three strands apart and focuses on each of them in turn.

Of the three, the first, oldest, and most prominent is the demand for reform of the Church 'in head and members' and the belief that this reform could best be achieved and consolidated through the periodic assembly of general councils. Rooted, as we have seen,[16] in the defensive reaction of the provincial churches of Europe in the thirteenth century to what they had come ruefully to see as the remorseless progress of Roman centralization, it had taken on a tone of greater hostility to papal jurisdictional claims in the demands for church-wide reform elicited by the assembly of the Council of Vienne in 1311, and in William Durand the Younger's call at that time for the future assembly of general councils at regular ten-yearly intervals. But, as Jedin has said, it was to require 'the pitiful situation created by the Schism to bring about the alliance of Conciliar theory with the demand for reform'.[17] Once that alliance was concluded, however, the destinies of both were to be interwoven for the duration of the conciliar epoch itself and, periodically at least, during the centuries ensuing.

Although lacking in the *Epistola concordiae* (1380) of Conrad of Gelnhausen, this reformist strand was to appear as early as 1381 in the *Epistola concilii pacis* of his Parisian colleague, Henry of Langenstein, who, in advocating the assembly of a general council to settle the schism, also painted a graphic picture of the prevalence of corruption in the Church, ascribed its persistence to the absence of general councils, and saw reform as one of the major tasks of his council of reunion.[18] In so doing, he set the tone for much that was to follow. In his *Tractatus de materia concilii generalis* (1402–3), for instance, Pierre d'Ailly was to outline a whole plan for reform, and one which he was later to present to the fathers assembled

---

[16] See above, Ch. 1.   [17] Jedin, *History*, i. 9.
[18] *Epistola concilii pacis*, cc. 16–19; in Gerson, *Opera omnia*, ed. Dupin. ii. 835–40.

at Constance;[19] similarly, his colleague at Paris, Nicholas of Clamanges,[20] or, again, and more strikingly, the curial official Dietrich of Niem. As the very title of his *De modis uniendi et reformandi ecclesiae* (1410) suggests, Dietrich assumed that reunion and reform of the Church had to go hand in hand, and that a council was necessary to achieve both.[21] Like d'Ailly, he was to repeat many of these ideas at Constance where, indeed, as later on at Basel, the conviction most widely shared among council fathers of different backgrounds and (otherwise) differing opinions was the heartfelt sense that the frequent assembly of general councils was a necessary precondition for any truly effective and enduring reform of the Church: thus, for example, at the time of Pisa and Constance, Jean Gerson and Francesco Zabarella; at the end of Pavia–Siena or later on at Basel, John of Ragusa, Andrew of Escobar, John of Segovia, Nicholas of Cusa, and Panormitanus (Nicholas de Tudeschis). Constance itself gave official expression to that conviction when it promulgated the decree *Frequens,* thus mandating (and seeking to render automatic) the future assembly of general councils at regular, stipulated intervals. It should be noted, however, that the councils it envisaged—at least in the absence of future schisms—were to be councils presided over and acting in concert with their papal head. In the minds of its framers, *Frequens* may well have been closely associated with the superiority decree *Haec sancta,* but it did not itself necessarily presume any assertion of the superiority to the pope alone of the council membership acting apart from or in opposition to its papal head.

This, then, was the most prominent strand in the conciliarist thinking of the classical era. Given the fact that the type of reform it envisaged was most persistently conceived of as reform of the Roman curia and the limitation of its authority over the universal Church, it is hardly surprising that the second of the three main strands in conciliarist thinking was a less prominent one. That strand sought to give institutional expression to the Church's corporate nature by envisaging its constitution in quasi-oligarchic terms, its government ordinarily in the hands of the curia, and the pope being in some measure limited in the exercise of his power by that

---

[19] Ed. Oakley in *The Political Thought of Pierre d'Ailly* (New Haven and London: Yale University Press, 1964), app. III, 244–342 (at 314–42); see also app. V and VI, 346–9. The plan is described briefly in Oakley, *Western Church,* 307–10.

[20] For whom, see now C. M. Bellitto, *Nicholas de Clamanges* (Washington, DC: Catholic University Press, 2001).

[21] The work has been edited by Heimpel (*Dietrich von Niem, Dialog über Union und Reform der Kirche 1410*), who with Johannes Schwab, put an end to its centuries' old attribution to Gerson. See G. H. M. Posthumus Meyjes, *Jean Gerson* (Leiden: E. J. Brill, 1999), 342–5; Stump, *Reforms,* 6–7.

of the cardinalate, with whose 'advice, consent, direction, and remembrance' he had to rule.[22] This was the point of view which inspired the dissident cardinals in 1378 when they rejected the demand for a general council and took it upon themselves to pass judgement on the validity of Urban VI's election, thereby precipitating the Great Schism.[23] Those outside the ranks of the cardinalate who were already convinced that the general council alone was the proper forum for deciding so grave a question were understandably unimpressed by the claims being made for the Sacred College. Certainly, one would look in vain for any trace of sympathy with such quasi-oligarchic sentiments in the writings of Conrad of Gelnhausen and Henry of Langenstein.

With the passage of time, however, and as the events that had led to the onset of schism receded now into history, it became possible for conciliarists to attempt to harmonize what had previously seemed dissonant and to concede to the cardinals as well as the general council a constitutional role in the governance of the universal Church. Thus, describing the Church as a 'polity' or 'mixed government', Gerson referred to the Sacred College as 'imitating' the aristocratic component of that polity.[24] But he did not develop the idea, and it is understandable that it is among those conciliarists who were themselves cardinals that the quasi-oligarchic strand is most clearly evident. In the years immediately preceding Constance, then, that position was advocated with great clarity and force by Francesco Zabarella, the most distinguished canonist of the day; at Constance itself Pierre d'Ailly defended it; among the conciliarists of Basel Nicholas of Cusa did likewise. In that, he was joined by Denys van Rijkel (the Carthusian), and both men, interestingly enough, drew their views on the matter directly from the case d'Ailly had made at Constance.[25] It

---

[22] These words, cited by d'Ailly in his *Tractatus de ecclesiastica potestate*—in Gerson, *Opera omnia*, ed. Dupin, ii. 929–30—are taken from the alleged *professio fidei* of Boniface VIII. For which, see S. Baluzius and J. D. Mansi, *Miscellanea* (Lucca, 1781–4), iii. 418.

[23] And it was the point of view which may have inspired the behaviour of some of them later on when, while refusing to join John XXIII in his flight from the Council of Constance, they none the less balked at that council's claim to be superior in authority to the pope.

[24] Gerson, *De potestate ecclesiastica*, consid. 13, in *Œuvres complètes*, ed. Glorieux, vi. 248.

[25] Denys van Rijkel's dependence on d'Ailly's views extends to verbatim copying. See his *De auctoritate summi pontificis et generalis concilii*, in *Opera omnia* (Tournai, 1896–1935), xxxvi. 613–27 (esp. 615 and 624–5). For Cusa's position, see *De concordantia catholica*, 2:18 in *Opera omnia*, ed. Kallen (Leipzig: F. Meiner, 1932–63); xiv. 199; English tr. by P. Sigmund, *Nicholas of Cusa: The Catholic Concordance* (Cambridge: CUP, 1991), 124–6. Cf. Sigmund, *Nicholas of Cusa and Medieval Political Thought* (Cambridge, Mass.: Harvard University Press, 1963), 103–7, 167–8. He notes (103–4 n. 64) that d'Ailly's *Tractatus de potestate ecclesiastica* is 'listed as No. 165 in the library at Cues' and that it may be the case that 'part of the manuscript was transcribed by Nicholas himself'.

was not d'Ailly, however, but Zabarella who, in his *Tractatus de schismate* (1403–8), gave this quasi-oligarchic strand its most coherent and, indeed, classic expression.

That this should have been the achievement of a canonist is not, given the earlier development of such views, altogether surprising. We have already seen[26] that those views were rooted in traditional curial claims based on the *de facto* share increasingly taken by the cardinals in the day-to-day government of the universal Church. In the anonymous apparatus on Gratian's *Decretum* which bears the name *Ecce vicit Leo* and which was written early in the thirteenth century, these traditional claims received what appears to have been their first theoretical formulation. And although their line of argument was not to command universal agreement among the canonists, the decretalists Hostiensis (d. 1271) and Johannes Monachus (d. 1313) gave that formulation more explicit expression. Taking as their premiss the idea that 'Pope and cardinals together formed a single corporate body subject to the normal rules of corporation law', so that 'the Pope stood in exactly the same relationship to the cardinals as any other bishop to his cathedral chapter', they maintained that the cardinals shared with the pope the exercise of the *plenitudo potestatis*. And for them it should be noted, 'authority in a corporation was not concentrated in the head alone but resided in all the members', so that 'the prelate could not act without the consent of the members in the more important matters affecting the well-being of the whole corporation'. From this point of view, then, the cardinals' claim to an intimate and vital role in the decision-making process was not to be gainsaid.[27]

Such was the point of view that writers like the Dominican theologian, John of Paris (d. 1304), in the early fourteenth century, or Pierre d'Ailly, Francesco Zabarella, and Nicholas of Cusa during the Councils of Constance and Basel were to appropriate and extend. And, in so doing, they were to rely in part upon the college of cardinals for the imposition of some continuously operating constitutional restraints upon the pope's exercise of his power. Thus, in his *Tractatus de potestate regia et papali*,

---

[26] See above, Ch. 1.

[27] Following in this the interpretation proposed by Tierney, *Foundations*, 68–84, 117, 149–53, 180–90 (the words cited appear at 184 and 117), J. A. Watt, 'The Constitutional Law of the College of Cardinals', *Mediaeval Studies*, 33 (1971), 127–57, has claimed to the contrary that, however much these canonists stressed the importance of the cardinals' 'especial and advisory position' in the papal government of the Church, they stopped short of giving them 'authority to limit papal power' and did not advance, therefore, 'a theory of curial constitutionalism'. Cf. G. Alberigo, *Cardinalato e collegialità* (Florence: Vallechi, 1969), 97–109, 144–57.

John of Paris argued that the cardinals, 'whose consent in place of the whole Church, makes a pope', could equally act in the place of the whole clergy and people in accepting his abdication or even deposing him for heresy, incapacity, or wrongdoing.[28] Earlier in the same tract, evoking the Aristotelian notion of the mixed constitution, he had also argued that the best and most practicable form of government for the universal Church would be that form of kingship which contains an admixture of aristo-cratic and democratic elements as well—such a regime being the best because 'all would participate in some way in the government of the Church'.[29] That is certainly congruent enough with what he says about the power of the cardinals, but he himself does not go on explicitly to identify the latter with the aristocratic element in his ideal ecclesiastical constitu-tion. That particular move it was left for Pierre d'Ailly to effect a century later. 'It seems manifest', he tells us (using without acknowledgement John's very words), 'that it would be the best regimen for the Church if, under one pope, many men were elected by and from every province', and (going now one step beyond John) if 'such men should be cardinals, who, with the pope and under him, might rule the Church and temper the use of [the pope's] *plenitudo potestatis*'.[30] And while Nicholas of Cusa does not seem to have been impressed with d'Ailly's vision of the Church as a 'mixed monarchy', he did borrow from him the notion that the cardinals should serve as representatives of the Church's provinces, assisting the pope in the day-to-day government of the universal Church itself—whence, he notes, echoing an old canonistic phrase, they are commonly said to be 'part of the pope's body', *partes corporis papae*.[31]

Drawing on the quasi-oligarchic tradition in canonistic thinking, d'Ailly moved beyond these generalities and went into somewhat greater detail in his own effort to describe the precise role played by the cardinals in ecclesiastical governance in their role as successors to the 'Sacred

---

[28] *Tractatus*, cc. 24 and 25, in Johannes Quidort von Paris, ed. F. Bleienstein (Stuttgart: Ernst Klett Verlag, 1969), 200–1, 206–7. I cite the Watt tr., *On Royal and Papal Power* (Toronto: PIMS, 1971), 241–3, 249–50. Cf. c. 13, in Bleienstein ed., 138 (Watt, 159).

[29] *Tractatus*, c. 19, in Bleienstein ed., 175; tr. Watt, 206–7. Cf. the discussion in J. M. Blythe, *Ideal Government and the Mixed Constitution in the Middle Ages* (Princeton: Princeton Uni-versity Press, 1992), 139–57.

[30] *Tract. de eccl. pot.*, in Gerson, *Opera omnia*, ed. Dupin, ii. 946; John of Paris, *Tractatus*, c. 19, in Bleienstein ed., 175 (Watt, 207). Cf. the discussion in Oakley, *Political Thought of d'Ailly*, 118–19.

[31] *De concordantia catholica*, ii. 18, in *Opera omnia*, ed. Kallen, xiv. 199; Sigmund ed. and tr., *Catholic Concordance*, 124. The members of the Roman Senate had been called *pars corp-oris imperatoris*, and the term *pars corporis papae* had made its first appearance in the 11th cent. See W. Ullmann, *The Growth of Papal Government* (London: Methuen, 1955), 321.

College or Senate of the Apostles'.[32] But in this he is not as systematic as his fellow cardinal, Francesco Zabarella who in his *Tractatus de schismate*—a work of pure canonistic scholarship—gives that tradition a forceful and classic expression.[33] The expression 'apostolic see' does not refer, he says, to the pope alone, but to the pope and cardinals who together form a single body of which the pope is the head and the cardinals the members. Thus, if, under the deplorable circumstances of schism, the pope were to refuse to summon a general council, that right would devolve upon the cardinals. Again, and under any circumstances whatsoever, it is the case that 'without the cardinals the pope cannot establish a general law concerning the state of the universal Church';[34] nor, without consulting them, can he act in matters of importance. For their own part, however, if circumstances warrant it, the cardinals can exercise their authority even to the extent of withdrawing allegiance from the pope. Moreover, during a vacancy or even a 'quasi-vacancy' (which occurs when the pope cannot effectively rule the Church), they succeed to the full power of the Apostolic See. And they do so because the Sacred College in electing the pope represents the universal Church and can act in its place.[35]

By the end of the fourteenth century this last sentiment had become quite common. Common enough, indeed, to help explain how men like d'Ailly and Zabarella, though they were at pains to stress the supreme authority in the Church of the general council, could still embrace also the quasi-oligarchic curialist position that others viewed as being in tension with conciliarist views. It reflects the fact that if Zabarella (and, less clearly, d'Ailly) saw the (local) Roman church or Apostolic See as itself a corporate body composed of pope and cardinals—with all that that might imply constitutionally—they also saw it as the head, in turn, of a greater corporate body, the universal Church, from which it derived its authority and the well-being of which it existed to promote.[36] By so doing, of course, they were affirming the third, most fundamental, and most enduring strand in the conciliarist pattern of thought, a strand that to avoid confusion I will refer to henceforth as 'the strict conciliar theory'.

[32] *Tract. de eccl. pot.*, in Gerson, *Opera omnia*, ed. Dupin, ii. 929–30.
[33] *Francisci Zabarellis Cardinalis … de ejus Schismate Tractatus*; printed in S. Schardius, *De jurisdictione* (Basel, 1566), 688–711. I paraphrase here the analysis of Zabarella's position in Tierney, *Foundations*, 220–37; cf., similarly, Ullmann, *Origins*, 191–231.
[34] Zabarella, *Tractatus de schismate*, in Schardius, 692–3, 702.
[35] Zabarella, *Tractatus de schismate*, in Schardius, 690. 'Collegium cardinalium repraesentat universalem ecclesiam, et ejus vice funguntur'. Cf. ibid. 698, 711.
[36] For a concise appraisal, see Tierney, *Foundations*, 236–7.

Whatever the controversialist descriptions of later years might suggest, this strict conciliar theory possessed no monolithic unity. Even if one declines Juan de Torquemada's essentially polemical invitation to identify it with the views expressed by Marsiglio of Padua[37] and restricts oneself to the classical age of Constance and Basel, one quickly finds that the conciliar theory of that era encompassed a variety of formulations. Common to all of them, however, were the beliefs that the pope, however divinely instituted his office, was not an absolute ruler or incapable of doctrinal error but in some sense a constitutional ruler and therefore susceptible to correction; that he possessed a merely ministerial authority delegated to him by the community of the faithful (*congregatio fidelium*) for the good of the whole Church, which itself alone possessed the gift of indefectibility; that that community had not exhausted its inherent authority by the mere act of electing its ruler but had retained whatever residual power was necessary to preserve the truths of the Christian faith and to prevent its own subversion or ruin; that it could exercise that power through its representatives assembled in a general council, could do so in certain cases acting alone and against the wishes of the pope, and, in such cases, could proceed if need be to judge, punish, and even depose him.

In the thinking of the various conciliarist authors, shaped usually by contextual factors of one sort or another,[38] one finds woven around this shared pattern of belief theories of different textures and dimensions. The variations involved reflect the differing temperaments of their authors, the differing callings—canon lawyer, theologian, curial official—that had helped shape them, and the differing capacities (cardinals; bishops; theological and canonistic advisers; representatives of kings, princes, councils, universities, and religious orders) in which they were actually serving when they made their particular conciliarist pronouncements. They also reflect the particular circumstances—political and diplomatic as well as strictly ecclesiastical—under which they wrote: the confused two or three years immediately following the outbreak of schism, when a conciliar judgement on the disputed papal election was the main desideratum and when Conrad of Gelnhausen, Henry of Langenstein, and the youthful Pierre d'Ailly made their contributions; the vigorous decade of Pisa and Constance, when energies were focused, hope ran high, and figures like the mature d'Ailly, Gerson, Dietrich of Niem, and Zabarella rose to

---

[37] See below, pp. 100–4.
[38] Thus Watanabe, Black, Kaminsky, Nörr, Swanson, Alberigo have all rightly stressed the importance of taking shifting circumstances into account when coming to terms with the views expressed by the various conciliar thinkers.

prominence; the conflicted years from 1431 to 1434, when the Council of
Basel under the leadership of Cesarini and fellow spirits was bringing
Eugenius IV to heel and Nicholas of Cusa was finishing his *De concordantia
catholica*, the greatest of all conciliar treatises; the bitter decade after 1439,
when such leading conciliarists as John of Ragusa, Panormitanus, and
John of Segovia were pushed into the role of diplomats or public relations
men, struggling against skilful papal propaganda to win from the German
princes and emperor a recognition of Basel's continuing legitimacy, of
the rightfulness of its deposition of Eugenius, the wisdom of its election of
Felix V.

It would not be too difficult to trace the workings of such factors and it
would be all too easy to do so at unconscionable length.[39] Three illustrations, however, should suffice, all of them involving differences of considerable significance.

First, in the context of the protracted confrontation with Eugenius and
the council's concomitant insertion of itself into the day-to-day government of the universal Church, some of the conciliar theorists of Basel (and
notably John of Segovia) moved beyond their predecessors at Constance
and edged into somewhat more radical territory. Evoking the analogy of
the civic republic and fusing corporation theory with the ideals of the
commune, they turned from notions of mixed monarchy and divided sovereignty to that of community sovereignty, attributing, therefore, what
amounted to an 'unlimited jurisdiction . . . to the *Church-in-council*, with
the pope as its merely executive servant (*primus minister*)'.[40]

---

[39] Thus, e.g. Conrad of Gelnhausen can define the general council as an assembly composed of representatives of all the different estates, ranks, persons, and sexes of Christendom,
and Pierre d'Ailly was at least willing to extend the vote to kings, princes, and their ambassadors as also to doctors of theology and canon law. Jean Gerson, on the other hand, limited
the council's voting membership to the ranks of the clerical hierarchy (including the lower
clergy), though others were to be allowed to play a consultative or advisory role. And Nicholas
of Cusa—in this, despite his doctrine of universal consent, somewhat more conservative—
appears to have viewed the council as essentially a general assembly of bishops including, of
course, the bishop of Rome. See Gelnhausen, *Epistola concordiae*, in E. Martène and V. Durand, eds., *Thesaurus Novus Anecdotorum* (Paris, 1717), ii. 1217–18; D'Ailly, *Oratio de officio imperatoris*, in Gerson, *Opera omnia*, ed. Dupin, ii. 921, and *Disputatio de jure suffragii quibus
competat*, in H. von der Hardt, *Rerum concilii oecumenici Constantiensis* (Leipzig, 1697–1700),
ii. 225–7; Gerson, *De potestate ecclesiastica*, in Glorieux, vi. 241; Cusa, *De concordantia catholica*,
ii. 1–2, iii. 14, in *Opera omnia*, ed. Kallen, xiv. 93–4, 385. Cf. Oakley, *Political Thought of d'Ailly*,
169–54; Posthumus Meyjes, *Gerson*, 284–5, 309–13; Sigmund, *Nicholas of Cusa*, 161.

[40] Following here the interpretation proffered by A. J. Black, in *Monarchy and Community* (Cambridge: CUP, 1970), as well as in his *Council and Commune* (London: Burns &
Oates, 1979), and 'The Conciliar Movement', in J. H. Burns, ed., *The Cambridge History of
Medieval Political Thought* (Cambridge: CUP, 1988), 573–87. The words cited above appear in
this last at 580.

natural law [handwritten annotation]

Second, although the conciliarist literature at large (and not only that of the classical era) reveals the deep impress made by arguments drawn from the glosses of the canon lawyers, Decretists and Decretalists alike,[41] the theologians were in general much more prone than were the lawyers to ground their theories not only in canon law, or ecclesiastical custom, or scripture and Church history (though, of course, they did all of those things), but also and more fundamentally in the universal mandates of the natural law.[42] Thus, in some of the conciliarists of the classical era—Zabarella, Andrew of Escobar, Denys van Rijkel, Gregor Heimburg—natural law is barely mentioned or mentioned not at all. In others—Gelnhausen, Langenstein, Dietrich of Niem, Panormitanus, John of Segovia—while natural law arguments are certainly invoked, they contribute but little to the mainstream of argument and relate most often to issues of a tributary nature. Only in John of Paris and Nicholas of Cusa do they come close to occupying the central position accorded to them by d'Ailly and Gerson (and, glancing ahead, by Jacques Almain, John Mair, and Edmond Richer, their successors among the 'divines of Paris').[43] And that fact must necessarily loom large in any attempt to assess the significance of the contribution which conciliarist ideas made to the history of political thought.[44]

Third, there is a related point, somewhat more complex but equally pertinent to the impact of conciliarism on the development of secular political thinking. I have already noted[45] that A. J. Black, Joachim Stieber, and, more recently, J. H. Burns, have all stressed the complex interaction of ideology and diplomacy that led in the 1430s and 1440s to a vigorous papal counter-offensive involving the damaging portrayal of the Baselian conciliarist ecclesiology, and especially the version advocated by John of Segovia, as 'constituting a subversive, even revolutionary challenge to the very principle of monarchical authority . . . in the temporal as well as in the spiritual realm'. And, further than that, this counter-offensive was 'propagated, not only in context of theoretical discussion, but also, and even more vigorously, in serious and energetic diplomatic efforts to establish a monarchical alliance with temporal rulers against the radical attack'.[46] Somewhat less emphasis has been placed, however, on the degree to

---

[41] See below pp. 106–10.

[42] Echoing here Oakley, 'Natural Law, the *Corpus Mysticum*, and Consent', *Speculum*, 56 (1981), 796–8.

[43] See below, Chs. 3 and 4.   [44] See below, Ch. 6.   [45] See above, Ch. 1.

[46] Burns, *Lordship, Kingship and Empire*, 9. Cf. Black, *Monarchy and Community*, esp. ch. 3, pp. 85–129, and also his *Council and Commune*; similarly, Stieber, *Eugenius IV*, 132–250.

Papal Counter-Offensive seek monarchical alliance with temporal rulers [handwritten annotation]

some conciliarists frame their theories to render them less relevant to political matters

which, partly in response to that counter-offensive and in an attempt to deflect the charge that the so-called 'democratic' ideas of the conciliarists posed a threat to every form of monarchy, some of these conciliarists (Panormitanus, Andrew of Escobar, Thomas Strempinski, and, above all, John of Segovia) were led to frame their conciliar theories in such a way as to render them *less* relevant, or, indeed, *irrelevant* to matters political.[47]

Indicative of this doctrinal shift is the fact that appeals to natural law, though not strictly lacking, as we have seen, play a less crucial role in the arguments of these Baselian conciliarists than in those of their predecessors. Similarly, the distinction between the powers of order and jurisdiction is less insistently and less effectively evoked, even at moments when it would have helped clarify and advance the line of argument. Again, whereas the concilar theorists of Constance (notably Dietrich of Niem, Jean Gerson, and Pierre d'Ailly), in describing the universal Church as a mystical body (*corpus mysticum ecclesiae*), used that term as a synonym for 'moral and political body' (*corpus morale et politicum*) and certainly regarded arguments drawn from secular political practice as applicable to the Church and vice versa, some of the conciliarists at the time of Basel (John of Segovia and, to a lesser degree, Panormitanus and Escobar) adopted a more cautious approach. The terms *corpus mysticum* and *corpus politicum*, instead of being used in the earlier conciliarist fashion as synonyms, were now contrasted and employed in such a way as to distinguish the universal Church from all other communities in precisely those dimensions most relevant to the strict conciliar theory and to set it apart from political societies in general. And the distinction now drawn between the Church as a 'mystical' and as a 'political' body was aligned with the familiar distinction between the whole membership of the universal Church considered 'collectively' and 'distributively'—that is, as a single, corporate body and as a mere aggregate of individuals (*omnes ut universitas/omnes ut singuli*).

Thus, in formulations like that of John of Segovia (Black describes them as constituting 'the essence of Baslean Conciliarism'), the Church assembled in general council was identified with the *corpus mysticum* and papal sovereignty seen in contrast as pertaining 'to a somewhat lower, merely "political" order of things'.[48] Parallels between Church and secular polity

---

[47] And that despite Segovia's evocation in his conciliar thinking of the civic republican tradition. I draw here and in what follows on the line of argument developed in my 'Natural Law', to which reference may be made for the pertinent texts and for some extracts from the unprinted manuscripts.

[48] Black, *Monarchy and Community*, 14; idem, 'The Realist Ecclesiology of Heimerich van de Velde', in E. J. M. van Eijl, ed., *Facultas S. Theologiae Lovanensis* (Louvain: Louvain

were to be admitted as valid only in so far as the Church was itself regarded as a *corpus politicum*, a collection of particular churches and individual members ruled in accordance with human judgement and reason, the governance of which, like the governance of any kingdom, God assists by a 'general' rather than a 'special' influence. But the Church congregated in a general council was to be regarded rather as a *corpus mysticum* animated and protected by divine grace and not dependent on a merely natural judgement. As a result, it was precisely to the Church as a mystical body directed by the Holy Spirit, as a unique community in which Christ rules by a special and not merely general influence, that the Baselian arguments for the superiority of council to pope pertained.[49] Their relevance, then, to the mundane realm of secular principalities and powers was understandably remote and kings, princes, and their advisers were properly to perceive them as such.[50]

And so on. Variations such as these make it well-nigh impossible, without coercing the texts, to move beyond the general description of the central pattern of conciliarist belief already given in order to construct a more detailed account faithful to the views of all the conciliarists of the classical era—let alone those representative of the broader range of conciliar theorists extending from John of Paris in the early fourteenth century to Matthias Ugonius in the mid-sixteenth. But if such differences do undoubtedly exist, they range, none the less, only within certain, fairly clearly defined limits, and what remains possible, certainly, is a somewhat closer analysis of the views advanced by Pierre d'Ailly, Jean Gerson, and Francesco Zabarella. This is not only possible, indeed, but also highly desirable, given their distinction and the influence all three exerted at Constance and, in the case of the two 'divines of Paris', given also the enduring role their views came to play in the continuing tradition of conciliarist thinking all the way down to the latter half of the nineteenth century.[51]

D'Ailly, Gerson, Zabarella, then—their views were comparatively centrist ones, widely shared by the council fathers at Constance and clearly reflected (or so I will argue) in the superiority decree *Haec sancta*. I do not

University Press, 1977), 273–91 (speaking with specific reference to the formulation of Heimerich van de Velde = de Campo, d. 1460).

[49] See esp. John of Segovia's speech at Mainz in 1441, in *Deutsche Reichstagsakten*, ed. H. Weigel *et al.* (Gotha and Stuttgart, 1898–1939), xv. 648–759 (at 682–3). For a discussion of this and of related texts, see Black, *Monarchy and Community*, 14–15, 45–7, 109–12.

[50] All of which is directly pertinent to any appraisal of the role conciliarist ideas played in the history, specifically, of secular political thinking. See below, Ch. 6.

[51] See below, Ch. 5 for a discussion of the views expressed by Bishop Henri Maret on the eve of the First Vatican Council.

wish to suggest that their views were simply identical. Although Gerson had been a student of d'Ailly's at Paris and appears to have remained closely attached to him, differences not only of nuance but also of fundamental grounding distinguish their respective theories, not least of all those stemming from Gerson's commitment to a fundamentally hierarchical vision of the Church.[52] Zabarella, moreover, writing a canonistic treatise with a very specific objective, does not range as widely as either of the other two. What is explicit in their work is sometimes only implicit in his. Nevertheless, it is possible without misrepresentation to align for purposes of examination the fundamental conciliarist commitments of all three.[53] And what is basic to those commitments—an assumption shared, of course, with their papalist adversaries—is that of the divine institution of all ecclesiastical power. That power they divide, again like the papalists and in accordance with established canonistic practice,[54] into a sacramental power of order and a power of ecclesiastical jurisdiction. About the former they have very little to say. That power may well come from above. It may well leave on the souls of those who possess it an indelible character that even the authority of a general council is powerless to efface. But then, the pope does not ground his claim to pre-eminence in the Church on his possession of any particular sacramental power. The papacy is not a distinct sacerdotal order; nor does the pope possess the *potestas ordinis* in any degree higher than other bishops. His pre-eminence and his claim to invulnerability rest, and have to rest, on the nature of his jurisdictional power.[55] More precisely, they rest on the degree of jurisdictional power he

[52] See Posthumus Meyjes, *Gerson*, esp. chs. 9 and 10, pp. 247–313; Pascoe, *Gerson*.

[53] This analysis is based upon an examination of the following works: Zabarella, *Tractatus de schismate*, in Schardius, 688–711; all of Pierre d'Ailly's conciliar tracts but especially *Tractatus de ecclesiastica potestate* (in Gerson, *Opera omnia*, ed. Dupin, ii. 925–60) and *Propositiones utiles* (in E. Martène and V. Durand, eds., *Veterum Scriptorum et Monumentorum* (Paris, 1724–33), vii. 909–11), as well as his *Tractatus de materia concilii generalis* (ed. Oakley, *Political Thought of d'Ailly*, app. III, 244–342); Gerson's *De auferabilitate papae*, *Tractatus de unitate ecclesiae*, *De potestate ecclesiastica*, *Sermo 'Ambulate dum lucem habetis'*, and *Sermo 'Prosperum iter faciet nobis deus'* (ed. Glorieux, iii. 294–313; vi. 136–45, 210–50; v. 39–50, 471–80). Of the numerous secondary works on the ecclesiology of these men, the following may be referred to: for Zabarella, Tierney, *Foundations*, 220–38, Ullmann, *Origins*, 191–231, Friedrich Merzbacher, 'Die ekklesiologische Konzeption des Kardinals Francesco Zabarella (1360–1417)', in A. Haidacher and H. E. Mayer eds., *Festschrift Karl Pivec* (Innsbruck: Sprachwissenschaftliches Institut, 1966); for Gerson, Posthumus Meyjes, *Gerson*, Pascoe, *Gerson*, J. B. Morrall, *Gerson and the Great Schism* (Manchester: MUP, 1960); for d'Ailly, Oakley, *Political Thought of d'Ailly*, Pascoe, 'Theological Dimensions of Pierre d'Ailly's Teaching', *Annuarium Historiae Conciliorum*, 11 (1979), 357–66.

[54] See above, Prologue.

[55] While Gerson would agree with this statement, he does insist (in this unlike d'Ailly and others who followed in the juristic tradition) that the papal *plenitudo potestatis* presupposes

possessed in the external forum (*potestas jurisdictionis in foro exteriori*—
the coercive, truly governmental power that pertains not to any merely
voluntary society, but to the public authority; the power, in effect, that
d'Ailly sometimes refers to simply as 'the governmental power' (*potestas
regiminis*),[56] and that John of Paris, a century earlier, had described as 'in
a certain way natural'.[57]

It is this type of jurisdictional power, and this alone, that these conciliar
theorists have in mind when they assert the superiority of council to pope.
For not even the highest of papalists would deny that the pope was subject
to ecclesiastical jurisdiction in the internal or penitential form (did he,
too, not have his confessor?). And not even the most radical of conciliarists would claim that the general council *as such* was possessed of the
power of order. Upon an analysis, then, of this jurisdictional or governmental power and of the precise manner of its distribution throughout the
ranks of the faithful these men bend their efforts. That the fullness of such
power (the *plenitudo potestatis*) must be conceded to reside in the pope
alone they simply deny. By that denial they do not wish to deny also that
the pope is head of the Church or that the papal primacy is of divine origin. Nor, in fact, do they wish the council to encroach more than is absolutely necessary upon the normal day-to-day operation of the papal
monarchy. But if the pope is indeed head of the Church (*caput ecclesiae*),
that headship they understand as a 'secondary' or ministerial one. As such,
it is to be understood as a headship subordinated to that of Christ, the 'primary', 'true and supreme', 'principal and essential head', from whom immediately 'the body of the Church derives its authority and the privilege of
being unable to err in matters of faith'.[58] Moreover, though the papal
office itself is of divine institution, its conferral upon a particular individual is the work of men. And when the cardinals elect a pope, they are to be

the possession not only of the *potestas jurisdictionis* but also of the *potestas ordinis*. Until he
has been consecrated as bishop, he says, while the pope-elect can exercise some jurisdiction
he should not be called supreme pontiff. See his *De potestate ecclesiastica*, consid. 10, in
Glorieux, vi. 227. Contrast d'Ailly, *Tract. de eccl. pot.*, in Gerson, *Opera omnia*, ed. Dupin,
ii. 950, where he does not hesitate to refer to the fullness of power as the *plenitudo jurisdictionis*.
See the discussion in Posthumus Meyjes, *Gerson*, 255–73.

[56] D'Ailly, *Ultrum Petri ecclesia lege reguletur*, in Dupin, i. 667–8.

[57] *Tractatus*, c. 25, ed. Bleienstein, 209: 'ea quae sunt jurisdictionis non sunt super naturam
et conditionem negotii et super conditionem hominum, quia non est super condicionem
hominum quod homines praesint hominibus, immo naturale est aliquo modo.' Tr. Watt,
252.

[58] Gerson, *Propositio facta coram Anglicis*, in Glorieux, vi. 128–9, D'Ailly, *Propositiones
utiles*, in Martène et Durand, *Veterum Scriptorum*, vii. 909–10, and *Tractatus de materia*, in
Oakley, *Political Thought of d'Ailly*, 307–9.

understood as doing so, not in their own right, but as representatives of the community of the faithful. For the final authority in the Church, as in other subsidiary ecclesiastical corporations, resides in the whole body of its corporate membership.[59]

Further than that, it would be improper to regard that final authority as being exhausted by the act of electing a head. Even after a papal election (and in this connection all concur in evoking a notion of 'divided sovereignty'),[60] the fullness of power still in some sense resides in the Church itself as well as the pope. In what precise sense that is so, the complex formulations to which these men resort do not succeed in conveying with total clarity. Given, however, the frequency with which they allude to the procedures normally followed in the more particular ecclesiastical corporations of the day (cathedral chapters, for example), those formulations may well have been clearer to contemporaries than they tend to be to us today. Thus, as Zabarella put it before *Haec sancta* was promulgated and in a succinct version later to be echoed by such as Frederick of Parsberg, the plenitude of power resides fundamentally in the whole Church as in a corporate body, but also derivatively in the pope in his capacity as 'principal minister' of that corporation.[61] Or, as d'Ailly was to put it later on in the context of discussions among the council fathers about the precise implications of the superiority decree they had promulgated the year before, even if the plenitude of power belongs 'properly speaking' to the pope alone, since he is the one who generally exercises it, it is still possessed, nevertheless, by the universal Church and the general council representing it 'figuratively and in another way equivocally' (*tropice et in alio modo equivoce*). Or, put somewhat more precisely, and echoing here the formulation which the theologian Maurice of Prague had already introduced into the conciliar debate at Constance, the plenitude of power must be said to reside *inseparably* in the universal Church as the final end to which it is ordained, and *representatively* in the general council which as a matter of course (*regulariter*) orders it, but *separably* in the pope as in the

[59] Gerson, *De potestate ecclesiastica*, in Glorieux, vi. 232–3; D'Ailly, *Tractatus de ecclesiastica potestate*, in Gerson, *Opera omnia*, ed. Dupin, ii. 942–3, where in the application to the universal Church of the rules of corporation law which the canonists had applied to individual collegiate churches, he follows closely on the heels of John of Paris, *Tractatus*, c. 6, ed. Bleienstein, 90–6. Tr. Watt, 96–102. Cf. Tierney, *Foundations*, 166.

[60] See Tierney, '"Divided Sovereignty" at Constance', *Annuarium Historiae Conciliorum*, 7 (1979), 238–56.

[61] Zabarella, *Tractatus de schismate*; in Schardius, 703, cf. 708–9. For Frederick of Parsberg, see Vooght, *Les Pouvoirs du concile*, 44 no. 40.

subject who receives it and the minister who exercises it.[62] Or, yet again, in Gerson's congruent formulation, which he shared with the council a year later, the plenitude of power is in the whole Church and the council representing it as in the goal to which it is ordained, as in the medium whereby power is conferred upon individual office holders, as in the means whereby the (papal) exercise of that power is regulated.

Although, by virtue of his superiority to any other single ecclesiastic and his normal exercise of the *plenitudo potestatis*, that power may indeed be ascribed to the pope, it is his duty to exercise it for the good of the entire Church and he cannot be viewed as superior either to that Church or the general council which represents it. It follows, then, that the council, acting in this like any subsidiary ecclesiastical corporation in relation to its head, has the right to set limits to the papal exercise of the *plenitudo potestatis* in order to preclude its being abused to the very destruction of the Church.[63]

That fundamental right these conciliarists envisaged as capable of exercise both under emergency conditions and on a more continuing basis. The emergency situation they most readily and frequently envisaged (though it was far from being the only one)[64] is that which occurs when the pope lapses into heresy or, by being the occasion of schism, imperils the faith of the entire Church—or, again, by 'open tyranny' or other 'notorious crime' threatens incorrigibly the destruction of that Church. Under such circumstances the entire community of the faithful which, unlike the pope, possesses the gift of doctrinal inerrancy, retains the continuing power to prevent its own ruin. While infallibility is not necessarily to be ascribed to the particular doctrinal decisions of a general council,[65] in the determination of orthodoxy (and even acting apart from him) the council does possess an authority superior to that of the pope, can stand in judgement over him, correct him, and even, if need be, depose him.[66]

---

[62] D'Ailly, *Tractatus de ecclesiastica potestate*, in Gerson, *Opera omnia*, ed. Dupin, ii, esp. 945–6, 950–1. Cf. the discussion in Oakley, *Political Thought of d'Ailly*, 115–21, 147–54; Pascoe, 'Theological Dimensions'.

[63] Gerson, *De potestate ecclesiastica*, in Glorieux, vi. 232–3.

[64] Thus Gerson argued that for appropriately compelling reasons (and he listed several) a pope could be deposed even when he was guiltless. See *De auferabilitate papae*, consid. 19, in Glorieux, iii. 310–11, and *Prosperum iter*, in Glorieux, v. 475.

[65] To d'Ailly that ascription was no more than a matter of pious belief. See Oakley, 'Pierre d'Ailly and Papal Infallibility', *Mediaeval Studies*, 26 (1964), 354.

[66] Zabarella, *Tractatus de schismate*; in Schardius, 696–7, 708–9; D'Ailly, *Tractatus de materia*, ed. Oakley, *Political Thought of d'Ailly*, 305–10, *Tractatus de ecclesiastica potestate*, in Gerson, *Opera omnia*, ed. Dupin. ii. 951, 956–7, 959–60; Gerson, *De auferabilitate papae*, consid. 12, in Glorieux, iii. 302. Gerson is particularly clear on the point that, should it come to this unhappy pass, the deposition involved would result from an 'authoritative act' on the part of the council not from a merely 'declarative' judgement making clear that the pope in

Concerning the exercise of this inherent ecclesiastical authority on a continuing basis and under non-emergency conditions, these conciliarists are understandably less precise. All three being advocates of the second strand in conciliarist thinking, they viewed the cardinals as sharing with the pope in the exercise of the reduced fullness of power they still ascribed to him. The cardinals were to serve, accordingly, as a continuously operating institutional restraint on any potential abuse of that power. In addition to that, however, and by virtue of their unambiguous adherence to the strict conciliar theory, these conciliarists also ascribed some sort of continuing constitutional role to the general council itself. To the latter, accordingly, they assigned the task of limiting and regulating by known laws the pope's exercise of his power. This is certainly true in matters which touch the faith itself. It is also true, it seems, in relation to decisions which affect the general state or well-being of the Church.[67] 'What touches all by all must be approved'—or, as d'Ailly reformulated that old Roman legal maxim, 'What touches all by all must be approved, or, at least, by many and by the more notable ones.'[68] As early as 1403 he had urged, accordingly, that in the future general councils should assemble automatically and at regular intervals, with or without special mandate from the pope. Twelve years later, in the sermon *Prosperum iter faciat nobis* which he delivered to the fathers assembled at Constance, Gerson was to express similar sentiments.[69]

THE CONSTANCE DECREES *HAEC SANCTA* AND *FREQUENS*:
STATUS, MEANING, SIGNIFICANCE

Delicately poised though it may be, the position thus summarized stands out, when placed in the context of debate at Constance as very much a centrist one. Certainly, it appears to have been one which generated widespread sympathy among the council fathers during those critical weeks at

question, having fallen into heresy, had for that reason already forfeited *ipso facto* his office. See *De auferabilitate papae*, consid. 14, in Glorieux, iii. 304–5.

[67] See D'Ailly, *Tractatus de materia*, ed. Oakley, *Political Thought of d'Ailly*, 261 and 312–13, and Zabarella, Commentaria *ad* 1. 6. 4, fo. no. 4 v *a*, for the claim that papal decisions on matters that touched the *universalem statum ecclesiae* were subject to the conciliar authority. The text is reproduced in Tierney, *Foundations*, 232.

[68] D'Ailly, *Additio circa tertiam viam supratactam*, in F. Ehrle, ed., *Martin de Alpartils Chronica Actitatorum* (Paderborn: F. Schöningh, 1906), 506.

[69] D'Ailly, *Tractatus de materia*, ed. Oakley, *Political Thought of d'Ailly*, 317; Gerson, *Prosperum iter*, in Glorieux, v. 480. See Brandmüller, *Konzil von Konstanz*, ii. 339–42, for other contemporary calls for the assembly of general councils at regular intervals.

the end of March and the beginning of April 1415, when, deserted by the pope on whose authority the council had depended, they summoned up the resolution to find its legitimacy elsewhere and, at the fifth general session (6 April), and with solemn unanimity, they promulgated the decree *Haec sancta*. In its broad outlines that centrist position had been expressed, or was soon to be expressed by a broad array of participants in the council, ranging from Cardinal Fillastre and Gérard du Puy, bishop of Carcassonne, to Stephen (Thierry) of Münster and Frederick of Parsberg, canon of Ratisbon.[70] If it did not go far enough for those at the council who were most radically conciliarist in their sympathies, it clearly went a bit too far for some of the more conservative among them. The cardinals, certainly, were divided among themselves and some had misgivings about the course events were taking. In both cases, however, and as the various interventions make clear, the reason was the same. The focus of disagreement, it turns out, was not the strict conciliar theory itself but, rather, the prerogatives traditionally enjoyed by the cardinals. For some of the more radical thinkers at the council the college of cardinals was too thoroughly discredited and itself too badly in need of reform to be accorded, as it stood, any constitutional role in the limitation of papal power analogous to that being claimed for the council. On the other hand, for some, at least, of the cardinals themselves, aligned as they were with the quasi-oligarchic curialist tradition, the circumstances in which they found themselves, grievous though they might be, were not yet of a gravity sufficient to warrant an appeal beyond the Roman church of pope and cardinals to that residual power possessed by the universal Church itself—a power which, they themselves admitted, a general council could in certain extremities be called upon to exercise.[71]

Between these opposing tendencies, the position at which d'Ailly, Gerson, and Zabarella had arrived, and which was shared by many another at the council, occupied what amounted to middle ground.

[70] See the statements of these authors and others printed in Finke, *Acta*, ii. 403–10, 701–5, iii. 116–22. Note especially the passage at ii. 406 where Gérard du Puy, stressing (11 March 1415) that the council's authority is superior to that of the pope in cases of heresy, schism, and matters touching the reformation or general *status* of the Church, remarks that 'concilii autem deliberacio, eciam si papa solus vel cum paucis eciam cardinalibus contradicat, est omnino tenenda et papae voluntatis preferenda'. He adds: 'multi asserunt in conciliis generalibus papam esse sicut episcopum particularis ecclesiae'. Vooght, *Les Pouvoirs du concile*, 40–7, having analysed these and other relevant memoranda and interventions, concludes (47) that 'On pourrait multiplier les citations de textes. Le témoignage en faveur du succès des thèses sur les pouvoirs conciliaires en serait plus massif.'

[71] See Vooght, *Les Pouvoirs du concile*, 47–54; cf. T. E. Morrissey, 'The Decree "Haec Sancta" and Cardinal Zabarella', *Annuarium Historiae Conciliorum*, 10 (1978), 145–76.

Paul de Vooght has contended that it is this mediating stance that is reflected in the provisions of *Haec sancta*, and a straightforward reading of the crucial central section of the decree would certainly appear to vindicate that contention. That section goes as follows:

In the name of the holy and undivided Trinity, Father and Son and holy Spirit. Amen. This holy synod of Constance, which is a general council, for the eradication of the present schism and for bringing unity and reform to God's church in head and members, legitimately assembled in the Holy Spirit to the praise of almighty God, ordains, defines, decrees, discerns and declares as follows, in order that this union and reform of God's church may be obtained the more easily, securely, fruitfully and freely.

First it declares that, legitimately assembled in the holy Spirit, constituting a general council and representing the catholic church militant, it has power immediately from Christ; and that *everyone of whatever state or dignity, even papal*, is bound to obey it in those matters which pertain to the faith, the eradication of the said schism and the general reform of the said church of God in head and members.

Next, it declares that *anyone of whatever condition, state or dignity, even papal*, who contumaciously refuses to obey the past or future mandates, statutes, ordinances or precepts of this sacred council *or of any other legitimately assembled general council*, regarding the aforesaid things or matters pertaining to them, shall be subjected to well-deserved penance, unless he repents, and shall be duly punished, even by having recourse, if necessary, to other supports of the law.[72]

Clear enough, it might seem. But, then, given the enormous freight of theological anxiety with which the interpretation of the decree has been burdened, as well as the degree of uneasiness, confusion, strain, anachronism, and dialectical gymnastic evident in the pertinent strain of discussion, 'straightforward reading' has hardly been characteristic of the long, rich, but deeply conflicted tradition of efforts to decode it.[73] And certainly not characteristic of the more recent and by now extensive body of interpretative literature which the historian, Paul de Vooght, and the theologian, Hans Küng, stimulated when, during the Vatican II era, they revived (and for the first time in a century) the claim that *Haec sancta* was enacted by a legitimate general council and was possessed of an enduring dogmatic validity.[74]

---

[72] Alberigo and Tanner, *Decrees*, i. 409. Italics mine.

[73] For which, see esp. Schneider, *Konziliarismus*.

[74] In his *Les Pouvoirs du concile et l'autorité du pape* (1965), restating the case which he had developed in a series of articles beginning in 1960 with 'Le conciliarisme aux conciles de Constance et de Bâle' (in *Le Concile et les conciles*), De Vooght, having argued that *Haec sancta* met all the conditions necessary to make it a dogmatic decree and one which 'in its authentic sense' binds in faith, concluded (198) 'there is no longer today any motive for maintaining the

For the historian, then, sensitive as always to the threat of anachronism and concerned to avoid the intrusion into the task of *historical* interpretation of extraneous judgemental criteria, the decree represents something of an interpretative minefield. In the crucial section of the conciliar text printed above, then, some phrases have been italicized in order to signal the neuralgic points which, if they certainly cannot be sidestepped, have to be approached with a heightened degree of circumspection.

Of the various factors conspiring to render the historian's interpretative task on this matter so very challenging and hazardous, three may be singled out for comment. First, the tumultuous atmosphere of crisis precipitated by John XXIII's flight from the council on 20 March 1415, and by his subsequent disruptive behaviour. If the decree was certainly not 'the hasty product of a day', for it drew on ideas long since current among canonists and theologians and was the product of a complex drafting process that stretched out for more than two weeks, nor was it altogether 'the well-chosen fruit of wise delay'. In this connection, one historian has cogently suggested that Zabarella's hesitations about the version finally proclaimed reflected less any objection to the decree 'as a whole' than the reservations of a crisp and precise juristic mind about the continuing presence in that text of ambiguities likely, if not eliminated, to give rise to subsequent interpretative confusion.[75] The second factor complicating the interpretative

[traditional] ostracism of a dogmatic decree which clarifies and confirms a point of doctrine always admitted in the Church and always taught in the schools'. In 1962 Hans Küng had endorsed the same conclusion in his *Structures of the Church* (New York: Thomas Nelson & Sons, 1964), 270, 284–5, 301–2 (a tr. of the original *Strukturen der Kirche*). During the 1960s these claims gave rise to a very vigorous debate, with a whole series of historians entering the lists—among them, Remigius Bäumer, Walter Brandmüller, Karl August Fink, August Franzen, Joseph Gill, Heinz Hürten, Hubert Jedin, Francis Oakley, Isfried H. Pichler, Helmut Riedlinger, and Brian Tierney. Most of their contributions are listed, described, and analysed in F. Oakley, *Council over Pope?* (New York: Herder & Herder, 1969), 118–31, and Vooght, 'Les Controverses sur les pouvoirs du concile et l'autorité du pape', *Revue théologique de Louvain*, 1 (1970), 45–75. Of the subsequent contributions to what has become a matter of no more than intermittent interest, mention should be made of Oakley, 'The "New Conciliarism" and its Implications', *Journal of Ecumenical Studies*, 8 (1971), 815–40; Tierney, '"Divided Sovereignty" at Constance' (a particularly fine article); Schneider, *Konziliarismus*, 239–339; Morrissey, 'The Decree "Haec Sancta"' (detailed and thoughtful); M. Fois, 'Il valore ecclesiologico del decreto "Haec Sancta"', *Civiltà Cattolica*, 126/2 (1975), 138–52; Alberigo, *Chiesa conciliare*, 165–205; and Brandmüller, *Konzil von Konstanz*, i. 237–59. More briefly, Tanner, *Councils of the Church*, 69–71.

[75] Thus Morrissey, 'The Decree "Haec Sancta"', esp. 167, 170, 176. Note, however, that one of the ambiguities on which Morrissey lays considerable stress (157–8) is something of an artefact created by the omission of a word in the defective edn. of the text on which he was relying, as a result eliciting from Brandmüller, *Konzil von Konstanz*, i. 253 n. 56, a tart rebuke for having generated thereby what is 'in truth, a non-existent problem'. For the arguments at

effort is the persistence with which, even in treatments purporting to be historical, theological and canonistic criteria of judgement have been permitted to intrude on the discussion.[76] And the third complicating factor is the common failure to signal clearly at the outset of the interpretative quest the assumptions being brought to the task on such crucial issues as whether or not John XXIII is being taken to be a legitimate pope and Constance as a legitimate general council at the very moment when *Haec sancta* was promulgated.[77] Such omissions are compounded by the further failure to distinguish with sufficient clarity the bundle of related but separable questions concerning the decree's dogmatic status, its validity, and its meaning.[78]

Focusing first in what follows, then, on this third factor, my own point of departure is the concrete historical situation described above in the previous chapter,[79] a state of affairs in which the greater part of Latin Christendom had recognized as legitimate the decisive action taken by the Council of Pisa, and in which the bulk of the fathers assembled at Constance had similarly recognized the legitimacy of John XXIII's papal title and, as Gerson later insisted, had regarded him accordingly as 'true pope' until the very moment at which they deposed him.[80] Not to have done so, after all, would have been to concede that the Council of Pisa had done no more (or had not possessed the power to do any more) than add to the two existing lines of doubtful claimants to the papacy, Roman and Avignonese, a third and equally doubtful Pisan line. Had that been the

---

the council and the successive redrafts eventuating in the final version, see Schneider, *Konziliarismus*, Beilage 1, and Alberigo, *Chiesa conciliare*, 165–205 (who both print the successive drafts side by side), Brandmüller, *Konzil von Konstanz*, i. 237–59, Vooght, *Les Pouvoirs du concile* , 31–47.

[76] Thus, e.g. in their attempts to decide whether or not *Haec sancta* constituted 'a dogmatic decree' or 'norm of faith', both H. Jedin, *Bischöfliches Konzil oder Kirchenparlament* (Basel and Stuttgart: Helbing & Lichtenhahn, 1965), 15, and Franzen, 'Council of Constance', 59, and 'Das Konzil von Einheit', in Franzen and Müller, *Konzil von Konstanz*, 103–4, do not hesitate to invoke the standard set by Vatican I.

[77] Thus, e.g. Tierney, 'Hermeneutics and History', in T. A. Sandquist and M. Powicke, eds., *Essays in Medieval History for . . . Bertie Wilkinson* (Toronto: University of Toronto Press, 1969), and Morrissey, 'The Decree "Haec Sancta"'.

[78] In this respect, I would fault my own attempt (thirty years ago) to come to terms with *Haec sancta* for its failure to discriminate more clearly between the general question of the decree's validity and the much more specific claim that it amounted to an assertion of unchanging dogmatic truth—see my *Council over Pope?*, 105–31. Similarly, Küng, *Structures*, 268–88.

[79] See above, Ch. 1.

[80] Gerson, *An liceat in causis fidei a papa appellare*, in Glorieux, vi. 286, where he also rejected the notion that a pope who had fallen into heresy ceased *ipso facto* to be pope without having to be formally judged, sentenced, and deposed as John XXIII had been. Cf. Harold Zimmermann, 'Die Absetzung der Päpste auf dem Konstanzer Konzil', in Franzen and Müller, *Das Konzil von Konstanz*, 113–37 (at 126 ff.).

case, why should they assume that they themselves possessed any greater power to achieve any end different from that achieved by their predecessors at Pisa? If Gregory XII was to prove willing to abdicate and John XXIII to accept his own deposition, Benedict XIII obdurately refused to do either. And yet the fathers at Constance went on, nevertheless, to elect Martin V and, in so acting, certainly thought they were doing something other than creating yet another potential line of doubtful claimants. But on what grounds would they have permitted themselves to conclude that they themselves possessed a power that they were prepared to deny to their predecessors at Pisa? On the grounds (or so would say the advocates of what appears to be the current curialist position)[81] that the Roman line of claimants had been the sole legitimate line of popes all along, and that only Gregory XII's convocation of the council and subsequent abdication had cleared the decks and transformed the Constance assembly into a true ecumenical council which, having eliminated the Avignonese line of antipopes, certainly possessed the power to proceed to the election of an indubitably legitimate pope.

There is little or nothing, however, to suggest that the fathers assembled at Constance were themselves disposed to think in such a way. When they proceeded to depose John XXIII they did so not as a doubtful claimant to the papacy but as a pope who had been brought to judgement and found guilty of criminal and incorrigible behaviour. In their very sentence of deposition they referred to him as 'the lord pope John XXIII' while speaking of the rival claimants as 'Angelo Correr' and 'Peter de Luna, called Gregory XII and Benedict XIII by their respective obediences'.[82]

This, certainly, also appears to have been the stance adopted later on by Martin V. In his registers, John XXIII (no less than Alexander V) is dubbed simply as 'our predecessor' or 'formerly pope', whereas the popes of the Avignonese and Roman lines (the Roman pontiff Gregory XII not excluded) are referred to, rather, as 'popes so-called in their obediences'

---

[81] See below, Epilogue.

[82] See the text in Alberigo and Tanner, *Decrees*, i. 417–18—esp. 418 where, after John XXIII's deposition, the council moved to preclude the possibility of any future re-election to the papacy of 'dominus noster Balthasar de Cossa nuper Joannes XXIII' or of '*Angelus de Corario, Gregorius XII, nec Petrus de Luna, Benedictus XIII, in suis oboedientiis nuncupati*' (italics mine). Similarly, in the later sentence of deposition handed down against the Avignonese pontiff, he is referred to as 'Peter de Luna called by some Benedict XIII (Petrus de Luna, Benedictus XIII a nonnullis nuncupati)', ibid. 437. Cf. the similarly differentiated terminology used in conciliar debate at Constance by Leonard Statius, master general of the Dominicans, when he said that 'concilium praesens Constanciense habuit potestatem execucionis ad deponendum *olim Joannes XXIII*, et par racione habet ad deponendum Benedictum XIII *in sua obediencia nuncupatum*' (italics mine), Finke, *Acta*, ii. 713.

(*papae in suis obedientiis sic nuncupati*).[83] Had that not been the case, and had John not been generally regarded as the true pope upon whose convocation the assembly's legitimacy as a general council had been predicated, it would be hard indeed to explain the panic and disarray that his flight from Constance engendered among the council fathers. Nor should their later willingness to go through the charade of allowing Gregory XII to convoke the assembly be permitted to lend credence to the notion that they regarded John's title to office as questionable—no more so, in effect, than their subsequent willingness for similarly diplomatic purposes to extend the same privilege to Benedict XIII of the Avignonese line whose title to office their later sentence of deposition (as we have seen), reveals them to have viewed as invalid. Despite the notion's rise to prominence in the nineteenth century and its widespread currency in the post-Vatican I era, it took the lapse of two centuries after Constance before it occurred to a high-papalist writer to build a bold case on the startling retroactive assumption that the Roman line of claimants had been the legitimate line of popes all along, and that Gregory XII, therefore, had been the true possessor of the papal dignity when Constance had assembled.[84] All of this serves in general, then, to mark the interpretative perimeter within which any attempt to come to terms with the nature, validity, meaning, and significance of *Haec sancta* must take place. And all of this serves in particular, and for example, to exclude the possibility of resolving the problem of interpretation by simply dismissing John XXIII as no more than an anti-pope and Constance, therefore, as something other than a legitimately assembled general council at the moment in 1415 when it promulgated the decree.[85]

So far as nature, validity, and meaning are concerned, it is important to realize that not one but at least four distinct (if closely related) questions are involved. First, did Constance in promulgating *Haec sancta* intend to

[83] I cite these texts from Fink, 'Zur Beurteilung', 341–2.

[84] Izbicki, 'Papalist Reaction', 7–20 (at 14), where he cites the claim advanced by André Duval (d. 1638), a Sorbonne theologian of papalist sympathies. Even in the late 18th cent. that view was still regarded as something of a novelty, but Izbicki notes (11–12), none the less, that the canonist Antonius de Cannario, writing in the last years of the Council of Basel, had 'argued that there had never been any reason for doubting the legitimacy of the Roman line'. He notes, too, that Torquemada conceded the possibility that 'Pope Eugenius may have held a personal belief that his uncle, Gregory XII, . . . had been the true pope, and that Gregory's convocation of the Constance assembly therefore had made it a general council'. That fact, however, 'did not divert Torquemada [himself] from his [own] fundamental argument that Constance was not a true council until after the followers of Benedict XIII, who included the young friar, Juan de Torquemada, had arrived'.

[85] This is the argumentative tactic adopted by Gill, 'Fifth Session', and idem, 'Il decreto *Haec sancta synodus* del concilio di Costanza', *Rivista di storia della Chiesa in Italia*, 12 (1967), 123–30.

define an unchanging dogmatic truth? Second, if that was not the case, is validity in general to be accorded to the decree and, if so, what sort of validity? Third, still more precisely, was that validity understood as extending only to the emergency situation prevailing at that time or was it intended to possess some more enduring import? Fourth, if the latter, then what precise import? Was it asserting the superiority in principle of a council united with its papal head to the pope acting alone, or the superiority to the pope (at least on certain specified matters) of the council acting apart from its papal head? The enormous body of commentary that *Haec sancta* has elicited over the centuries since its proclamation strongly suggests that it has usually proved easier to appreciate why the last three questions should be teased apart than it has to maintain the distinction between the two first. But, as Thomas Morrissey has done well to insist, while 'it is obvious . . . that if it were a dogmatic definition it would have to claim permanent validity, . . . the converse is not true'.[86] That is to say, the permanent validity being claimed might be other than doctrinal.

What, then, and in the first place, are we to conclude in relation to the question of dogmatic definition? For those willing to turn to the definitions of the First Vatican Council as a timeless (and, therefore, retroactively applicable) touchstone for such matters, the question is easy enough to answer: clearly, Constance could not have been attempting to establish anything of such moment as an irreformable and infallible norm of faith. But if some theologians may well have proved comfortable with such an approach, it is hardly an option which historians can properly choose—even if some have done precisely that.[87] For the latter, and absent that choice, the question turns out to be a surprisingly difficult one to answer in straightforward historical terms. Even modern Catholic theologians themselves have had to wrestle mightily with the tricky issue of deciding in the wake of Vatican I which of the papal or conciliar pronouncements of the past are to be viewed as 'dogmas of faith in the modern sense of the term'. And part of the problem they have had to face stems from the incontrovertible historical fact that all such terms—seemingly transparent words like 'faith', 'dogma', 'heresy', 'define', and so on—were used more loosely in centuries past than they have come to be used more recently.

---

[86] Morrissey, 'The Decree "Haec Sancta"', 162.

[87] Thus Jedin, *Bischöfliches Konzil*, 11–12; Franzen, 'Council of Constance', 59, and 'Das Konzil der Einheit', in Franzen and Müller, *Konzil von Konstanz*, 69–112 (at 103–4). The Vatican I touchstone also seems to hover in the background of Tierney's discussion in 'Hermeneutics and History', 362–4, as to whether or not *Haec sancta* was enacted as an 'immutable dogmatic decree', one 'infallible and so irreformable'.

Until the eighteenth century, indeed, 'doctrine' or 'dogma' could be used
without any intimations or irrevocability to mean nothing more that
'teaching'.[88] Accordingly, we have to be very careful to avoid the inadvert-
ent reading back into earlier centuries of theological notions, definitions,
and modalities of judgement that are, in fact, of much more recent provenance. And we certainly need to be clearer than we currently appear to be
about what exactly it would have taken in the early years of the fifteenth
century to frame a conciliar pronouncement in such a way as to make it
constitute a formal dogmatic definition.[89]

With such caveats in mind, historians have compared the language employed in *Haec sancta* with the terminology used in the dogmatic constitutions of the general councils which preceded it as well as that used at
Constance itself in the condemnations of the Wycliffite and Hussite heresies. And such comparisons have been evoked as serving to exclude the
possibility of classifying *Haec sancta* as a declaration of dogma. It has similarly been argued that no 'dogmatizing' force should be attributed to the
imposing array of enacting verbs that that decree itself employs (ordain,
define, decree, discern, declare). In the juristic terminology of the day they
proclaim, it seems, nothing more portentous than a conciliar resolution
or decision at large.[90]

Arguments of this sort command serious attention. In its hour of
trial, after all, the Council of Basel did not view it as a redundant gesture
when, reissuing *Haec sancta* yet once more, it attempted a clarification
of the interpretative situation by explicitly insisting that its teaching was
to be embraced as an article of faith.[91] And yet, long years before the
fathers assembled at Basel were to move finally to put that claim beyond
dispute, they still appear themselves to have regarded the council's 'earlier
reaffirmations of "Haec Sancta". . . as mere reiterations of existing

[88] See F. A. Sullivan, *Magisterium* (New York: Paulist Press, 1983), esp. 106–7. For a judicious overview of the meanings attaching in the Middle Ages to words and phrases like 'faith',
'dogma', 'articles of faith', 'heresy', see Heft, *John XXII and Papal Teaching Authority* (Lewiston, NY: Mellen, 1986), 106–10, 136–42, 152–8, 181–2. He notes (154–7) that the term 'articles
of faith' was used with a more restricted meaning than was 'dogma' and alluded to unchanging and scripturally based credal statements.
[89] Schneider, *Konziliarismus*, 328–30.
[90] Brandmüller, 'Besitzt das Konstanzer Dekret *Haec sancta* dogmatische Verbindlichkeit?', *Römische Quartalschrift*, 62 (1967), 4–6; idem, *Konzil von Konstanz*, i. 250–2; J. H.
Pichler, *Die Verbindlichkeit der Konstanzer Dekrete* (Vienna: Herder, 1967), 29–51; Tierney,
'Hermeneutics and History', in Sandquist and Powicke, *Essays*, 362–4; Schneider,
Konziliarismus, 288–95.
[91] It did so on 16 May 1439, at its thirty-third session. For the text of the decree, see J. Mansi,
Sacrorum conciliorum nova et amplissima collectio (Leipzig, 1759–1927; Florence, 1724–1937),
xxix, 178–9; cf. Stieber, *Eugenius IV*, 54–5.

dogma'.[92] It seems, in effect, that they and others in the early fifteenth century were already inclined to view the decree as embodying an 'unbreak-
able truth',[93] a 'truth founded on the rock of holy scripture' and one that
it would be heretical to gainsay.[94] This last characterization (dating to 1417)
being the work of none other than Gerson himself, it, too, has to be
weighed with great seriousness.

What, then, on this question of *Haec Sancta's* dogmatic status, can one
safely conclude: nothing very crisp, it has to be confessed, and certainly
nothing very satisfactory. The intricacy, ingenuity, and density of the pertinent argumentation notwithstanding, one is left with the uneasy sense
that on this matter[95] modern commentators may sometimes have suc-
cumbed to a degree of clarity and decisiveness not available to people at
the time. For the historian (if not, it may be, the theologian) the best available, though admittedly sobering, conclusion may well be that the question has simply to be left open, conceding to Schneider, as a result, the
rectitude of his claim that in this aspect of the interpretation of *Haec
sancta* 'the last word has not as yet been spoken'.[96]

No similarly craven abstention is called for in relation to the second
(and broader) question concerning the validity of the decree in general.
Constance being in its own estimate a legitimate general council and being
viewed by contemporaries as such, it clearly intended to claim some sort
of validity for a decree so solemn in its promulgation and so foundational
in its import. Even if one would be wise to leave open the question of

[92]   Thus Stieber, *Eugenius IV*, 53–4, arguing that 'only a formal declaration that these decrees were articles of faith would transform the charge in its [i.e. Basel's] legal proceedings
against Eugenius from one of contempt for the superior authority of a general council to one
of heresy'. Stieber also insists (53) that already in 1437 and 1438 Basel had emphasized 'that it
regarded the superior authority of a general council not as a new principle of church
discipline which had been introduced by the Council of Constance but as a tenet of faith
grounded in the words of Christ himself'.

[93]   Indeed, an 'irrefragibilis veritas'—thus Joannis Palomar, cited in Morrissey 'The Decree "Haec Sancta"', 168 n. 103. Morrissey describes Palomar as being 'in general a pro-
papalist writer in this tract'.

[94]   Gerson, *Sermo in Festo S. Antonii*, in Glorieux, v. 384–5, at which point he has just
quoted the central section of *Haec sancta*. Cf. his *Resolutio circa materiam excommunicationum et irregularitatum*, consid. 8, in Glorieux, vi. 295: 'haeresis damnata per constitu-
tionem expressissimam et practicatam in concilio . . . Constantiensi'. Note, too, that when
Eugenius IV himself came finally to impugn *Haec sancta* as the work of John XIII's obedience
alone, he still conceded that the Constance fathers in promulgating the decree had believed
themselves to be proclaiming a *veritas fidei catholicae*. See Vooght, *Les Pouvoirs du concile*,
96–7.

[95]   As also on the matter of the alleged status of Gregory XII and his successors in the
Roman line of claimants as representatives of the sole legitimate line of papal succession.

[96]   Schneider, *Konziliarismus*, 328.

whether or not it intended to claim validity for it as a declaration of dogma (in the modern sense of that term), no obstacles stand in the way of accepting the view that Bishop Henri Maret was to put forward on the very eve of Vatican I[97] and that has been expressed independently and more recently by a series of twentieth-century commentators. Namely, that *Haec sancta* was, in effect, 'a licit enactment of positive constitutional law'.[98] So long, of course, as one recognizes the fact that it possessed also an important doctrinal penumbra, that it was rich in 'theological consequences', and, implying 'an ecclesiological concept', 'touched upon the very nature of the Church'.[99]

Valid certainly as a constitutional law, then, but law extending to what? The Church as it would endure through time or simply the Church under the wholly extraordinary crisis conditions prevailing at the very moment in which the decree was passed? Over the centuries, this third question has evoked one of the oldest and most durable of stratagems deployed in the ongoing attempt to deflect, or at last contain, the potentially subversive constitutional implications attaching to the decree. That stratagem goes back, perhaps, to one of Torquemada's subsidiary arguments,[100] was revived in the 1920s by Johannes Hollnsteiner and, of more recent years, has been employed with force and ingenuity by Hubert Jedin and Walter Brandmüller.[101] It pivots on the assumption that the fathers at Constance did not recognize (or in 1415 no longer recognized) John XXIII as true pope, and believed themselves to be confronting, therefore, an extraordinary situation in which there were three contenders for the papal office, all three of them, however, no more than claimants of doubtful legitimacy. 'This circumstance', Jedin has said, 'is in my judgment decisive.' Why? Because 'in the light of the definitions of the First Vatican Council only the legitimate successor of Peter is endowed with infallibility and with the

---

[97] See below, Ch. 5.

[98] Or, 'a permanently binding statement of positive constitutional law'. Thus Tierney, 'Hermeneutics and History', 363, and his introduction to the new (1998) edn. of *Foundations*, p. xxiii. Similarly, Morrissey, 'The Decree "Haec Sancta"', 172–3, and his 'After Six Hundred Years', *Theological Studies*, 40 (1979), 500–1. Cf. Pichler, *Verbindlichkeit*, 48–51, where, while dismissing the decree as invalid, he categorizes the intent of the council fathers in similar terms.

[99] I draw these words from Morrissey, 'After Six Hundred Years', 501, and idem, 'The Decree "Haec Sancta"', 173; Pichler, *Verbindlichkeit*, 50–1. Vooght, 'Les Controverses sur les pouvoirs du concile et l'autorité du pape', *Revue théologique de Louvain*, 1 (1970), 46: 'il est indéniable que le décret est doctrinal par son objet'.

[100] Thus Izbicki, 'Papalist Reaction', 19.

[101] Hollnsteiner, 'Konstanzer Konzil' (1929), 395–420, the full statement of a position he had adumbrated already in 1925 (see Schneider, *Konziliarismus*, 226–31); Jedin, *Bischöflicher Konzil*; Brandmüller, 'Besitzt', and his *Konzil von Konstanz*, i. 237–59.

pastoral power over the whole Church'. In the absence of such a successor, then, the type of emergency situation arises in which, as the canonists had long insisted, the interest and well-being of the whole Church must come before that of the pope himself. Confronted with such an emergency situation (and in aggravated form), the fathers at Constance framed *Haec sancta*. It is, therefore, no 'universal as it were free-floating definition of belief', but has to be understood, rather, as 'an emergency measure [intended] to meet a quite definite exceptional case'.[102]

Against this interpretation, however, it is necessary to lodge two fundamental objections. First, and as we have seen, the Council of Constance itself (and, therefore, at least the bulk of its membership) recognized John XXIII as himself the true pope. That being so, the emergency situation which existed has to be understood as one calling for an assertion of conciliar authority, not simply over three rival papal contenders all of them of doubtful legitimacy, but, more tellingly, over the pope who had himself called the council into being but was now threatening its very existence, and was doing so before its task of reunion and reform had been completed. Second, *Haec sancta* itself is quite explicit, after all, on the crucial point that, in matters pertaining to the faith, the ending of the schism, and reform of the Church in head and members, its claim to be possessed of an authority superior to that of the pope alone was one advanced, not simply for itself, but for any other legitimately assembled general council in the future.[103]

In relation to that second point, Jedin himself ruefully conceded the difficulty it posed for his own interpretation of the decree as an emergency measure of limited applicability. He was led, therefore, to speculate that the decree's drafters could conceivably have been envisaging merely the possibility that it might take another council to complete the basic work of ending the schism that Constance had begun.[104] And that point Brandmüller, in asserting similarly that *Haec sancta* was no more than a time-bound emergency measure, has pushed a little further. He has insisted, in novel and (it must be confessed) somewhat strained fashion, that the customary way of rendering the two phrases *etiam si papalis exsistat* and *cujuscumque alterius concilii generalis* is misleading. They should more properly be translated, he argues, in such a way as (respectively) to underline the fact that in April 1415 the council recognized there to be a

---

[102] Jedin, *Bischöfliche Konzil*, 11–12.
[103] See above, p. 83, the words italicized in the third paragraph of the decree.
[104] Jedin, *Bischöfliches Konzil*, 37–9 (postscript to the 2nd (1965) edn. of the work).

quasi-vacancy in the papal office, and to suggest that the ongoing claim to superiority was being advanced not for any other council in the future but only for a further council charged with the task of completing Constance's current effort to end the schism.[105]

An ingenious argument, no doubt, but one that ultimately fails, and indeed, has failed to convince.[106] *Haec sancta*, it seems clear, was much more than a time-bound emergency measure. Far more universal in intent than that, it set out to lay down nothing other than a constitutional order for the future. That the second clause makes quite clear, indicating, as it does, that the superiority being claimed under certain circumstances for the council is one claimed, not just for Constance or for another council confronting the same unresolved crisis, but for any legitimately assembled council in the future. It makes clear, too, that the circumstances it has in mind extend beyond the grievous circumstances of the moment. Moreover, its definition of those circumstances is remarkably wide, involving the ascription to the council of a superior jurisdiction in matters pertaining not merely to the ending of the present schism but, more broadly, to the faith, the reform of the Church in head and members, and even (more broadly still, it seems) 'things pertaining to' the three matters stipulated.

Clear enough it may be, but a fourth and still more refined question has to be asked. Conceding a universal validity to the decree, even if not necessarily validity as an unambiguous definition of dogma, one may still be moved to ask: what sort of jurisdictional superiority did it claim for the council? Or, more accurately, for what sort of council or assembly was

---

[105] See above, p. 83, where I have italicized the two phrases which Brandmüller addresses in *Konzil von Konstanz*, i. 252–6. There, of *etiamsi papalis existet* he insists that: 'This *must* be translated: "even if a holder of the papal diginity should exist"' (italics mine). But, in so doing, he fails to note that in the sermon *Ambulate dum lucis habetis* it was Gerson who had first used that particular phrase. He did so in the context of the March–April conciliar crisis. And Gerson we know (see above, Ch. 2 n. 80) to have had no doubt that John XXIII was *verus papa*. Schneider, *Konziliarismus*, Beilage 1, sets out helpfully the pertinent section of Gerson's sermon in parallel with the successive drafts of *Haec sancta*. In relation to the phrase *cujuscumque alterius concilii generalis legitime congregati*, and ignoring the force of *cujuscumque*, Brandmüller places great emphasis on the fact that the drafters chose to employ *alterius* rather than *alii*, viewing it as a word intended to denote simply the further council that might be needed to complete the work began at Constance.

[106] See Schneider, *Konziliarismus*, 290–2, 325 n. 80; Vooght, 'Les Controverses', 48; Stump, *Reforms*, p. xiv n. 6; Morrissey. 'The Decree "Haec Sancta"', 162–5; Alberigo, *Chiesa conciliare*, 184, n. 100. Earlier on, however, Tierney, 'Hermeneutics and History', 367 n. 19, had hinted at a similar understanding when, pointing out that 'some members [of the Council of Constance] believed that they were claiming authority for the council at a time when no true pope existed', he went on to assert that '[t]his position was provided for in the rather roundabout wording of *Haec sancta* with its reference to any rank, state, or dignity, even if it be the papal'.

superiority being claimed? And that question has, in fact, been asked—by none other than Brian Tierney, the distinguished historian of canon law to whom conciliar studies owe so much. In answering it, he has advanced an argument that is at once novel,[107] intriguing, and possessed of considerable persuasive force. If I myself do not find it conclusive, I believe, none the less, that it deserves more focused attention than it appears, in fact, to have received.

'The all-important point to grasp on interpreting *Haec sancta*', he says, but one 'that has been overlooked in modern interpretations', is that

the decree used the word 'council' in an ambiguous fashion and that the ambiguity was probably deliberate. *Haec sancta* certainly did not state, and its framers probably never intended to state, *that the members of a council acting in opposition to a certainly legitimate pope, could licitly enforce their will on such a pope in any circumstances* [under any circumstances whatsoever?]. As regards the immediate situation, the prelates of Constance claimed authority for themselves at a time when there were three 'popes,' all of doubtful legitimacy. As regards the future, *Haec sancta* laid down that all popes were to be subject to the decrees of lawfully assembled councils in certain defined spheres. But in normal circumstances, once the schism was ended, a lawfully assembled council would not consist of the members alone—bishops and other representatives—but of pope and members together. The decrees of future councils, which were to be binding on the pope, would, in normal times, be decrees of pope-and-council acting jointly, not decrees of the members acting against the head. There was nothing revolutionary in claiming supremacy for such an assembly.

At Basel, he adds, 'the claim of the members to override a legitimate head' was certainly advanced. But that was 'a radically different claim from that of *Haec sancta*'.[108] If some of the fathers assembled at Constance had doubtless favoured that claim, 'they did not succeed in enacting it into law'.[109]

Tierney rightly insists that the distinction he draws between 'council' understood as pope and members conjoined and 'council' as members alone acting apart from (or in opposition to) this papal head is no modern invention but one deeply embedded in the canonistic tradition and one

---

[107] Tierney, 'Hermeneutics and History', 366–70; also his 'Roots of Western Constitutionalism in the Church's Own Tradition', in J. A. Coriden, ed., *We, The People of God* (Huntington, Ind.: Canon Law Society of America, 1968), 124–6, '"Divided Sovereignty" at Constance', 243–53. He has recently (1998) reaffirmed his position in the introduction to the new edn. of *Foundations*, pp. xxii–xxvii.

[108] 'Hermeneutics and History', 367.

[109] Tierney, introduction to the 1998 edn. of *Foundations*, p. xxiv, where he also refers to his own position as involving 'a strict intepretation of *Haec sancta*'.

certainly well-known to those participating in the debates at Constance. His argument, therefore, is an important one, calling into question as it does the way in which *Haec sancta* has been for centuries commonly understood.[110]

For that very reason, of course, it must perforce labour under a formidably heavy burden of proof. And that burden of proof extends to what is being claimed in relation to 'the immediate situation' at Constance as well as to the 'normal circumstances' that would prevail after the schism had been terminated.

In the first place, and in relation to the former, Tierney's formulation strikes me as slightly ambiguous. But if in the words italicized above he is in fact saying (as would seem to be the case[111]) that under no circumstances whatsoever were the framers of *Haec sancta* claiming for a council acting apart from and in opposition to a certainly legitimate pope the authority licitly to impose its will on him, then I am compelled to disagree. To argue thus would surely be, with Jedin and Brandmüller, to reduce the decree to the status of a time-bound emergency measure of limited applicability, and that despite Tierney's own explicit rejection of such a position and his own interpretation of the measure as a 'licit enactment of positive constitutional law'.[112] For Jedin's interpretation of *Haec sancta* as an emergency measure, it will be recalled, the circumstances that in 1415 all three contenders for the papal office (John XXIII himself included) were of doubtful legitimacy was 'decisive'. And with that understanding of the situation in 1415 Tierney would appear to agree.[113] But, as I have more than

[110] For which, see the painstaking discussion in Schneider, *Konziliarismus*.

[111] 'Hermeneutics and History', 366–7; '"Divided Sovereignty" at Constance', 242–4; 'Roots of Western Constitutionalism', in Coriden, *We, The People of God*, 124–6.

[112] 'Hermeneutics and History', 363. Cf. his introduction to the 1998 edn. of *Foundations*, p. xxiii.

[113] Though in one place he speaks as if the doubtfulness of John's claim sprang not from the circumstances of his election but from the fact that he himself had put his legitimacy in question 'when he threatened to prolong the schism by fleeing from the Council' (introduction to the 1998 edn. of *Foundations*, pp. xxiii–iv). The remark is made only in passing and it would probably be unwarranted to conclude that it aligns him with the position carved out at Constance by the papalist, Leonard Statius de Datis, who spoke of John XXIII as having 'illegitimated himself' by his flight, and to whom his conciliarist opponent ascribed, therefore, the view that 'a council could never really depose a pope; it could only declare that a pope had forfeited his office by his own behavior'—thus Tierney, '"Divided Sovereignty" at Constance', 247–50. Cf. Finke, *Acta*, ii. 719, for Statius's claim that 'quia presens Constanciense concilium pape caret, habet sacrum concilium plenariam gladii spiritualis potestatem et eandem semper habuit post illegitimacionem prefati olim domini Johannis ac per consequens, quod presens concilium potuit dictum Johannen velud illegitimatum post fugam eius de dicto concilio a papatu deponere'. And his opponent's concomitant conclusion, ibid. 709: 'Unde sequitur, quod nullo casu concilium potest ferre sentenciam deposicionis contra

once insisted, for the bulk of the fathers assembled at Constance
John XXIII was certainly far more than another 'dubious claimant' to the
papacy. To have supposed, after all, that he was anything less than the legitimate pope would also have been to question the legitimacy of the Council
of Pisa's claim to have deposed the Avignonese and Roman pontiffs, and to
have questioned that would of necessity have been to question in turn the
legitimacy of Constance's claim to be a legitimate council possessed of the
authority to judge and depose its own recalcitrant pontiff, or even, for that
matter, to promulgate such a decree as *Haec sancta*, however restrictively
interpreted. Not too happy a line of thought for a body of churchmen
anxious to see Constance put an end to the schism. It is not surprising,
then, and as Fink, Franzen, and Zimmerman have all insisted, that 'by far
the greater part of Christendom maintained the legitimacy of the Council
of Pisa and its popes'. So that John XXIII when he convoked Constance
did so as 'a legitimate and generally accepted pope', and when his fortunes
waned 'was deposed, not because people doubted his legitimacy, but
because they objected to his simoniacal intrigues at his election, his
immorality, his faithless utterances and his irreligious conduct'.[114] This
the very wording of the council's sentence of deposition makes clear—the
more so, indeed, when compared with the wording of the later sentence
handed down in relation to the Avignonese claimant, Benedict XIII. For
unlike 'the lord pope John XXIII' whom Constance acted to 'remove, deprive and depose', Benedict XIII, having been condemned for his conduct,
was declared deprived and deposed only (and explicitly) 'as a precaution-
ary measure, since according to himself he actually holds the papacy'.[115]
Nor was the anonymous conciliarist adversary of Leonard Statius de
Datis, the Dominican master-general, alone when, during the conciliar
debates of 1416, he insisted that what Constance had done in John XXIII's
case was actually to depose a pope, not simply to issue a declaratory sentence confirming the fact that that pope had 'illegitimated' himself by fleeing the council and had, as a result and *ipso facto* forfeited the papal

papam, ita quod ipsum deponat, set solum declaracionis, per quam declarat, ipsum esse
verum papam vel non aut esse depositum vel non, quod est contra determinata et practicata
in isto concilio, in quo Johannes primo fuerit suspensus ab administracione papatus et
postea depositus a papatu.' Though it is not, admittedly, the point with which Tierney is immediately concerned, one of the interesting things about this exchange is that both men appear to have assumed that, prior to his deposition (or self-deposition), John XXIII was
indeed a true and legitimate pope.

[114] Fink, 'Zur Beurteilung', esp. 340–3; Franzen, 'Council of Constance', 42–3; Zimmermann, 'Die Absetzung der Päpste auf dem Konstanzer Konzil', in Franzen and Müller, *Konzil
von Konstanz*, 113–37.

[115] Alberigo and Tanner, *Decrees*, i. 417–18, 437–8.

office.[116] In 1418, as we have seen, when arguing for the existence of a right of appeal from the sentence of a pope to that of a future general council, Gerson was to do likewise.[117]

Gerson's argument, moreover, is pertinent, and in the second place, to what Tierney claims for *Haec sancta* in relation to the 'normal circumstances' pertaining after the ending of the schism. For it was precisely under such normal circumstances as they prevailed in 1418 with Martin V now safely ensconced as pope that Gerson was writing. He was doing so in an attempt to vindicate *in principle* the right of appeal from pope to council. And what that had to mean was a right of appeal from an undoubtedly legitimate pope, acting alone, to the judgement of a general council acting, of necessity, apart from him. If one were to deny such a right, he argued, then one would have to deny also the 'most express constitution' of the Council of Constance and the moves which that council had made acting apart from and in opposition to 'a true pope', John XXIII.[118] And that means, of course, that he was taking the word 'council' to denote (at least at moments of pope–council disagreement) the same sort of assembly under 'the normal circumstances' of his day as it had during the immediate circumstances of crisis which Constance had had to confront. The same, moreover, appears to have been true of Cardinal Cesarini later on when, in 1431–2, resisting Eugenius IV's attempt to dissolve the Council of Basel, he pointedly reminded that pope of the provisions of *Haec sancta* and of the fact that the very legitimacy of his own papal title depended upon the legality and validity of the actions which Constance had taken in accord with it.[119]

According to Tierney, however, when they used the word 'council' in the third paragraph of *Haec sancta*, the fathers at Constance intended it to denote an assembly different in kind than that alluded to as a 'council' in the second paragraph. Or, more precisely, they either intended to denote by it a general council acting in harmony with its papal head or were being deliberately and diplomatically ambiguous in their use of the word in order to leave unresolved the question (much debated in the canonistic tradition) concerning the extent of the authority wielded under normal

[116] See above, n. 113.

[117] Gerson, *An liceat in causis fidei a Papa appellare*, in Glorieux, vi. 283–90 (at 286) where, having rejected the notion of *ipso facto* loss of office, he adds (speaking of the judicial process leading up to the deposition of John XXIII): 'Unde et in toto processu usque post sententiam definitivam suae depositionis, reputatus est ab eodem concilio [Constantiensis] verus papa.'

[118] See the texts cited above in nn. 94 and 117. See also Gerson, *Dialogus apologeticus*, in Glorieux, vi. 302–3.

[119] G. Christianson, *Cesarini* (St Ottilien: EOS-Verlag, 1979), 58.

circumstances by the members of a general council acting apart from their papal head. But nothing in the actual wording of the decree itself suggests that they were choosing to use the word in two such different ways. Nor do the immediate circumstances under which they were operating provide any real ground for imputing to them so very complex an intention. After all, they framed the decree at a time when, because of John XXIII's flight, they were acting alone and in opposition to a pope the legitimacy of whose title they themselves recognized. The whole immediate context powerfully suggests, indeed, that it was the authority of a council acting apart from such a pope on matters pertaining to the faith, the ending of schism, and reform in head and members that they had in mind throughout, and in relation no less to the longer future than to the immediate crisis.

Moreover, though here one moves onto more speculative ground, given the fact that many of the council fathers were later to insist that the council, having disposed of all the rival claimants and acting, therefore, apart from any papal head, should go on to enact a programme of reform *before* proceeding to the election of a new pope, one could surmise that it was their intention in the latter part of the decree to make sure that no future pope could question the validity of the steps they had taken while acting alone. And the decree *Frequens*, promulgated as a central part of the reform package which they approved prior to proceeding to the election of Martin V, and imposing on future popes as a matter of legal obligation the assembly of general councils at stated and regular intervals, may be read as an attempt to translate into a disciplinary regulation the conviction which underlay *Haec sancta*. That disciplinary regulation moreover, they buttressed with various enforcement mechanisms designed to prevent the pope's avoidance of that obligation and (in the companion decree *Si vero*) automating the speedy assembly of a general council in the unhappy event of any disputed papal election or future schism.[120]

So far, then, as the validity and meaning of *Haec sancta* go, even if one leaves open the question of its status as any sort of dogmatic decree, it seems clear that Constance intended it to be something more universal and less time-bound than a mere emergency measure cobbled together to cope with the crisis at hand. It mandated for the future an understanding of the nature of the Church and of its constitution that entailed not only a rejection of 'the fourteenth century curialist doctine of the Church',[121] but also the

---

[120] Alberigo and Tanner, *Decrees*, i. 439–42. See the analysis of these measures in Stump, *Reforms*, 104–8, and, for the drafts of these decrees produced by the first and second reform committees at Constance, ibid. 317–19, 382–5.

[121] Tierney, 'Hermeneutics and History', in Sandquist and Powicke, *Essays*.

attribution to the general council—even one acting apart from the pope—of a jurisdictional authority in certain crucial matters superior to that possessed by the pope alone. That, certainly, was the way in which it was for centuries to be understood, both by the papalist theologians of the Roman school who rejected it and by the broad array of theologians and churches north of the Alps who 'received' and accepted it as an integral part of their Catholic commitments.[122] Arresting enough, no doubt, but what we finally make of the nature of the theory reflected in the decree, as also the historical significance we choose to attach to it, both depend in no small measure upon what we conclude about its origins and what we conclude also about its career subsequent to the ending of the Council of Basel in 1449. To the latter question I will be turning in the chapters which follow. In this chapter it remains, then, and by way of conclusion, to address the question of origins.

THE MATTER OF ORIGINS

In 1867, addressing the reform programme of the Council of Constance, the historian Bernhard Hübler delivered himself of the opinion that the conciliar theory which that council had striven to translate into practice marked a great departure from the past and, from the point of view of late medieval canon law, constituted nothing less than 'the grossest heresy'. In 1869, Ignaz von Döllinger, who was fighting via the celebrated Janus papers a futile rearguard action against the infallibilists of the day, viewed the decisions taken at Constance as together constituting 'the most extraordinary event in the whole dogmatic history of the Christian church'. To John Neville Figgis similarly, delivering his splendid Birkbeck Lectures at Cambridge some thirty years later, the council's claims were so breathtakingly radical that *Haec sancta* itself (which he viewed as 'striving to turn into a tepid constitutionalism the Divine authority of a thousand years') was 'probably the most revolutionary official document in the history of the world'.[123]

For the next half-century or so, subsequent historians may well have winced a little at Figgis's hyperbole. But, writing as they were in the long historiographical shadows cast by the First Vatican Council, they also tended to concur in the understanding giving rise to his no less than to

---

[122] For the principle of 'reception' see below, Epilogue, at n. 43.

[123] B. Hübler, *Die Constanzer Reformation und die Concordate von 1418* (Leipzig: B. Tauchnitz, 1867), 362: 'die ärgste Ketzerei'. The whole of Exkursus ii. 360–88 is pertinent. Döllinger (alias 'Janus'), *The Pope and the Council* (London, 1869), 302. Figgis, *Political Thought*, 41–70 (at 41). The original lectures were delivered in 1900 and the book 1st published in 1907.

Hübler's and Döllinger's sense of the extraordinary, even revolutionary, nature of *Haec sancta*. Hence the marked degree to which the problem of origins preoccupied and puzzled historians all the way down to the publication in 1955 of Brian Tierney's path-breaking book, *Foundations of the Conciliar Theory*.[124]

It would be hard, I think, fully to sense the importance of the contribution that book made without having had some personal acquaintance with the state of the field prior to its publication. 'In conciliar studies', E. F. Jacob had grumbled in 1943, 'we are frequently told that this or that view is to be found in Ockham and there the matter is unsatisfactorily left.'[125] On that score, nothing much had changed by 1955. By that time nobody was any longer content, with some of the earlier historians of conciliarism, to regard the positions staked out by Conrad of Gelnhausen and Henry of Langenstein at the start of the schism as simply the product of their own pragmatic efforts to come to terms with the grievous difficulties occasioned thereby. Nor did much enthusiasm attach to Figgis's unargued assumption that what conciliar theory in fact reflected was the bold and radical extension to the universal Church of principles already being hammered out in the national kingdoms on the anvil of constitutional unrest and finding expression all over Europe in the erection of parliamentary bodies and assemblies of estates.[126] E. F. Jacob's twinge of asperity notwithstanding, more sympathy was extended to the efforts of other historians to push back beyond the immediate context in which Gelnhausen and Langenstein had framed their position and to claim an earlier source for conciliarist views in the great efflorescence of publicistic literature occasioned in the first half of the fourteenth century by the bitter clash between the Avignonese papacy and Lewis of Bavaria, and especially in the tracts which the two leading imperialist propagandists, William of Ockham and Marsiglio of Padua, had contributed to the cause.[127]

The implications, however, of this attribution should not escape us. In the last great medieval dispute between the supreme spiritual and temporal authorities in Latin Christendom these two men had sided with the temporal and neither was destined to be in particularly good standing with the leading Catholic theologians of the modern era. Along with Eugenius IV himself, indeed, it was the Dominican theologian, Juan de Torquemada, who, in his role as papal ideologist and propagandist at the Council of Basel, had first attached to conciliarism this highly suspect and

---

[124] Republished in 1998 with a new introductory essay.
[125] E. F. Jacob, *Essays in the Conciliar Epoch* (Manchester: MUP, 1953), 85.
[126] Figgis, *Political Thought*, 46–8, 56.   [127] See above, Ch. 1.

radical genealogy.[128] If the strict conciliar theory was really rooted in the thinking of Ockham and Marsiglio, then a considerable cogency would attach to Torquemada's claim (one dear to modern commentators of ultramontane sympathies) that what conciliar theorists were really involved in was nothing less than an attempt to foist upon the Church an unorthodox ecclesiology of revolutionary vintage.[129] The facts of the matter, however, in all their irritating complexity, turn out to tell a very different story.

So far as Ockhamist ideas go, part of the difficulty one encounters in attempting to assess their alleged influence is that it is often difficult to identify in Ockham's publicistic writings, amid the complex interplay of opinions adduced and analysed, those views that are truly his own. In those works, moreover, there is a certain ambivalence that makes it possible to read him in more ways than one. If later conciliar thinkers[130] could find in them a good deal of piecemeal support for their views, we should not miss the fact that those same works contained also some crumbs of hope for their opponents. On the one hand, his anti-papal critique is as extensive as it is devastating. It is election by the faithful or their chosen designees, he argues, that confers the papacy on the person elected, and the need for such consent serves further to limit the reach of the papal power. The universal Church is itself nothing other than that consenting congregation of the faithful, and to that Church alone, and not to the (local) Roman church of pope and cardinals, belongs the indefectibility that Christ promised his apostles. Whereas the universal Church can never lapse wholly into heresy, history itself proves that the pope can. If popes have done so in the past, they may well do so again in the future and, if they do, they will of course be subject to judgement. Canon law may well stipulate that the pope alone may summon a general council, but simple equity requires that in the event of papal heresy a council can be assembled by other means, can stand in judgement on the pope, and can remove him from office. Further than that, the council itself is not to be seen as composed of members of the clerical hierarchy alone. Because 'the Church is not the pope or the

---

[128] Izbicki, 'Papalist Reaction', 7–20; idem, *Protector of the Faith*, 19, 42–4, 53. For Eugenius, see Bäumer, 'Die Stellungnahme Eugens IV, zum Konstanzer Superioritätsdekret in der Bulle "Etsi non dubitemus"', in Franzen and Müller, *Konzil von Konstanz*, 337–56 (at 345).

[129] Hence the anxious attempts of such historians as Bäumer and Franzen to construct classificatory schemata distinguishing the 'moderate' *conciliar* viewpoint of the theorists of Constance from the 'extreme', or 'radical *conciliarism*' associated with Ockham and Marsiglio. For which, see above, at nn. 5, 6, and 7.

[130] And quasi-conciliar thinkers such as Jean Courtecuisse (d. 1423). See Oakley, 'The "Tractatus de Fide et Ecclesia..." of Johanne Breviscoxe', *Annuarium Historiae Conciliorum*, 14 (1982), 99–130 (esp. 121–3).

congregation of priests but the congregation of the faithful', and 'since what touches all ought to be discussed and approved by all', the elected representatives at the council should include lay folk and even women.[131]

All of this certainly smacks of radicalism. But it is now clear, and on the other hand, that too much was made in the past of Ockham's references to the role of the general council. It was not, it turns out, really central to his ecclesiology at all. De Lagarde has insisted, indeed, that it would be futile to turn to his works for 'a coherent theory of the rights of a general council', and, of recent years, something of a scholarly consensus has developed to the effect that Ockham was not, according to the usual understanding of the term, a conciliarist at all.[132] Even under circumstances of crisis he does not necessarily attribute to the council the supreme jurisdictional power in the Church. That it *can* judge and replace an heretical pope he has no doubt. But, at least according to his final opinion on the matter, he does not view it as *necessarily* the pope's 'natural judge'. For, at that point, he was inclined to conclude that 'a heretical pope was *ipso facto* deposed and so subject to the judgment of any Catholic'—bishop, assembly of bishops, or, even, the emperor.[133] General councils do indeed represent the universal Church, but representatives do not necessarily enjoy all the powers pertaining to the community they represent. The council no more enjoys the prerogative of infallibility than does the pope, whose office, after all, is of divine origin, who himself represents the Church, and who is normally charged with the task of convoking councils.[134] If a heretical pope can be subjected to the 'declaratory' judgement (at least) of a general council, the members of such a council would equally be subject to the pope's judgement if they all lapsed into heresy and he did not.[135] And so on. The complexity of his argumentation is daunting and that a taint of heresy came to attach itself to what were thought to be his views is not altogether surprising. But, for our purposes, it is sufficient to note that, had the conciliarists indeed drawn their central commitments from Ockham, to do so they would have had to simplify and distort what he actually had to say.

If Ockham is something less, or other, than a conciliarist, Marsiglio of Padua is something more than that, and it would be a salutary clarification if, by general agreement, we could decide henceforth to withhold that

---

[131] Ockham, *Octo quaestiones de potestate papae*, qu. 1, dist. 17, ed. Sykes in *Opera politica*, i. 60.

[132] Lagarde, *Naissance*, v. 53.

[133] Tierney, 'Ockham, the Conciliar Theory, and the Canonists', *Journal of the History of Ideas*, 15 (1954), 60–1.

[134] Ockham, *Dialogus*, 1. 5. 25, in Goldast, *Monarchia*, ii. 494.

[135] Ockham, *Dialogus*, 1. 6. 64, in Goldast, *Monarchia*, ii. 571.

designation from both of them.[136] Certainly, as evidenced in Marsiglio's major work, the *Defensor pacis* (1324), the thrust of his thinking is vigorous and its direction unmistakable—so much so, indeed, that Pope John XXII lost no time and, as early as 1327, moved formally to condemn him as a heretic. In so doing, he was not lacking in cause. It appears to have been Marsiglio's instinct to go straight for the jugular of the traditional medieval ecclesiology. In company with Ockham and others of unimpeachable orthodoxy, he insists that the Church is not to be defined as the clerical body alone but as 'the whole body of the faithful who believe in and invoke the name of Christ'.[137] Unlike Ockham, however, and unlike those others, Marsiglio moves on to conclude from this that faith being a voluntary thing the congregation of the faithful must lack the type of coerced unity that is possessed by truly political bodies. For him, then, the Church is 'a purely spiritual congregation of believers, connected by no ties but their common faith and participation in the sacraments'.[138] As a result, there is no place in that Church for the exercise by its ministers of any coercive jurisdictional power at all, any *potestas jurisdictionis in foro exteriori*. The very distinction, indeed, of ecclesiastical power into disparate powers of order and jurisdiction is itself excluded, for the latter, he insists, is the prerogative of the temporal political authority alone.[139]

The existence of a divinely established priesthood Marsiglio does not call into question and he devotes attention to the role of the priest in the administration of the sacraments of penance and holy orders. But to that latter sacrament the attitude he displays is revealing. The 'bestowal of orders' is a power that pertains, he says, not to bishops alone but to all priests. The inequalities evident in the clerical hierarchy of his own day he viewed as having no divine basis whatsoever. Christ alone, its founder, is the real head of the Church. The great hierarchical structure of bishops, archbishops, and pope is not of divine provenance at all. It is, instead, a human contrivance, explicable only in terms of administrative convenience and justifiable only to the extent to which it is grounded in the

---

[136] See Oakley, 'Conciliarism in the Sixteenth Century', 130–2, where it is suggested that, while the effect of classifying Marsiglio as a conciliarist was formerly to make conciliarism in general look more radical than it was, the effect of late has been to make the conciliar thinkers of the classical era look by comparison more conservative as a group than they were and certainly to obscure the differences that existed within their ranks.

[137] *Defensor pacis*, 2. 2. 3, ed. Previté-Orton, p. 117. I cite Gewirth's translation, ii. 103. See the useful introductory synopsis in ibid. ii, pp. xix ff.

[138] Ibid. i. 277.

[139] Marsiglio, *Defensor pacis*, 2. 4, ed. Previté-Orton, pp. 128–43, tr. Gewirth, ii. 113–26. The whole of Marsiglio's second discourse is devoted to exploring the implications of this claim.

consent of the faithful. And that consent is to be expressed by direct election of priests, bishops, and 'head bishop' (that is, the pope). It is to be expressed, also, by the general council. And that council is to be an elective body made up of laity as well as clergy. Its supreme prerogative is to be able, as the body representation of Christian believers, to express itself on matters of faith with that authority which Christ promised neither to Peter or his supposed successors, nor the apostles or their clerical succession, but to the whole congregation of the faithful alone.

It would be redundant to belabour the novelty and radicalism of so many of these positions. If this Marsilian ecclesiology were indeed the source of conciliar theory, then that theory was doomed to heterodoxy from its very birth and its traditional dismissal by Catholic theologians and historians alike as a revolutionary deviation in the history of the medieval Church would be wholly comprehensible. But the positions we have seen carved out by the leading conciliarists of the classical era suggest the improbability of any such lineage. Borrowings from Ockham, it is true, there are many, and they extend in the case of Pierre d'Ailly to outright, verbatim copyings.[140] Such borrowings, however, are piecemeal in nature. If they reflect the willingness of the conciliarists to cash in on Ockham's freewheeling critique of the traditional high-papalist ecclesiology, they reflect also their blindness to the equally destructive effects of that critique when turned upon the conciliarist ecclesiology they themselves wished to promote. And signs of Marsilian influence are much less in evidence. Admittedly, Dietrich of Niem and Nicholas of Cusa both drew some fragmentary material from the *Defensor pacis*,[141] but the presence even of piecemeal borrowings in the works of most of the conciliarists of the classical era has proved hard to detect. If it was once common to link Gerson with Marsiglio, that was because Dietrich's *De modis uniendi et reformandi ecclesiam in concilio universali* had been attributed to him, but incorrectly so. Gerson had, in fact, and in this he was like Jacques Almain a century later, taken explicit exception to Marsiglian views.[142] The

---

[140] Oakley, *Political Thought of d'Ailly*, 200–4.

[141] P. Sigmund, 'The Influence of Marsilius of Padua on XVth-Century Conciliarism', *Journal of the History of Ideas*, 23 (1962), 392–402. In neither case were the borrowings extensive and Heimpel, *Dietrich von Niem*, 77–121, stresses the eclecticism of Dietrich's views.

[142] Posthumus Meyjes, *Gerson*, 226, 246, 289, 311–12, 318, 342–8. Almain, *Expositio circa decisiones Magistri Guilelmi Occam super potestate ecclesiastica*, in Gerson, *Opera omnia*, ed. Dupin, ii. 1037, 1041, and *Tractatus de auctoritate ecclesiae et conciliorum*, ibid. 980. Cf. Oakley, 'Conciliarism in England: St. German, Starkey and the Marsiglian Myth', in T. M. Izbicki and C. M. Bellitto, eds., *Reform and Renewal in the Middle Ages and Renaissance* (Leiden: E. J. Brill, 2000), 225–39.

radicalism of the Marsiglian vision was simply too much, it seems, for most of these conciliarists to take.

Of the three strands that combined in the conciliarist thinking of the classical era, we have already seen that two had perfectly orthodox origins amid the established respectabilities of the pre-Ockhamist and pre-Marsiglian era.[143] It remains to be established, then, that much of the same was true also of the third and remaining strand—what I have referred to as the strict conciliar theory. Even if we were to persist in the quest to trace that theory back to the bitter conflicts between the spiritual and temporal authorities in the early fourteenth century and to the great efflorescence of publicistic literature which those conflicts stimulated, while the trail would not lead us to Ockham and Marsiglio, it would point us back a little earlier to John of Paris, writing in 1301–2 in the context of the great clash between Boniface VIII and Philip IV of France, his *Tractatus de potestate regia et papali*.[144]

In the modern era, interest in this tract has characteristically focused on what it has to say about church–state relations. But it also incorporates a very important set of theoretical statements about the internal constitution and government of the Church itself. They involve the insistence that, while the papal authority itself was conferred by God, the decision as to which particular individual was to be called upon to exercise it was made by the Church—or, rather by the college of cardinals standing in the place of the whole Church. The pope so chosen was to wield his authority for the common good of the Church which had called him to his high office. Should he fail to do so, whether because of a lapse into heresy, or criminal behaviour, or simply though sheer incompetence, he could be called to account, tried, judged, and even deprived of his office. And while John certainly viewed the college of cardinals as 'adequate' or 'competent' to effect the deposition of such a heretical, criminous, or incompetent pontiff, he also thought that for the discharge of so solemn a responsibility a general council would be 'more appropriate'.[145]

Commenting on this teaching, Tierney has pointed out that John's 'work provides by far the most consistent and complete foundation of conciliar doctrine before the outbreak of the Great Schism', one which 'not only influenced subsequent publicistic arguments,[146] but also penetrated

---

[143] See above, pp. 66–71.

[144] Ed. Bleienstein; English tr. with a very good introduction in Watt. For the general context, see above, Ch. 1.

[145] John of Paris, *Tractatus*, c. 24, ed. Bleienstein, 201–2; tr. Watts, 242–4. John also discusses the issue of papal correction and deposition in cc. 6, 13, 22, and 25.

[146] Not least among them the conciliarist writings of d'Ailly and Gerson. On which, see

into the technical compilations of the canonists themselves'.[147] And if that was indeed the case, it was so because John himself, theologian though he was, had so absorbed the ideas of the earlier canonists on matters pertaining to the internal governance of the Church and 'so thoroughly appreciated their inner logic'. That claim Tierney advances as part of the overall argument concerning the roots of conciliarism which he developed in his *Foundations of the Conciliar Theory* and which was to make the publication in 1955 of that classic work a major turning point in conciliar studies.[148]

That argument, at once both powerful and subtly nuanced, is grounded firmly in an intensive examination of the canonistic materials, some of them as yet unprinted. Prior to 1955, scholars had long pointed out the frequency with which the earlier canon lawyers were cited in the conciliarist tracts, and the growth since the Second World War of interest in the history of medieval canon law helped focus attention on those citations. Insisting that the borrowings from Ockham and Marsiglio to be found in the conciliarist tracts usually reflected the use to which those two authors had themselves made of the canon law, Tierney argues that the strict conciliar theory, far from being a reaction *against* canonistic teaching or an alien importation onto ecclesial soil of secular constitutional notions, had instead deep (and impeccably orthodox) roots in the ecclesiological tradition of the pre-Marsiglian era. It unquestionabley drew a great deal of inspiration from the *communio* ecclesiology and synodal practice of the first millennium of Christian life, and especially from the essentially conciliar mode of governance that had characterized the ancient Church for long centuries after the Council of Nicaea (325). That phase of Church history had left as its enduring legacy not only the doctrinal decrees and disciplinary canons of the great ecumenical councils but also the memory of the work accomplished by a whole series of pivotal provincial councils, prominent among them those held at Toledo in Visigothic Spain. Much of that legacy was embedded in the texts which Gratian assembled later in his *Decretum*, and the older conciliar material to be found there was very much on the minds of

Oakley, *Political Thought of d'Ailly*, 49–51, 117–18, 204–5, 241–2; Posthumus Meyjes, *Gerson*, 359–63. Tierney, *Foundations*, 177.

[147] Tierney, *Foundations*, 177 and 164 and n. 1, where he points out that 'the canonist Joannes Andreae followed John of Paris literally in his *Novella* on the *Sext. ad* I, vii, 1 fo. 32 n. 2'.

[148] In connection with the book should also be consulted Tierney's subsequent article, 'Pope and Council: Some New Decretist Texts', *Mediaeval Studies*, 19 (1957), 197–218, as well as the introductory essay to the 1998 edn. of *Foundations*, pp. ix–xxix. The observations which follow are based largely on these works and upon Moynihan.

the great conciliar theorists as they laboured to meet the great ecclesiastical challenges of their own day.[149] But if it unquestionably drew rich sustenance from that ancient conciliar past, it is Tierney's claim that conciliar theory, none the less, was to derive much of the structural precision crucial to its practical implementation from certain elements in the body of canon law itself and in the vast ocean of glosses on that law produced during the twelfth, thirteenth, and fourteenth centuries.

During the century and more preceding the onset of the Great Schism, he says, the Decretalists (commentators on the body of decretals or statute laws produced in the thirteenth century by Pope Gregory IX), turning to the Roman law of corporations in their attempts to rationalize the structure, first of the individual churches of Christendom, then of the (local) Roman church, and finally of the universal Church itself, had been led to develop not *one* but *two* separate doctrines of the universal Church's unity. 'The more conspicuous one', he says, 'which has usually been regarded as the canonistic doctrine *par excellence* insisted that the unity of the Church would be secured only by a rigorous subordination of all the members to a single head'. Hence the doctrine of absolute papal monarchy that admittedly dominated most of the canonistic glosses of the fourteenth century.

But side by side with this [familiar doctrine of papal sovereignty] there existed another theory [developed notably by the great thirteenth-century decretalist, Hostiensis] applied at first to single churches and at the beginning of the fourteenth century, in a fragmentary fashion, to the Roman church and the Church as a whole, a theory which stressed the corporate association of the members of the Church as the true principle of ecclesiastical unity and which envisaged the exercise of corporate authority by the members of the Church even in the absence of an effective head.[150]

If, through the agency of the cardinals, therefore, the members of the Church had endowed the pope with authority, they retained the power, should he fall into error on a matter of faith or abuse his authority in a manner detrimental to the common good of the entire Church, to withdraw that authority.

Or so, as we have seen, John of Paris was to conclude in the early fourteenth century, appropriating Hostiensis' corporatist understanding of the Church's unity and using it to provide the framework for his own succinct and precociously complete formulation of conciliar theory. And

---

[149] This is very evident, for example, in the battery of references one finds in a work like Pierre d'Ailly's *Tractatus de materia concilii generalis* (1402/3), ed. Oakley, *Political Thought of d'Ailly*, 252–342.

[150] Tierney, *Foundations*, 240.

it was that same corporatist understanding that was to be expressed so forcefully in Gerson and d'Ailly and, with such depth of canonist erudition, in Zabarella. Their arguments, however, like those of John of Paris before them, drew also on another and older strand in canonistic thinking that went back to the commentaries written on the *Decretum* of Gratian in the twelfth and early thirteenth centuries, especially to their discussion of the case of the heretical pope. The 'Decretists', or canonist commentators on the *Decretum*, denied to the pope himself, and to the (local) Roman church of pope and cardinals, the prerogative of inerrancy which they accorded to the universal Church. On the basis of this, some of them (most notably the author of the *glossa ordinaria*—the influential standard commentary on the *Decretum*) concluded that the general council must be 'above the pope' in matters of faith. By this they probably meant to imply no more than that on such matters the decisions of pope-in-council (pope and council acting together, as they normally would) were superior to the decisions of the pope acting alone.[151] But what if a pope lapsed into heresy? Gratian had included in the *Decretum* the ancient legal maxim which, though it is now known to stem from a sixth-century forgery, was still enshrined in the 1917 *Code of Canon Law*, namely, that 'the pope can be judged by no one'.[152] He had also included, however, the qualification appended to that maxim in the eleventh century—namely, 'unless he [the pope] is caught deviating from the faith'. But if the pope is indeed accused of heresy (or, for that matter, of any notorious crime tantamount to heresy), by whom will he be judged? On this tricky point there was no single Decretist theory and Tierney is careful to insist that many important canonistic texts still await assessment.[153] It is possible, however, to identify what appear to be two main 'schools' of canonistic thinking on the matter.

According to the first of these schools a pope who lapsed into heresy ceased *ipso facto* to be pope. If he contumaciously persisted in his heresy, resource to a judicial superior might be necessary in order to make it clear that he was, in fact, guilty of heresy and in order to have proclaimed, therefore, a *declaratory* sentence of (self-inflicted) deposition. But the judicial superior in question might be the college of cardinals and not the general council. The principal spokesman for this school of thought was Huguccio

---

[151] For the pertinence of this point to the controversy surrounding the interpretation of the Constance decree *Haec sancta*, see above, pp. 94–5.

[152] *Decretum Gratiani*, D. 40, c. 6; ed. Friedberg, i. 146; *Codex Juris Canonici* (1917), can. 1556. Similarly, the 1983 *Code*, can. 1404. For that canon with useful comment, see Beal *et al.*, *New Commentary on the Code of Canon Law*, 1618.

[153] Though, as he indicates in the introductory essay written in 1997 for the 1998 edn. of *Foundations*, he sees no reason to qualify his original argument.

(d. 1210). According to the second school, a heretical pontiff did not cease *ipso facto* to be pope; he had instead to be subjected to trial, judgement, and deposition. And the body possessing the requisite authority to stand in judgement was the general council since, even acting in opposition to the pope, it possessed a jurisdiction superior to his in matters pertaining to the faith. The leading advocate of this point of view was Alanus Anglicus (*c.*1202). On this crucial point, the teaching of Johannes Teutonicus (d. 1246), author of the *glossa ordinaria*, turns out to be ambiguous. But many seem, at least, to have understood him to back the latter school of thought. Certainly, even in 'the most cautious glosses' of the late thirteenth and fourteenth centuries that latter school prevailed. In those glosses,

> there was little trace of Huguccio's cautious distinctions indicating that a pope had ceased to be pope before being brought to trial, and thus eliminating the necessity of a strict papal trial as such. Rather, the conciliarist doctrine of Alanus came to the fore during this period, and his view was [later] presented in a cogent synthesis by the great canonist, Franciscus Zabarella.[154]

According to Tierney, it was in the combination of *both* of these strands of canonistic thinking—the second 'corporatist' view of the Church's unity and the second of the two Decretist theories of papal liability—that we find the foundation of the strict conciliar theory. The ambivalence of the canonistic heritage hindered the development of a coherently constitutionalist understanding of the Church's unity until the imperative necessities of a protracted schism called such an understanding into being. That understanding crystallized in the formulations of the great conciliarists of Pisa, Constance, and Basel, theologians no less than canonists—not least of all those formulations characteristic of 'the most notable and harmonious of the conciliar theories, that of Nicholas Cusanus'. But it remains, none the less, true that what made those formulations possible was nothing other than 'impregnation of Decretist ecclesiology by Decretalist corporation concepts'.[155]

Despite the surfacing of some oblique (and not so oblique) scholarly grumbling, I would judge that the great tide of literature on conciliar and related matters that has been flowing during the nearly fifty years since Tierney propounded his thesis has really done little or nothing to shake it.[156] As our knowledge of the thinking of individual conciliarists has

---

[154] J. M. Moynihan, *Papal Immunity and Liability in the Writings of the Medieval Canonists* (Rome: Gregorian University Press, 1961), 142.

[155] Tierney, *Foundations*, 36 and 245.

[156] On which, see Oakley, *Politics and Eternity*, 73–6, and Tierney's own remarks in his introduction to the 1998 edn. of *Foundations*, pp. xi–xv. It should be noted that not all of

grown, so, too, has the body of evidence for the deep impress made on the full range of conciliarists of arguments drawn (either directly or at one remove or another) from the glosses of Decretists and Decretalists alike. That this should be true of works written by those who were themselves lawyers is hardly surprising; more striking is the degree to which some of the theologians, too—d'Ailly and Gerson among them—reveal their acquaintance with, or indebtedness to, the canonistic literature.[157] And if one is willing to accord a measure of deference to the understanding of conciliar theory evinced by commentators who lived closer in time to the conciliar epoch than do we, one would do well to take note of the fact that the English Protestant divines, John Ponet in the mid-sixteenth century and John Bramhall in the mid-seventeenth, unhesitatingly labelled the conciliar theory as a canonistic teaching. So, too, did the seventeenth-century English parliamentarian, William Prynne.[158] And such men, it need hardly be insisted, had themselves not even a remotely conciliarist axe to grind.

What this solution to the problem of origins means, of course, is that conciliar theory did not represent (as Figgis and others assumed) some sort of radical intrusion—in Tierney's words, 'something accidental and external, thrust upon the Church from the outside'. It was, instead, 'a logical culmination of ideas that were [deeply] embedded in the law and doctrines of the Church itself'.[159] That being so, and it being clear that the conciliar theory of the classical age was neither as recent nor as revolutionary in its origins as for long we were encouraged to assume, we are now in a position to explore the congruent possibility that the demise of that theory was neither as sudden nor as final as formerly we were accustomed to suppose. To that exploratory task, which will take the story down as far as the late nineteenth century and into conciliarist territory that is less familiar and (accordingly) more controverted, I propose to devote myself in the four chapters ensuing.

---

those who praised Tierney's book appear to have absorbed (or understood) his argument. Thus Franzen and Bäumer both pass over in silence his fundamental stress on the contribution of Decretalist corporation theory to conciliar thinking and focus instead and exclusively on the Decretist strand. See Oakley, *Politics and Eternity*, 84–6.

[157] Oakley, *Political Thought of d'Ailly*, 163–4, 209–10; Posthumus Meyjes, *Gerson*, 220–32; Morrall, *Gerson and the Great Schism*, 120, Oakley, 'Gerson and d'Ailly', 81.

[158] Ponet, *Shorte Treatise of Politicke Power*, [103]–[104]; Bramhall, *The Serpent-Salve*, in *Works*, iii. 316, *A Just Vindication of the Church of England*, in *Works*, i. 248, *A Replication to the Bishop of Chichester*, in *Works*, ii. 249, Prynne, *The Sovereign Power of Parliaments and Kingdoms*, 73.

[159] Tierney, *Foundations*, 13. The words are written in relation to the conciliar movement in general.

3

Cajetan's Conundrum: Almain, Mair, the Divines of Paris, and their English Sympathizers

The question at issue . . . is whether the supreme pontiff is above the universal council or the universal Church, which is represented by the council. On this question there are opposing ways of speaking, one of which holds that the pope is above the universal council. This view has been and is held by some of the cardinals and by the Thomists generally; and in Rome (it is said) no one is allowed publicly to maintain the contrary. The other has always been followed by our University of Paris since the days of the Council of Constance, so that any member taking the other view, upon being challenged, is compelled to recant it.

(John Mair, 1518[1])

I cannot deny that I am a Frenchman, nurtured at the University of Paris where the authority of the council is held to be above that of the pope and where those who hold to the contrary are censured as heretics. [Nor can I deny] that in France the Council of Constance is viewed as general in its entirety, the Council of Basel is likewise recognized, but that of Florence held to be neither legitimate nor general.

(Charles de Guise, cardinal of Lorraine, 1563/4[2])

[T]he Councell [of Constance] did not reject him [John XXIII] as disorderly chosen, nor disclaime him for no Bishop, but removed him from the function which he had, as unworthy [of] the same. And their generall decree, by which they define the Pope to be subject to

---

[1] Mair, *Disputatio de auctoritate concilii supra pontificem maximum*, in Gerson, *Opera omnia*, ed. Dupin, ii. 1150. I cite the translation in Burns and Izbicki, *Conciliarism*, 285–6.

[2] Charles de Guise, letter to his agent at Rome, in Le Plat, *Monumentorum*, v. 658.

> the Council [i.e. *Haec sancta*], must not be referred to wrongfull in-
> vaders, but wholly restrained to lawfull possessors of the Romane
> See: else, no masterie for the Councell to be superiour to those that
> were no Popes, but only usurpers.

(Thomas Bilson, 1585[3])

> I believe that if there had been Popes with a great reputation for
> wisdom and virtue, who had wanted to follow the measures taken at
> Constance, they could have remedied the abuses, prevented the
> rupture [occasioned by the Protestant Reformation], and sustained
> or even advanced Christian society.

(Gottfried Wilhelm Leibniz, 1715[4])

It would, I suppose, be an egregious understatement if I were to say that the
council which met in 1511–12, first in Pisa then in Milan, had not enjoyed,
over the centuries, a very good press. The fact of the matter is that it enjoyed
hardly any press at all, and what little it did receive was bad. Convoked
by several dissident members of the college of cardinals, derided by
papalists as the *conciliabulum* of Pisa, and disdained by the Italian, Spanish, German, English, and Polish hierarchies, it was engineered into
existence by Louis XII of France, whose purpose it was to extend his anti-
papal offensive from the military and political spheres into the ecclesiastical.[5] Short of duration and poorly attended, it was composed throughout
almost entirely of French prelates and its activities devoted almost exclusively to the assertion and reassertion of its own legitimacy, the endorsement yet once more of the Constance superiority decree *Haec sancta*, and
the mounting of an accusatory process directed against Pope Julius II. Its
most significant achievement, ironically enough, was that of stimulating
that pope to convoke, by way of defensive reaction, the rival and papally
dominated assembly that has gone down in history as the Fifth Lateran
Council—a council often credited with having added to earlier papal pro-
hibitions of appeals from the judgement of the pope to that of a future
general council, 'a condemnation of the conciliar theory itself'.[6] And on
that theory of the jurisdictional superiority of council to pope, Pisa, of
course, had staked its own legitimacy.

---

[3] T. Bilson, *The True Difference betweene Christian subjection and Unchristian Rebellion*
(Oxford, 1585), 89.
[4] 'Observations on the Abbé de St. Pierre's "Project for Perpetual Peace" (1715)', in Leibniz, *Political Writings*, tr. and ed. Riley (Cambridge: CUP, 1988), 180.
[5] For the historical background to Pisa and the Fifth Lateran Council, see above, Ch. 1.
[6] Thus Jedin, *History*, i. 133.

A record of achievement, admittedly, that is eminently forgettable; but the *conciliabulum* of Pisa constituted a very important moment in the history of conciliarist constitutionalism in the Latin Church. It did so for two reasons. First, the very success of its convocation—and it was not the first such attempt during the post-conciliar half-century that has come to be known as the era of papal restoration[7]—witnesses dramatically to the enduring vitality of the conciliar tradition on the very eve of the Reformation itself. Second, by stimulating the ire of Thomas de Vio, the Dominican Master-General and future Cardinal Cajetan, it called forth from the Parisian theologians Jacques Almain (d. 1515) and John Mair or Major (d. 1550) particularly clear and powerful restatements of conciliar theory. By so doing, it functioned in effect, as the first in a notable series of ideological relay stations, picking up from the past a gradually attenuating conciliarist signal, clarifying, strengthening, and boldly transmitting it forward in updated and re-energized form to the receptors of future generations.

ECCLESIOLOGICAL AMBIGUITIES IN THE ERA OF PISA AND
LATERAN V

The urgent need to end the Great Schism, the push for sweeping reform of the Church in head and members, the emerging Hussite threat, the beguiling dream of restoring communion with the beleaguered Orthodox Churches of the Byzantine East—these and other issues had preoccupied the generations of churchmen assembled at the four general councils called into existence between 1409 and 1449. But at none of them was the pressing constitutional question of the relationship of conciliar to papal jurisdictional authority off the agenda for very long. Martin V had not directly challenged the constitutional implications of the Constance superiority decree, *Haec sancta*. How could he, indeed? The very legitimacy of his own papal title was directly dependent upon it. In the end, however, after years of struggle with the conciliarists at Basel, his successor Eugenius IV had issued, in effect, precisely such a challenge.[8] His attempt, first, to dissolve the Council of Basel shortly after its assembly in 1431, and then, later, to translate it to Florence, had led the council fathers to reissue and reconfirm *Haec sancta* on no less than three occasions. In 1439, finally, they had declared the superiority of council to pope to be nothing less than an

---

[7] For which, see above, Ch. 1.   [8] For which, see above, Ch. 1.

article of the Catholic faith. But, by that time, Eugenius had succeeded in splitting the ranks of the conciliarists, inducing some of the most distinguished among them to align with his rival council of Florence, and depriving the diminished assembly soldiering on at Basel of much of the political support it had earlier received from the leading European powers. And when those powers, in return for the concessions embodied in very favourable papal concordats finally abandoned a posture of neutrality and rallied clearly to the papal cause, the game was up. The rump assembly enduring at Basel had little choice but to follow their lead and the conciliar movement of the fourteenth and fifteenth centuries came to an end.

In the high-papalist constitutive narrative that was embedded until recent years in most of our standard ecclesiastical histories, this outcome is portrayed as nothing less than a triumph for the papacy, the ending of a long nightmare of debilitating constitutional confusion with the Church, and the dawn of the more bracing era of papal restoration. As recently as a quarter of a century ago, Paul Ourliac could depict the year 1440 as the great turning point after which theologians and canonists alike turned energetically to what he called (revealingly enough) the 'constructive' task of vindicating the papal monarchy.[9] So far as conciliar theory was concerned, it was seen to have been banished into the outer darkness of heterodoxy with the promulgation in 1460 of Pius II's bill *Execrabilis* prohibiting the appeal from the judgement of the pope to that of a future general council. If conciliar sympathies did indeed linger on into the age of the *conciliabulum* of Pisa, any enduring doubts about the heterodoxy of conciliar theory itself were destined soon to be dissipated at the Fifth Lateran Council, when in 1516 the decree *Pastor aeternus* declared that the Roman pontiff had 'authority over all councils'.[10] And if, in later centuries, distant conciliarist echoes were still detectable in the French- and German-speaking world in the context of Gallican, Febronian, and Josephinist statist propaganda, they should properly be recognized for what they truly were— nothing more than pallid harmonics of a discredited ideology long since consigned to the junk heap of ecclesiological history.

The growing body of historical scholarship focusing on the aftermath of the conciliar epoch has come of recent years, however, and with growing

---

[9] Ourliac and Gilles, 'La Problématique de l'époque: Les Sources', in Le Bras, ed., *Histoire du Droit*, 13, 1:51, cf. Ourliac, 'La Victoire de la papauté', in Delaruelle *et al.*, *L'Église*, i. 285.

[10] Alberigo and Tanner, *Decrees*, i. 642: 'cum etiam solum Romanum pontificem pro tempore existentem, tanquam auctoritatem super omnia concilia habentem, conciliorum indicendorum, transferendorum, ac dissolvendorum plenum jus et potestatem habere.'

insistence, to point in a very different direction.[11] It strongly suggests that we can no more take for granted the weakening of the conciliarist impulse in the late fifteenth and early sixteenth centuries than could the watchful popes of the period. It is only, it must once more be insisted, our familiarity with the papalist outcome that suggests the necessity of the process. If the temporal powers had been induced to reject Basel and side finally with the pope, it was only after a period of neutrality during which the French in the Pragmatic Sanction of Bourges and the Germans in the *Acceptatio* of Mainz had adopted as their own much of the reforming legislation of Basel, not excluding its reconfirmation of the Constance decrees *Haec sancta* and *Frequens*. *Execrabilis*, moreover, and as we now know, was viewed less in its own day as an authoritative pronouncement than as a propagandistic proclamation of the view of one particular faction. It encountered robust opposition, and it was in vain that subsequent popes felt impelled to renew its prohibition of appeals to a future council. The crucial phrases of the 1516 decree *Pastor aeternus*, moreover, were simply too restricted in meaning to constitute any unambiguous condemnation of conciliar theory. Addressing the issue of the legitimacy of Basel after Eugenius IV had translated that council to Ferrara, it spoke only of the papal right 'to convoke, transfer, and dissolve councils'. It did not spurn the conciliar superiority decrees of Basel, nor is there any mention of Constance or any rejection of *Haec sancta*. And that, as previously noted,[12] was not because such a move would have been regarded as redundant at the time. Ferdinand the Catholic of Spain, indeed, in the instructions he had given to his representatives at the Fifth Lateran Council, had explicitly urged the need for such a formal repudiation of *Haec sancta*.

The fact that no such move was made is consonant with the marked degree to which the papalism of those churchmen who rejected the conciliarist assembly at Pisa and rallied to the pope's Lateran Council was highly qualified in nature.[13] So qualified, indeed, as to be compatible with a continuing adhesion to some, at least, of the ecclesiological commitments

---

[11] See esp. Jedin, *History*, i. 1–165; J. Klotzner, *Kardinal Domenikus Jacobazzi und sein Konzilswerk* (Rome: Apud Aedes Universitatis Gregorianae, 1948); Brosse, *Le Pape et le Concile*; Bäumer, *Nachwirkungen*; R. Bäumer, ed., *Von Konstanz nach Trient* (Munich: F. Schöningh, 1972); Fink, 'Die konziliare Idee in späten Mittelalter', in Mayer, *Die Welt zur Zeit des Konstanzer Konzils* (Constance and Stuttgart, 1965); Oakley, 'Natural Law', with full bibliographical listing of pertinent works down to 1981.

[12] See above, Ch. 1.

[13] Vooght, 'Le Conciliarisme aux conciles de Constance et de Bâle', in B. Botte *et al.*, *Le Concile et les conciles* (Chevetogne and Paris: Éditions de Chevetogne, 1960), 179; Bäumer, *Nachwirkungen*, 16, 261–6.

embedded in the conciliar thinking of the classical era. That was true even of Cajetan himself, and it confronted him with something of a conundrum when, in October 1511, he entered the lists against the *conciliabulum* of Pisa and set out to refute its conciliarist claims.

The conundrum which he faced reflects the presence within the triumphantly restored papal monarchy of the late fifteenth and early sixteenth centuries of some complex and debilitating tensions that were at least partly constitutional in nature. But if the picture which emerges is, indeed, a complex and sometimes confusing one, I would suggest that these complexities correspond in marked degree to the complexities of conciliarism itself. Once that is realized, the confusion, if it cannot totally be dispelled, can be diminished, or, at least, domesticated.

In the previous chapter I argued for the presence within the conciliar thinking of the classical era of three broad strands woven momentarily and fatefully into a meaningful configuration.[14] In the late fifteenth and early sixteenth centuries those three strands, just as they had been distinct in their origins, were turning out now to be distinct also in their subsequent careers.

The first and most prominent of those three strands, it may be recalled, was the demand for reform of the Church 'in head and members', and the belief—eventually reflected, of course, in *Frequens*—that the reform could best be achieved and consolidated through the periodic assembly of general councils. During the years of schism that type of reforming programme had come to be closely allied with the strict conciliar theory itself. But given the failure of the conciliarists at Basel to deliver effectively on reform, by the mid-fifteenth century that alliance was beginning to crumble—a development well reflected in the careers of the Cardinals Cesarini and Nicholas of Cusa who, having begun in the conciliarist camp, ended, without giving up their commitment to reform, by abandoning Basel and aligning themselves with Eugenius IV.[15] As the century wore on, moreover, those who continued to espouse the strict conciliar theory were not necessarily as fervently committed to the reforming cause as the Italian conciliarist and curialist, Giovanni Gozzadini, was to be at the time of the Fifth Lateran Council.[16] In its formal pronouncements, the *conciliabulum*

---

[14] See above, Ch. 2.

[15] See Christianson, *Cesarini*; Watanabe, *Concord and Reform*; idem, *Political Ideas*; Sigmund, *Nicholas of Cusa*; E. Vansteenberghe, *Le Cardinal Nicolas de Cues* (Paris: Champion, 1920).

[16] Gozzadini combined conciliar theory with a fervent appeal for sweeping reform. His conciliarist tract, *De electione romani pontificis* (Ms. Vat. lat. 4144, fos. 1ʳ–307ʳ) has yet to be edited and printed. See Jedin, 'Giovanni Gozzadini, ein Konziliarist am Hofe Julius II', in Jedin, *Kirche des Glaubens*, ii. 17–74.

of Pisa strove to give a different impression, but the real ecclesiastical evil it had met to remedy was nothing more spiritual than Pope Julius II's adoption of a diplomatic stance hostile to the French presence in Italy, and in the tracts of its most prominent apologists—Almain and Mair themselves not excluded—the matter of reform does not occupy a prominent place.

At the same time, those who believed that the necessary reform of the Church in head and members could be achieved only by means of a general council had come increasingly to recoil from advocacy of the strict conciliar theory itself, and it was with the Lateran Council, rather than Pisa, that most chose to align themselves. But it must be insisted that their rejection of the conciliarist ideas of men like Almain did not necessarily mean an abandonment of the first strand of conciliarist thinking. Of course, given the use made of *Frequens* by the initiators of the Council of Pisa,[17] it is not surprising that Julius II should seek, when he in turn invoked the Lateran Council, to prevent any misunderstanding of his action by pointing out that that decree had long since lost its force and that, even if it had not, extenuating circumstances would have rendered it inapplicable in his own day.[18] Nor is it surprising that Cardinal Cajetan should denounce the idea of the periodic assembly of councils as an infringement on the legal rights of the papacy.[19] Given the context of events, what *is* surprising is the demand of Ferdinand of Spain for a pledge that general councils be assembled every ten or fifteen years. This demand was made (not without reference to *Frequens*) in the instructions given to the Spanish envoys to the council.[20] And it was a demand made again and more forcefully in 1516, when the two Camoldolese monks, Tommaso Giustiniani and Vicenzo Quirini, presented to the pope their *Libellus ad Leonem X*. For in that great programme for reform they stated quite explicitly that they regarded it as nothing less than vital to the recovery and maintenance of the Church's health that general councils be held every five years.[21]

These are striking and important manifestations of the persistence of one strand of conciliarism in the thinking of supporters of the Lateran Council whom we tend to classify as 'papalists'. But what about the

---

[17] Jedin, *History*, i. 108–9.
[18] Hefele, *Histoire*, viii. 299. The bull is printed in Baronius *et al.*, *Annales*, xxx: ann. 1511, nos. 9–15; see esp. no. 11.
[19] Cajetan, *De comparatione auctoritatis papae et concilii*, c. 16, no. 237, ed. Pollet, 110. English trans. in Burns and Izbicki, *Conciliarism*, 72.
[20] Printed in Doussinague, *Fernando*, app. 50, 539.
[21] *Libellus ad Leonem X*, in J. B. Mittarelli and A. Costadoni, eds., *Annales Camaldulensis* (Venice: Apud Jo Baptistam Pasquali, 1755–73), xi. 708.

second, or oligarchic, strand, which, it may be recalled, was rooted in thirteenth-century canonistic corporation theory and in the traditions of the Roman curia? It had envisaged the pope as being limited in the exercise of his power by that of the cardinals. Its synthesis with the more 'democratic' conciliarist views had occurred only later on, during the classical age of conciliar theory, and that synthesis did not turn out to be a very stable one. The years after the collapse of Basel were to witness its disintegration, and by the time of the Pisan crisis and the convocation of the Lateran Council, such advocates of the strict conciliar theory as Almain and Mair, though they drew heavily on Pierre d'Ailly's conciliar thinking, were quick to dissociate themselves from the specifically oligarchic elements in his ecclesiology.[22]

Their reason for doing so is not too hard to detect. The old curialist oligarchic tradition was by no means defunct. But by their day it had come to find its home where it had found it originally—not, that is, among those of recognizably conciliarist commitment but in the Roman curia itself. In his great *Summa de ecclesia* of 1453, Juan de Torquemada had reproduced verbatim (though naturally without acknowledgement) much of d'Ailly's discussion of the role of the cardinalate in the government of the universal Church. The advocacy of these views by the dean of papalists himself (as well as by the curialist Domenico Domenichi and others) had been a factor of some importance in the struggle for power that raged between the college of cardinals and the popes during the latter half of the fifteenth century.[23] In that struggle, the efforts of the cardinals had not met with much success. The electoral capitulations, the faithful observance of which they sought to impose on pope after pope, were, as Jedin has said, 'rearguard actions, not offensive strokes'.[24] But that old curialist tradition was still alive at the time of Pisa and the rival Lateran Council and was clearly reflected in the tendency, widespread even among those who rejected the strict conciliar theory and who denounced the Pisan adventure, to ascribe to the cardinals a right to convoke a general council in cases of emergency even against the expressed wish of the pope.[25]

[22] See esp. Jacques Almain, *Tractatus de auctoritate ecclesiae*, in Gerson, *Opera omnia*, ed. Dupin, ii. 1011; cf. ibid. 996 and F. Oakley, 'Almain and Major', *American Historical Review*, 70 (1965), esp. 686 ff.

[23] Compare Juan de Torquemada, *Summa de ecclesia*, lib. 1, cc. 80–1 (no foliation) with d'Ailly, *Tractatus de ecclesiastica potestate*, in Gerson, *Opera omnia*, ed. Dupin, ii. 929 ff. For Domenichi, see Jedin, *History*, i. 83 n. 1.

[24] Jedin, *History*, i. 90.

[25] For an elaboration of this line of argument by a supporter of the Lateran Council, see Domenico Jacobazzi, *De concilio*, esp. lib. 3 and lib. 7, in Mansi, *Sacrorum conciliorum*

We must be careful, moreover, in our choice of those to whom we ascribe the rejection of that strict conciliar theory, as also, indeed, in what we
take the rejection to involve. That theory, the third and most crucial strand
in the conciliarism of the classical era, involved the assertion of the jurisdictional superiority to the pope, in certain critical cases, of the general
council acting apart from him, and of its ability, therefore, to judge, chas-
tise, and even depose him. This was the very premiss, of course, on which
the *conciliabulum* had assembled, but we should not assume that all of
those who rejected Pisa and aligned themselves with the rival, papally convoked Lateran Council—those, in effect, whom we usually classify as papalists—necessarily espoused an ecclesiology totally alien to that of the
conciliarists. For those responsive to the canonistic teaching of the day, it
was perfectly possible to 'grant, in the abstract, the cardinals' right to convoke a Council in certain emergencies while contesting the lawfulness of
the [particular] summons to Pisa, and especially the continuation of that
venture after the convocation of the Lateran Council'.[26] Gozzadini, after
all, unambiguously conciliarist though his views were, none the less threw
his support to the pope, and the position of others of more robustly
papalist sympathies was far more finely nuanced than we tend to assume.

That this should be so reflects the persistence after Basel of elements of
the strict conciliar theory even in the thinking of those prominent in the
advocacy of a high-papalist ecclesiology. Juan de Torquemada himself is a
case in point. While he had come firmly to deny the validity of the Constance decrees *Haec sancta* and *Frequens*, and to reject the Decretalist corporational element in the strict conciliar theory, he none the less affirmed
a version of the older Decretist element concerning the case of the heretical pope or of the pope guilty of crimes against the *status ecclesiae* or general well-being of the Church. And he ascribed to the general council in
that connection, as also in the case of disputed papal elections, quite extensive powers of an investigative and declaratory nature.[27] Something
similar is true of his contemporary, the curialist Antonio de' Roselli,
staunch advocate of the papal monarchy though he was,[28] as also, later on,
of the reformer Vicenzo Quirini at the time of the Lateran Council. In his
Tractatus super concilium generale Quirini could insist, of course, that 'the

---

collectio, i: 'Introductio'. See esp. 112–18 and 286 ff., where he questions the applicability of the
emergency doctrine to the Pisan assembly. For his career, see Klotzner, *Jacobazzi*. For a similar line of march, but one adopted by a member of the Pisan camp, see Philippus Decius,
Consilium . . . de auctoritate papae et concilii, in Goldast, ii. 1667–76, esp. 1673 ff.

[26] Jedin, *History*, i. 109.   [27] Izbicki, *Protector of the Faith*, 93.
[28] Jedin, *History*, i. 26; Burns, *Lordship, Kingship, and Empire*, 107 ff.

pontifical authority is above the council',[29] for that had long been the motto of those who adhered to the papalist position. But, as De Vooght has said, their papalism was often more qualified (*nuancé*) than the slogan under which they served.[30] That did not prevent Quirini's insisting also on a clear role for general councils in the removal of heretical popes.[31] Even Ferdinand of Spain, while arguing for a formal repudiation of *Haec sancta*, did not think that the pope's superiority to the council extended to a heretical pope or a pope whose title was in doubt.[32] And as late as the end of the sixteenth century, as we know from the testimony of the English Catholic apologists Robert Persons and Cardinal William Allen, one or other version of the Decretist teaching on the deposability or loss of office by a pope guilty of heresy was a matter taught publicly in the schools, even those in Rome itself.[33]

CAJETAN, ALMAIN, AND MAIR

Against the background of these hesitancies and complexities in the monarchical ecclesiologies of the era of papal restoration, the complexities and moments of fragility in the anti-conciliarist position which Cajetan himself hammered out in October 1511, in his *De comparatione auctoritatis papae et concilii*, become more readily comprehensible.[34] It may well have been, as Hubert Jedin once proclaimed, 'a momentous event, when, in the person of Cajetan, a theologian—perhaps the greatest theologian of his time—intervened in the debate [over Pisa] and pushed the canonists aside'.[35] Certainly, the Pisan fathers, now removed for French protection to Milan, seem to have seen it in this light, for early in 1512 they referred the book for examination to the University of Paris, and

---

[29] Quirini, *Tractatus super concilium generalium*, in Mittarelli and Costadoni, *Annales*, ix. 606 § 25: 'Auctoritas pontificis sit supra concilium'; similarly 606 § 23: 'Concilium Generale superius non est pontifice Romano auctoritate, immo inferius.'

[30] Vooght, 'Le Conciliarisme', in Botte *et al.*, *Le Concile et les conciles*, 175.

[31] Quirini, *Tractatus super concilium generalium*, in Mittarelli and Costadoni, *Annales*, ix. 599–611.

[32] See Doussinague, *Fernando*, app. 50, 539. The text in question is reproduced above at Ch. 1 n. 90.

[33] Oakley, 'Constance, Basel and the Two Pisas', 99 n. 45.

[34] Ed. Pollet. There is now a conveniently available English tr. in Burns and Izbicki, *Conciliarism*, 1–134, along with (201–84) his *Apologia* written in response to Jacques Almain's attack on his position. In the quotations I usually follow the Burns–Izbicki tr. For an analysis of Cajetan's position, see Pollet, 'Le Doctrine de Cajetan sur l'Eglise', *Angelicum*, 11 (1934), 514–32, and 12 (1935), 223–44.

[35] Jedin, *History*, i. 114.

Jacques Almain's vindication of the conciliarist position was a direct outcome of that chain of events. But in the course of his cogent, powerful, and
sweeping rejection of the legitimacy of Pisa and of the ecclesiology that
sustained it, Cajetan left himself open to attack on two grounds. Both are
in some measure surprising. The first concerns the deposability of popes;
the second, Cajetan's apparent desire to ground his position in the mandates of the natural law.

About the firmness of his rejection of the strict conciliar theory itself,
there was nothing at all ambiguous. The claim that 'the council is superior
to the pope, has coercive power over him, can impose laws on him about
the use of power, suspend him for the exercise of it, and depose him with
or without fault'—that claim he dismisses as an 'exceedingly dangerous . . .
new fantasy of Jean Gerson'.[36] Why? Because in the absence of papal convocation and papal concurrence, the actions of a council lack the absolute
perfection which alone would guarantee its freedom from error in matters
of faith.[37] By embracing Gerson's fantasy in its decree *Haec sancta*, Constance had fallen into error, and Basel, however 'legitimately assembled',
by reaffirming that decree had gone further and lapsed into notorious
error.[38] As successors of the apostles the bishops may well wield collectively a sort of 'governing authority' or 'executive power'. But it was to
Peter alone that Christ gave the 'sovereign', 'ruling authority', involving
'power unconditionally over all'. It is the pope alone, then, who as Peter's
successor wields the supreme power in the Church, which is, in effect, a
monarchical system.[39] To argue, as Gerson and the conciliarists had, that
'the Church has authority over the pope' does nothing less than 'pervert'
the Church's 'constitutional order', turning it into a democratic or popular one, in which all authority resides with no one person but with the
whole community.[40] And so on.

All of that said, however, Cajetan was anxious to portray himself, not as
carving out any extreme position, but as occupying some sort of mediating ground.[41] And, like other papalists of his day, or like Torquemada before him, he was sensitive enough to the possibility of papal malfeasance

---

[36] Cajetan, *De comparatione auctoritatis papae et concilii*, c. 10; ed. Pollet, 77–80. Tr. Burns
and Izbicki, *Conciliarism*, 47–9.

[37] Ibid., c. 16; ed. Pollet, 104–6; tr. Burns and Izbicki, 67–8.

[38] Ibid., c. 11; ed. Pollet, 90; tr. Burns and Izbicki, 58.

[39] Ibid., c. 3; ed. Pollet, 25–30; tr. Burns and Izbicki, 10–13.

[40] Cajetan, *De comparatione auctoritatis papae et concilii*, c. 6; ed. Pollet, 46–7; tr. Burns
and Izbicki, 25–6.

[41] See esp. ibid., cc. 16 and 20; ed. Pollet, 104–11, 125–32; tr. Burns and Izbicki, 67–73,
82–8.

even to open up the ideological door to some of the component elements of the strict conciliar theory. Thus, though he insisted that 'no notorious and scandalizing crime, apart from unbelief' could lead to pope's removal from office, he was at one with Torquemada and other papalists of his own day in echoing a version of the old Decretist teaching that the universal Church itself, via the agency of a general council, did indeed have a role to play in the deposition of a heretical pope.[42] But whereas Torquemada, taking the safer route, had argued (with the thirteenth-century Decretist Huguccio) that a pontiff who lapsed into heresy ceased *ipso facto* to be pope, and had limited the role of the council, accordingly, to that of investigating the matter and issuing a merely *declaratory* judgement to that effect, Cajetan bluntly rejected that position and insisted, rather, that in accordance with canon law (as he understood it) such a heretical pope had actually to be deposed.[43]

But by what authority? Having been wholly unambiguous in his insistence that the pope had no superior on earth, he was now forced, willy-nilly, to argue that it was for an *inferior* power, the universal Church or the general council, to fulfil this function. But how could that be? Only, it turned out, if one were willing with Cajetan to take the traditional canonistic distinction between the papacy or papal office itself and the person of the individual pope who serves in that office, and stretch it out to include a third distinct term—namely, the joining together of the two. Thus, while acknowledging that the papal office is immediately from God and the person of the pope is from his human father, it becomes possible to argue that the third essential element, the joining together of the two, is from neither, but comes about instead from the undeniably human process of election. When, therefore, the council acts to depose a heretical pope, it does so neither because it possesses any authority over the papal office, nor by virtue of any power superior or even equal to that of its papal incumbent, for he himself has no superior on earth and the power of the universal Church and of the general council is, in fact, inferior to his. If the council is able to act in this way it is, rather, not by an absolute but by a merely ministerial power, one which reaches no further than the third element—the conjunction of the person of the pope with the papal office. What man has joined together man, it seems, can put asunder—or, at least, can do so in this particular case.[44]

---

[42] Cajetan, *De comparatione auctoritatis papae et concilii*, cc. 17–22 and 26; ed. Pollet, 112–49, 167–75 (words cited at 175); tr. Burns and Izbicki, 73–101, 113–19 (words cited at 119).

[43] Ibid., cc. 17–19; ed. Pollet, 112–24; tr. Burns and Izbicki, 73–82.

[44] Ibid., cc. 20–2; ed. Pollet, 125–49; tr. Burns and Izbicki, 82–101.

This ingenious gambit of Cajetan's represents a somewhat desperate attempt to seek middle ground,[45] and those commenting on him, when they come to it, have sometimes tended chastely to avert their eyes and walk past it, whether because they are embarrassed by the fact that he accorded any power of judgement and deposition to a council or because they find his moves, on this particular point, to be altogether too nimble. Whatever the case, this quintessentially scholastic exercise in the drawing of exceedingly refined distinctions was necessitated by Cajetan's determination to maintain, along with his assertion of the jurisdictional supremacy of pope over Church, the seemingly incompatible canonistic teaching based on dist. 40, ch. 6, Gratian's *Decretum* to the effect that a heretical pope could be judged by the Church. In any other context, that distinction would surely have been as redundant as it was implausible. Moreover, it inserted a moment of weakness into the complex structure of his argument by making possible a worrying degree of ideological overlap with the rival conciliarist approach, a degree of overlap extended by his use of language redolent of natural law and suggesting, therefore, that he, too, viewed the ecclesiastical and secular polities as in some significant measure really analogous. This matter clearly came to give him some concern and led him to do a certain amount of complex backing and filling when he returned to it in his later *Apologia* responding to Almain's attack.[46] Understandably so, because that moment of weakness and that compromising degree of ideological overlap had been one upon which Almain had been quick to pounce in the spring of 1512 when, at the behest of the Parisian Faculty of Theology, he undertook in his *Tractatus de auctoritate ecclesiae et conciliorum generalium* to refute Cajetan's claims.[47] As in his other ecclesiological writings, and in sharp contrast with Gerson and d'Ailly, the great Parisian conciliarists of the previous century to whom he was otherwise deeply indebted, he makes no mention of the reforming strand and explicitly rejects the oligarchic strand, both of which in their thinking had been interwoven with the strict conciliar theory itself.[48] It is on that latter theory alone that

---

[45] See Pollet, 'Le Doctrine de Cajetan', 224–9. The simpler distinction (embraced by all conciliarists) between the papal office and the person of the pope was, of course, an ancient one. See Ullmann, *Principles*, 37–8, 50, 102–5.

[46] For which, see below, Ch. 4.

[47] For Almain's life and thought see R. G. Villoslada, *La Universidad de Paris* (Rome: Apud aedes Universitatis Gregorianae, 1938), 165–79; Brosse, *Le Pape et le Concile*, 70–3; Oakley, 'Almain and Major', 673–81; Friedrich Merzbacher, 'Die Kirchen und Staatsgewalt bei Jacques Almain', in H. Lentze and I. Gampl, eds., *Speculum Juris et Ecclesiarum* (Vienna: Herder, 1967), 301–12.

[48] See above, Ch. 2.

he, as also, a little later, his former teacher John Mair, concentrate with a clarity and intensity of focus that was to characterize conciliarist constitutionalism in its sixteenth-century silver age, as also what may for convenience be called the bronze-age conciliarism of subsequent centuries.

Both in his reply to Cajetan and in his other ecclesiological tracts, Almain is careful to concede that the Church differs from the secular polity in that it is ordained to no merely natural end but to the supernatural goal of life eternal, and that its power, accordingly, is not of human institution but from God alone. The appeal to natural law, none the less, and to the analogy of the secular polity, remains central to the powerful case he makes for the strict conciliar theory, as well as to his essentially constitutionalist understanding of the governance structure of the universal Church.[49] That Church, admittedly, is for him 'one mystical body whose head is the pope'. That papal headship, moreover, is to be regarded as subordinated to that of Christ, himself 'the true and principal head of the Church'.[50] But we should not miss the revealing fact that, in the course of arguing thus for a merely 'ministerial' papal headship and insisting that 'the whole Church is not said to be the body of Peter, but the body of Christ alone',[51] he does not hesitate to cite the same text from Paul (Rom. 12: 5) that he cites elsewhere with reference to the unambiguously political powers possessed by any civil community.[52] The *corpus Christi mysticum* the Church may well be, but with Almain, as with his fifteenth-century Parisian predecessors, that term itself had shed its original eucharistic associations, taken on corporational and political connotations, and become a term well-nigh synonymous with 'moral and political body'. If the priestly power of order pertained to 'the true body of Christ' in the eucharist, it is to the mystical body that the power of jurisdiction in the external or public forum pertains. As was also the case with his conciliarist predecessors, Almain's focus, then, is on that truly governmental power, and, as he proceeds to discuss it, we are confronted again and again with arguments, analogies, and expressions indicating that, whatever its unique characteristics, the Church or 'ecclesiastical polity' was still to be regarded as 'one of a class, political societies'.[53]

[49] Almain, *Tractatus de auctoritate ecclesiae*, in Dupin, ii. 993; *Quaestio resumptiva . . . de dominio naturali*, ibid. 972; *Expositio circa decisiones Magistri Guilelmi Occam super potestate ecclesiastica et laica*, ibid. 1019.

[50] Almain, *Expositio*, in Gerson, *Opera omnia*, ed. Dupin, ii. 1027.

[51] Almain, *Tractatus de auctoritate ecclesiae*, in Gerson, *Opera omnia*, ed. Dupin, ii. 896.

[52] Almain, *Tractatus de auctoritate ecclesiae* and *Quaestio resumptiva . . . de dominio naturali*, in Gerson, *Opera omnia*, ed. Dupin, ii. 977, 964.

[53] See above, Ch. 2.

The line of march he follows is, therefore, clear enough and can be traced quite briefly. In insisting on the truth of the proposition that the Church or general council is superior in this power of jurisdiction to the pope, he refers of course to the superiority decrees of Constance and Basel in view of which, he says, that proposition should be venerated 'just as the Holy Gospel'.[54] But because Cajetan 'blasphemously' rejected the validity of those decrees, Almain does not dwell on them. Instead, he seeks to establish his case on three principal and closely related grounds.

First, just as the coercive civil power is present in a political body as a whole before it is wielded by any of its members, so, too, is it with the Church. The supreme ecclesiastical power, which Christ admittedly conferred directly upon Peter, he had earlier conferred 'in its plenitude' on the Church.[55] So true is this, indeed, that had he failed after the Resurrection to institute anyone as his supreme pontiff or vicar general, the Church, being possessed already of the 'supreme coercive power', could itself have done so.[56]

That being so, and secondly, the ecclesiastical power residing in the Church is 'greater in extension' than is that residing in the pope. When Christ conferred upon Peter the keys of the kingdom of heaven, he gave them to him not as a private person but 'as a sign and figure' or representative of the universal Church.[57] Hence it is by the authority of the Church and in its place that Peter and his successors have wielded the power of the keys—'just as kings exercise the power of jurisdiction in place of the community'.[58] But the general council immediately represents the universal Church and it has the power of the keys 'more directly than does Peter'.[59] So true is this for Almain that when he compares the jurisdictional powers of pope and Church he regards it as a matter of indifference whether one has in mind the Church itself or the general council which,

[54] *Tractatus de auctoritate ecclesiae*, in Gerson, *Opera omnia*, ed. Dupin, ii. 1067, 1070.

[55] Ibid. 993; *Quaestio resumptiva . . . de dominio naturali*, in Gerson, *Opera omnia*, ed. Dupin, ii. 971–2.

[56] *Tractatus de auctoritate ecclesiae*, in Gerson, *Opera omnia*, ed. Dupin, ii. 993; *Quaestio resumptiva . . . de dominio naturali*, ibid. 972; *Expositio*, ibid. 1019.

[57] *Tractatus de auctoritate ecclesiae*, in Gerson, *Opera omnia*, ed. Dupin, ii. 990; *Expositio*, ibid. 1069.

[58] 'Petrus et quilibet ejus Successor, utitur clavibus vice Ecclesiae Universalis quam significat, sicut Rex quilibet, vice Communitatis exercet Jurisdictionis actus, ita quod Summus Pontifex excommunicat, confert Beneficia, similiter et Indulgentias, et sic de aliis actibus Ecclesiasticae Potestatis, auctoritate totius Ecclesiae' (*Tractatus de auctoritate ecclesiae*, in Gerson, *Opera omnia*, ed. Dupin, ii. 991; cf. 996).

[59] *Expositio*, in Gerson, *Opera omnia*, ed. Dupin, ii. 1069, 1074. Also *Tractatus de auctoritate ecclesiae*, ibid. 1004, where he describes the pope as representing the Church *remote* whereas the general council represents it *propinquissime*.

even when the pope is not (or chooses not to be) included, faithfully represents that Church.[60]

Third, the ecclesiastical power which resides in the Church is not only 'greater in extension' than that residing in the pope, it is also 'greater in perfection' too.[61] For it resides in the Church with constancy (*indeviabiliter*) so that the Church 'is unable to err in those things that pertain to the faith and to good morals, nor can it err in passing sentence [on such matters] ... since it is assisted always by the Holy Spirit, doctor of truth and infallible director'.[62] And the same is true of a legitimately assembled council representing the universal church.[63] It pertains, therefore, not to the pope but to the universal Church, or to the general council representing it, to determine in an authoritative or judicial fashion—not merely, that is to say, in the fashion proper to a scholar or expert—what pertains to the faith. For popes can err, and manifestly *have* erred in matters of faith, and have done so in their official public capacity as well as in their private personal beliefs, whereas from that danger the Holy Spirit protects the general council, representing truly as it does that council of apostles and disciples which was the recipient of Christ's promise that he would be with us always even to the consummation of the world.[64]

Given these basic general commitments, the transition to more specifically conciliarist conclusions is easy enough to make. After all, if power over the Church had been conferred on the pope in such a way that the whole Church could not punish or depose him even if he exercised that power in a way conducive not to its well-being but its destruction, then the ecclesiastical polity would be less well-ordered than is 'the purely civil polity' and also be deprived of a power which by natural law pertains to 'any community' whatsoever.[65] Clearly, for Almain, an unimaginable situation, and he proceeds at once to demolish the multiple arguments with which Cajetan had sought to bolster his own misguided position. Thus, for example, the assertion that the whole Church or general council is superior in power of jurisdiction to the pope does not entail, as Cajetan

[60]   *Tractatus de auctoritate ecclesiae*, in Gerson, *Opera omnia*, ed. Dupin, ii. 989; cf. 987.

[61]   *Quaestio resumptiva ... de dominio naturali*, in Gerson, *Opera omnia*, ed. Dupin, ii. 972.

[62]   Ibid.

[63]   *In tertium Sententiarum lectura*, dist. 24, qu. 1; in Almain *Opuscula*, fos. 78ᵛ–79ʳ. This text constitutes Almain's most extensive discussion of the respective claims of Church, general council, and pope to an infallible magisterial power.

[64]   *Tractatus de auctoritate ecclesiae*, in Gerson, *Opera omnia*, ed. Dupin, ii. 1001–5; *Quaestio resumptiva ... de dominio naturali*, ibid. 972; *In tertium Sententiarum lectura*, dist., 24, qu. 1, in *Opuscula*, fo. 79ʳ.

[65]   *Quaestio resumptiva ... de dominio naturali*, in Gerson, *Opera omnia*, ed. Dupin, ii. 973. Cf. *Tractatus de auctoritate ecclesiae*, ibid. 991.

suggested, the belief that the constitution of the Church is an aristocratic one, in which the authority resided in no single man. But while agreeing that that constitution is immutably monarchic, Almain insists that a political society is not said to be monarchical (that is, be a *politia regalis*) because it is ruled by one man who is superior in authority to the whole community, but simply because he is superior in authority to any other single person in that community. And the power that the monarch possesses is the power of the community, a power indeed in place of the whole people which, under normal circumstances, cannot assemble together.[66] Nor, again, is it proper to conclude that to deny to the pope a power superior to that of the Church or general council is to believe that there are two plenitudes of power, for that would indeed be impossible. It is simply to assert that there is one plenitude of power, but that it is in the Church more fully than in the pope, in that it extends to some actions of which the pope is incapable.

Of these, the crucial instance is the Church's possession (and in this unlike the pope) of the power to depose a supreme pontiff.[67] Seizing upon Cajetan's admission that a pope guilty even of open heresy did not cease *ipso facto* to be pope but had to be subjected to judgement and formal deposition at the hands of a general council, Almain dismissed as simply nonsensical any idea that what was involved was not an authoritative power over the pope's person but rather a merely ministerial power over the conjunction of the person and the papal office.[68] Christ gave the Church and the general council representing it 'authoritative power' to act as ordinary judge of the pope, not only in such cases as heresy, but in every case of notorious sin. Had he not done so, then the Church would not be as well-ordained as 'the purely natural and civil polity', which, if its ruler abuses his position, has the power to deprive him and even punish him with death. Christ did not deprive the Church of this natural power. Not only can it depose a pope who is guilty of notorious crimes against its well-being and go on to deprive him of his life if he persists in his wrongdoing, it can also impose constraints on him in the exercise of his prerogatives, force him to conform his actions to its laws and constitutions, and, further, should it be for the good of the Church, depose him even if he is guiltless.[69]

---

[66] *Tractatus de auctoritate ecclesiae*, in Gerson, *Opera omnia*, ed. Dupin, ii. 996–7; cf. 979. *Expositio*, ibid. 1074–5. *Quaestio resumptiva . . . de dominio naturali*, ibid. 966, 970. Cf. Blythe, *Ideal Government*, 258–9.

[67] *Tractatus de auctoritate ecclesiae*, in Gerson, *Opera omnia*, ed. Dupin, ii. 997. On this and the points immediately following, see Oakley, 'Almain and Major', 679–81.

[68] *Tractatus*, 1005–7. *Expositio*, in Gerson, *Opera omnia*, ed. Dupin, ii. 1072, 1075–6.

[69] Ibid. 1008–11.

To many of these same points John Mair, Almain's former teacher, returned (and not without an eye on Cajetan's claims) in the context of a commentary on St Matthew's Gospel which he published in 1518 in the wake of the Franco-papal concordat of 1516 and several years after the collapse of the *conciliabulum* of Pisa. He is quite straightforward in his conclusions. A general council he defines as 'a congregation [of representatives] from every hierarchical rank which it concerns, convoked by those whose duty it is, and assembled in order to deal according to the common intention with matters pertaining to the public utility of Christendom'. Such a council, 'properly assembled and representing the universal Church, is superior to the supreme pontiff' (the council, in this specific instance, being taken to exclude that pontiff).[70] To this conclusion he attaches many of the corollaries, parallel assertions, and supporting arguments to be found in Almain, notably those concerning the convocation of a council under emergency conditions when a pope is unwilling to do so and one is needed for the correction of evident abuses,[71] as well as the right of such a council to judge and depose a pope for heresy and other notorious crimes.[72] In common again with Almain, Mair also devotes considerable effort to refuting arguments opposed to his own position, many of them drawn from Cajetan. Here, three particular emphases should be noted.

First, going even further on the point than Almain, he rejects out of hand the idea that conciliar supremacy means that the Church has an aristocratic constitution rather than that monarchical form which, he says, Aristotle proclaimed to be the best. 'Some people', he says, 'maintain that the ecclesiastical polity is a mixed one, but I do not say so.'[73] Second, he is even more forceful than Almain in grounding his conciliarist claims in the dictates of natural law and in treating the ecclesiastical and secular polities almost univocally. 'It is more in conformity with the natural light', he

---

[70] 'Concilium . . . est Congregatio ex omni statu hierarchico, quorum interest, convocata ab iis quibus incumbit, ad tractandum communi intentione, de utilitate publica Christiana . . . Concilium rite congregatum, Universalem Ecclesiam repraesentans, est super Maximum Pontificem, et capio Ecclesiam, pro Ecclesia ab eo separata' (Mair, *Disputatio de auctoritate concilii*, in Gerson, *Opera, omnia*, ed. Dupin, ii. 1132).

[71] Thus, Mair argues (*Disputatio de auctoritate concilii*, in Gerson, *Opera omnia*, ed. Dupin, ii. 1137–8) that though it normally pertains to the pope to convoke a general council, if, in times of evident need he is unable or unwilling, then the Church itself has from God the authority to do so. Cf. Almain, *Tractatus de auctoritate ecclesiae*, in Gerson, *Opera omnia*, ed. Dupin, ii. 1012.

[72] Mair, *Disputatio de auctoritate concilii*, in Gerson, *Opera omnia*, ed. Dupin, ii. 1134–5.

[73] Ibid. 1141; cf. 1135 and 1139.

argues, that an incorrigible head should be deprived of his authority, nor is it 'true to say that God did not leave [this fundamental] power in the Church in the same way as this political power resides among the men of one Kingdom', and he buttresses his case, accordingly, with precedents drawn from the custom and practice of France, of the Spanish Kingdoms, and, above all, of Scotland.[74] Third, surfacing now a formulation that was to be echoed again and again by such as Paolo Sarpi and George Lawson in the seventeenth century, Louis Ellies du Pin in the eighteenth, Henri Maret in the nineteenth—all the way down to the very eve of the First Vatican Council—Mair affirmed that there were among Christians in his day not one but two contending opinions concerning the relationship of pope to council: the one, that the pope is above the council, being espoused by the Thomists and professed above all at Rome, where no public dissent from it was permitted; the other opposing and conciliarist point of view having none the less been maintained stoutly by his own University of Paris ever since the time of the Council of Constance.[75]

CONCILIARISM IN SIXTEENTH-CENTURY ENGLAND

Given the intensity of their focus on the strict conciliar theory and the clarity and force with which they restated it, it is no more than appropriate that Almain and Mair have begun at long last, in the more recent interpretations of early modern political thought, to emerge from the historiographic shadows.[76] But I would not want that fact, or my own choosing to concentrate on them here, to give the impression that they were even remotely alone, in the opening decades of the sixteenth century, in their advocacy of that position. The Pisan crisis had served to reveal that such views were current enough even in Italy as to find a series of advocates among the Italian jurists from Philippus Decius and Zaccaria Ferreri to Matthias Ugonius, bishop of Famagusta, Marco Mantova at Padua, and Gianfrancesco Sannazari della Ripa, teaching at Avignon. So current, indeed, as to find two robust defenders—Giovanni Gozzadini and Girolamo Massaimo—in the unlikely setting of the papal court itself.[77]

---

[74] Ibid. 1136. Cf. Burns, '*Politia regalis et optima*', 31–61.

[75] *Disputatio de auctoritate concilii*, in Gerson, *Opera omnia*, ed. Dupin, ii. 1132.

[76] See Burns, '*Politia regalis et optima*'; Skinner, *Foundations*, 2: chs. 2, 4, and 9; idem, 'Origins of the Calvinist Theory of Revolution', in Malament, *After the Reformation*, esp. 312, 324–36; Burns and Izbicki, *Conciliarism*.

[77] For such latter-day advocates of conciliar theory and the growing body of scholarly literature concerning them, see Oakley, 'Natural Law', 786–810. Also, Jedin, 'Giovanni

Such views, however, had understandably put down deeper roots in northern Europe—Germany and Poland as well as France and Scotland—than in Italy. And concern about the danger to the papacy which they still posed helped, accordingly, to bolster reluctance at Rome to respond to the Protestant challenge in Germany by summoning the general council for which so many Catholics pleaded. When the Council of Trent did finally meet in 1545, it was not only suspicious representatives of the evangelicals who turned out to want the matter of the superiority of pope to council placed on the agenda.[78] Apprehension about the potential recrudescence of conciliarism, very much on the minds of the papal legates, was also, as Paolo Sarpi was to note later on in his ascerbic history of Trent, widespread among the council fathers themselves.[79] And not, it turned out, without good cause. Given the way in which events were to unfold, one is forced to concur in the judgement that 'there was . . . scarcely any set problems that was so controversial at Trent or that brought the council so close to collapse as the question of primacy and the relationship between the primate and episcopate'.[80] Disagreement about the respective powers of pope and council, though partially downplayed in response to the threat posed by Protestant dissent, rumbled on through the council's first two periods in the 1540s and 1550s, rising to the level of something more than a subdominant whenever the issue of reform in head and members came to be discussed. And in 1562–3, during the council's last phase when a French delegation of some significance had finally joined the ranks of the participants, the issue helped precipitate what was clearly Trent's greatest crisis.

During that last phase a bitter dispute broke out at the ecclesiological intersection of three complexly related issues: the sacrament of holy orders and the episcopal power of jurisdiction (whether conferred on the recipient immediately by Christ or delegated by the pope); the duty of bishops to reside in their dioceses (whether that obligation was *jure divino*

Gozzadini: Ein Konziliarist am Hofe Julius II', in Jedin, *Kirche des Glaubens*, ii. 17–74; Nelson H. Minnich, 'Girolamo Massaino: Another Conciliarist at the Papal Court, Julius II to Adrian VI', in Minnich *et al.*, *Studies*, 520–65; T. F. Mayer, 'Marco Mantova, a Bronze Age Conciliarist', *Annuarium Historiae Conciliorum*, 14 (1984), 385–408; idem, *Thomas Starkey and the Commonweal* (Cambridge: CUP, 1989), 172–87 (for Mantova and della Ripa).

[78] For a lengthy and detailed account of the unfolding of these ecclesiological tensions at Trent, see K. Ganzer, 'Gallikanische und Römische Primatsauffassung im Widerstreit', *Historisches Jahrbuch*, 109 (1989), 109–63; Jedin, *Geschichte*, ii. and iii. W. Brandmüller, 'Papst und Konzil auf dem Tridentinum', *Annuarium Historiae Conciliorum*, 5 (1973), 198–203, provides a useful brief conspectus of material on the topic of pope and council in Jedin's third volume, and there is a good brief account in Schneider, *Konziliarismus*, 49–56.

[79] Sarpi, *History of the Council of Trent*, ii. 216; v. 433; vi. 482–3, 529.

[80] Schatz, *Papal Primacy*, 128. Cf. Alberigo, 'L'ecclesiologia del Concilio di Trente', 227–42.

and so integral to the episcopal office as to preclude the widespread practice of papal dispensation from it); the precise nature of the papal primacy and the prerogatives attaching to it (whether, as the pope certainly wished, the council should reaffirm the definition embedded in the Council of Florence's decree, *Laetentur coeli*). Here, the level of disagreement was such as to preclude not only that papally sponsored redefinition but also any decree at all on the controverted nature of the Christian Church. So menacing, indeed, was the atmosphere at the council, and so rancorous the dissent, that it was something of a triumph for the diplomacy of the papal legates to have succeeded finally in sidestepping the pursuit of that issue in a compromising context in which appeals were being made to the superiority decrees of Constance and Basel (among others, by one of John Mair's former pupils),[81] and in which the celebrated Charles de Guise, cardinal of Lorraine, proudly proclaimed himself to be a Frenchman, one nourished at the University of Paris where, he noted, the Councils of Constance and Basel (but certainly not that of Florence) were held to be fully legitimate and ecumenical in status, and where those rash enough to deny the superiority of council to pope could expect to be censured as heretics.[82]

On that score there was really nothing exceptional about the nature of his claims—except, perhaps, the unselfconscious forthrightness with which he formulated them. In France, especially, the great fifteenth-century councils continued to cast an exceedingly long shadow. It is not surprising, then, glancing back now to the period prior to the assembly of Trent, that it had been to the theologians of Paris that Henry VIII of England had turned thirty and more years earlier, when, in the quest for the royal divorce, he and his advisers had set out to explore the political and diplomatic leverage that an advocacy of the conciliarist ecclesiology might well afford them.[83]

English churchmen of the fifteenth century had not played a leading role at either Constance or Basel. If they certainly had had access to

[81] Robert de Ceneau—see Burns and Izbicki, *Conciliarism*, p. x.

[82] Le Plat, *Monumentorum*, v. 658. For the role of the French at Trent and the depth of their commitment to conciliarist views, see A. Tallon, *La France et le Concile de Trente* (Rome: École Française de Rome, 1997), esp. 770–811. Tallon concludes (424) that 'l'heritage conciliariste est devenu constitutif de l'identité gallicane'.

[83] For succinct accounts, see Becker, *Appellation*, 264–9; Oakley, 'Constance, Basel and the Two Pisas', 92–7. The basic studies are those of P. A. Sawada, 'Das Imperium Heinrichs VIII, und die erste Phase seiner Konzilspolitik', in E. Iserloh, ed., *Reformata Reformanda* (Münster: Aschendorff, 1965), ii. 476–507; idem, 'The Abortive Council of Mantua and Henry VIII', *Academia*, 27 (1960), 1–15; idem, 'Two Anonymous Tudor Treatises on the General Council', *Journal of Ecclesiastical History*, 12 (1961), 197–214. Cf. Baumer, *Early Tudor Theory*, 49–56; J. J. Scarisbrick, *Henry VIII* (Berkeley and Los Angeles: University of California Press, 1963).

conciliarist publicistic literature and had shown 'a striking preference' for
the works of d'Ailly and Gerson, there was 'no standard orthodoxy' on the
respective standing of pope and council, and the bishops themselves
appear still to have felt a persistent measure of sympathy for the type
of episcopalism favoured long ago by Robert Grosseteste, the great
thirteenth-century bishop of Lincoln.[84] It is reasonable to surmise that a
similar climate of opinion had continued to prevail on into the early years
of the sixteenth century. Given the degree to which the convocation in 1511
of the Council of Pisa had reflected the exigencies of French diplomacy,
and given Henry VIII's subsequent alliance with the pope in the Holy
League, the lack of English participation in that ill-attended assembly
provides no ground for speculation about the ecclesiological proclivities
of English churchmen. Still less does England's subsequent adhesion to
the Fifth Lateran Council. Given the behaviour of most of the English
bishops during the crisis years of the Reformation Parliament, there is no
reason to believe that the clarity of the papalism that brought John Fisher,
bishop of Rochester, to his untimely death was anything but exceptional
among the higher clergy of England.

At the same time, the evidence is also lacking to suggest any similar clarity of commitment to views that could properly be called conciliarist. In
this respect, the characteristic ecclesiological posture of the English
bishops may well have had more in common with that of Sir Thomas More
who, at least in the years prior to the composition of his *Confutation of
Tyndale's Answer* (1534), while affirming the authority of general councils,
had not really concerned himself with the quintessentially conciliarist
issue of the authority of such councils acting in the absence of (or even in
opposition to) their papal head.[85] Certainly, even after the passage of the
crucial Act in Restraint of Appeals (1533) and after the publication later in
that same year of Henry VIII's appeal to a future general council, the royal
council was clearly unsure about the views of the English bishops on the
matter of whether 'he, that is now called the Pope of Rome, ys above the
Generall Counsaile or the General Counsaile above him'. So unsure,

---

[84] Thus M. Harvey, *England, Rome and the Papacy* (Manchester: MUP, 1993), 214–16, 222,
and 242. C. M. D. Crowder, 'Constance *Acta* in English Libraries', in Franzen and Müller,
Konzil von Konstanz, 477–517, who notes (479) that among the Constance publicists, the English showed 'a striking preference … for two works of Pierre d'Ailly, his *De potestate ecclesiastica* and *De reformatione ecclesiae*, with Gerson's treatise on the Church, published during
the council, next in favour'. In what follows, I draw on the more detailed account in Oakley,
'Constance, Basel and the two Pisas'.
[85] Gogan, and the other works referred to in Oakley, 'Constance, Basel and the Two Pisas',
91–2 n. 16.

indeed, as to mandate that they be examined on that very point.[86] And yet, by that time, the king's conciliar strategy had been under way for several years and, having succeeded in renewing and broadening the acquaintance of Englishmen with the conciliarist tradition, had begun also to stimulate a degree of sympathy towards it. As a result, by the end of the century things had changed quite markedly, and the growing familiarity of English people, Protestant as well as Catholic, with the history of the fifteenth-century councils and the writings of the conciliarists may serve as a final, if perhaps unexpected, testimony to the enduring vitality of the tradition of conciliarist constitutionalism on into the seventeenth century.

Already in 1529–30, during Reginald Pole's successful mission to secure from the theologians of Paris a satisfactorily supportive opinion on the question of the king's marriage, the members of the English delegation, especially Edward Foxe, Thomas Starkey, and John Stokesly, 'showed a great deal of interest in individual conciliarists and conciliarist ideas'. Stokesly met with John Mair and a *librum conciliorum* was acquired for Edward Foxe, who was later to fold conciliarist arguments into his *Collecteana satis copiosa*.[87] In the wake of Henry's excommunication and subsequent appeal (November 1533) to a general council, moreover, an official propaganda campaign was launched, designed not only to wring tactical advantage from the legal manœuvre itself but also to reinvigorate the conciliarist tradition and to acquaint English people with its central claims concerning the relationship of pope to council.[88] Thus such early (1533) propagandists as the anonymous authors of *A Glasse of Truthe* and of the *Articles devised by the hole consent of the Kynge's most honourable counsayle* evoked the authority of Jean Gerson, the words of the Constance superiority decree *Haec sancta*, and the authoritative practices of Constance and Basel.[89] And they were bolstered throughout the 1530s by a significant flow

[86] *State Papers of the Reign of Henry VIII*, i. 411–12 ('Minutes for the Privy Council', 2 Dec. 1533).

[87] On which see Mayer, *Thomas Starkey*, 78–80.

[88] Thus it was ordered that copies of the appeal were to be disseminated throughout England (and abroad), and that sermons be preached affirming that general councils were superior to all bishops, the pope included. See above, n. 86, and *Letters and Papers Foreign and Domestic of the Reign of Henry VIII*, vi. 600–2, nos. 1487 and 1488. No. 1488 is a speech on general councils attributed to Archbishop Cranmer. It invokes Gerson's *De auferabilitate papae* and notes, among other things, that 'the Council of Constance and the divines of Paris had declared the Pope to be subject to a General Council' (602). Cf. Sawada, 'Das Imperium Heinrichs VIII, und die erste Phase seiner Konzilspolitik', in Iserloh, *Reformata Reformanda*, ii. 476–507.

[89] Printed, respectively, as nos. 320 and 350 in Pocock, *Records of the Reformation*, ii. 385–421, 523–31.

of publicistic writing likewise evoking *Haec sancta*, the authority of
Gerson and d'Ailly, and the great deeds of Constance and Basel.[90]

Nor can all of those in England who began, around this time, to express
quasi-conciliarist or outright conciliarist views simply be dismissed as
royal propagandists deftly responding to the shifting imperatives of their
royal master's policy. That was certainly not the case with Christopher
St German, author of the most distinguished of Tudor legal treatises,
whose 'stature was that of an independent scholar in contact with, but not
a pensioner of, the circle of Thomas Cromwell'.[91] His familiarity with the
thought of d'Ailly and Gerson (in the latter case quite extensive) is evident
from his widely read twin dialogues, *Doctor and Student* (1523–31),[92] and,
in two later works of controversy, he quotes at length (though attributing
the tract incorrectly to Gerson) from Henry of Langenstein's *Consilium
pacis*.[93] He was familiar enough, then, with the conciliarist authors, and we
know that as late as 1537 he spoke to the authority of general councils in his
*A Dyalogue shewinge what we be bounde to byleve as thinges necessary to
salvacion and what not*.[94]

Thomas Starkey, similarly, in the one work of his published in his own
lifetime (*c.*1500–38), like St German ascribed to the prince the right to
summon councils and to give force to their decrees.[95] But he appears to
have had a somewhat more intense engagement with conciliarist ideas
than can be claimed for St German, and has been described as having

[90]   See Oakley, 'Constance, Basel and the Two Pisas', 94–5.

[91]   Thus J. Guy *et al.*, eds., *The Debellation of Salem and Byzance*, in *The Complete Works of
St Thomas More* (New Haven: Yale University Press, 1963–87), x, p. xxix. Cf. Guy, *Christopher
St German*, 33. Francis Oakley, 'Conciliarism in England: St German, Starkey and the Mar-
siglian Myth', in Izbicki and Bellitto, *Reform*, 225–9.

[92]   Ed. Plucknett and Barton. Cf. Z. Rueger, 'Gerson's Concept of Equity and Christopher
St. German', *History of Political Thought*, 3 (1982), 1–30, who sees St German as deeply indebted to Gerson. In the *Doctor and Student* St German cites, among other works, Gerson's
De vita spirituali animae, De unitate ecclesiastica, and *Regulae morales*. See also Oakley, 'Conciliarism in England', in Izbicki and Bellitto, *Reform*, 224–39.

[93]   St German, *A treatise concernynge the division betwene the spiritualtie and temporaltie*
(1532), ed. J. B. Trapp, in *Complete Works of St Thomas More*, ix. 175–212 (at 182–5), and
A dialogue betwixte two englyshemen, whereof one was called Salem and the other Byzance
(1533), ed. J. Guy *et al.*, in *Complete Works of St Thomas More*, x. 323–92 (at 378–9, 382–3).

[94]   As yet unprinted. The manuscript is to be found in the Public Records Office, London,
State Papers, Henry VIII, 6/2, Theological Tracts, 89–168. Although St German's name is
written on it, it is a newly discovered work, 'a major treatise hidden away for centuries in
Cromwell's papers'—thus Guy, *Christopher St German*, 68–9. Cf. Oakley, 'Conciliarism in
England: St German, Starkey and the Marsiglian Myth', in Izbicki and Bellitto, *Reform*,
224–39, for a critique of Guy's claim that the *Dyalogue* 'encourages a return to . . . Baumer's
view that St. German had studied [Marsiglio of Padua's] *Defensor pacis*'.

[95]   Mayer, *Thomas Starkey, passim*, and his 'Thomas Starkey, an Unknown Conciliarist',
207–22.

preserved 'a record of nearly unspotted conciliarism in the midst of all the smoke and fire of propaganda'. During the course of his legal education in the 1530s he had studied, it seems likely, with Marco Mantova Benevides in Padua and Gianfrancesco Sannazari della Ripa in Avignon—both of them 'contemporary conciliarists of some stature' and both sympathetic to the classical version of conciliar theory expounded at Constance by the great canonist, Francesco Zabarella.[96] Some years earlier, moreover, Starkey appears to have become acquainted with the conciliarism of the Parisian school[97] and, towards the end of his life when he undertook a critique of Albertus Pighius's *Hierachiae ecclesiasticae assertio*, he made a point of rebutting Pighius's attack on the assertion by Gerson and the Councils of Constance and Basel of the superiority of council to pope. 'Both councils and Gerson and the Parisian school', he said, 'stand on the contrary, to which I thus far stand fast.'[98]

By the time he wrote those words in 1538, Starkey's religious commitments, like those of St German for that matter, were from the standpoint of the old faith unquestionably heterodox. But the same can hardly be said of the Sir Thomas More who, out of office, out of royal favour, and finally imprisoned, came to focus more intently than heretofore on the teaching function of the general council and on its role as ultimate legislative authority in the government of the universal Church. Thus, in his *Confutation of Tyndale's Answer* (1534) he returned repeatedly to that role. He described the council as representing 'the congregacyon of all the whole chrysten people', so that its decrees and determinations were 'of lyke strength and power as yf they [i.e. the *congregatio fidelium*] hadde ben all assembled there to gether on a grene'. He drew the analogy of Parliament which, in comparable fashion, 'represented the hole realme' and as a result speaks for it when it acts in a legislative capacity. And, by fairly clear implication, he assigned to the council the prerogative of admonishing and, if need be, deposing an incorrigible pope.[99] As he wrote in that same year

[96] Mayer, 'Thomas Starkey, an Unknown Conciliarist', 208, 221. He concedes however (208) that 'only once did Starkey trim his beliefs to the dictates of policy'. Idem, *Thomas Starkey*, esp. 172–87; cf. idem, 'Marco Mantova'.

[97] Mayer, 'Thomas Starkey, an unknown Conciliarist', 221–7; idem, *Thomas Starkey*, 81–3.

[98] Pighius's *Assertio*, lib. 6, fos. ccix[r]–cclxvii[r], is concerned with the power of councils and dwells lengthily on Gerson and the superiority decrees of Constance and Basel. Starkey's critical notes on the *Assertio* remain unpublished. The manuscript is in the Public Records Office, London, State Papers, Henry VIII 1/141, fos. 188[v] ff. I cite the words in the text from Mayer, 'Thomas Starkey, an Unkown Conciliarist', 29. Cf. the lengthier discussion in his *Thomas Starkey*, 82–3, 266–71.

[99] Ed. L. A. Schuster *et al.*, in *Complete Works of St Thomas More*, viii/2 (in order of citation): 940/31–941/7; also 937/13–938/23; viii/1: 146/15–21; viii/2: 520/13/15. His exact words are: 'There

to Cromwell from the Tower: '[N]ever thought I the Pope above the generall counsaile nor never have in any boke of myn put forth among the Kynges subjectis in our vulgare tunge avaunced greatly the Pope's authoritie.'[100]

More's conciliarist leanings do not appear to have had any impact upon those who came *after* him,[101] but they may serve (should that indeed be necessary) to disabuse us of any easy assumption that those in England who rejected the royal supremacy over the English church and rallied to the old faith necessarily rejected also the conciliarist ecclesiology. In 1560, certainly, at the very start of Queen Elizabeth's reign, that was an assumption that John Jewel, later bishop of Salisbury, found to be fallacious when he tried to engage in disputation with Dr Henry Cole, formerly dean of St Paul's during the reign of Mary Tudor. Deprived now of that office and jailed for refusing the Elizabethan Oath of Supremacy, Cole none the less insisted that in relation to the papal primacy and on the particular matter of the superiority of council to pope he held still to Gerson's position. Which response irritated Jewel mightily and stimulated him to embark on an effort to prove to Cole that if he held to that position he was as much of a heretic in Catholic eyes as was he (Jewel) himself.[102] On that score, however, Cole knew better, and it was as a recusant prisoner in the Tower that he was to die some twenty years later. Not even the leading Roman Catholic apologists who emerged in England later on in the reign—Cardinal William Allen and the Jesuit priest, Robert Persons—were indeed to take as simple an ecclesiological stance as Jewel might have desired of them, and both evoked the Decretist teaching on the deposition or loss of office by a pope guilty of heresy.[103]

are orders in Christes churche, by which a pope may be both admonished and amended and hathe be for incorrigible and lacke of amendment finally deposed and chaunged.'

[100] See *The Correspondence of Sir Thomas More*, ed. E. F. Rogers (Princeton: Princeton University Press, 1947), 499. That statement lacks precision and could be taken to ascribe coordinate powers to pope and council. But B. Gogan, *The Common Corps of Christendom* (Leiden: E. J. Brill, 1982), 293, comments that 'the burden of his [More's] expressed attitudes [overall] would tend to place him closer to contemporary conciliarists such as Jacques Almain and John Major rather than with papalists such as Catharinus or Cajetan'.

[101] Gogan concludes (ibid. 380) that More's theology of the Church in general had no 'great influence on subsequent developments within Roman Catholic circles'.

[102] For the whole exchange, see *The Works of John Jewel*, ed. J. Ayre (Cambridge: CUP, 1845–50), i. 64–9. *The Apology of the Church of England by John Jewel*, ed. J. E. Booty (Ithaca, NY: Cornell University Press, 1963), p. xxviii, gives the background to the incident.

[103] Allen, *A true, sincere and modest defence of English Catholiques*, 73; Parsons, *Elizabethae Angliae Reginae . . . Edictum*, §§ 221, 152, and his *A Treatise tending to Mitigation towards Catholicke Subiectes*, §§ 52–3, 180–1. For a discussion, see T. C. Clancy, *Papist Pamphleteers* (Chicago: Loyola University Press, 1964), 51 and 94.

As for the English churchmen who had by then accepted the breach with Rome, at least from the time of the conciliarist flurry of the 1530s they did not lose sight of the constitutional revolution that the council fathers assembled at Constance and Basel had threatened when they took their stand on the conciliarist affirmation of the jurisdictional superiority under certain circumstances of council to pope. In 1556, for example, John Ponet, bishop of Winchester until Queen Mary's accession, made lengthy appeal to the conciliar theory, which he attributed to the canonists and saw as grounded in the law of nature itself. Writing from exile, he made that appeal in an attempt to bolster a case for legitimate resistance to tyranny by driving home the point that 'the lawe of nature to depose and punishe wicked gouvernours, hathe not been only received and exercised in politicke matters, but also in the churche', where 'the canonists (the popes owne championes)' had themselves argued that popes 'maie be de-pryved by the body of the churche'. So that 'at one clappe, in the counsail holden at Constance in Germanie, in the yeare of our Lorde 1415, were three popes popped out of their places'.[104]

Seven years later, in the first English edition of the famous work he, too, had begun to assemble in exile, John Foxe, the great English martyrologist, devoted a great deal of attention to the histories of the Councils of Constance and Basel. In the nineteenth-century Cattley edition, which reproduces the contents of the 1563 version, over a hundred pages are devoted to that topic.[105] So far as Constance is concerned, Foxe concludes his account of its general proceedings before going on to describe the trials of John Hus and Jerome of Prague, by noting 'that in this council of Constance nothing was decreed or enacted worthy of memory but only this, that the pope's authority is under the council, and that the council ought to judge the pope'.[106] Nevertheless, he gives 'a recapitulation of Matters done in each Session of the council', including the resignation of Gregory XII and the deposition of John XXIII and Benedict XIII, and, in his discussion of the fourth and fifth sessions, reproduces much of the language of *Haec sancta*.[107] He cites that decree again (with a reminder that John XXIII was deposed, not for heresy, but for his crimes) in his lengthy account of the proceedings at Basel, much of that account consisting of a (rather uneven) translation into English of material drawn from Aeneas Sylvius Piccolomini's pro-conciliar *De Gestis Concilii Basiliensis Commentariorum*,

---

[104] Ponet, *Shorte Treatise of Politicke Power*, [103]; cf. [60], [102]–[106], [111].
[105] Foxe, *Actes and Monuments*, ed. Cattley, iii. 416–23 (for Constance), 605–700 (for Basel).
[106] Ibid. iii. 423.
[107] For this last, ibid. iii. 418.

libri duo, a significant segment of which focused on the arguments of
Panormitanus, John of Segovia, Thomas de Courcelles, and Alfonso
Garcia, bishop of Burgos, concerning the resolution that 'it is a matter of
the faith that the holy general council holds power over the pope and
anyone else'.[108]

Given the enduring popularity of the *Actes and Monuments* (the *Book of
Martyrs*)—it was frequently reprinted, a copy being kept along with the
Bible at the pulpit of many an English parish church—it must have done
more to draw attention to conciliarist teachings and the dramatic deeds
done at Constance and Basel than anything else since the episode of royal
flirtation with conciliarism in the 1530s. It should not surprise us, then, to
find, two years *after* the publication in 1583 of yet another edition of the
Actes and Monuments, that Thomas Bilson (later bishop of Winchester) in
his widely read and much-cited work, *The True Difference between Christian Subjection and Unchristian Rebellion,* devoted significant attention to
the histories of Pisa, Constance, and Basel.[109] In so doing, he proffered an
English translation of *Haec sancta,* affirmed that Basel had decreed conciliar superiority to be 'a truth of the catholicke faith', and noted (citing
Gerson) that the opposition of 'the Divines of Paris' to papal pretensions
dated back to the fourteenth century and had manifested itself as recently
as 1518 when the University of Paris had appealed 'from the Pope and
his assembly [i.e. the Fifth Lateran Council] to a generall and free
Councell'.[110]

Nor should we be surprised at the marked degree of explicit familiarity
which the Anglican controversialist Matthew Sutcliffe (1550?–1629)
showed with the writings of such prominent conciliarist sympathizers as
Nicholas de Clamanges, Pierre d'Ailly, Jean Gerson, Francesco Zabarella,
Nicholas of Cusa, Panormitanus, Aeneas Sylvius Piccolomini, and Jacques
Almain. A learned churchman who disposed of an impressive degree
of scholastic and canonistic erudition, Sutcliffe mined the conciliarist

[108] This runs in the Cattley edn. of the *Actes and Monuments,* iii, from 605–51. Cf. Piccolomini, *De Gestis Basiliensis Commentariorum,* 13–187 (Latin text of book 1 with English tr.).
This work is not to be confused with the same author's *De rebus Basiliae gestis commentarius,*
written in 1450 after he had become a bishop and from a more pro-papal viewpoint.

[109] Bilson, *The True Difference,* esp. 85–94, 270–3, 310–11. C. H. McIlwain, ed., *The Political
Writings of James I* (Cambridge, Mass.: Harvard University Press, 1918), p. xxxiii n. 3, comments that 'this long dialogue . . . was a storehouse of facts and arguments for later disputants,
probably including James I himself'.

[110] i.e. after the bull *Pastor aeternus,* promulgated at the Fifth Lateran Council, had
declared the Pragmatic Sanction of Bourges to be null and void and after the compromising
concordat of 1516. See Bilson, *The True Difference,* 87–8, 90, 92–4. For the context, see above,
Ch. 1.

and quasi-conciliarist literature to illustrate from the testimony of Catholics themselves the corruption of the old Church, the contradictions embedded in its teaching, its long-standing recognition of the possibility that the pope might lapse into heresy and be liable to judgement, and, above all, the sheer novelty in terms of traditional Catholic teaching of contemporary papist claims that the pope was superior in authority to the general council.[111] In his *De conciliis* and other Latin writings intended presumably for a learned and international readership, he evoked the history of Pisa, Constance, and Basel to establish the fact that heretical and criminous pontiffs had indeed been subjected to judgement and deposition by general councils laying formal claim to their own jurisdictional superiority to all ranks of the faithful, the papal not excluded.[112] But it is in his English writings intended for broader domestic consumption that he is most emphatic about the novelty of contemporary papalist attempts to explain away such unwelcome facts. That the Council of Florence had felt it necessary to declare the pope 'head of the universall church' he took (and used) as evidence of 'the noveltie of the papacie', and the teaching 'that the Pope is above all generall councels' as something that 'no church ever believed . . . for a thousand four hundred yeares'. After all, 'the Doctoures assembled at Constance and Basel [had] decreed the contrary doctrine to be more Christian'. Indeed, 'that the pope was above the councell was decreed', in effect,

only in our fathers' time by Leo the tenth, in the Councell of the Laterane, which showeth that till then, it was commonly holden, that the government of the universall church was aristocraticall, and not monarchicall, and that the councell was reputed supreme judge of controversies of faith, and all ecclesiasticall matters, and not the pope.[113]

Small wonder, then, that in the *Lawes of Ecclesiasticall Polity*, Richard Hooker himself called in 1593 for the revival of the practice of holding ecumenical councils. In the eighth book of that great work, moreover, when

---

[111] For a full listing of the works of Sutcliffe upon which I base these judegments, see Oakley, 'Constance, Basel and the Two Pisas', 101–2 n. 53.

[112] The whole line of Sutcliffe's argument in his *De conciliis* (directed against Cardinal Bellarmine) seems intended to lead up to the two final chapters establishing the Catholic commitment to the proposition that 'the Roman Pontiff is not superior to the general council', and rebutting Bellarmine's arguments to the contrary. See *De conciliis*, lib. 2, cc. 5 and 6, fos. 76ʳ–82ᵛ.

[113] These words I draw from Sutcliffe's *The Subversion of Robert Parsons*, 97, and his *A New Challenge*, 41–2, in which place he refers also to 'the later councell of Pisa, where Alexander the fifth was chosen pope, and . . . the Councell of Constance where three popes were deposed'.

claiming that 'the natural subject [i.e. the natural possessor] of power civill all men confesse to be in the bodie of the Commonwealth', he made an explicit appeal to conciliarist views.[114] That particular book was not destined to be published until 1648, but we have in addition rough notes written for a chapter in it in which he purposed to set forth arguments, pro and con, concerning the correction of an erring king. And in those notes, he also quotes (in company with John Foxe and more than one Jacobean successor) the famous pro-conciliarist speech delivered at Basel by the bishop of Burgos which Aeneas Sylvius Piccolomini had reproduced in his own pro-conciliar *De gestis Concilii Basiliensis Commentariorum libri duo*.[115]

Small wonder, too, that by the end of James I's reign in 1625 people in England had come to be better acquainted with conciliar history and the writings of the conciliarists than at any previous time—the fifteenth century, or so I would judge, not excluded.[116] But fully to account for that state of affairs we will have to factor in the impact of the great, Europe-wide ideological upheaval spawned by events in Venice, England, and France, an upheaval which coincided with that king's reign and which constituted the second great ideological relay-station re-energizing the conciliarist signal and transmitting it forward with renewed clarity and force to long generations to come.

[114] Hooker, *Of the Laws of Ecclesiastical Polity*, bk. 8, ch. 6; in *The Folger Library Edition of the Works of Richard Hooker*, iii. 385–7. I am much indebted to Arthur S. McGrade for drawing these interesting passages to my attention. See also W. B. Patterson, 'Hooker on Ecumenical Relations: Conciliarism in the English Reformation', in McGrade, ed., *Richard Hooker and the Construction of Christian Community* (Tempe, Ariz.: Medieval and Renaissance Texts and Studies, 1997), 281–303.

[115] For a pertinent extract from the speech, see below, Ch. 4, and for its citation by others in the 17th and 18th cents., Ch. 4, and Ch. 6. Cf. Foxe, *Actes and Monuments*, iii. 611–12; Piccolomini, *De Gestis Basiliensis Commentariorum*, ed. Hay and Smith, 32–3.

[116] Patterson, 'Hooker on Ecumenical Relations', in McGrade, *Richard Hooker*, 288, comments that 'Conciliarism, though it left its mark on the leading reformers and on Rome, took root in the theology of the English church to a much greater extent than in that of Lutheranism or Calvinism.'

4

Bellarmine's Nightmare: From James I, Sarpi, and Richer to Bossuet, Tournély, and the Gallican Orthodoxy

[W]hile in Rome it is not permitted to hold the doctrine of Panormitanus which maintained the superiority of the council, neither does the University of Paris tolerate the upholding of the contrary position. . . . [And] an opinion which enjoys the concurrence of as many famous scholars as may have held to the contrary, and which has the support of an equal, if not greater, number of universities, regions and kingdoms, can hardly be said to be proposed without reason or authority, still less audaciously.

(Paolo Sarpi, 1606[1])

The Pope is in the Church as a King is in his Kingdome, and for a King to be of more authority than his Kingdome, it were too absurd. Ergo. Neither ought the Pope to be above the Church . . . And like as oftentimes Kings, which doe wickedly governe the commonwealthe and expresse cruelty, are deprived of their Kingdoms; even so it is not to be doubted but that the Bishop of Rome may be deposed by the Church, that is to say, by the General Councell.

(William Prynne, 1643[2])

That the plenitude of power in matters spiritual possessed by the Apostolic See and the sucessors of St Peter, Vicars of Christ, is such that the decrees passed by the holy ecumenical council of Constance in its fourth and fifth sessions [i.e. the successive versions of *Haec*

[1] P. Sarpi, *Apologia per le opposizioni fatte dall'illustrissimo . . . cardinale Bellarmino*, in *Opere*, ed. M. D. Busnelli and G. Gambarin (Bari: Gius Laterza e Figli, 1931–65), iii. 117–18.
[2] W. Prynne, *The Soveraigne Power of Parliaments and Kingdoms* (London, 1643), 6.

sancta synodus], approved by the Apostolic See, confirmed by the
usage of the Roman pontiffs and of the entire church, and observed
with reverence down through time by the Gallican church, also remain unchanged and in force; and that the Gallican church does not
approve of the views of those who diminish the force of those decrees
by implying that their authority is doubtful, that they are not approved, or that they pertain only to the time of the schism.

(The second Gallican article of 1682[3])

I am no Papist, nor is my religion Popery. [Whereas] Catholic is an
old family name, which we have never forfeited, the word *Roman* has
been given to us to indicate some undue attachment to the See of
Rome.

(Joseph Berington, 1781[4])

'A generall councell is a Congregation of Pastors, Doctors and Elders, or
others, met in the name and authority of Jesus Christ, out of all Churches,
to determine according to the word of God, all controversies in faith,
Church-government or manners, no faithfull person who desireth being
excluded from reasoning and speaking.' The author of this definition correctly noted that the definitions given across the two centuries and more
preceding by the conciliar theorists Jean Gerson and Jacques Almain did
not differ much from his own 'save that they thinke that councells are lawfully convened, if such and such onely, as are of the Hierarchike order be
members thereof . . . as also the Pope president . . . [which] we disclaime'.
And, even so, he goes on to point out, Almain had indicated that under
certain circumstances a general council could be convened without the
pope and, if necessary, take action against him. Such an argument, he says,
'is grounded upon the necessitie' of councils, a point of view which 'our
brethren' think of as 'popish'. None the less, 'councells as councells are no
popish devices, but rather hated by right downe, and well died Papists, as
is clear from [the complaints of Gerson and Zabarella that] . . . wicked
Popes neglecting generall councells, have undone the Church'. In any
case, he adds, 'our brethren are forced to acknowledge their necessitie by
way of counselling and advising', so that 'we hold [to] the authoritie of
Councils, but ascribe to them as much power over the conscience as there
is reason in them from God's Word, and no more'.

[3] Tr. from the Latin and French versions in A.-G. Martimort, *Le Gallicanisme de Bossuet*
(Paris: 'Editions du Cerf, 1953), 466 and n. 2. See below, n. 140, for the Latin text.
   [4] J. Berington, *The State and Behaviour of English Catholics*, preface to the 1st edn.
(London, 1781), p. vi.

These comments are drawn from *The Due Right of Presbyteries* which Samuel Rutherford, the Scottish Presbyterian, published in 1644.[5] I do not believe it fanciful to suggest that they reflect in intriguing fashion the knowledge of, interest in, and sympathy with the long conciliarist tradition which had been so marked a feature of Scottish ecclesiological thinking since the first quarter of the fifteenth century, and of which, in the early sixteenth, John Mair had been the 'outstanding representative'.[6] Of course, it has proved easy enough to exaggerate or misrepresent Mair's influence in Scotland,[7] but as J. H. Burns has properly noted, 'the mere fact that he and his pupils were teaching in Scottish universities and teaching Scottish students at Paris throughout the last generation before 1550 suggests that conciliarist ideas were part of the mental equipment of educated Scots as the Reformation approached'.[8]

George Buchanan, one of those students both at St Andrews and Paris (and later to become tutor to the young James VI) we know to have conceded to the Lisbon inquisition in 1550 his own earlier adhesion to the doctrine of the superiority of council to pope,[9] and his familiarity with the tradition of conciliarist constitutionalism was to be clearly reflected in his celebrated resistance tract *De jure regni apud Scotos*.[10] Significant elements of this conciliar ecclesiology are evident also in the *Catechism* which John Hamilton, archbishop of St Andrews, published in 1550, and they were later reflected also in such official statements of the Reformed Scottish Kirk as the Scots Confession of 1560 and the Second Book of Discipline, this last drawn up in 1578 and recognized by James VI's government in

[5] S. Rutherford, *The Due Right of Presbyteries* (London, 1644), 332–3, 336–7, 342–3, a discussion punctuated not only by citations of the works of Gerson, Zabarella, Almain, Aeneas Sylvius Piccolomini, Cajetan, and Bellarmine, but also by references to the actions taken at Constance and Basel. Cf. J. Coffey, *Politics, Religion and the British Revolution* (Cambridge: CUP, 1997), 74, where he notes that Rutherford also appeals to Gerson, Almain, and Mair 'for their conciliar view of the church and papalist account of the origins of government', in his *A Preamble and Temperate Plea for Paul's Presbytery in Scotland* (London, 1643), 3. For his ecclesiology in general, see Coffey, *Politics*, 188–224.

[6] J. H. Burns, 'The Conciliarist Tradition in Scotland', *Scottish Historical Review*, 42 (1963), 89.

[7] In that connection I have had my own *mea culpa* to make, having been unaware in 1961/2, when I first wrote about John Mair, of the strength of the conciliarist tradition in Scotland during the 15th cent. For which, see J. H. Burns, 'John Ireland and "The Meroure of Wyssdome"'; *Innes Review*, 6 (1955), 79–98; idem, *Scottish Churchmen and the Council of Basel* (Glasgow: J. S. Burns & Sons, 1962); idem, 'Conciliarist Tradition in Scotland.'

[8] Burns, 'Conciliarist Tradition in Scotland,' 89.

[9] J. M. Aitken, *The Trial of George Buchanan before the Lisbon Inquisition* (Edinburgh: Oliver & Boyd, 1939), 22–5.

[10] *De jure regni apud Scotos*; in Buchanan, *Opera omnia* (Edinburgh, 1715), i. 36. Cf. F. Oakley, 'On the Road from Constance to 1688', *Journal of British Studies*, 1 (1962), 13–26.

1592.[11] This Second Book of Discipline, indeed, affirmed the general council to be an integral part of the Kirk's organization, a capstone, as it were, to the structure of local, regional, and national or general assemblies. It was to be called together in times when schism or doctrinal confusion threatened, and it constituted 'an uther mair generall kynd of assemblie quhilk is of all nationis or of all estaitis of personis within the kirk representing the universall kirk of Chryst quhilk may be callit properlie the generall assemblie or generall counsall of the haill kirk of God'.[12]

Though demonstration proves elusive, one may at least surmise, then, that the degree of familiarity James I himself was to show in his writings with the Parisian conciliarist tradition (he alludes specifically to the events at Constance and to the works of John of Paris, Gerson, Almain, and Mair) had at least some roots in his earlier encounter with the Scottish conciliar tradition.[13] Certainly, he does not appear to have found alien the emphasis such Anglican divines as Bilson, Sutcliffe, and Hooker were placing on the role of the general council in the governance of the universal Church and on the promise it might hold for the restoration of the fractured unity of Christendom. Within a year of his becoming king of England, after all, and even before he told his first parliament that he acknowledged 'the Romane Church to be our Mother Church, although defiled with some infirmities and corruptions' and expressed, accordingly, his own heartfelt desire to help promote 'a generall Christian union in Religion', he had proposed to the papal curia via diplomatic backchannels that the pope should 'summon a General Council, which, according to the ancient usage' would be 'superior to all Churches, all doctrine, all Princes, secular and ecclesiastic, none excepted'.[14] And if he believed the pope to be subject in jurisdiction to that of the general council (as the Council of Constance had demonstrated), he still insisted that he regarded hierarchy as 'essential' to the Church, and the pope 'the first Bishop in it, President and Moderator in Council, but not head or superior'.[15]

---

[11] W. B. Patterson, *King James VI and I and the Reunion of Christendom* (Cambridge: CUP, 1997), 59–60.

[12] *The Second Book of Discipline*, ed. James Kirk (Edinburgh, 1980), 205–6, cited from Patterson, *King James*, 60.

[13] See his *A Premonition to all most mightie Monarches* and *A Remonstrance for the Right of King's, and the Independence of their crownes*, in *The Political Works of James I*, ed. C. H. McIlwain (Cambridge, Mass.: Harvard University Press, 1918), 119–20, 202, 205–6, 263–4 (for Gerson) and 202–4 for Almain, Mair, and John of Paris. Cf. Burns, 'Conciliarist Tradition in Scotland.'

[14] Patterson, *King James*, 35–7.   [15] Ibid. 39.

Understandably enough, neither this nor subsequent calls of his for a council of reunion met with the desired response from Rome. The last such calls, embedded in the texts of his *Apologie for the Oath of Allegiance* and his *Premonition to All Most Mightie Monarches*, were advanced in 1607 and 1609, respectively, and directed this time, not to the pope himself, but to the kings and civil states of Europe.[16] They were so directed as part of the great ideological battle concerning the reach of the pope's authority that lasted from 1606 right down to the early 1620s.[17] This battle was to constitute, as I have suggested, the second of what I have called ideological relay-stations, picking up and clarifying the conciliarist signal and transmitting it forward in amplified form to future generations. It is to this second relay-station as also to the third—the great struggle between Pope Innocent XI (1679–89) and Louis XIV of France over the king's regalian rights which precipitated the famous *Declaration of the Gallican Clergy* of 1682— that I wish in this chapter to direct attention.

LONDON, VENICE, PARIS: THE OATH OF ALLEGIANCE
CONTROVERSY AND RELATED UPHEAVALS

Although it generated an enormous ideological fallout, the first of these episodes—at least in its multinational totality—has yet to find its historian. The ideological energy which it involved was released by a dramatic series of events occurring in three countries during a four-year period at the start of the seventeenth century. The events in question, each fully

---

[16] Ibid. 50–74, 96, 110–20.

[17] The most complete recent discussion of the Venetian side of the controversy is W. J. Bouwsma, *Venice and the Defense of Republican Liberty* (Berkeley and Los Angeles: University of California Press, 1968), esp. 359–482. For good shorter accounts, see F. C. Lane, *Venice* (Baltimore and London: Johns Hopkins University Press, 1973), 481–96, and L. Salvatorelli, 'Venezia, Paolo V e fra Paolo Sarpi', in V. Branca, ed., *Storia della civiltà Veneziana* (Florence: Sansoni, 1979), iii. 23–36. Cf. A. D. Wright, 'Why the Venetian Interdict?', *English Historical Review*, 89 (1974), 536–50. The most complete discussion of the English and French aspects of the controversy is still that of McIlwain in the lengthy introductory essay he wrote for his edn. of *The Political Works of James I*, pp. xxxv–lxxx. Of recent years, J. H. M. Salmon has touched upon these aspects very helpfully in his 'Gallicanism and Anglicanism in the Age of the Counter Reformation', in Salmon, *Renaissance and Revolt* (Cambridge: CUP, 1987), 155–88, and in 'Catholic Resistance Theory, Ultramontanism, and the Royalist Response, 1580–1630', in J. H. Burns and M. Goldie, eds., *The Cambridge History of Political Thought 1450–1700* (Cambridge: CUP, 1991), 219–53. Though P. Prodi, *Il sacramento del potere* (Bologna: Il Mulino, 1992), 398–414, touches interestingly on all three (cf. his *The Papal Prince*, Cambridge and New York: CUP, 1987), I know of no full account of the complete controversy in all its Venetian, French, and English dimensions. I draw in what follows on Oakley, 'Constance, Basel, and the Two Pisas'; idem, 'Complexities of Context', idem, 'Bronze-Age Conciliarism'.

comprehensible only in terms of the issues and developments native to the countries involved, can best be understood as a group in the context of the rise to prominence in relation to England, Venice, and France of the doctrine of the *indirect* power of the pope in matters temporal—a doctrine of medieval provenance but refurbished by Francisco de Vitoria (d. 1566) and transformed into a commonplace by Robert, Cardinal Bellarmine (d. 1621).[18]

The story begins in England after November 1605, when the discovery of the Gunpowder Plot stimulated Parliament before its adjournment in May 1606 to impose on Catholic recusants an Oath of Allegiance requiring them (among other things) to reject as 'impious and heretical' the teaching that princes who had been excommunicated or deprived of their office by the pope might lawfully be deposed by their subjects.[19] In Italy, almost immediately thereafter, Pope Paul V allowed to go into effect the sentences of excommunication of the Venetian doge and senate and of interdict on all Venetian territories that had already been issued on 17 April 1606, in response to the senate's attempt to extend to the *terraferma* (or mainland territories) the restrictive laws pertaining to Church property long since enforced within the city of Venice itself. That interdict was to remain in effect until 21 April 1607, and for the Republic of Venice the decade and more ensuing was to be characterized by political insecurity and ideological tension.[20] Finally, in France, in the wake of Henry IV's murder in 1610 at the hands of a Catholic assassin, the Third Estate at the meeting of the Estates-General in 1614–15 attempted to impose on churchmen, royal officials, and others an oath which its opponents portrayed as modelled on the earlier English Oath of Allegiance.[21]

None of these events occurred in a vacuum. The Jacobean Oath of Allegiance has to be seen against the background of the divisions which had emerged among English 'Roman' Catholics during the previous reign and which, in the so-called 'stirs of Wisbech', had generated a surge of tension among the recusant clergy interned at Wisbech Castle.[22] Notable among

[18] F. de Vitoria, *Political Writings*, ed. A. Pagden and J. Lawrence (Cambridge: CUP, 1991), 45–108 (esp. 82–101); J. C. Murray, 'St Robert Bellarmine on the Indirect Power', *Theological Studies*, 9 (1948), 491–535.

[19] Salmon, 'Catholic Resistance Theory', Burns and Goldie, in *Cambridge History*, 247–53; *Political Works of James I*, ed. McIlwain, pp. xxxv–lxxx.

[20] Bouwsma, *Venice*, 339–555. The papal sentence was handed down in an attempt to coerce the Venetian Republic into abrogating the traditional subjection of the clergy to state jurisdiction as well as into lifting the restrictions imposed on the Church in relation to the acquisition of property.

[21] *Political Works of James I*, ed. McIlwain, p. lxvi.

[22] J. Bossy, *The English Catholic Community* (New York: OUP, 1976), 33–48, Salmon,

those divisions was that between one group of laity and secular clergy reluctantly willing to put up with the Elizabethan religious settlement in return for even a restricted measure of toleration, and a younger, growing, and more aggressive group, including some converted to the old faith under Jesuit influence. The latter usually adhered to Cardinal Bellarmine's doctrine of the indirect power of the pope in matters temporal, yearned for nothing less than the restoration of England to the papal allegiance, and were willing to accept the intervention of a foreign power to achieve that happy end. Fearful of Jesuit involvement in the campaign for reconversion, and viewing the members of that order as foreign agents scheming to advance the cause of the Spanish enemy, the Elizabethan and Jacobean bishops laboured mightily to widen this particular division among English Catholics, and the 1606 Oath of Allegiance may well have been intended to further that end.[23] But, whatever the case, it clearly involved a frontal attack on the prerogatives of the papacy as traditionally conceived as well as an outright rejection of any papal power to intervene in the temporal affairs of the secular states of Europe—even if presented in the more modern and fashionable guise of a power that was merely indirect.

In the case of Venice, the latter years of the sixteenth century had seen a deepening of age-old tensions between the aspirations of a proud and ancient republic, self-consciously intent upon the preservation of its freedoms and independent traditions in matters ecclesiastical as well as temporal, and the deepening clericalism and growing militancy of a Counter-Reformation papacy concerned to subordinate the episcopacy to its own direct control, and concerned also to project its claim to worldwide leadership and jurisdictional oversight even into the realm of temporal affairs.[24] The crisis of the interdict, then, involved far more than the cluster of intricate legal issues concerning Church property, clerical immunity, and the precise reach of Venetian civil jurisdiction which had precipitated it. It fanned into flame some very fundamental and contentious issues about the nature and extent of the jurisdictional power attaching to the papal primacy, issues that had burnt fiercely during the conciliar epoch, had continued to smoulder on into the era of papal

'Catholic Resistance Theory', in Burns and Goldie, *Cambridge History*, 243–4. Cf. Clancy, *Papist Pamphleteers*. For a discussion of the views of the Appellants see P. Holmes, *Resistance and Compromise* (Cambridge: CUP, 1982), 186–223.

[23] McIlwain, introduction to *The Political Works of James I*, pp. xxv–xxvi. Cf. p. xlix, where he says of the oath: 'It was England's answer to the Jesuit challenge contained in Bellarmine's theory of the Pope's indirect power.' Cf. Bossy, *English Catholic Community*, 46.

[24] See the thoughtful analysis in Bouwsma, *Venice*, 293–338.

restoration, and, as we have seen, had provoked something of a crisis at the Council of Trent itself.

The subsequent chain of events in France was destined to produce a similar effect. There the murder of Henry IV imparted new strength to the long-established and widespread suspicion that the Jesuits were the sinister force behind the assassinations and attempted assassinations of rulers ever since the inception of the Catholic League. Coming at a time when ultramontane sympathies and a real commitment to the Tridentine reform had been growing among the French clergy and had found, even among the theologians of the Sorbonne, a notable champion in the person of André Duval (d. 1638),[25] it helped boost the fortunes of Gallicanism, at least in its theological if not necessarily its political variant.[26] In the years immediately preceding, Edmond Richer (1559–1631), syndic of the Sorbonne, had worked hard to wean his colleagues from their ultramontane sympathies and to rally them, with the help of Jacques Leschassier, procureur général of the Parlement de Paris, to a form of Gallicanism that contrived (albeit uneasily) to combine both variants, political as well as theological.[27] In 1611 the Parlement rallied to his support after he came out in opposition to a Dominican attempt to vindicate the principles of papal infallibility and the superiority of pope to council. But Richer's own forceful assertion of Gallican principles in his *Libellus de ecclesiastica et politica potestate* (1611) proved in the end to be too extreme even for his theological colleagues and he was forced to relinquish his position as syndic. It is significant, none the less, that it was a friend of his, the magistrate Le Prêtre, who was to be responsible for the (ultimately) abortive attempt at

---

[25] Stern adversary of Edmond Richer, Duval wrote against him in 1612 his *Libelli de ecclesiastica et publica potestate, Elenchus pro summa romani pontificis in Ecclesiam auctoritate*, a work which drew praise from Bellarmine and the Roman Inquisition. See A. Ingold, in *Dictionnaire de théologie catholique* (Paris: Letourzey & Ané, 1935–65), iv/2: 1967, s.v. 'Duval, André'.

[26] So far as relations between pope and clergy were concerned, L. Willaert, *Après le concile de Trente* (Paris: Bloud & Gay, 1960), 369–70 n. 1, distinguishes in Gallicanism between a *theological* anti-Romanism involving (among other things) the claim to superiority of council over pope, and a *political* anti-Romanism, involving an assertion of the absolute nature of the royal power, its direct reception from God, and its independence of the papal spiritual authority, as well as a *liturgical* anti-Romanism, insisting on local autonomy in matters concerning the liturgy. He also notes that while *theological* and *political* Gallicans both insisted on the absolute independence of the royal power of papal authority, *royal* Gallicanism was not always on this matter as intransigent as the Gallicanism characteristic of the lawyers of the Parlement de Paris. For a comparable though not identical typology linked, however, with the claim that 'le Gallicanisme est un phénomène purement français', see V. Martin, *Les Origines du Gallicanisme* (Paris: Bloud & Gay, 1939), ii. esp. 325–39 (words quoted at 325).

[27] See Oakley, 'Bronze-Age Conciliarism', 65–86.

the Estates General of 1614–15 'to enact a fundamental law safeguarding the crown against papal intervention'.[28]

London, Venice, Paris—it is understandable, then, that the events described above contrived to generate in each case an outburst of controversialist writing that came in the end to involve (among a host of others) participants of the distinction, or notoriety, of Richer himself, the Servite monk, Paolo Sarpi (d. 1623), at that time official legal and theological adviser to the Venetian Republic, and the former Huguenot, Jacques Davy, Cardinal du Perron (d. 1618), as well as Francisco Suarez (d. 1617), the great Spanish philosopher and theologian, Cardinal Bellarmine, and none other than King James I of England himself. The story of this great outpouring of publicistic literature, which lasted on into the 1620s, is at once both intricate and fascinating, but for our purposes it must suffice to emphasize three of its dominant characteristics.

First, its sheer dimensions and extraordinarily high profile. The importance that contemporaries attached to this great upheaval of the spirit is exemplified by the fact that about three-quarters of the formal writing that James I devoted to matters political is concerned with the defence of the Oath of Allegiance. And Milward's listing of almost 200 works, most of them published between 1605 and 1620, conveys some sense of the sheer dimensions of the dispute—the more so in that he is concerned only with the English and French phases and does not include the related literature of controversy generated by the Venetian interdict.[29] Hence McIlwain's conclusion (and his analysis also brackets the Venetian phase): 'The England oaths of allegiance controversy ... [gave] rise to a paper warfare in Europe the like of which has never been seen since and is hardly likely ever to be seen again now that the common language of that warfare has fallen into disuse.'[30] The hyperbole, if real, is doubtless pardonable.

Second, scarcely less striking than the sheer scale of the controversy is the rapidity with which it ramified into a genuinely Europe-wide phenomenon, as also the multiplicity and intimacy of the interconnections that developed among the English, French, and Venetians in their efforts to cope with the onslaught of the ultramontanes and their Jesuit champions. Similarly striking is the ease and speed with which tracts and ideas circulated among them—whether in Latin works (or Latin translations) intended for a learned international readership or in more precisely

[28] Salmon, *Renaissance and Revolt*, 188.
[29] P. Milward, *Religious Controversies of the Jacobean Age* (Lincoln, Neb., and London: University of Nebraska Press, 1978), 82–136.
[30] *Political Works of James I*, ed. McIlwain, p. lvii.

targeted translations from English into French, French into English and Italian, Italian into English and French, and so on. Once James I himself had responded to the papal challenge by publishing in 1607 his *Triplici nodo, triplex cuneus or an Apologie for the Oath of Allegiance*,[31] it is not surprising that the controversy captured a Europe-wide audience and stimulated entry into the lists, on one side or another, of a whole series of English, German, Italian, and French controversialists. The most prominent among them was Cardinal Bellarmine himself, writing under the name of Matthaeus Tortus in his *Responsio* of 1608. This work evoked in turn from the King a reissue of his *Apologie*, prefaced this time by a lengthy address to the princes of Europe.[32]

But the rapid internationalization of the dispute was very much advanced by the complex web of diplomatic links, intellectual affiliations, and mutual sympathies (much of it already in place) which joined together London, Venice, and Paris, imparting a certain cohesion to the anti-papal cause and nourishing, not only in Venice but also in England, a heightened susceptibility to the attraction of traditionally Gallican commitments.[33]

Thus a marked reciprocity characterized the ideological relationships between England and France and, again, between England and Venice. James I himself, who had taken a keen interest in the Venetian affair,[34] took an even greater interest in the unfolding of events in France. In his

[31] Written in response to the papal letters of 1606 and 1607 commanding English Catholics to refuse the oaths and to a letter of Cardinal Bellarmine to the Archpriest Blackwell, the English Catholic leader, rebuking him for his own acceptance of the oath and denouncing it as contrary to the faith. The *Apologie* is reprinted in *Political Works of James I*, ed. McIlwain, 71–109.

[32] The fuller title of Bellarmine's work is *Responsio ad Librum Inscriptum Triplici Nodo Triplex Cuneus, sive Apologia*. James entitled his prefatory address: *A Premonition to all most mightie Monarches, Kings, Free Princes, and States of Christendome*, in *Political Works of James I*, ed. McIlwain, 110–68.

[33] For the English–Venetian connection, see G. Cozzi, 'Fra Paolo Sarpi', *Rivista storica italiana*, 63 (1956), 556–619. For the Franco-English connection, see *Political Writings of James I*, ed. McIlwain, esp. pp. lxv–lxx. John Bossy, 'Henry IV, the Appellants and the Jesuits', *Recusant History*, 8 (1965), 80–112, and Salmon, 'Gallicanism and Anglicanism in the Age of the Counter Reformation', ch. 7 of his *Renaissance and Revolt*, 155–88. For the Franco-Venetian connection, see Ulianich's lengthy introduction to his edn. of Sarpi, *Lettere ai Gallicani*, esp. pp. xix–xxxvii, and W. J. Bouwsma, 'Gallicanism and the Nature of Christendom', in A. Molho and J. A. Tedeschi, eds., *Renaissance Studies* (Dekalb, Ill.: Northern Illinois University Press, 1971), 809–30. All of these intricate linkages are judiciously assessed in Salmon, 'Catholic Resistance Theory', in Burns and Goldie, *Cambridge History*, 219–53.

[34] It appears to have renewed his earlier hopes for the assembly of a general council of the entire Christian world to reunite Christendom and reform the Church—see Bouwsma, *Venice*, 392. For James's earlier efforts to encourage the pope to summon such a general council, see Patterson, *King James*, 35–43.

Remonstrance for the Right of Kings, and the Independence of their Crownes (1615) he responded to Cardinal du Perron's oration to the Third Estate attacking the proposed French oath ('c'est le serment d'Angleterre tout pur!'), and he made sure that that response appeared in French and Latin as well as English.[35] Under the shadow of the Armada, Anglican royalism had long since 'found common ground with politique and Gallican responses to the alliance of Spain, the pope and the [Catholic] League', and 'Gallican and Anglican theory' had increasingly 'converged in response to the Ultramontane threat'. Similarly, during the years of the Venetian interdict and its uneasy aftermath, Paolo Sarpi came to be regarded not only as 'some sort of republican Gallican' but also as 'an honorary member of the Church of England'.[36] Within a few months of its original publication his *Considerazioni sopra le censure* had been republished in English translation as well as in French.[37] In 1614, in turn, Sarpi rose to the defence in Venice of the Catholicity of two books which the English Benedictine, Thomas Preston, had written in support of the Oath of Allegiance and in opposition to Bellarmine's doctrine of the pope's indirect power of deposition.[38]

Among the traditionally Gallican commitments reflected in much of these writings, considerable prominence attached to the affirmation of unambiguously conciliarist principles, and the third dominant characteristic of the body of controversialist literature we have been discussing (as well as the one most pertinent to the subject at hand) is the marked degree to which it served to focus attention on the conciliarist tradition and to disseminate conciliarist writings. As the Venetian and Gallican controversies converged on the English Oath of Allegiance,[39] the tide of controversialist literature and the arguments of those opposing the ultramontanes—Venetians, Anglican, English Catholic supporters of the Oath of Allegiance—certainly had the effect of further familiarizing English people with the history of the fifteenth-century councils and the

[35] Printed in *Political Works of James I*, ed. McIlwain, 169–268.

[36] Thus Salmon, *Renaissance and Revolt*, 155 and 166–7; cf. Cozzi, 'Fra Paolo Sarpi', 559–619 (esp. 584–93).

[37] Under the title *A Full and Satisfactorie Answer to the late Unadvised Bull thundered by Pope Paul V against the renowned State of Venice* (London, 1606).

[38] The works in question (written under the alias of 'Roger Widdrington') were his *Apologia Cardinalis Bellarmine pro Jure Principum. Adversus ipsius rationes pro auctoritate Papali Principes in ordine ad bonum spirituali deponendi* (1611) and *Disputatio Theologica de Juramente Fidelitatis Sanctissimo Patri Paolo Papae Quinto Dedicata* (1613). Both works had been placed on the Index. Cf. Sarpi's letter to Jacques Leschassier, dated 23 July 1613, in *Lettere ai Gallicani*, ed. Ulianich, 123–4, and Ulianich's n. 120 (at 275–6).

[39] *Political Works of James I*, ed. McIlwain, p. xlv.

writings especially of the Parisian conciliarists, from John of Paris, via Pierre d'Ailly and Jean Gerson, to Jacques Almain and John Mair.

In both respects, though in his recent and very useful history of Catholic conciliar ideas from the age of Reformation to that of the Enlightenment Hermann Joseph Sieben passes over them in silence,[40] these years of controversy proved to be very fruitful. Richer's publication in 1606 of his new edition of Gerson made readily available not only Gerson's own conciliarist tracts but also the *Tractatus de regia potestate et papali* of John of Paris, as well as the most important conciliarist writings of Pierre d'Ailly and those of his sixteenth-century successors, Almain and Mair.[41] It was this edition, presumably, that James I presented in 1612 to the library at St Andrew's University, and one may surmise that it was in its pages that he himself had made his acquaintance with the Parisian conciliarists whom he cites so readily in his own writings.[42] It is the edition, moreover, to which Cardinal du Perron drew attention in his celebrated *Oration* of 1614, identifying it as the source to which 'the Maisters of the Kinges retinue of the Parliament of Paris, do remit and refer their Readers, to understand what be the batteries and strongest defenses of the Jurisdiction Spiritual and temporal [i.e. against the pope]'.[43] And, only five years after its appearance, as the controversy over the indirect power continued to unfold, the Calvinist author Melchior Goldast published the first volume of his enormous *Monarchia Sancti Romani Imperii* which included, along with William of Ockham's *Dialogus* and a host of other works, John of Paris's *Tractatus de regia potestate et papali*, several of the conciliarist tracts of Gerson, Gregor Heimburg, Matthias Doering, Philippus Decius, and Jacques Almain, Richer's *Libellus de ecclesiastica et politica potestate* (with its own evocation of conciliar theory), as well as Latin versions of several contemporary Venetian efforts to vindicate the *Serenissima Repubblica* against papal condemnation.[44]

In the controversialist literature of the day, then, the conciliarist tradition was very much in play. The evocation of that tradition, certainly, the English and Scottish writers (Protestant no less than Catholic), who for

[40] H. J. Sieben, *Die Katholische Konzilsidee von der Reformation bis zur Aufklärung* (Paderborn: F. Schöningh, 1988). Schneider's excellent book, which takes up the conciliar story in full detail only with the advent of Febronius in the 18th cent., is similarly silent on this particular episode.

[41] *Joannis Gersonii ... Opera*, esp. ii. 675–934.

[42] See above, Ch. 4 n. 13. For James's gift to St Andrews, see Z. Rueger, 'Gerson, the Conciliar Movement and the Right of Resistance', *Journal of the History of Ideas*, 25 (1964), 484.

[43] I quote from the contemporary English translation of the Oration. See J. D. Perron, *An Oration ...* (St Omer, 1616), 49–50; cf. 121–2.

[44] Goldast, *Monarchia*, *passim*.

one reason or another contributed to the Oath of Allegiance controversy, were quick to make their own. James I himself, insensitive, it may be, to the broader constitutionalist implications of conciliar theory, was no exception.[45] Noting that John XXIII had been tried and deposed in 1415 by the Council of Constance, that the *conciliabulum* of Pisa had moved in 1511 to depose Julius II, and insisting (with citation of the crucial text from Gratian's *Decretum*) that the popes themselves had conceded the possibility of papal heresy, he triumphantly demanded, 'How can he, that may be infected with damnable heresie . . . be judge of heresie in a King or depose an Orthodoxe King for heresie?'[46]

In posing that question he was not alone. Among other Anglican writers, for example, the conciliarist authors and the history of the fifteenth-century councils were likewise discussed, sometimes at great length, by Lancelot Andrewes, David Owen, Robert Burhill, John Buckeridge, Richard Field, and John White. Similarly among the Catholics, by the Archpriest George Blackwell, William Warnington, William Barclay, Thomas Preston (alias Roger Widdrington), William Barret, and John Floyd. And one may find similar discussions also in Richard Sheldon and Marc Antonio de Dominis—men who, in the course of their lives, crossed or even recrossed the Roman Catholic–Anglican divide.[47]

In the works of these authors the range of conciliarist writings cited is very broad (extending from Dietrich of Niem and Zabarella to Nicholas of Cusa and Panormitanus), but it is the members of the so-called 'School of Sorbonne' or the 'Divines of Paris' who top the list—from John of Paris via Pierre d'Ailly to Almain and Mair, with Gerson's writings and authority being called upon more frequently than anyone else's.

Nor did the winding down of the Oath of Allegiance controversy in the 1620s signal the end of the English interest in the conciliarist tradition. The ideological turbulence of the Civil War era in mid-century stimulated something of a revival of that interest, with conciliarist authors, the history of the fifteenth-century councils, and the conciliar analogy to secular constitutional struggles being discussed by royalists and parliamentarians alike—from Robert Baillie in 1640 to Henry Ferne, William Bridge, John Bramhall, William Prynne, John Maxwell, and Samuel Rutherford in the crucial 1642–4 period, as well as by Rutherford again in 1648. Bramhall

[45] Oakley, 'On the Road', 8–9; Salmon, *Renaissance and Revolt*, 184.
[46] *A Remonstrance for the Right of King's*, in *Political Works of James I*, ed. McIlwain, 181, 198, 298–9.
[47] For a complete roster of the pertinent references in the writings of these men, consult Oakley, 'Constance, Basel and the Two Pisas', 113–14 nn. 94, 95, 96, and 97.

again in the 1650s, and George Lawson in 1660.[48] Thus, in the course of a broad-gauged discussion that reached into ecclesiology as well as political theory, arguing that 'the primary subject of the Power of the Keys is the whole Church' and referring back to the evocation by Lancelot Andrewes of d'Ailly, Gerson, 'the school of Sorbonne', Nicholas of Cusa, and the Council of Constance, Lawson conceded that 'some determine the pope as Peter's successor, to be the visible head and universal monarch of this church'. But 'others', he reminded his readers, such 'as the Councils of Constance and Basle, Cameracensis [i.e. Pierre d'Ailly], Gerson and the faculty of Paris, give this power to the whole church to be exercised in general councils'.[49]

During the Oath of Allegiance controversy and later such conciliarist authors were called upon with the object of documenting from unimpeachably Catholic testimonies the obvious corruption of the old Church (thus Sir John Hayward, Richard Field), or of triumphantly underscoring the contradictions and instability embedded in the Catholic doctrinal tradition (thus Bilson, Sutcliffe), or of debunking the idea that a pontiff who was himself capable of heresy and subject to conciliar judgement could presume to claim any power of judging and deposing kings (thus Sheldon and James I himself).[50] But they were called upon also (and by those of Catholic as well as Calvinist sympathies) to help make the case for an ecclesiology of episcopalist or conciliar bent, or, alternatively, to strengthen the argument for a non-episcopalist but synodal form of Church government. Thus, among the Calvinist divines making the latter case, mention should be made of Robert Parker as well as Samuel Rutherford.[51] And among the Catholics making the conciliarist or episcopalist case, one may cite Blackwell, Warmington, Marc Antonio de Dominis, and Widdrington—this last reminding his readers that 'the ancient Doctors of Paris, as Joannes Major, and Jacobus Almainus, who wrote against Cardinall Cajetane concerning this question, thought the opinion, which held the Pope to be above a Generall Councell, to be improbable, yea and other Doctors, as Cardinalis Cameracensis [i.e. Pierre d'Ailly] and John Gerson thought it to be erroneous and hereticall'.[52]

---

[48] Oakley, 'Constance, Basel and the Two Pisas', 115–16.

[49] G. Lawson, *Politia Sacra et Civilis*, ed. C. Condren (Cambridge: CUP, 1992), 164–5, 185–6.

[50] For the pertinent references see Oakley, 'Constance, Basel and the Two Pisas', 116–17 nn. 102, 103, 104.

[51] Parker, *De Politeia Ecclesiastica Christi*, II, 24, 26, 41–2, 78–9, 104–5; for Rutherford, see above, n. 5.

[52] Blackwell, *A large Examination*, 96–167; Warmington, *Moderate Defense*, 38–9, 59; Dominis, *Papatus Romanus*, 35, 114–16, 163, 175; idem, *De republica ecclesiastica. Libri X*,

About this last move there was nothing at all surprising, given the marked reservations evident among the English recusant clergy concerning the more extreme claims being made at the papal curia for the reach of papal power not only in the temporal but also in the spiritual domain. Antipathy to such claims manifested itself among the so-called Appellant clergy who in 1600 challenged the authority of their papally appointed archpriest, whom they viewed as a lackey of those doughty ultramontane colleagues, the zealous priests of the Jesuit mission to England. It was evident also in the willingness of some of the seculars to propose in 1600 an Oath of Allegiance comparable to that later imposed by Parliament in 1606, and of others, including the Archpriest Blackwell himself, to take the 1606 oath.[53] It was evident, further, in the staunch support extended to the episcopalism of the secular clergy later on in the century by the 'Blackloists'—the Catholic churchmen who coalesced around that strange figure Thomas White (alias Blacklo), friend of Hobbes and critic of ultramontane claims.[54] Indeed, it constituted something of a persistent, if fluctuating, characteristic of recusant Catholic opinion in England, especially among educated lay folk and segments of the secular clergy, all the way down to the era of Catholic emancipation in the nineteenth century.

This strain of 'Old', or 'Cisalpine', or 'Anglo-Gallican' Catholicism, as it has variously been called, was to reach its moment of greatest prominence during the closing decades of the eighteenth century when, from 1782 onwards, groups of Catholic gentry—men like Sir Richard Throckmorton, Lord Petre, and Charles Butler—organized themselves into successive Catholic committees and, later, into the appropriately (and deliberately) named Cisalpine Club.[55] Seeking relief from the penal laws, anxious to be freed to take what they viewed as their rightful place in English society, and drawn, it has been said, from 'the oldest and best Catholic families of the day', their characteristic mode of thinking was 'neither as outrageously new nor as limited in appeal as has sometimes been assumed'.[56]

249–53, 256, 600–3, 620, 675, and *De republica ecclesiastica. Pars secunda*, 36–8, 464; Widdrington, *A Cleare, Sincere and Modest Confutation*, 34.

[53] Bossy, *English Catholic Community*, 33–48; Holmes *Resistance*, 186–204.

[54] See R. I. Bradley, 'Blacklo and the Counter-Reformation', in C. H. Carter, ed., *From the Renaissance to the Counter Reformation* (New York: Random House, 1965), 348–70; Bossy, *English Catholic Community*, 62–7.

[55] Duffy, 'Ecclesiastical Democracy Detected', 1 and 2; Chinnici, *English Catholic Enlightenment*; shorter accounts in Bossy, *English Catholic Community*, 330–7; E. Norman, *Roman Catholicism in England* (Oxford: OUP, 1988), 48–68.

[56] Duffy, 'Ecclesiastical Democracy Detected: 1', 194; J. Pereiro, *Cardinal Manning* (Oxford: OUP, 1998), 262, 265, notes that as late as 1862 Manning still regarded Gallicanism as posing a more serious threat to Roman Catholicism in England than did Anglicanism.

Along with such learned clerical sympathizers as John Lingard and Joseph Berington, they came, it is true, to be denounced by some of the more conservative among the clergy as quasi-schismatic fellow-travellers with Scipio Ricci and the malcontents of the Synod of Pistoia (1786),[57] and as determined to foist upon the Church a republican form of ecclesiastical government.[58] But their sympathies appear to have been somewhat more moderate than that and more specifically Gallican. They are better understood as the inheritors of an indigenous and English recusant tradition stretching back all the way to the Appellant clergy of 1600.[59] 'I am no Papist,' Joseph Berington did indeed proclaim, 'nor is my religion Popery.' Whereas '*Catholic* is an old family name, which we have never forfeited', it should be recognized that 'the word *Roman* has been given to us to indicate some undue attachment to the See of Rome'.[60] His own attachment to that see of Rome was clearly not very warm—no warmer, perhaps, than was that of the great Irish 'Liberator', Daniel O'Connell, later on.[61] But like the other Cisalpines he was clear enough in his commitment to the notion of a divinely instituted papal primacy, which he (and they) understood, moreover, not simply as a primacy of honour or rank, but as in some measure a primacy of jurisdiction, too.[62] Where he (and they) parted company with the ultramontanes or 'transalpines' of the Roman curia was not on the *fact* of the papal primacy but, rather, on its *nature*.

---

[57] For which, see below, Ch. 5. Chinnici, *English Catholic Enlightenment*, 59, notes that Berington himself detected something of an affinity between his own ideas concerning ecclesiastical government and those of Ricci.

[58] Ibid. 58.

[59] Thus Norman, *Roman Catholicism*, 47 and 55, where he describes Berington's attack on papal authority as having 'summed up two centuries of English Catholic loyalism to the Crown', and Lord Petre's Catholic Committee as standing 'in the long tradition of the Appellants of 1600'.

[60] Berington, *State and Behaviour*, p. vi.

[61] Watkin, *Roman Catholicism in England* (New York: OUP, 1957), 161, citing O'Connell's proclamation: 'I am sincerely a Catholic but I am not a papist. . . . In spiritual matters the authority of the Pope is limited.'

[62] Berington, *State and Behaviour*, 152; idem, *Reflections addressed to the Rev. John Hawkins* (London, 1785), 69; cf. C. Butler, *The Historical Memoirs of the Church of France* (London: W. Clarke & Sons, 1817), 35–6: 'It is an article of the Roman Catholic faith, that the pope has, by divine right, 1st, a supremacy of rank; 2ndly, a supremacy of jurisdiction in the spiritual concerns of the roman-catholic church; and 3rdly, the principal authority in defining articles of faith. In consequence of these prerogatives, the pope holds a rank, splendidly preeminent, over the highest dignitaries of the church . . . To the pope, in the opinion of all Roman-catholics, belongs also a general superintendence of the concerns of the church'. For Lingard's comparable views, see Chinnici, *English Catholic Enlightenment*, 90–1. He notes that Lingard emphasized the pope's possession, not only of a primacy of honour, but one of jurisdiction, and attributed to him an authority, 'superior to that of every one of his brethren individually considered'. This last is a familiar and important qualification.

Like their fifteenth-century conciliarist predecessors, they emphatically denied that there was anything 'absolute' about the pope's jurisdictional power, or that the jurisdiction of bishops, rather than being itself of direct divine institution, was instead derived by delegation from his. Indeed, those divines who argued to the contrary Lingard denounced as being nothing better than 'sycophants', 'flatterers', 'leaden headed dunces'.[63]

Resonating, as they all clearly did, to the English constitutional tradition, the ecclesiological stance of these Cisalpines was an essentially constitutionalist one, and the government of the universal Church they saw, accordingly, as one limited by law.[64] If, as Berington readily confessed, the pope is by divine right and 'under Christ its founder' the 'head' or 'supreme head' of the Church, he also specified the limited nature of the powers attaching to that secondary leadership by describing the pontiff as 'the first ecclesiastical magistrate', 'the principal executive power', 'the head of . . . [the] . . . constitution'.[65] As he wrote in his later (and somewhat more radical) phase, '[I]t has pleased the community, for the sake of unity and good order', to surrender into his pontifical hands 'a limited superintendence'. But to him, none the less, 'belongs no *absolute* or despotic jurisdiction', and 'he is as much bound by the laws of the constitution as is the lowest member of it'.[66] It is hardly surprising, then, that the conciliarist tradition should have succeeded in drawing these Cisalpines into its enduring magnetic field. In Lingard and Butler especially, one encounters explicit endorsements of that tradition as it had been expressed at the Council of Constance and in the superiority decree *Haec sancta*. Thus, having first delineated the ecclesiological commitments which 'Transalpine' and Cisalpine' shared in common, Butler went on to discriminate the latter from the former as follows:

The Cisalpines affirm that in spirituals, the pope is subject in doctrine and discipline, to the church, and to a general council representing her; that he is subject to the canons of the church, and cannot, except in an extreme case, dispense with them; that, even in such a case, his dispensation is subject to the judgment of the

---

[63] Cited by Chinnici, *English Catholic Enlightenment*, 89–92, cf. 59–60; Berington, *State and Behaviour*, 152; Butler, *Historical Memoirs*, 37–8.

[64] On this see, with reference to Berington, Butler, and other Cisalpines, as well as to Lingard, the discussion in Chinnici, *English Catholic Enlightenment*, esp. 43–60.

[65] Berington, *State and Behaviour*, 3 and 152, where he adds that, like that of 'the first magistrate in every well-regulated state', it is the pope's 'duty to attend to the execution of ecclesiastical laws, and to take care that the Christian republic receive no injury'.

[66] Berington, *Reflections*, 69–70.

church, that the bishops derive their jurisdiction from God himself immediately, and not derivatively through the pope . . . They affirm [also], that a general council may, without, and even against the pope's consent, reform the Church. They deny his personal infallibility, and hold, that he may be deposed by the church, or a general council, for heresy or schism; and they admit, that in an extreme case, where there is a great division of opinion, an appeal lies from the pope to a future general council.[67]

Harmonics, if not direct echoes, of such views can be detected also in the fleeting affirmations of one of Berington's sympathizers abroad, none other than the robustly independent (and at least quasi-Gallican) John Carroll, bishop of Baltimore and the first Roman Catholic bishop to be appointed in the newly established United States of America.[68] And, Chinicci has insisted, such views were certainly not unusual at the time. But, in so doing, and contemporary accusations of Cisalpine dependence on Febronius and Ricci notwithstanding, he has also affirmed that the guiding inspiration for the Cisalpines was (rather) the Gallican ecclesiological tradition in general and the authority of Bishop Bossuet in particular[69]—the man whose biography Butler himself wrote, whose words he and Lingard cited, and whose role in the framing of the 1682 Declaration of the Gallican Clergy and of what came to be 'the Gallican orthodoxy' I shall address later on in this chapter. But that said, and with the Gallican tradition firmly in mind, we must return first to roots and to the great ideological upheaval of the early seventeenth century, but approaching it this time, not from the English side of the equation, but from the continental angle—Venetian no less than French.

[67] Butler, *Historical Memoirs*, 38. For Lingard's comparable affirmations, made with explicit reference to Constance, to the second Gallican article of 1682, and to Bishop Bossuet, see Chinicci, *English Catholic Enlightenment*, 90; cf. 59–60.

[68] Carroll had made extensive use of Berington's *State and Behaviour*. He wrote to the latter praising his stance on toleration and Church government and urging him to probe further in order to ascertain 'the boundaries of the spiritual jurisdiction of the Holy See'. For which, see P. Guilday, *The Life and Times of John Carroll* (New York: Encyclopedia Press, 1922), 129–30; J. T. Ellis, *Catholics in Colonial America* (Baltimore and Dublin: Hellicon, 1965), 418–19; J. Hennesey, *American Catholics* (New York and Oxford: OUP, 1981), 69–100. Hennesey notes (88 and 98) that the failure of Carroll's plans for a national church, 'in communion with the bishop and see of Rome but internally autonomous, self-perpetuating, and free from the last taint of foreign manipulation', did not preclude the lay trustees of Charleston and Norfolk from appealing in support of their claims to administrative independence to the authority of such conciliarist figures as Gerson, Sarpi, and even Febronius. For this last, see below, Ch. 5.

[69] Chinnici, *English Catholic Enlightenment*, 59–60, 93.

BELLARMINE, SARPI, AND RICHER

During the turmoil of the French Wars of Religion, ultramontane views had succeeded in colonizing even that erstwhile citadel of conciliarist doctrine, the Faculty of Theology at Paris. To that fact, the change in ecclesiological commitments of the Parisian theologian, Edmond Richer, bear ironic witness.[70] As late as 1592 he himself had been a supporter of the Catholic League, a staunch admirer of Bellarmine's writings, and a person of distinctly ultramontane sympathies. Within a few years, however, he was to shift his position and to become a defender of the rights of Henry IV.[71] Moreover, having combed the scriptures, the Church fathers, the histories of general councils, and the ecclesiological writings of his late medieval predecessors in the Faculty of Theology, he was eventually to modulate into a convinced, vigorous, and dogged proponent of 'a Gallicanism that reconciled the teachings of the councils of Constance and Basle with those of the theorists of the divine right of kings'.[72] While certainly making common cause with the *politique* Gallicans of the Parlement de Paris,[73] it was his great aim to reinvigorate the theological heart of the Gallican tradition by reviving and disseminating the knowledge of the old Parisian doctors, from John of Paris, via d'Ailly and Gerson, down to Almain and Mair, and by reinstating the conciliarist vision they all shared in common (that is, their endorsement of the strict conciliar theory) as the official ecclesiological doctrine of the Parisian Faculty of Theology.[74] Though it should be noted that for him, as for Almain and Mair a century earlier, but in this unlike the great Parisian conciliarists of the classical era, the oligarchic and reformist strands play no role. The entire focus, then, is on the third strand—the strict conciliar theory itself. And that was to set something of a pattern for much of the future.[75]

[70] For Richer's life and achievements the fullest treatment is still the old standard account by Puyol, *Edmond Richer* (Paris: Th. Olmer Librairie, 1876). See also E. Préclin, 'Edmond Richer (1559–1631)', *Revue d'histoire moderne*, 51 (1930), 241–9, 321–36; Monique Cottret, 'Edmond Richer (1559–1631): Le Politique et le sacré', in H. Méchoulan, ed., *L'État Baroque* (Paris: Librairie Philosophique J. Vrin, 1985), 159–77; Oakley, 'Bronze-Age Conciliarism'. For the general background, see Willaert, *Après le concile de Trente*, 363–407.

[71] Préclin, 'Edmond Richer', 243–4.

[72] Ibid. 251, 329–36. Cf. Cottret, 'Edmond Richer'.

[73] Who defended as ancient and imprescriptable the liberties of the Gallican church, and deployed the legal machinery at their disposal to preclude any intrusion by the Roman curia that they viewed as incompatible with those liberties. See Willaert, *Après le concile de Trente*, esp. 369–70 n. 2, for the various forms of Gallicanism current at the time.

[74] Préclin, 'Edmond Richer', 251–2, 326–8.

[75] For the three strands in question, see above, Ch. 2, and for the differences between the positions of Almain and Mair and those of their 15th-cent. predecessors, see Ch. 3.

To that end, and throughout his career, Richer drew repeated attention to the views of his Parisian predecessors and, by his editions and works of compilation, laboured assiduously to make their ecclesiological writings readily available to a broad public. The fruit of his most important editorial endeavour, an edition of Gerson's works, he published in 1606, a serendipitous moment in that it coincided with the onset of the era's great ideological upheaval. As the first complete edition of those works and one that contained also the critical conciliarist writings of d'Ailly, Almain, and Mair, it was to prove to be a very significant and influential publication. To that fact, as we have seen, Cardinal du Perron himself bore witness.[76] And around the same time, just when that edition had been completed, Richer himself was led by the crisis unfolding at Venice to frame his own first affirmation of the strict conciliar theory—in some respects a more coherent and powerful affirmation than that embedded in his later, much reprinted, much better known, and much more influential *Libellus de ecclesiastica et politica potestate* of 1611.

It was Bellarmine, in fact, who by vigorously asserting the papalist ecclesiology had stimulated that first affirmation of 1607. But the Bellarmine in question was not the great 'administrator of doctrine',[77] the systematic controversialist of the earlier *Disputationes de controversiis Christianae Fidei* who had moved firmly and serenely to nudge the conciliarist ecclesiological tradition into the outer darkness of heterodoxy as it was construed, at least, in Rome.[78] Instead, it was the harried (and sometimes confused) respondent to the war of words that the Venetian Republic had unleashed by way of self-defence after the proclamation of the papal interdict in 1606. The first blow struck in that war of words was the anonymous publication in Italian translation of two short Latin tracts of Gerson's which he had directed against the abuse of ecclesiastical censure. Their republication in the vernacular was, in fact, the work of Paolo Sarpi and it had drawn Bellarmine into the fray, eventuating in a tangled series of polemical exchanges between the two men in which (or so I would judge) Sarpi, a far less attractive figure than Bellarmine, may be said to have had the edge.[79]

---

[76] See above, Ch. 4 n. 43.

[77] Bouwsma, *Venice*, 297, is responsible for this felicitous designation.

[78] *Disputationes . . . de controversiis Christianae Fidei* constitute the first four tomes (in 5 vols.) of Bellarmine, *Opera omnia*. See ii, lib. 2: *De conciliorum auctoritate*, in *Opera omnia*, ii. 43–72 (esp. 63, where he notes that the ecumenicity of Lateran V was still in his day a matter of dispute among Catholics).

[79] For a more detailed examination of this revealing exchange, see Oakley, 'Complexities of Context'.

The tracts in question addressed the characteristically late medieval topos of the abuse of the power of excommunication. The second of them, *Esamine di quell'asserzione: Sententia pastoris, etiam injusta, timenda est,*[80] though it refers glancingly to the Council of Constance, makes no mention at all of the relative jurisdictional standing of council and pope. And if the first does so in its eighth *considerazione*—and does so, indeed, quite force-fully—it still devotes no more than a single, 150-word paragraph (about a tenth of the whole text)[81] to the matter. That this should be so is not alto-gether surprising, given the fact that both tracts had postdated the election of a pope of undoubted legitimacy and the ending, therefore, of the long agony of the Great Schism. They had been written, in effect, in April 1418, either during the very last days of the Council of Constance or in the days im-mediately subsequent to its dissolution.[82] If Gerson, in the first of them, had been moved to insist that it was heretical to deny the right of an appeal from pope to council, he had done so only in passing and in the context of speak-ing (ironically enough, and as Sarpi was quick to point out and Bellarmine was forced later to concede) 'in favor of the Apostolic See'.[83] But what little he had said was now enough to goad Bellarmine, hyper-sensitive to what he clearly intuited to be a continuing conciliarist threat, into condemning Ger-son's claim as 'manifestly erroneous' and denouncing the translator who had put it forward as pertinent to the present Venetian situation as having, by so doing, revealed himself to be 'not much of a Catholic' (*si dimostra poco Catholico*).[84] By so doing, and by devoting a full third of his critique of Ger-son's first tract to a refutation of the strict conciliar theory, Bellarmine in fact succeeded in promoting what it had clearly been his intention to de-flect: nothing less, that is, than the insertion of the old conciliarist claim into the growing body of publicistic literature now being generated by the Venetian interdict, and by that republic's effort to defend itself and to rally support for its cause not only at home but also in London and Paris.[85]

[80] Printed in Sarpi, *Opere*, ed. Busnelli and Gamberin, ii. 180–4. The original, *De sententia pastoris semper tenenda* is to be found in Gerson, *Œuvres*, ed. Glorieux, vi. 294–6.

[81] *Resoluzione circa la materia della scommuniche ed irregolarita*, in *Opere*, ed. Busnelli and Gambarin, ii. 175–9 (with the eighth consideration at 177–8). The original: *Resolutio circa materiam excommunicationem et irregularitaten* is to be found in Gerson, *Œuvres*, ed. Glorieux, vi. 294–6 (at 295).

[82] See Gerson, *Œuvres*, ed. Glorieux, i. 133 ('Essai biographique').

[83] Bellarmine (instinctively, it seems) had taken Gerson to be speaking, not of the height-ened danger attaching to the contempt for the power of the keys when that contempt was dir-ected *against* the pope, but rather when it sprang from the abuse of that power *by* the pope. For which, see Oakley, 'Complexities of Context', 382–3, 386.

[84] Bellarmine, *Risposta . . . ad un libretto intitulato Trattoto, e resolutione*, 71.

[85] Bellarmine, *Risposta alle oppositioni di Fra Paolo Servita*, printed with continuous

That Bellarmine's subsequent exchanges with Sarpi (and Richer's affiliated response) made abundantly clear. In Bellarmine's eyes, Gerson's greatest offence in the brief paragraph in question was that of having insisted that Constance had pronounced it heretical to deny the right of appeal from pope to council, and therefore, at least by implications the superiority of council to pope.[86] The superiority decree *Haec sancta*, Bellarmine argued, dated to a time when there was no unquestioned pope; it had not received papal approbation; it had no pertinence to anything but the remediation of the Great Schism itself. As a result, Pius II and Julius II (and subsequent popes in their annual reissue of the bull *In coena domini*) had imposed a sentence of excommunication on anyone appealing from pope to general council. Reason and the teaching of the scriptures both served to underline the 'manifestly erroneous' nature of Gerson's position. So, too, did the general councils of the Church. The Fifth Lateran Council, for example, had expressly affirmed in 1516 that the pope is above any council whatsoever. In any case (and with this Bellarmine steered his dialectical ship into what he obviously thought would be a welcoming harbour), 'the Holy Church is not like the Republic of Venice which can be said to be . . . above the prince'. 'Nor is it like a worldly kingdom', where the power of the monarch is derived from the people. Instead, it is 'a most perfect kingdom and an absolute monarchy, which depends not on the people . . . but on the divine will alone'.[87]

Thus Bellarmine in 1606, writing in his *Risposta . . . ad un libretto di Giovanni Gersone*, a work which in turn evoked two responses from Sarpi. In the first of these, the *Trattato del Interdetto*, while he was at pains to insist that the old question of the superiority of council to pope (or vice versa) had 'not yet been decided but remains in doubt in the Church of God',[88] he did so very much by way of conclusion to an examination of the limits of the obedience owed to ecclesiastical superiors in general, of the notion that not even the pope's powers were unlimited and absolute, of the

---

pagination and after the tract of the title in his *Risposta . . . al Trattato di i setti Theologi di Venetia sopra l'Interdetto*, 77; idem, *Risposta . . . ad un libretto intitulato Trattato, e resolutione*, 64–71. Cf. Oakley, 'Complexities of Context', 382–6.

[86] For what follows, see Bellarmine, *Risposta . . . ad un libretto intitulato Trattato, e resolutione*, 72–7.

[87] Ibid. 76.

[88] In support of this position he invoked the witness of John Mair as well as the fact that Bellarmine had himself conceded the ecumenical status of Lateran V to be in doubt among Catholics (on which, see above, n. 78). Paolo Sarpi, *Trattato del' Interdetto del Santita di Papa Paulo V*, in *Opere*, ed. Busnelli and Gambarin, iii. 3–41 (at 17–18). Though signed by seven Venetian churchmen the *Trattato* was, in fact, Sarpi's work.

possibility that popes might be wrong in particular legal judgements and might even fall into heresy.[89] But what was in the *Trattato* very much the conclusion of a long line of reasoning became in the second work, his *Apologia per le opposizioni fatte dall'illustrissimo . . . Signor cardinale Bellarminio*, nothing less than the point of departure for a lengthy exploration of conciliar history and conciliarist claims.[90] A full quarter of it, indeed, being devoted to a long rebuttal of Bellarmine's attack on Gerson's eighth *consideratio*, it clearly continued the process that Bellarmine had hoped to derail but had unwittingly succeeded in fuelling—namely, that of drawing to the attention of a new generation of Europeans the enduring presence in the Church of a strong tradition of conciliarist thinking. Similarly, Sarpi helped reacquaint contemporaries with the nature and history of that tradition and the degree to which it was grounded in modalities of Catholic ecclesiological thinking dating back to a very distant past.

The line of argument he pursues is long and sometimes convoluted, involving the chalking up of many a specific historical point—as, for example, when he needled Bellarmine by reminding him that there was little point in his flourishing the authority of the Fifth Lateran Council now to demonstrate the superiority of pope to council when he himself had earlier conceded the ecumenicity of that particular council still to be a matter in dispute among Catholics.[91] Or, again, when he issued a tart reminder to Bellarmine that his dismissal of the contemporary pertinence of Gerson's arguments (on the grounds that the latter had been writing at a time of schism when there were three claimants to the papal office) hardly held much water in view of the fact that Gerson had written the two works in question after the Council of Constance was over, and after Martin V had been accepted as the sole legitimate pope.[92] Nevertheless, there is nothing particularly complicated about Sarpi's basic tactical move in this work. It is simple enough and, in effect, two-pronged.

First, he insists that the arguments which Bellarmine had directed against Gerson's conciliarist commitments had already been assessed and rebutted, either by Gerson himself or by such subsequent and like-minded

[89] Sarpi, *Trattato del Interdetto*, in *Opere*, ed. Busnelli and Gambarin, iii. esp. 3–17.

[90] This work of Sarpi's runs to some 146 pp. in the Busnelli and Gambarin edition of the *Opere* (iii. 43–189), about 44 of them devoted to the conciliar issue. Its full title is: *Apologia per le oppozitione fatte dall' illustrissimo e reverendissimo Signor cardinale Bellarminio alli Trattati e Risoluzioni di Giovanni Gersone sopra la validità della scommuniche*. For its dating, see *Opere*, ed. Busnelli and Gambarin, iii. 284.

[91] Sarpi, *Apologia*, in *Opere*, ed. Busnelli and Gambarin, iii. 135, 146–69.

[92] Ibid. 171–3. He is commenting here on Bellarmine's response to the twelfth *consideratio* of Gerson's first tract in *Risposta . . . ad un libretto intitulato Trattato, e resolutione*, 80.

thinkers as Almain and Mair.[93] If he (Sarpi) was now reproducing these rebuttals (and he certainly was), it was 'solely to show that the question needed to be treated on more solid grounds, and that writers as outstanding in learning and piety [as were these conciliarists] were not so easily to be condemned'.[94]

Second, he also insists, not that Gerson was necessarily right in his affirmation of the jurisdictional superiority of council to pope, but rather that Bellarmine was certainly wrong in his stubborn refusal to acknowledge what John Mair, Melchior Cano, and so many other theologians of repute had persistently emphasized, namely, that the question of the relationship of pope to council had continued to be a matter of controversy, so that 'while in Rome it is not permitted to hold the doctrine of Panormitanus which maintained the superiority of the council, neither does the University of Paris tolerate the upholding of the contrary position'. 'For, surely, an opinion which enjoys the concurrence of as many famous scholars as may have held to the contrary, and which has the support of an equal, if not greater number of universities, regions, and kingdoms, can hardly be said to be proposed without reason or authority, still less audaciously.'[95]

None of which was destined, of course, to bring much cheer to Bellarmine, who felt compelled to return (somewhat wearily and testily) to the fray with responses both to the *Trattato* and to the *Apologia*. On those responses it is unnecessary to dwell,[96] beyond noting his blustering insistence (in the teeth of every evidence to the contrary) that there simply was not any doubt among Catholics about the superiority of pope to council, and that to dare to set the teachings of Constance and Basel against that of the Fifth Lateran Council and to suggest that legitimate general councils could actually disagree one with another smacked of nothing less than 'the reasoning of heretics'. If those who toyed with such noxious ideas were 'really Catholic teachers', they would finally recognize where true legitimacy resided, and realize that both Constance and Basel were of dubious legitimacy at the moment when they issued their superiority decrees. For (triumphantly now) 'legitimate general councils do not contradict one another, and that [council] alone is legitimate which has asserted the authority of the pope to be superior to all councils'.[97] This argument, its

---

[93] Sarpi, *Apologia*, in *Opere*, ed. Busnelli and Gambarin, iii. 120.

[94] Ibid. '. . . e non dannare con tanta facilità gli scrittori di eccelente santità e dottrina.'

[95] Sarpi, *Apologia*, in *Opere*, ed. Busnelli and Gambarin, iii. 117–18.

[96] See Oakley, 'Complexities of Context', 392–3.

[97] Bellarmine, *Risposta . . . al Trattato de i setti theologi di Venetia*, 22–8, concluding with the words: 'Et cosi non sono tra se contrarii, li Concilii legittimi, et quello solo è legitimo che afferma l'autorità del Papa essere superiore à tutti li concilii.'

elegant circularity notwithstanding, seems to have exercised in some theological circles an irresistible charm all the way down to the late twentieth century.[98]

Meanwhile, back in Paris, the Venetian ambassador Pietro Priuli reported in January 1607 that he had finally induced the 'principalissimo theologo' there to write in support of Venice. Though at the time he refused to acknowledge the fact, the person in question turns out to have been none other than Edmond Richer, and the work that resulted, the short *Apologia pro ecclesiae et concilii auctoritate*, was first printed in Italy in 1607. Published at that time in badly proof-read form, without author, publisher, or place of publication indicated, it was (and is) hard to find, did not enjoy in its own day a wide circulation, and, perhaps because of that, elicited no reply.[99] And yet, like Sarpi's *Apologia* (though far more blunt and forceful than that work) it was a direct response to Bellarmine's harsh attack on Gerson, and witnesses even more powerfully than Sarpi's controversialist writings to the damage Bellarmine had done to his own papalist cause by his disproportionate emphasis on the glancing conciliarist remarks in Gerson's first tract on excommunication. Anxious now to rebut Bellarmine's portrayal of Gerson's conciliarism as erroneous and evocative of contemporary heretical positions, Richer was moved to devote the bulk of his own *Apologia* to the Church's constitution in general and the central role of general councils in particular, turning only in the last three pages of a forty-eight page discourse to the matter of the abuse of the power of the keys which had, in fact, been Gerson's own topic and the reason, presumably, for Sarpi's having chosen to translate the two tracts in the first place.

Bellarmine's attack on Gerson had moved on two levels, the one theoretical, the other historical. Richer's reply is framed in similar fashion, though the theoretical aspect of his work is much more fully and coherently developed,[100] and he gives something of a dismissive backhand to Bellarmine's historical arguments. After all, he says, had Bellarmine read the final version of the superiority decree *Haec sancta*, which had been

---

[98] See below, Epilogue.

[99] The full title of the work is *Apologia pro ecclesiae et concilii auctoritate, adversus Joannis Gersonii doctoris christianissimi obtrectatores*. Richer was careful to dissociate his name from the work and refrained from republishing it. For its publishing history see Oakley, 'Bronze-Age Conciliarism', 76 n. 41.

[100] Bellarmine's argument 'della raggione' had involved little more than the insistence that the Church was 'not a kingdom of this world' or a polity comparable to the Republic of Venice, but was 'a most perfect kingdom and an absolute monarchy, which depends ... solely on the divine will'. See above, p. 162.

approved at the *fifth* general session at Constance (and not simply the earlier version approved at the fourth), he would have been forced to admit that it applied to *any* general council whatsoever, and not merely to pontiffs of dubious legitimacy but to those whose titles were wholly uncontested.[101] Moreover, tiresome wrangling about the ecumenicity of Constance, Basel, and Lateran V notwithstanding, if Bellarmine were correct in his imputation of heresy to Gerson's teaching on the superiority of council to pope, then what on earth, Richer wondered, was to be made of the similar teaching of those three great cardinals Pierre d'Ailly, Francesco Zabarella, and Nicholas of Cusa, or, for that matter, of the congruent views of such other distinguished conciliarists as Panormitanus, Almain, and Mair? Or what, indeed, of the posture of the Gallican church itself, which had 'always received and defended the teaching of Gerson as Catholic and orthodox?'[102] And, as if anticipating a responsive question as to why that was indeed the case, Richer sets forth the answer in the fifty-three axiomata that together constitute the heart of his *Apologia*.

Intended to prove that Gerson's conciliarist doctrine was 'altogether in conformity with natural, divine, and canon law',[103] and bolstered with invocations not only of Gerson's own writings but also of the conciliarist arguments of d'Ailly, Almain, Mair, and the divines of Paris in general, these axioms elaborate in somewhat fuller and more systematic fashion the core ecclesiological commitments that Richer was to incorporate a few years later in his far better known and/or notorious *Libellus de ecclesiastica et politica potestate*.[104] And in them, it should be noted, he gives even less salience than he was to do in that later work to the more 'democratic' or 'populist' notions that his critics were subsequently to identify with what came in the eighteenth century to be denounced as *richérisme*—identify, indeed, to such a degree as to blind them to the centrality to his thinking of his somewhat more traditional conciliarist commitments. The notions in question (no novelty in the fifteenth let alone the seventeenth century) pivot on the view that the *curés* or parochial clergy were, as successors of the seventy-two disciples of Christ, an integral part of the divinely established hierarchy of the Church, possessed, therefore, of their own

---

[101] Richer, *Apologia*, 11, 38–9. For the formation of the decree *Haec sancta* and the difference between the texts approved at the fourth and fifth sessions of the Council of Constance, see Alberigo, *Chiesa conciliare*, 165–86. See also above, Ch. 2.

[102] Richer, *Apologia*, 3.

[103] Ibid. 10.

[104] To which work, accordingly, I will give cross-references in what follows, using the version printed in Goldast, *Monarchia*, iii. 797–806.

jurisdictional powers and entitled accordingly to a say in the government of the Church.[105]

Stipulating, then, at the outset that absolute or despotic government (papal no less than secular) is repugnant to natural and divine law,[106] he goes on to insist (the best political regiment being monarchy tempered by aristocracy) that the universal Church is, accordingly, a monarchical polity instituted by Christ for a supernatural end and, via the instrumentality of the general council, participation in which is not limited to bishops alone, tempered in its government by an aristocratic element.[107] Its 'essential monarch', 'absolute' or 'essential head', being none other than Christ himself, Peter and his papal successors must properly be viewed as no more than 'mutable', 'secondary', 'ministerial', and 'accidental' heads.[108] Moreover, it is not on the pope but on the universal Church and the general council representing it that Christ, its founder and head, has directly conferred the infallible teaching power. Similarly, the Council of Constance, by decreeing that general councils should be assembled at regular and frequent intervals, has underlined the degree to which the Church's well-being depends on them.[109] Capable of performing every act of jurisdiction that the pope can,[110] and by virtue of the fact that it has its power immediately from Christ, the general council is 'superior to the pope in infallibility and authority', and is possessed also of the power of assembling itself without, and even in opposition to, the pope.[111] The right, then, of appeal from the judgement of the pope to that of a general council is not to be gainsaid. The council is undoubtedly empowered to correct a scandalous and incorrigible pope and to curb the abuse of the power of the keys—as, indeed, the Council of Constance had quintessentially demonstrated when it tried and deposed Pope John XXIII.[112]

---

[105] For some comments on which, see Oakley, 'Bronze-Age Conciliarism', 70–2. In Richer's own day, and sometimes, indeed, later on, his insistence on the divinely established and hierarchical status of the parish clergy was recognized for what it truly was—no bold novelty but the echoing of a theme prominent in the thinking of Gerson, and so long established in the latter's day that the novelty lay not in its affirmation but in the willingness of some members of the mendicant orders to deny it.

[106] Richer, *Apologia*, 14; *Libellus*, c. 9, in Goldast, *Monarchia*, iii. 802 (11–14).

[107] Richer, *Apologia*, 15, 20; cf. *Libellus*, cc. 3, 6, and 15, in Goldast, *Monarchia*, iii. 799 (18–22), 800 (16–18), 804 (58–62).

[108] *Apologia*, 17; cf. *Libellus*, cc. 1, 3, 4, and 15, in Goldast, *Monarchia*, iii. 758 (24–6), 799 (27–30, 33–8), 804 (49–51). And as such as Richer was later to argue (see below, p. 169) possessed of the power of jurisdiction in only a partial fashion.

[109] *Apologia*, 10–11, 32–3; cf. *Libellus*, cc. 5 and 8, in Goldast, *Monarchia*, iii. 800 (5–7), 801 (41–4).

[110] *Apologia*, 33.   [111] Ibid. 28, 31, 35–6.

[112] Ibid. 26–7, 34–6; cf. *Libellus*, cc. 7 and 16, in Goldast, *Monarchia*, iii. 801 (30–4), 85 (1–11).

Thus, with many an invocation of the deeds and decrees of Constance and Basel, and many a reference to 'the doctors of Paris' (Gerson, d'Ailly, Mair, and, above all, Almain), Richer laboured mightily to vindicate against Bellarmine the Catholicity of Gerson's advocacy of the strict conciliar theory. But Bellarmine, as he had ruefully acknowledged in the opening paragraph of the *Apologia*,[113] was by no means the only papalist to have impugned the orthodoxy of that most Christian teaching. A hundred years earlier, after all, during the crisis occasioned by the assembly of the *conciliabulum* of Pisa, Cajetan had done likewise. That duly noted, when he returned some years later to matters conciliar in his *Defensio libelli de ecclesiastica et politica potestate* (*c.*1622), Richer, while observing that Almain had swiftly risen to the defence of the Parisian ecclesiology against Cajetan's attack, noted also that Cajetan had returned to the fray in his *Apologia de comparata auctoritate papae et concilii* (1512) and that Almain's premature death in 1515 had prevented his responding to *that* work. That task, accordingly, Richer now undertook himself a full century later, boldy proclaiming, moreover, that he would respond further to *all* of Cajetan's arguments,[114] including those set forth in his *De comparatione auctoritatis papae et concilii* (1511), the work to which Almain had originally replied in his *Tractatus de auctoritate ecclesiae.*[115] It would doubtless be possible to argue about the quality of these responses—sometimes dogmatic, not infrequently condescending, occasionally bordering on outright abuse. But as Richer works his way remorselessly, first through the successive chapters of the *Apologia*, then those of the *De comparatione*, carefully summarizing Cajetan's arguments and then stating his own responses to them, a wearying measure of credibility comes to attach to his claim.

He divides his rebuttal into some seven *quaestiones*, on only the first of which will we need to dwell at any length. The other six questions constitute a sort of dialectical mopping-up operation designed to dispose of Cajetan's residual arguments, many of them drawn not from the *Apologia* but from his earlier *De comparatione*. The argumentation they contain is highly repetitive, circling back again and again to a handful of claims central to Richer's earliest formulations of his conciliarist commitments

---

[113] Richer, *Apologia*, 3.

[114] *Defensio*, lib. III, c. 3, 311. Richer devotes the whole of ch. 3 (311–40) to that refutation of Cajetan.

[115] Modern edited versions of both of Cajetan's works are to be found in Cajetan, *De comparatione auctoritatis papae et concilii*, ed. Pollet. The Latin text of Almain's *Tractatus de auctoritate ecclesiae* is most really available in Gerson, *Opera omnia*, ed. Dupin, ii. 976–1012. All three works are now conveniently available in English tr. in Burns and Izbicki, *Conciliarism*.

in 1607 and 1611: namely, that it is Christ himself who is the only 'internal and essential head' of the Church; that Peter was no more than an 'external, ministerial and mutable head' charged with the external work of hierarchical administration; that the same is true, accordingly, of his papal successors; that upon them, as upon other prelates taken individually, Christ conferred the keys (the power of jurisdiction) only 'partially', in so far as it pertains to 'use, exercise', and 'the execution of natural, divine, and canon law'. It was, rather, upon the sacerdotal Church as a whole that he conferred that jurisdictional power 'in its totality' and in 'the architectonic fashion that pertains to lordship and proprietary right'. That being so, it is of course 'the power of the pope [that] is subordinated to the power of the Church and the council, just as a part [is subordinated] to the whole, and not *vice versa*'.[116] This line of argument Richer bolsters with frequent appeals not only to the case he himself had made in 1607 in his *Apologia pro ecclesiae et concilii auctoritate*, or to such 'private doctors' as John of Paris, Gerson, Nicholas of Cusa, Almain, and Mair, but also to the historic decrees of Constance and Basel affirming the jurisdictional superiority of council to pope—decrees which, as he reminds us yet once more, 'the whole School of Paris' had long held and 'doggedly defended' as a tenet of the Catholic faith itself.[117]

But, then, it was precisely that traditional Parisian ecclesiology that Cajetan had set out to attack. He had done so, especially, in the first and most important chapter of his own *Apologia*, where he had gone to the very heart of the matter by challenging its claim to be grounded in the law of nature itself. Long ago, in advancing his classic argument that conciliarist thinking had played an important role in the history of late medieval and early modern political and constitutional thinking, John Neville Figgis argued that the crucial move made by the conciliarist thinkers was that of having treated 'the Church definitively as one of a class, political societies'.[118] That some (though by no means all)[119] of them were led, as a result, to ground their case in the mandates of the natural law itself was only to be expected. That move was certainly characteristic of such great Parisian theologians as d'Ailly and Gerson at the time of the Council of Constance. A century later, as Burns and Skinner have emphasized, it was

---

[116] Richer, *Defensio*, lib. III, c. 3, qu. 3, 6, and 7, 321, 334–5, 337, 339; cf. qu. 1 and 2, 313, 314, 317, 319. The words quoted occur (in order) at 335, 321, 339, and 317.

[117] Ibid., qu. 7, 337–9; cf. qu. 5 and 6, 332 and 335.

[118] Figgis, *Political Thought*, 56.

[119] For the differences among conciliar thinkers in this respect, see Oakley 'Natural Law', and above, Ch. 2.

characteristic also of their sixteenth-century Parisian successors, Almain and Mair.[120] Had that not been the case, indeed, the willingness of Calvinist monarchomachs in the sixteenth century and English parliamentarians in the seventeenth to deploy conciliarist ideas in an attempt to bolster their own constitutionalist claims to a right of resistance against tyrannous monarchs would have been totally inconceivable.[121]

As we have seen,[122] Almain had been particularly forceful in this respect, and despite an opening bow in his *Tractatus de auctoritate papae et concilii* in the direction of acknowledging the features that serve to distinguish the universal Church from secular political societies, he had come close (like Mair, his former teacher) to treating the ecclesiastical and secular polities univocally. In his *De comparatione auctoritatis papae et concilii*, Cajetan had employed language that could be taken to suggest a degree of compatibility with that approach, and by the time he came in 1512 to respond to Almain's treatise he may conceivably have felt a bit rueful about the degree of ideological overlap that others might thereby assume.[123] Whatever the case, he certainly chose, in his *Apologia*, to try to blunt the force of Almain's argument from natural law.

A century later, when forced to confront the similar challenge posed by Paolo Sarpi's invocation of secular political analogies, Bellarmine (as we have seen) was to content himself with a firm insistence on the *supernatural* grounding of ecclesiastical power: 'The Holy Church', he was to insist, is 'a most perfect kingdom and absolute monarchy, which [unlike worldly monarchies] depends not on the people but on the divine will alone.'[124] Cajetan's response, on the contrary, while more complex and scholastically sophisticated, was somewhat less robust. Unlike Bellarmine, he chose not to contrast supernature with nature, but to try to operate within the orbit of the argument from natural law which his conciliarist

---

[120] Burns, '*Politia regalis et optima*'; idem, '*Jus gladii* and *jurisdictio*'; idem, 'Scholasticism: Survival and Revival', in Burns and Goldie, *Cambridge History*, 132–55; idem, *Lordship, Kingship, and Empire*, 124–5. Skinner, *Foundations*, ii, chs. 2, 4, and 9; idem, 'Origins of the Calvinist Theory of Revolution', in Malament, *After the Reformation*.

[121] See below, Ch. 6.   [122] Above, Ch. 3.

[123] This Katherine Elliott van Liere has suggested in her stimulating analysis, 'Vitoria, Cajetan, and the Conciliarists', *Journal of the History of Ideas*, 58 (1997), 597–616 (at 605): 'Jacques Almain's reply to Cajetan', she says, forced the latter 'to confront the paradox that his own arguments shared some fundamental presuppositions with the radical conciliarists. Cajetan had unwittingly played into the conciliarists' hands by using language that was comprehensible only if one imagined the Church as being in some sense analogous to a secular monarchy.' Cf. T. M. Izbicki, 'Cajetan's Attack on Parallels between Church and State', *Cristianesimo nella Storia*, 20 (1999), 80–9.

[124] See above, p. 162.

opponent had pursued. He did so by insisting that 'the nature of government' had to be considered at a level deeper than the one to which Almain had penetrated. Government, he said, 'takes different forms according to the *source* of its nature' (italics mine). It being (as is the case with other things) 'the natural propagation of a government' that reveals 'the nature of the thing produced', it should be recognized that 'the Church derives the first principle of [its] origin, perfection and power, not from individuals or the community but from the head who shares its nature, Jesus Christ'. 'So far', then, 'as the right of ruling' is concerned, the Church is not 'a free community' like more ordinary political communities. Hence, and 'as a consequence of natural law', it is for Christ, the natural head and 'prince' of the ecclesiastical community, and not for the community itself 'to provide for a vicar'. So that that vicar, who is none other than the pope, draws his authority *naturally* 'not from that community but from Jesus Christ', and 'the [alleged] foundation from natural law for the Church's power over the pope' is altogether 'rooted up'.[125]

To this rather indirect line of argument, Richer's response, in turn, is nothing if not blunt in its confident reaffirmation of the direct pertinence to ecclesiological discourse of secular political analogies. Cajetan, he concedes, was correct in his insistence on the importance of focusing on the very nature of any governmental regime and, accordingly, 'on the essential causes of its institution'. But 'with respect both to its nature and its exercise', the papal primacy 'is clearly a moral and political entity, not something metaphysical'. Disputation concerning its institution, then, should be pursued in moral and political terms not in terms of scholastic metaphysics, and certainly not in terms of the vain cavillings and sophistic subtleties favoured by Cajetan.[126] That said, it is easy enough to recognize that the papal primacy is something altogether different from any absolute monarchy. If it is, indeed, of divine institution, so too is the Church's aristocratic form of government. Neither can be abrogated by the other, but it has to be recognized that the aristocratic government of the Church can in practice *limit* the exercise and execution of the primacy. For just as the kingdom of Poland confers authority on someone by electing him as king, so too does the Church when it chooses someone as pope, for it is the Church as a totality which possesses ecclesiastical authority architectonically and,

---

[125] Cajetan, *Apologia de comparata auctoritate papae et concilii*, c. 1, ed. Pollet, 204–7. My quotations in most cases follow the English tr. in Burns and Izbicki, *Conciliarism*, 201–84 (at 202–5).

[126] Richer, *Defensio*, lib. III, c. 3, qu. 1, 312.

as it were, by proprietary right. Far from being irrelevant to ecclesiological discourse, then, such arguments drawn from the analogy of political bodies are to be regarded as entirely apposite to the matter at hand.[127]

Of course, when he made that case in the 1620s, writing in one of the many works of compilation or controversy that he cautiously refrained from publishing during his lifetime, Richer was addressing himself to an imagined Gallican posterity. By that time, that was all that in prudence he could do. He had been forced out of his position as syndic of the Sorbonne because the views he had expressed in his *Libellus* of 1611 had proved too bitter a pill for the papal nuncio, such leading French churchmen as the Cardinal du Perron, and even some of his own theological colleagues to swallow. However conciliarist the ecclesiology embedded in the species of Gallicanism later to be espoused by the Parisian theologians and enshrined in what came to be referred to as 'the maxims of Paris' or 'the doctrine of the School of Paris', during the earlier part of the seventeenth century,[128] at least, papal influence in France was at something of a high point and the doctors of the Sorbonnne were by no means united in their adhesion to those maxims. That the writings of even so moderate a papalist as Richer's determined opponent, André Duval (d. 1638), make perfectly clear.[129] Still less were they united in their willingness to frame those maxims unambiguously, and to do so with authority, clarity, and force. Unity and consistency on that matter were not a secure legacy from the past, but a gradually won achievement of the future. Precisely because of that, and in relation to the salience of conciliarist constitutionalism in the ecclesiology of the eighteenth- and nineteenth-century Gallican church, a very considerable importance attaches to that church's official endorsement of the conciliarist ecclesiology embedded in the 1682 Declaration of the Gallican Clergy, as also to Bishop Bossuet's great defence of that solemn declaration—both of which together constitute the third great relay-station transmitting the conciliarist signal forward to future generations.

---

[127] Richer, *Defensio*, lib. III, c. 3, qu. 1, 313–14.

[128] Willaert (*Après le concile de Trente*, 394) claims indeed that '1614/15 marks the apogee of papal influence in France under the Old Regime'.

[129] Duval, while refraining from any explicit condemnation of the traditional Parisian adhesion to conciliarist views, did not himself hesitate to affirm the personal infallibility of the pope. See Martimort, *Le Gallicanisme de Bossuet*, 31; Louis Cognet in W. Müller *et al.*, *The Church in the Age of Absolutism and Enlightenment* (New York: Crossroad, 1981), 60–1; Préclin, 'Edmond Richer'.

BOSSUET, TOURNÉLY, AND THE GALLICAN ORTHODOXY

It is true that anti-curial ideas cognate to those espoused by the political, if not necessarily the theological, Gallicans, were prevalent not only in Venice, but in the Kingdom of Naples and Sicily too, as also, for that matter, in Spain itself. And a form of pragmatic episcopalism which was yet to find any explicit doctrinal expression was firmly rooted in the German empire.[130] But given 'the capital role played by the French church in the history of the post-Tridentine church' at large,[131] a particular importance attaches to the crystallization across the first half of the century of an ecclesiological stance deemed henceforth as proper to France. A similar importance attaches to the energy invested in the task of putting 'in order the archives of Gallicanism',[132] as well as to the further dissemination of the fifteenth- and sixteenth-century Parisian conciliarist writings occasioned by the publication in the latter half of the century of the works of compilation which Richer had produced in the last years of his life.[133] Already in the 1630s, in pursuit of his own complex ends and his dream of engineering the creation of a semi-independent 'patriarchate of the Gauls', Richelieu had exploited the traditional Gallican reservations about any too robust an exercise of the papal jurisdictional power and had facilitated, accordingly, the publication of explicitly Gallican writings.[134] And with the death of Mazarin and the onset in 1661 of Louis XIV's period of absolute personal rule, the royal court came close to adopting as its own the tenets of theological Gallicanism. With Louis XIV, in effect, and as it has more than once been claimed, Gallicanism came to occupy the throne.[135]

In the more bracing ecclesiological atmosphere that ensued, and provoked by an unambiguous flicker of ultramontane sympathy on the part of several regular clerics defending theological theses at Paris, the Faculty

[130] Following here the discussion of Willaert, *Après le concile de Trente*, 367–424, which hinges on the premiss (367–8): 'On représente parfois le gallicanisme comme un mouvement né en France et qui se serait communiqué aux pays voisins... Mais... il s'agit d'éruptions diverses d'une même lave souterraine. L'anti-romanisme et un phénome européen, des causes semblables produisant des effets semblables.' Cf. Louis Cognet in Müller *et al.*, *Age of Absolutism*, 57–65. Martin, *Les Origines du Gallicanisme*, esp. ii. 325–39, takes a very different tack.

[131] Willaert, *Après le concile de Trente*, 367.

[132] Thus Martimort, *Le Gallicanisme*, 77–8.

[133] For descriptions of these works and a publication history, see the 'Notice bibliographique sur les œuvres de Richer', in Puyol, *Richer*, ii. 419–33.

[134] Martimort, *Le Gallicanisme de Bossuet*, 116–25; Willaert, *Après le concile de Trente*, 400–7; Louis Cognet, in Müller *et al.*, *Age of Absolutism*, 61–5.

[135] Willaert, *Après le concile de Trente*, 406. Louis Cognet, in Müller *et al.*, *Age of Absolutism*, 65, notes that 'a revival of Gallican ideas can be perceived from the very beginning of the grand monarch's absolute rule'.

of Theology there was moved in 1663 to issue a declaration of six articles, the first four of which (three of them reflecting positions hammered out already in 1611 and 1614) affirmed that the king had no superior save God alone, repudiated accordingly any claim of the pope to possess over the king any authority in temporal matters, rejected any possibility that subjects of the king could be dispensed from the fidelity and obedience they owed him, and asserted the traditional liberties from papal intrusion in the affairs of the Gallican church. In the final two articles, which were the ambivalent product of difficult debates within the faculty, it was asserted 'that is was *not* the doctrine of the Faculty that the pope was above the ecumenical council', and 'that it was *not* the doctrine nor a dogma of the Faculty that the pope's doctrinal teachings were infallible, absent the consent of the Church'.[136] If the former reflects a distinct retreat from the forthrightness of earlier, unambiguously conciliarist affirmations, the latter marks the first time that the faculty had officially declared itself on the subject of papal infallibility. As a whole, moreover, the six articles represented 'the first great synthesis of Gallicanism',[137] and one which provided a foundation for the propositions promulgated some nineteen years later in the form of an official Declaration of the French Clergy.

When it came to that formal declaration, the work of representatives of the French clergy gathered together in a quasi-national assembly (1681–2) at the behest of the royal administration, while the six articles of 1663 did indeed serve for them as a model, the degree of expository timidity evident in the merely negative formulation of the last two articles gave way to a forthrightness that admitted of little ambiguity. The context was the protracted (and, in the end, inconclusive clash) between pope and king that precipitated, before it ended, yet another appeal from the judgement of the pope to that of a future general council. That clash was occasioned by Louis XIV's determination to extend the regalian rights conceded by the Concordat of 1516 to parts of his kingdom which they had previously not affected, as well as to monasteries and no less than sixty bishoprics hitherto, for one reason or another, exempted.[138] As early as 1673 he had

---

[136] For the incidents of 1663 see Martimort, *Le Gallicanisme de Bossuet*, 216–36 (233–5 for the text of the six articles). Shorter accounts in Martimort, *Le Gallicanisme*, 79–82; Louis Cognet, in Müller *et al.*, *Age of Absolutism*, 65–70.

[137] Thus Martimort, *Le Gallicanisme*, 82.

[138] 'This presupposed a broadening of the right of regalia, the spiritual regalia which enabled the King to fill the benefices of a bishop while the bishopric was vacant, and the secular regalia enabling the King to gain the possession of the income of vacant bishoprics.' Thus Louis Cognet, in Müller *et al.*, *Age of Absolutism*, 67; Martimort, *Le Gallicanisme de Bossuet*, 361–442.

moved to make that extension of his rights official, but, in the wake of the election of Pope Innocent XI in 1676 he had found himself forced into the position of having to vindicate those rights in the teeth of stubborn papal opposition. The convocation for October 1681, then, of a quite extraordinary 'general assembly of the clergy of France' was a policy move designed to bring pressure to bear on the pope. And the central involvement in the work of that assembly of the much-admired Jacques-Bénigne Bossuet (1627–1704), bishop of Meaux, former tutor of the Dauphin, and, in intellectual circles certainly, the leading light of the leading national church of Latin Catholic Christendom, did much to ensure its enduring celebrity.[139]

Having delivered at the assembly a much-admired, learned, and essentially conciliatory opening sermon on the mystery of the Church, one that somehow managed to combine with a recognizably sincere veneration for the Roman primacy the called-for measure of episcopalist firmness, he was inevitably drawn into the complex and delicate diplomatic manœuvres that occupied the assembly during the winter months of 1681–2. Having sought, with only partial success, to induce his episcopal colleagues to adopt a conciliatory stance *vis-à-vis* the papal position, he found himself in the end charged with the task of redrafting the four articles that were to make up the historic declaration of 19 March 1682. And though he framed them with characteristic judiciousness, eschewing the jargon of the scholastic theologians and favouring the more capacious Latin of the Church fathers, the message those articles conveyed was clear, unambiguous, and historic in the force of its impact on generations to come. In so far as civil or temporal matters were concerned, and in line with the first three articles of 1663, the autonomy and independence of kings and sovereigns was asserted—thus Article One. So far as spiritual jurisdiction was concerned, the pope's authority was declared to be limited by the canons of the Church—thus Article Three, a modified version of the fourth article of 1663. Similarly, his decisions on matters of faith, however important, were stated to be irreformable only if they enjoyed the concurrence of the Church—thus Article Four. Finally—Article Two—the general council was in effect declared to be superior in authority to the pope.

For our purposes, the critical article is the second, which addressed the

---

[139] For a recent biographical appraisal of Bossuet and his historical significance, see Mayer, *Die Welt*. For his place in the history of Gallicanism, Martimort's lengthy and detailed *Le Gallicanisme de Bossuet* is the standard work. J. Orcibal, *Louis XIV contre Innocent XI* (Paris: J. Vrin, 1949), focuses specifically on the great clash of the 1680s and early 1690s. Briefer accounts in Martimort, *Le Gallicanisme*, 82–103, and Louis Cognet in Müller *et al.*, *Age of Absolutism*, 65–70. Cf. Costigan, 'Bossuet and the Consensus of the Church', *Theological Studies*, 56 (1995), 652–72.

conciliar issue.[140] It did so in moderate fashion. That is to say, it affirmed the papal plenitude of power provided that it was understood in accordance with the decrees which the Council of Constance had approved in its fourth and fifth sessions (the reference, of course, is to the successive versions of the superiority decree, *Haec sancta*). Those decrees, it said, had been confirmed 'by the usage of the Roman pontiffs and of the entire Church, and observed with reverence down through time by the Gallican church'. It affirmed that those decrees remained in force, and it rejected the opinion of those who sought to weaken them by impugning their authority, by saying that they were never officially approved, or by claiming that they pertained only to the time of the schism. What was involved, then, was basically a reaffirmation of the strict conciliar theory in the form hammered out by such as Gerson, d'Ailly, and Zabarella—in so far, at least, as that position had found expression in the version of the decree *Haec sancta* that had been approved at the fifth session.

In his *Defense of the Declaration*, the lengthiest of all his writings, which Bossuet wrote at the king's behest and which was eventually to command so attentive a readership and to exert so marked an influence that both were to reach well beyond the borders of France itself,[141] he repeatedly

---

[140]   The articles were written in Latin. For a French tr. see Dupin, *Histoire ecclésiastique*, iii. 533–56. This tr. is reproduced (with some corrections and along with the original Latin text) in Martimort, *Le Gallicanisme de Bossuet*, 461–75. The second (conciliarist) article (466 n. 2) goes as follows: 'Sic autem inesse Apostolicae Sedi ac Petri successoribus Christi vicariis rerum spiritualium plenam potestatem, ut simul valeant atque immota consistant sanctae oecumenicae Synodi Constantiensis a Sede Apostolica comprobata, ipsoque Romanorum pontificum ac totius ecclesiae usu confirmata, atque ab ecclesia Gallicana perpetua religione custodita decreta de auctoritate conciliorum generalium, quae sessione quarta et quinta continentur; nec probari a Gallicana ecclesia qui eorum decretorum quasi dubiae sint auctoritatis ac minus approbata, robur infringant, aut ad solum schismatis tempus Concilii dicta detorqueant.' When commenting on this article in 1953 (*Le Gallicanisme de Bossuet*, 466–9), Martimort implied that its careful wording precluded any explicit affirmation of conciliar superiority. When, twenty years later, he returned to the issue (*Le Gallicanisme*, 95), he conceded, however, that 'si les décrets de Constance ont une portée qui ne se limite pas au temps du schisme, c'est équivalement d'affirmer, sans la nommer, la superiorité des conciles sur le pape'.

[141]   The *Defensio Declarationis Conventus Cleri Gallicani A. D. 1682: De ecclesiastica potestate* occupies, with its *Appendix*, some 1243 pp. spread across vols. xxi and xxii of the *Œuvres complètes de Bossuet*, ed. Lachat. It is prefaced (xxi. 5–129) by Bossuet's *Gallia Orthodoxa sive Vindiciae Scholae Parisiensis totiusque Cleri Gallicani: Praevia et theologica dissertatio*, a product of his subsequent efforts to revise the manuscript of the original work. Bossuet had finished that manuscript by 1685, but, at that time, the king's wish to come to an accommodation with the papacy precluded its publication and it was not to appear in print during Bossuet's lifetime. In 1730 and 1745, respectively, Latin and French versions were printed in Amsterdam and it was frequently republished thereafter. Martimort, *Le Gallicanisme de Bossuet*, 549–96, 655–78, devotes several (not altogether uncritical) chapters to the original work and Bossuet's revisions. For the exceedingly difficult questions involved in establishing a definitive text of

deployed the prestige attaching to the names of those great conciliarists (as well as to those of Nicholas of Cusa, Denys the Carthusian, Panormitanus, Almain, and Mair),[142] in an effort to vindicate against ultramontane sniping the ecumenicity of Constance from the time of its first assembly to that of its dissolution, as also the orthodoxy and enduring validity, therefore, of its superiority decree *Haec sancta*, which, he argued, Martin V had himself confirmed.[143] That decree, he emphasized, was restrained and tightly focused in its formulations; it envisaged no routine, day-to-day assertion of conciliar supremacy in the governance of the universal Church but, as Mair had pointed out, an extraordinary superiority *casualiter* in precise cases.[144] When properly (and precisely) understood, then, the decree could be seen as constituting no novelty but as standing in direct continuity with the characteristically patristic intuition that the Church was, in its innermost essence, collegial.[145] Certainly, the doctrine of *Haec sancta*, unquestionably reaffirmed by the Council of Basel, had been the constant teaching of the school of Paris from that time onwards (here he evokes the witness of Almain, Mair, and Francisco de Vitoria). Indeed, it had been taught also beyond the borders of France by individual doctors and schools of theology right across Europe from Louvain to Cracow, and Vienna to Erfurt.[146] Moreover, if one were to reject that teaching one would find oneself in the uncomfortable position, after all, of having to call into question the very legitimacy of Martin V's election, with all that that would entail.[147]

Not exactly a happy thought. But if, in his firm endorsement of *Haec sancta*, Bossuet aligned himself with the conciliarists of the classical era and their silver-age successors, it should be noted that in three respects he also parted company from them, as also from Richer, whom he touched

the *Defensio* and for the differences in the structure and organization of the various editions of that work, see Martimort, *L'Établissement du texte de la Defensio*.

[142] *Defensio*, pars II, lib. 5, c. 6 (xxi. 562–5); *App*. III, lib. 1, cc. 5–10 (xxii. 476–96); *Praevia dissertatio*, c. 13 (xxi. 20–3).

[143] *Defensio*, pars II, lib. 5, cc. 13–29 (xxi. 587–631).

[144] *Defensio*, *App*. I, lib. 1, c. 17 (xxii. 523–4).

[145] *Defensio*, pars III, lib. 7, c. 5 (xxii. 7–9); lib. 10, c. 2 (xxii. 260–3). Cf. *App*. I, lib. I, cc. 8 and 10 (xxii. 488–92, 495–6).

[146] *Defensio*, *App*. I, lib. 1, c. 8 (xxii. 489–92); *Praevia diss.*, c. 13 (xxi. 20–3); *App*. III, c. 1 (xxii. 568–73). Also *Defensio*, pars II, lib. 6, c. 22 (xxi. 737–40).

[147] *Defensio*, pars II, lib. 6, c. 19 (xxi. 727–30). See esp. xxi. 729 where he says: 'Atque illud quidem Constantiense decretum est ejusmodi, ut ab eo caetera tanta concilii acta pendeant. Hinc Viclefi de primatu Romanae Ecclesiae error condemnatus: hinc destituti Pontifices, etiamsi qui a synodo totaque fere christiano orbe colebatur; hinc alter substitutus, eique creando forma praescripta.' Cf. Martimort, *Le Gallicanisme de Bossuet*, 593.

upon but briefly and with a distinct measure of chill reserve.[148] First, he is manifestly uneasy with the characteristically conciliarist practice of under-standing the Church on the analogy of the secular political organism.[149] Second, he is firmly episcopalist and unsympathetic with any classical or Richerist willingness to admit the lower clergy or laity to any deliberative voice in a general council.[150] Third, while *Haec sancta* is at the centre of his conciliar thinking, its companion Constance decree *Frequens*, which had sought to make general councils a regular and reformative part of the governance of the universal Church, is not. This is not altogether surprising. For Bossuet, general councils were to be no more in fact than extraordinary occurrences in the life of the Church. While necessary, they were for him only *relatively* necessary. So far as matters doctrinal were concerned, the extra-conciliar definitions of the episcopate dispersed throughout the world retained the infallibility attaching in his view to conciliar definitions themselves—so long, that is, as those bishops were morally united in those definitions with the determinative voice of their great fellow bishop, the pope.[151] In this respect, Bossuet reflects at once the depth of his veneration for the papal primacy and the strength of his countervailing (and essentially episcopalist) determination to vindicate the dignity of the episcopal order in the teeth of the overweening claims to jurisdictional superiority advanced by the denizens of the Roman curia. In this respect, too, the fourth Gallican article, with its insistence that the pope's judgements on matters of faith were not irreformable, absent the consent of the universal Church, emerges as really as central to Bossuet's commitments as was the second, and conciliarist, article.

That said, and notwithstanding Louis XIV's later change of direction, ambivalent settlement in 1693 with the new pope, and half-hearted promise to that pope to render moot for the future the Declaration of 1682 itself, it remains the case that the conciliarist constitutionalism stemming from the classical era drew renewed vigour from this whole episode. In 1706 the patristic scholar Louis Ellies Dupin made access to the classic

---

[148] *Defensio*, pars II, lib. 6, cc. 24–5 (xxi. 743–8).

[149] *Defensio*, pars III, lib. 8, c. 15 (xxii. 141): 'Demonstrandum enim erat, ecclesiasticam monarchiam, sub Christo praecipuo Monarcha constitutam, ad formam monarchiae saecu-laris penitus institutam esse; quod est falsissimum: id, inquam, Scripturis et traditione demonstrandum, non ex proprio cerebro, vanisque ratiocinationibus christianae reipub-licae forma effligenda erat.' Cf. R. Duchon, 'De Bossuet à Febronius', *Revue d'histoire ecclé-siastique*, 65 (1970), 380–1; Martimort, *Le Gallicanisme de Bossuet*, 552.

[150] *Defensio*, *Praevia diss.*, c. 76 (xxi. 97–100); pars III, lib. 8, c. 14 (xxii. 136–9). Cf. Marti-mort, *Le Gallicanisme de Bossuet*, 552–3.

[151] *Defensio*, pars III, lib. 7, c. 1 (xxii. 1–2). Cf. ibid., *App.* III, lib. 3, c. 2 (xxii. 574–6); Duchon, 'De Bossuet', 382–3, 406.

conciliarist writings easier than it had been by publishing a new edition of Jean Gerson's complete works and by including in it an even broader array of other conciliarist writings from the fourteenth, fifteenth, and sixteenth centuries than had Richer in his less complete 1606 edition.[152] A year later, moreover, in his *Traité de la puissance ecclésiastique*, a lengthy commentary on the Declaration of 1682, Dupin echoed the traditional mantra that the University of Paris had always held 'as a fundamental point of its ecclesiastical discipline' that the general council is superior in authority to the pope, and supported his case with a veritable battery of references to the works of d'Ailly and Gerson.[153]

Dupin himself was somewhat Jansenist in his inclinations. By and large, however, in the struggle over royal regalian claims the Jansenists had not chosen to side with the king against the pope. It should be noted, then, that as the century wore on, and even when they turned for support to the Gallican ecclesiological tradition, not all those of Jansenist sympathies were inclined to make much of the Four Articles of 1682. Dale Van Kley, indeed, has been at pains to emphasize that in the writings of such as Vivien de la Borde and Nicholas le Gros at the start of the eighteenth century, as well as those of Gabriel-Nicholas Maultrot and Claude Mey in mid-century, it was 'the . . . more radical scholastic conciliarism of Almain, Gerson, Major [Mair]' that was evoked, rather than 'the royal and episcopal Gallicanism of the Declaration of 1682' which had 'temporarily eclipsed' it.[154]

None the less, among those less heterodox in their sympathies, the conciliarist ecclesiology—so far, at least, as it had been enshrined in the superiority decrees of Constance and Basel—was destined from 1682 onwards to enjoy a novel status. Having been endorsed officially by the leadership of the French church, it now came to be taught in the nation's seminaries and theological schools and to constitute in the eighteenth century the orthodox Gallican norm in matters ecclesiological. Bossuet's great *Defense* of the 1682 Declaration, finally published in 1730 and 1745 in successive Latin and French editions, came also to constitute the very *summa* of the Gallican orthodoxy.[155] Similarly, the *Praelectiones theologicae* of Honoré Tournely

---

[152] Joannis Gersonii, *Opera omnia*, ed. L. E. Dupin, 5 vols. (Antwerp, 1706).

[153] Dupin, *Traité de la puissance*, 372–542 (esp. 441, 443, 450, 475–6, 487, and 537).

[154] D. K. Van Kley, *The Religious Origins of the French Revolution* (New Haven and London: Yale University Press, 1996), 79–80, 195–6. For the tangled story of Jansenist ecclesiological commitments and their intermittent and shifting relationship with traditionally Gallican positions, see Préclin, *Les Jansenistes du XVIIIe siècle*, who distinguishes no less than four different phases of ideological affiliation during this period.

[155] Martimort, *Le Gallicanisme*, 100, dubs it 'la somme la plus complète du gallicanisme'.

(d. 1729), which appeared in multiple volumes and successive editions from 1725 to 1739 and was later abridged for widespread use in the seminaries of France, served for the rest of the century to frame the theological formation of a goodly part of the French priesthood and to mediate that orthodoxy to them.[156] Tournély was a firm supporter of the controversial papal bull *Unigenitus* (1714) that had cut so undiscriminating a swathe through the thicket of Jansenist, quasi-Jansenist, and supposedly Jansenist views which by the early eighteenth century had come to flourish so luxuriantly on French soil.[157] At the same time, he was also one of the most important and effective disseminators of that moderate Gallican ecclesiology to which Bossuet had lent his formidable reputation and in which the conciliarist form of ecclesiastical constitutionalism was so firmly embedded.

In the republic of Venice, Tournély says, and by way of characteristic affirmation, 'the doge is superior to each individual magistrate and each individual member of the senate'. None the less, it remains true that 'he is inferior to and subject to the republic as a whole'.[158] So, too, is it with the universal Church. If its constitution is indeed monarchical 'in that councils are not always assembled while there is always [present] a supreme pontiff' who is charged with its 'common, ordinary, and habitual governance', there is nothing absolute about the monarchical authority. For 'the supreme, primary and infallible authority of ruling' resides in 'the universal Church alone, whether dispersed or united [in a general council]'.[159] Its monarchical element, then, is tempered by the aristocracy of the bishops who, no less than their papal head, derive their jurisdictional power immediately from Christ.[160] From the New Testament itself we learn that the authority of the apostolic college was exercised even over Peter,[161] and the episcopal successors to the members of that apostolic college stand in a similar relation to Peter's papal successors. To that fact,

---

[156] *Praelectiones theologicae quas in scholis sorbonicis habuit Honoratus Tournély*, published at Paris in 16 vols. (1725–30). The section pertinent to ecclesiology is *Praelectiones Theologicae de Ecclesia Christi quas in Scholis Sorbonicis habuit*. In his lengthy article on Gallicanism in the *Dict. de théol. catholique*, vi (Ie partie): 1096–1137, M. Dubruel summarizes its contents (at 1097–1103) and labels it as 'le résumé des doctrines alors professés par le clergé gallican'. For the Gallican nature of the textbooks used in the French seminaries, see J. McManners, *Church and State in Eighteenth-Century France* (Oxford: Clarendon Press, 1998), i. 205–6. And for the vogue of Tournély's work at the 'grands séminaires' of France right up to the eve of the Revolution, see Dégart, *Histoire*, ii. 250–75.

[157] J. Hild, *Honoré Tournély* (Freiburg: Herder, 1911), esp. 116–33. For the *Praelectiones theologicae*, see 157–66.

[158] Tournély, *Praelectiones*, ii. 294–5.

[159] Ibid. i. 554; cf. 566–72.

[160] Ibid. i. 543–4.

[161] Ibid. ii. 296–7.

across the course of time, the general councils of the Church have borne eloquent witness, no less by their actions than by their doctrinal affirmations. Constance, for example, not only stood in judgement over the rival papal claimants of the day but also deposed two of them. Further than that, it also formally proclaimed in the decree *Haec sancta* the subjection of the pope to conciliar jurisdiction and correction. In so doing, moreover, it was legislating in a way that looked beyond the immediate crisis circumstances of the day to the ongoing faith and future reform of the Church. Against the force of that decree, reiterated after all by the Council of Basel prior to the date of its (legitimate) dissolution and reaffirmed in 1682 by the Declaration of the Gallican Clergy, one can adduce the authority of no subsequent council of indubitable ecumenicity.[162]

And so on. To Tournély's Gallican orthodoxy, certainly, and, beyond it, to the older reaches of the conciliarist tradition, Henri Maret, titular bishop of Sura, was to recur a century and more later when, in 1869, he submitted as a preparatory memorandum to the Vatican Council then impending his own two-volume *Du concile général*.[163] That commonly overlooked work (the fruit of a decade's labour) amounted to nothing less than a calmly lucid attempt to vindicate once more, and against the increasingly aggressive high papalists of the day, Bossuet's reaffirmation of the dignity of the episcopal order, his insistence on the continuing validity of the superiority decree *Haec sancta*, his concomitant reiteration of the essentially constitutionalist understanding of the Church's government that went with it, and his carefully modulated responsiveness to the ecclesiological witness rendered by the theological tradition which had endured at Paris now for no less than half a millennium.

---

[162] Ibid. ii. 296–308. He cites (301–2) both the version of *Haec sancta* approved at the fourth session of the Constance and that approved at the fifth. And, in rejecting attempts to limit its reach to the emergency conditions of that time, he emphasizes that in its final version it referred not only to its own mandates but to those *cujuscunque alterius concilii generalis legitime congregati*.

[163] See below, Ch. 5.

5

De Maistre's Denial: Febronius, De Maistre, Maret, and the Triumph of Ultramontanism

The doctrine of the ultramontanes concerning the infallibility of the Roman Pontiff is not recognized by the other Catholic churches, nor does it have any practical utility.

(Febronius, 1763[1])

Infallibility in the spiritual order and sovereignty in the temporal are two words perfectly synonymous. Both express that high power which dominates all the others and from which they all stem, which governs and is not governed, which judges and is not judged.

(Joseph de Maistre, 1819[2])

We seek the true relations of the general council with the pope. It has seemed to us that they were demonstrated in a very clear and certain fashion in the fourth and fifth sessions of the Council of Constance. In conformity with the practice of [previous] general councils, with the teaching of the greatest popes and with the public law of the Church, these decrees [successive versions of *Haec sancta*] contain a constitutional law which regulates in authentic fashion the relation of general council to Sovereign Pontiff.

(Henri Maret, 1869[3])

Little name recognition attaches today to Johann Nikolaus von Hontheim, and even the evocation of the pseudonym 'Justinus Febronius', behind which, in his own day he tried unsuccessfully to hide, is unlikely to elicit all that many spontaneous confessions of comfortable familiarity

---

[1] Febronius, *De Statu Ecclesiae* (Stuttgart, 1765), c. 1, § x, p. 82.
[2] J. de Maistre, *Du pape*, bk. 1, ch. 1, ed. J. Lovie and J. Chetail (Geneva: Librairie Droz, 1966), 27.
[3] H. Maret, *Du concile général* (Paris: Henri Plon, 1869), i. 466.

either with the man himself or with his work. An unexceptionable figure for most of his comparatively uneventful life, he attained sudden notoriety only in his latter years, exerted (as we shall see) a very potent influence during the closing decades of the eighteenth century, but slipped over the course of the next hundred years into the unhappy role of an author whose fate it was to be more often denounced than read, the heedless begetter (it was alleged) of yet another deplorable 'ism',[4] not much more, in some ways, than a caricature useful for frightening the children. With the lapse of a further century and more, his name recognition has ceased to be such as even to sustain that stereotypical role, and interest in him has come to be confined to a somewhat isolated and dwindling group of historical specialists. Before focusing, then, on what exactly it was that he had to say, it will be necessary to draw him out from the historiographic shadows, to give some feel for the context in which his ideas came to flourish, and, having earlier focused attention largely on developments in France, Italy, England, and Scotland, to try to catch at least a glimpse of the ecclesiological landscape characteristic of the Habsburg territories and, more generally, of the Holy Roman Empire.[5]

EPISCOPALISM, FEBRONIUS, AND REFORM CATHOLICISM IN
THE GERMAN TERRITORIES

Born in 1701, student of canon law at Louvain under Bernhard van Espen (d. 1728—famously Gallican and Jansenist in his sympathies), and later, as auxiliary bishop of Trier, close associate of Georg Christoph Neller (d. 1783) who taught canonistics there and who was likewise markedly

---

[4] Along with 'gallicanisme', 'richérisme', 'multitudinisme', 'presbytérianisme', 'parochisme', and so on—all of them vigorously flourished by Puyol in his *Edmond Richer* (1876), a work quite explicitly shaped by what the author took to be the doctrinal implications of the 1870 decree on papal infallibility.

[5] Because of their authorship by Heribert Raab, who wrote so much on the topic, a considerable value attaches to the pertinent chapters (18 and 23) in Müller *et al.*, *Age of Absolutism*, 329–42, 443–89. See also Raab, *Die Concordata Nationis Germanicae* (Wiesbaden: F. Steiner, 1956); O. Chadwick, *The Popes and European Revolution* (Oxford: Clarendon Press, 1981), 391–444; D. Beales, *Joseph II* (Cambridge: CUP, 1987–9), i. 439–79; F. Vigener, 'Gallikanismus und episkopalistische Strömungen', *Historische Zeitschrift*, 111 (1913), 495–558. There is a useful survey of the shifting scholarly approaches to the Catholic Enlightenment and Reform Catholicism in Elizabeth Kovács, 'Katholische Aufklärung und Josephinismus: Neue Forschungen und Fragestellungen', in H. Klueting *et al.*, *Katholische Aufklärung* (Hamburg: Meiner, 1993), 245–59. See also Timothy Hochstrasser, 'Cardinal Migazzi and Reform Catholicism in the Eighteenth-Century Habsburg Monarchy', in R. Robertson and J. Beniston, eds., *Catholicism and Austrian Culture* (Edinburgh: Edinburgh University Press, 1999), 16–31.

responsive to the Gallican authors, Febronius' claim to fame springs from the fact that in 1763 he published a Latin best-seller.[6] It was a book that created something of a sensation, first in Germany and then, having been placed on the Index of Prohibited Books within a year and (one is tempted to say 'therefore') translated into German, French, Italian, Spanish, and Portuguese, went on then to create a similar sensation throughout Latin Christendom at large. Its title was *De statu ecclesiae et de potestate legitima Romani pontificis*—or, in full, *On the Constitution of the Church and the Legitimate Power of the Pope, a Book Composed for the Purpose of Reuniting in Religion Separated Christians.*[7] Sprinkled with a veritable embarrassment of quotation marks, it is essentially a work of learned compilation, though one punctuated, from time to time, by arresting moments of pungent proclamation. It is swollen with long extracts from Augustine, Cyprian, and Bossuet, from the *acta* of the ecumenical councils (especially Constance and Basel), from such prominent conciliarists of the classical era as Pierre d'Ailly, Jean Gerson, Francesco Zabarella, Nicholas of Cusa, Andrew of Escobar, the younger Aeneas Sylvius Piccolomini, and Denys the Carthusian, as well as from Jacques Almain and Honoré Tournély later on. And anyone venturing forth on this vast ocean of quotation must make something of an effort of the historical imagination, I suspect, in order to grasp why on earth a book of this sort could have had so wide an appeal to contemporaries or exerted so powerful an influence on those who followed immediately thereafter.

The explanation for that appeal and influence is, I believe, threefold. First, what the book had to say on a theoretical level turns out to have been in fundamental harmony with long-established episcopal practice and persistent clerical aspiration within the German imperial church. Second, so far as German 'episcopalism' is concerned, it clearly spoke to a pressing ideological need. Third, in a part of Europe troubled and fragmented by competing confessional allegiances long since locked into recalcitrant

---

[6] For Febronius himself see the comparatively recent biography by V. Pitzer, *Justinus Febronius* (Göttingen: Vandenhoeck & Ruprecht, 1976) and, for Febronius' ideas and the Febronian controversy, R. Duchon, 'De Bossuet à Febronius', *Revue d'histoire ecclésiastique*, 65 (1970), 375–422, and H. Raab, 'Episcopalism in the Church of the Empire', in Müller *et al.*, *Age of Absolutism*, 443–69. Also, Schneider, *Konziliarismus*, 69–80; and Chadwick, *Popes and Revolution*, 408–11. For Van Espen, Neller, and Febronius, see G. Leclerc, *Zeger-Bernard van Espen* (Zürich: Pas Verlag, 1964), esp. 196–208; Raab, 'Georg Christophe Neller und Febronius', *Archiv für mittelrheinische Kirchengeschichte*, 11 (1957), 185–206; and Vigener, 'Gallikanismus'.

[7] Febronius, *De Statu Ecclesiae et legitima potestate Romani Pontificis* (1765). This was the first part of a multi-volume set published between 1765 and 1773, the other volumes containing subsequent apologetic tracts vindicating the original work.

patterns of mutual alienation, it voiced an encouragingly irenic hope that an affirmation of regional autonomy, an emphasis on conciliar self-governance, and a concomitant de-emphasis on the exercise of centralized papal jurisdiction might, in the long run, facilitate the ecumenical goal of reuniting the whole of Christendom around a common religious allegiance.

In the fifteenth century, and the victory of the papacy over the Council of Basel notwithstanding, conciliarist commitments had been widespread in Germany.[8] But, given the dominating position attained by the Jesuits during the following century in the territories that remained Catholic, conciliarism as such does not appear to have retained any continuity of allegiance across the turbulent years of Protestant Reformation, Catholic Renewal, and Counter-Reformation. What did, however, persist across that period and on into subsequent years was a form of practical or *de facto* episcopalism. Just as Gallicanism in France had taken its stand on positions crystallized during the phase of weakened papal jurisdiction characteristic of the latter years of the Council of Basel, so, too, the more loose-limbed episcopalism of the German imperial church. In the case of the former, the Pragmatic Sanction of Bourges which, in 1438, had unilaterally endorsed the conciliarist superiority principle and much of the reforming legislation of Basel, provided a crucial grounding and persistent rallying point for those anxious to impose limits on the jurisdictional powers wielded by the Roman curia in France. In the case of the latter, the contemporaneous *Acceptatio* of Mainz (1439) did something similar—as also did the jurisdictionally compromising 'concordats of the German nation' which Pope Eugenius IV had seen fit to conclude during his frantic diplomatic campaign to deprive of secular support his conciliarist opponents at Basel.[9] On that basis (and recurring especially to the 1448 Concordat of Vienna), the bishops of the imperial church, and especially the great elector-bishops of Cologne, Trier, and Mainz, had persistently striven to defend against the supple (and sometimes not so supple) manœuvrings of the papal nuncios and the persistent intrusions of the papal curia such 'liberties of the German nation' as the right of cathedral chapters to elect their own bishops or the right of bishops to appoint to benefices. On that

[8] See above, Ch. 2.

[9] See above, Ch. 1; Vigener, 'Gallikanismus', 495–513. In the later 1750s attention had been drawn to the Mainz 'acceptance' of the Basel reforming decrees. In 1763 the text of the *Acceptatio* was printed for the first time and 'immediately became the charter of German episcopalism', and viewed henceforth as 'its basic law and program'—thus H. Raab, in Müller *et al.*, *Age of Absolutism*, 444 and 457; Raab, *Concordata*, 125–33. See also for the events culminating in the *Acceptatio* and the Concordat of Vienna, Stieber, *Eugenius IV*, esp. 158–73, 276–322.

basis, in effect, they may be said to have worked in general to achieve for Germany the much-envied degree of independence from Rome that the firm exercise of royal power had been able long since to secure for France and Spain.[10]

German imperial episcopalism, however, tended to be essentially pragmatic in nature; it lacked, that is to say, the extensive canonistic and theological foundations that the Gallicans had long since established in France. Not until the early eighteenth century, in fact, did it begin to acquire a supportive and unifying ideology, and then only as Gallican ideas began to make their way into Germany on the heels of an ascendant French culture. Propagated notably by the canonists Van Espen at Louvain, Neller at Trier, and Johann Kasper Barthel (d. 1761) at Würzburg,[11] the characteristically Gallican insistence on drawing its ecclesiological norms from the conditions prevailing in the early Church picked up an additional charge from the growing sophistication of historical studies and the maturing tradition of historical criticism. The latter brought with it the characteristically Gallican insistence on distinguishing in relation to the papal primacy what was essential and of divine institution from what was historically contingent, merely accessory, and the product of the simple accretion of time. It brought with it also the liberating message that the overweening claims currently being made for the reach of papal authority represented a far cry from the type of primacy accorded to Rome during the first eight centuries—during the period, that is, prior to the surfacing of the historic collection of forgeries now known as the Pseudo-Isidorean Decretals. For it was the Decretals that had come to furnish the papal ideologists with so beguiling a basis for their assertion of sweeping claims to a monarchical authority at once both absolute and universal.

Such ideas readily linked with and suggested mechanisms of practical support for the tradition of Reform Catholicism that we now know to have been gathering strength in mid-century, drawing particular inspiration from the efforts of Ludovico Antonio Muratori (d. 1750) to 'recover the basic purity of the Christianity of the Apostles and Church Fathers and reclaim the Church from the excesses of Baroque piety'.[12] That tradition

[10] It had even been rumoured that at the Imperial Diet held at Regensberg in 1663 an attempt would be made to institute a German patriarchate in order to introduce into Germany the norms and practices of the Gallican church. See H. Raab, in Müller *et al., Age of Absolutism*, 446–7.

[11] Vigener, 'Gallikanismus', esp. 520–9. For Barthel and the episcopalism of the Barthel (or Würzburg) school, see Raab, *Concordata*, 79–96.

[12] Thus Hochstrasser, 'Cardinal Migazzi and Reform Catholicism', in Robertson and Beniston, *Catholicism*, 391–407.

helped shape the reforms undertaken already in Austria during the reign of Maria Theresa (1740–80). It stimulated the participation in the work of reform of a man like Christoph Anton Migazzi, cardinal-archibishop of Vienna (d. 1803), in the years before the turn to a more rigorously 'statist' mode of reform in the 1760s transformed him into a stern opponent of the government's ecclesiastical policies. Moreover, even during the latter 'Josephinist' stage, historians are now inclined to argue that 'many of the state's aims in the field, and many of [the Emperor Josephy II's] . . . own, breathed the effort of Reform Catholicism and Catholic Enlightenment'.[13]

All such ideas and tendencies converged on and were indeed reflected in Febronius' massive work. There they were wedded to a genuine yearning for the unity of all German Christians, an ecumenical hope that a return to earlier Christian roots and a reform of the Church's constitution in such a way as to engineer a moderating of papal claims might smooth the way to the eventual attainment of that goal. There they were wedded also to a degree of deference to temporal rulers as divinely instituted guardians of the Church's well-being in such a way as to render the whole package very attractive to the imperial chancellor Prince von Kaunitz and to the Emperor Joseph II himself, architects both—or, better, elaborators—of the so-called Josephinist Austrian state-church system which, at its most 'statist' moments, based its reforming make-over of the Church in the Austrian territories not on powers technically conceded by papal privilege but more directly on the overriding sovereign power of the state. Because of this latter affinity, and because for the past century and more it has been Febronius' fate to be so little read, there has been something of a tendency among commentators to reduce what in the nineteenth century came to be called 'Febronianism' to the status of just one more aspect of what came also to be called 'Josephinism'.[14] But such an exercise in interpretative

[13] Beales, *Joseph II*, i. 479, for a description of the type of reform pursued in the late 18th and 19th cents. by what he prefers to call 'Enlightenment Catholicism', and for the degree to which its ultimate failure was to be determined by the absence of any structural reform in Church government of the sort advocated in the 15th century and, again, by Febronius in the 18th. See L. Swidler, *Aufklärung Catholicism* (Missoula: Scholars Press, 1978).

[14] Beales, *Joseph II*, i. 8 and 439, proffers the following description of 'Josephism' (or 'Josephinism'): 'a movement for change named after Joseph, "Joseph[in]ism", affecting many aspects of life, but especially associated with claims made and measures taken by the state to control and reform the Roman Catholic Church within its borders, invoking not only obviously ecclesiastical matters like the exclusion of papal bulls, the dissolution of the monasteries and the introduction of religious toleration but also wider issues such as the reform of education in all its aspects, the liberalization of censorship and the reorganization of poor relief'. At the end of his balanced and judicious discussion of the phenomenom (i. 439–79), Beales parts company with earlier scholars who had been prone to portraying the entire reforming effort of the period as nothing more (or other) than statist in its inspiration.

concision does less than justice to Febronius himself and to his earnest attempt to chart a complex middle ground between statist and papalist positions respectively, between, that is, an ecclesiological stance in harmony with a state established or controlled church system and one supportive of a system firmly subordinated to a centralized Roman jurisdictional authority.

We have seen that the theological version of Gallicanism (if not necessarily its political or judicial forms) had sought a comparable *via media*,[15] and its ideas had come to be disseminated in Germany during the first half of the eighteenth century, most energetically by the Würzburg school of canonists. Prominent among those who favoured such ideas were Van Espen of Louvain, Febronius' former teacher, and his friend at Trier, Georg Christoph Neller. Though the compilatory nature of the work has made it difficult to resolve the question in satisfactory fashion, Neller may well in fact have been Febronius' direct collaborator in the composition of the *De statu ecclesiae*.[16] But whether or not he was, Gallican ideas are certainly interwoven into the very fabric of the book and Gallican authors heavily invoked—not only the older 'divines of Paris' but also Bossuet himself, whom Febronius cites more frequently (forty-one times) than any author other than St Augustine (sixty-four times). And the Bossuet in question is almost exclusively the Bossuet of the *Defense of the Declaration of the Gallican Clergy of 1682*, the original Latin version of which had appeared in print for the first time in 1730, with a French translation following in 1745.[17]

That being so, one might expect to encounter in Febronius' book an echoing endorsement and enthusiastic dissemination of Bossuet's Gallican views. And in many ways, indeed, that is precisely what one does find.[18] Thus, in their efforts to vindicate what they believe to be the essential constitution of the universal Church, both men turn away from the abstractions of scholastic analysis to the concrete message conveyed by scripture, tradition, and history—especially the history of the early centuries before the Hildebrandine revolution, and the canonistic and curial elaboration of the ideology and jurisdictional machinery underpinning

---

[15] See above, Chs. 3 and 4.

[16] See Raab, 'Neller und Febronius', 185–206 (esp. 199–202), for Neller, Hontheim, and the authorship of the *De Statu Ecclesiae*. Cf. Pitzer, *Justinus Febronius*, 19–20, 146 n. 42.

[17] Duchon, 'De Bossuet', 377.

[18] For Bossuet's position, see above, Ch. 4, and, for a careful comparison of the ideas of the two men, see Duchon, 'De Bossuet'. (Note that Duchon's references are to the original 1730 edn. of the *Defensio*, in which the sequencing and numbering of the constituent books—and some chapters—differ significantly from that in the more readily accessible version printed in the standard Lachat edn. of the *Œuvres de Bossuet*.)

absolutist papal claims to universal monarchy. In scripture and tradition, that is to say, both men find clear confirmation of the papal claim to a divinely conferred primacy in the universal Church,[19] but it is nevertheless a Church, they both insist, that cannot be understood in terms of the profane categories proper to merely secular politics. For these are alien to the more appropriate (and profoundly scriptural) understanding of the Church as a mysterious community of salvation, the mystical body of Christ, the communion of saints, the very *sponsus Christi* or bride of Christ. Unless one has specifically in mind the kingship of Christ himself, to such a body the very notion of monarchy is alien.[20] No such monarchy, certainly, was conferred on Peter, let alone on his papal successors, nor any prerogative of personal infallibility. It was upon the Church itself, and not Peter alone, that Christ conferred the power of the keys. And it is the general council, not the pope, that most truly represents that Church. In that general council, which receives its powers directly from Christ, the bishops participating do so not as mere counsellors to the pope, but as his fellow bishops and, indeed, as co-judges with him of the matter at hand. As the Councils of Constance and Basel made totally clear in decrees which are in harmony with the Church's enduring tradition and which enjoy right down to the present a continuing validity, it is the general council which, under God, possessed the ultimate authority in the Church. That authority is superior to that of any Christian, the pope himself included, for the council can limit him in the exercise of his power, can judge him for the abuse of power, and can if need be depose him for the good of the Church.[21]

And so on. The overlap in the *De statu ecclesiae* with the position Bossuet had sought in his *Defensio* to vindicate is extensive, the tribute paid to his authority effusive, and the impetus given to the further dissemination of Gallican ideas in the German-speaking world beyond the borders of Francophonia accordingly strong. But Febronius is more—or other—than some sort of Bossuet 'look-alike', and one has to be sensitive to the fact that he sometimes hides behind the prestige of Bossuet in order to advance positions that are different from, perhaps more radical than,

---

[19] Febronius, *De Statu Ecclesiae*, c. 1, § 1, pp. 1–12; c. 2, § 1, pp. 89–95. Bossuet, *Defensio*, pars II, lib. 5, c. 1 (xxi. 548–50); lib. 6, c. 26 (xxi. 748–83). Cf. Duchon, 'De Bossuet'; Martimort, *Le Gallicanisme de Bossuet*, 549–50.

[20] Febronius, *De Statu Ecclesiae*, c. 1, § 1, p. 9, § 4, p. 24, § 8, pp. 56–7; c. 2, § 12, pp. 155–6. Duchon, 'De Bossuet', 380–1, Martimort, *Le Gallicanisme de Bossuet*, 552.

[21] Febronius, *De Statu Ecclesiae*, c. 3, § 1, pp. 157–62; c. 6, pp. 357–533 (good summary at §§ 1 and 2, pp. 357–77. For Bossuet, see above, Ch. 4, and Martimort, *Le Gallicanisme de Bossuet*, 553–60, for what he labels as Bossuet's 'rehabilitation théologique de l'episcopat'.

those espoused by his great mentor,[22] and closer, in fact, to those advanced
by the great conciliar thinkers of the fifteenth century. Of these, four
should be emphasized.

First, and as their differing titles perhaps suggest, Febronius' *De statu
ecclesiae* focuses more sharply and more exclusively upon the internal
constitution of the Church than does Bossuet's *Defensio*. The latter work
had emerged, after all, as had the four Gallican articles themselves, in the
context of a great crisis in church–state relations, and it is to such matters
that the *Defensio* (written at the command of Louis XIV)[23] is primarily devoted. Febronius, on the other hand, pauses only occasionally to address
issues pertaining to the relationship between the two powers, temporal
and spiritual. His goal, rather, in the *De statu ecclesiae* is 'to lead the eighteenth-century Church back to the [ecclesiological] principles which had
been those of the reforming councils of Constance and Basel in the first
half of the fifteenth century', to restore, in effect, a past which he hoped
would lead almost spontaneously to the reconciliation of all Christians
around a papal office 'reformed authentically' along scriptural lines.[24] His
focus, then, is very much on the pope–bishop or, better, pope–council relationship. Febronius is, if you wish, more obsessively conciliarist than
was Bossuet, and Duchon is very much on frequency when he refers to the
latter as 'the French episcopalist' but to the former as 'the episcopalist-
conciliarist'. The chapter devoted to general councils takes up, indeed, almost a quarter of the entire *De statu ecclesiae* and, put together with the
chapter on the episcopal office, more than a third.[25]

Second, impressed as he was by the distorting impact of the Pseudo-
Isidorean Decretals over the centuries on the constitution of the Church.[26]
Febronius was more insistent than Bossuet had been on the stringency
of the limits within which papal power should properly operate. Whereas
Bossuet, while he sought means to guarantee the free initiative of the episcopal corps and to put obstacles in the way of any arbitrary curial interference, was notably respectful of the papal primacy and perfectly willing (in
accord with the second Gallican article) to concede to the pope a plenitude

---

[22] In this respect, as Duchon currently observes ('De Bossuet', 421), close attention has to
be paid to *De Statu Ecclesiae*, c. 6, § 8 (pp. 413–35). It constitutes, he insists, 'la partie la plus
inattendue et la plus originale du *Febronius*'.

[23] See above, Ch. 4; Martimort, *Le Gallicanisme de Bossuet*, 361–563.

[24] Duchon, 'De Bossuet', 378.

[25] Ibid. 442. The crucial 'conciliarist-episcopalist' chapters of the *De Statu Ecclesiae* are
cc. 6 and 7, pp. 357–635.

[26] See e.g. *De Statu Ecclesiae*, c. 1, § 8, p. 60; c. 3, § 9, pp. 198–207; c. 8, §§ 2 and 4, pp. 641–7
and pp. 650–6.

of power,[27] Febronius, in discussing the matter, betrayed much greater reserve.[28] For him the pope is but first among the ministers who are called upon to exercise the power of the keys which Christ conferred upon his Church.[29] As 'guardian and protector' of the canons he is charged to secure their faithful observance throughout the universal Church.[30] He is basically, in effect, the focus of that church's unity (*centrum unitatis*), charged, when general councils are not assembled, with the responsibility for taking thought for the common good of all the churches.[31] Only in that sense can he be said to be 'universal bishop', and neither that title nor those of 'head of the church' or 'vicar of Christ' should be taken to imply any 'universal monarchy' or 'absolute superiority'.[32] The fuller authority he possesses does not extend to the exercise over the individual churches of any *jurisdiction*, properly so-called.[33] For his rule or pre-eminence (*principatus*) in the universal Church is not so much one of jurisdiction as one of order and association (*consociatio*) or unity.[34] And it was while it had continued to respect these original conditions (as it did for the first eight centuries) that the papal primacy had best served the overriding goal of unity.[35]

Third, along with that diminished sense of the legitimate reach of papal power went, in Febronius, a concurrently greater emphasis on the importance, indeed centrality, of the general council's constitutional role in the continuing governance of the universal Church. For Bossuet, it may be recalled, general councils were only *relatively* necessary. They pertained, not to the day-to-day government of the Church under ordinary conditions, but, rather, to extraordinary situations. Even in doctrinal matters, the definitions of the pope, so long as the bishops dispersed around the world were morally united with them, possessed for him the same infallibility as that attaching to their solemn definitions when assembled together in a general council.[36]

In none of this, however, did Febronius concur. At one with Bossuet in vindicating the legitimacy and continuing validity of the Constance

---

[27] Bossuet, *Defensio*, pars II, lib. 5, c. 1 (xxi. 548–50); lib. 6, c. 26 (xxi. 753); lib. 11, c. 1 (xxii. 359–60). Cf. Martimort, *Le Gallicanisme de Bossuet*, 549–55, and 392–427 for Bossuet's famous sermon on the unity of the Church, delivered on 9 Nov. 1681.

[28] Febronius, *De Statu Ecclesiae*, c. 3, § 1, pp. 157–62, §§ 9, 10, and 11, pp. 198–223.

[29] Ibid., c. 1, § 6, p. 32.   [30] Ibid., c. 2, §§ 7–10, pp. 119–46.

[31] *De Statu Ecclesiae*, c. 2, §§ 5 and 11, pp. 109–11, 144–51.

[32] Ibid., c. 3, §§ 1 and 6, pp. 157–62, 176–86; c. 2, § 11, pp. 144–51.

[33] Ibid., c. 5, § 4, pp. 297–314.   [34] Ibid., c. 2, § 11, pp. 144–51.

[35] Ibid., c. 2, § 12, pp. 152–6.

[36] Bossuet, *Defensio*, App. lib. III, c. 1 and 9 (xxii. 568–73, 586–90); App. lib. I, c. 17 (xxii. 521–6). Cf. Duchon, 'De Bossuet', 409–10; Martimort, *Le Gallicanisme de Bossuet*, 558–61.

superiority decree *Haec sancta*, he went beyond him in insisting also (and consistently) on the continuing validity of the related decree *Frequens* providing for the regular and frequent assembly of general councils. For him, that is to say, such councils were an absolutely necessary continuing component of the Church's ordinary governance. Moreover, 'the nature . . . of authority in the church' being for him 'essentially collegial', he insisted accordingly that doctrinal truth would be discerned and defined only in 'episcopal assembly' which will express—and here he looked back to the conciliarists of the classical era, still more, perhaps, to Richer—the consent, tacit or diffused or both, of the entire *congregatio fidelium*.[37] It was only, after all (and here he invoked the words of Zabarella and went on to cite *Frequens*), when popes had begun to behave more like temporal princes than apostles that the ancient practice of assembling councils to deal with difficult matters had been allowed to lapse, and with what disastrous consequences for the health of the universal Church.[38] All of which points, of course—and this is the fourth factor differentiating him from Bossuet—to Febronius' deep-seated preoccupation with the reform of the Church in head and members, his endorsement, in effect, of the oldest strand in conciliarist thinking, and his concomitant alignment with the conviction which had inspired *Frequens*. Namely, that it was only by making regularly assembled general councils an integral part of the Church's ongoing governance that such a reform could be achieved.[39]

The weight of historical learning that Febronius was able to deploy, and the degree to which he succeeded in presenting in summary form what so many of his contemporaries apparently wanted to hear, has led one historian to label his *De statu ecclesiae* as 'the most significant work of anti-curial opposition in Germany' prior to the notorious 'Janus' articles which the Munich church historian Ignaz von Döllinger was to publish over a century later on the very eve of the First Vatican Council.[40] Certainly, the nature of the book's impact in the quarter-century after its publication is not in doubt. The sheer number of theologians (more than twenty) who rushed to refute it testifies to the seriousness with which it was taken and the widespread apprehension in pro-curialist circles about the damaging nature of the influence it could well be expected to exert. That fear was not

[37] Febronius, *De Statu Ecclesiae*, c. 6, § 7, pp. 404–13; § 8, esp. pp. 413–15, 429–30. Cf. Duchon, 'De Bossuet', 409–10, (the words cited are his).

[38] Febronius, *De Statu Ecclesiae*, c. 6, § 8, p. 407.

[39] See e.g. ibid., c. 6, § 12, pp. 455–65; §§ 14 and 15, pp. 482–508.

[40] Thus Schneider, *Konziliarismus*, 69. The reference is to Ignaz von Döllinger's *The Church and the Council*, published as by 'Janus.'

misplaced. What Febronius had in fact done, it has rightly been observed, was to restart 'the old argument, once so hotly fought at the time of the great schism in the papacy but since the Reformation almost confined [in the Catholic world at least] to France and Belgium and Venice about the place of the Pope in the constitution of the Catholic Church'.[41] In the latter half of the century there was a rapid increase in the incidence of conflict between the German bishops and the Roman curia, and, therefore, of friction with the papal nunciatures. Those conflicts culminated in the so-called 'Punctuation of Ems' (1786), when the representatives of the German archbishops, having assembled in conference, committed themselves to what Klaus Schatz has described as 'the last great uprising of the German prince-bishops against Rome'.[42] There, having noted that it was now 'universally recognized' that the Pseudo-Isidorean Decretals were a forgery, and rejecting, therefore, all the 'privileges and reservations' that had accrued from those decretals to the papacy at the expense of episcopal jurisdiction, and looking back to the Church's first centuries for a true understanding of the reach of the papal primacy, the participants described the pope as simply the 'principal overseer' of the universal Church and 'the focus of its unity', and went on to attempt to translate into ecclesiastico-political reality many of the ideas to which Febronius had given voice.[43]

In that same year, moreover, something similar was attempted in Tuscany, where Leopold, son of the Empress Maria Theresa and a man whose reforming instincts had been shaped by the Catholic Enlightenment, had become grand duke in 1765 and had quickly moved to encourage the advocates of Reform Catholicism already active there.[44] Prominent among those reformers was Scipione de'Ricci (d. 1809), vicar-general of the Florence archdiocese, who in 1780 and at Leopold's nomination had become bishop of Pistoia and Prato, combined sees which had enjoyed reforming or, it may be, 'Jansenizing' leadership for almost half a century. And it was at Pistoia in the autumn of 1786 that 'the most famous of all diocesan synods' enacted, under Ricci's leadership, a sweeping set of reforming resolutions many of which seemed revolutionary at the time but some of which turned out to be very much at one with the pastoral ideals which came to inform post-Vatican II Catholic practice in the 1960s and 1970s. So far as

[41] Chadwick, *Popes and European Revolution*, 411, where he adds: 'What he began continued as a key issue within Germanic Catholicism until the first Vatican Council of 1870, which tried to kill the debate, and thought it had succeeded, but was later proved wrong.'

[42] Schatz, *Papal Primacy*, 141.

[43] Ibid. 141–2; H. Raab in Müller *et al.*, *Age of Absolutism*, 443–69.

[44] I follow here the account in Chadwick, *Popes and European Revolution*, 418–31 (see 426–8 for the resolutions enacted).

the constitution of the Church was concerned, however, the synod responded to a vision fundamentally at odds with papal and curialist views. Infallibility was seen to reside in the *congregatio fidelium*, with the general council rather than the pope being seen as its representative mouthpiece, and the four Gallican articles of 1682 were incorporated into the synod's resolutions.

Though a conservatizing reaction soon set in, the ideological ripples generated by Pistoia were enormous. They were felt as far away as England where, as we have seen,[45] they were not lost on Joseph Berington and other Anglo-Gallicans of self-proclaimed Cisalpine commitment. Never before, perhaps, at least since the era of Constance and Basel in the fifteenth century, had anti-curialist sentiment in general and conciliarist leanings in particular attained so widespread a currency or so salient a position. With the advent of the French Revolution, the humiliating capture of Pius VI, and his death in 1800 as a prisoner of the French, the very survival of the papal office itself seemed called into question.[46] Had not the Gallican principles embedded in the National Assembly's Civil Constitution of the Clergy (1790) been imposed on the French church over the protests of thirty of the thirty-five bishops in the Assembly and without benefit of formal consultation with the body of the French clergy (over half of whom refused, on oath, to accept it), the future of the Church might have been destined to lie with some sort of episcopalist-conciliarist system. Certainly, the endorsement of the Gallican articles of 1682 which Napoleon embedded in the 'organic articles' appended to his 1801 Concordat with Pius VI (along with the stipulation that they be subscribed to by all French teachers of theology)[47] seemed to point in that same direction. Only in retrospect, then, does the publication in 1799 of a work of triumphalist pro-papal advocacy, *Il Trionfo della Santa Sede* (*The Triumph of the Holy See and the Church over the Attacks of the Innovators*) by an obscure Camaldolese monk, Fra Mauro Cappellari,[48] destined, or so it seemed at the time, to perish unread, suggest a fugitive straw in the wind pointing in an ironically different and wholly unexpected direction.

The direction in question was the astonishing recovery in power and prestige of the papal office, the triumph of ultramontane views, and the

[45] See above, Ch. 4.
[46] Chadwick, *Popes and European Revolution*, 445–90; Leflon, *La Crise révolutionnaire* (Paris: Bloud & Gay, 1951), 37–158.
[47] For which, see Leflon, *La crise révolutionnaire*, 194–5.
[48] Cappellari, *Il Trionfo della Santa Sede e della Chiesa contro gli assalti degli Novatori* for his treatment of the Council of Constance, see 'Discorso preliminare', §§ L–LIX, 86–103.

almost total destruction in little more than half a century of a tradition of conciliarist constitutionalism which, admittedly waxing and waning across time, had still survived all ecclesiological and political vicissitudes for what was already the better part of half a millennium.

JOSEPH DE MAISTRE AND THE REVIVAL OF THE ULTRAMONTANE VISION

What, then, happened? What went wrong for those many of constitutionalist sympathies whose star seemed in the late eighteenth century to be so very much in the ascendant? At the start of this book, I suggested that it is only our familiarity today with the unambiguously papalist outcome that suggests the necessity of the process that was eventually to consign the long-standing tradition of conciliarist constitutionalism to the unlamented dust-heap of history. I suggested similarly that the really taxing question confronting the historian is not that of explaining how it was that that constitutionalist tradition had risen to such prominence in the Latin Church during the fourteenth and fifteenth centuries, but rather that of throwing some light on why it was, contrary to all expectations at the time, that that tradition went down to utter ruin in the latter part of the nineteenth century—at the very moment, ironically enough, when various forms of liberal constitutionalism were daily extending their purchase on public opinion and their sway over the secular kingdoms and polities of Europe.

It would take another book than this to shed an adequate measure of light on this great puzzle.[49] But of the many complex and intricately interrelated factors that would have to be addressed in order to come even close to that goal, three stand out and certainly call for comment here.

First, and most fundamental, was the enormously destructive impact upon the national church of the French Revolution itself. The seismic role of that historic upheaval and of its sequential after-shocks in transforming

---

[49] And one, I suspect, that would need to involve not simply the exploration of the theological and canonistic literature, but also the sort of in-depth study of the complex ideological cross-currents evident in French ecclesiastico-political life during the era of restoration that Richard F. Costigan has advocated. See his *Rohrbacher and the Ecclesiology of Ultramontanism* (Rome: Gregoriana, 1980), esp. pp. xx–xxvi, 243–7; and his 'Tradition and the Beginning of the Ultramontane Movement', *Irish Theological Quarterly*, 48 (1981), 27–45. Similarly Y. Congar, 'Bulletin de théologie', *Revue des sciences philosophiques et théologiques*, 59 (1975), 489–93, in remarks reacting to Hermann Josef Pottmeyer's reliance on canonistic and theological writings in his *Unfehlbarkeit und Souveränität* (Mainz: Matthias-Grunewald-Verlag, 1975).

the political and legal landscape of Europe has become so much of a historiographic cliché that one hesitates even to mention it. But only ecclesiastical historians, I sense, are acutely conscious of the devastatingly transformative effect that it had in particular on the age-old ecclesiastical practices, legal and institutional forms, and long-established modalities of religious education, spiritual formation, and religious life right across Europe. And especially so in France, the most populous of all the Catholic states, headquarters to a historic array of international religious orders, graced with a proud tradition and a distinguished corps of theologians and church historians, and possessed, moreover, of the best endowed, most prosperous, and most powerful church in Christendom. The downfall of that great church, the seizure of its properties, the suppression of its monasteries, the destruction of its ancient theological faculties, the humiliation, expulsion, exile, or execution of so many of its clergy, the reshaping of its dioceses and subsequent replacement of its entire episcopal cadre—these things together amounted, Owen Chadwick has recently observed, to nothing less than 'one of the most momentous events in modern history'.[50] And here, as also eventually in Germany, it meant also the striking dismantling of that whole regal church structure characteristic of the *ancien régime*, in the lee of which alone, at least from the sixteenth century onwards, persistent advocates of episcopalist or conciliarist constitutionalism had been able to find some measure of continuing shelter against the countervailing winds and waves of papalist and statist domination.

If it would be hard to overestimate the transformative impact of the revolution itself, it would be only a little less difficult, and in the second place, to make too much of Pius VI's condemnation of the Civil Constitution of the Clergy and the extraordinary nature of the accommodation his successor arrived at with Napoleon in the Concordat of 1801.[51] Confronted in 1790–5 first by the National Assembly's demand that they sign on to the essentially statist Civil Constitution of the Clergy and then by Pius VI's belated condemnation of that measure, over half the French clergy refused to take the required oath and French Gallicanism was irreparably split. Clerics of more *politique* leanings, inclining to understand the essence of

---

[50] Chadwick, *Popes and European Revolution*, 445. Cf. Y. Congar, 'L'Ecclésiologie de la Révolution Française au concile du Vatican sous le signe de l'affirmation de l'autorité,' in Nédoncelle *et al.*, *L'Ecclésiologie au XIXe siècle* (Paris: Éditions du Cerf, 1960), 76–114 (at 97–106).

[51] See the accounts in Chadwick, *Popes and European Revolution*, 487–94; Schneider, *Konziliarismus*, 89–103; Leflon, *La Crise révolutionnaire*, 37–86, 161–222.

their Gallican heritage as residing in something close to an identification of church and nation, found it possible to side with the new order and to be part of the 'constitutional' church. But seeing that heritage as lying, rather, in a tenacious adherence to the episcopal, collegial, and conciliar constitution of the pre-medieval Church, 'theological Gallicans' tended to be numbered among the non-jurors and, with that, to be nudged into beginning the long, involuntary trek that was eventually to induce so many of them to join the company of clerics possessed already of clearly ultramontane sympathies. For alignment with the papal stance of opposition to the Civil Constitution of the Clergy had now come to be 'the crucial confessional point for whose sake the non-jurors were persecuted and driven underground, sent into exile, or even put to death'.[52] And, critical as they were of the subservience to the state of the Gallican church under the restored Bourbon monarchy, it was to the papacy, again, that so many priests of the younger generation also chose to turn.[53]

Moreover, humiliating though its terms may have seemed at the time, the accommodation which Pius VII arrived at with Napoleon in the Concordat of 1801 not only ended the schism in the French church but also, ironically enough, did something more than that. Involving as it did what has been called the 'liquidation of the French past', it redounded ultimately more to the benefit of the curia than to that of the emperor.[54] In the long haul, that is to say, it led once more to the growth in stature of the papal office in the eyes of canonists and theologians alike, to the concomitant strengthening of papal authority, and to the progressive transformation that was to make the papacy the obvious rallying point for hard-pressed Catholics all over Europe as they struggled to prevent the subordination of their religious commitments to the all-encompassing allegiance increasingly being demanded by the secular bureaucratic state.[55] Under the terms of the concordat the pope was forced to wipe the episcopal slate clean, to depose all French bishops—non-jurors as well as jurors—to establish in their place an entirely new episcopate, and, by the bold redrawing of diocesan lines, a restructured distribution of bishoprics. Viewed at the time as a cruelly revealing sign of ultimate

---

[52] Schatz, *Papal Primacy*, 145.   [53] Costigan, 'Tradition'.

[54] Schneider, *Konziliarismus*, 90.

[55] The more so in that, after 1815, many more Catholics were subject to Protestant rulers. The more so, again, in that the humbling of the pope's potential rivals, such towering figures as the great prince-bishops of sees like Mainz, Cologne, and Trier, served further to elevate the stature of his own office. In effect, 'the Revolution hurt Catholic episcopalism even more than it hurt the popes'—thus Chadwick, *Popes and European Revolution*, 609; see also 541, 571.

powerlessness (the 'imperial chaplain' was the nickname sardonic diplomats began to attach to Pius VII), and bemoaned by Cardinal Consalvi as 'the massacre of a hundred bishops',[56] this extraordinary move was eventually recognized for what it really was: nothing less, in fact, than a historic and wholly unprecedented exercise of direct papal power over the universal Church. And it was to set the tone for the vigorous expansion of papal jurisdictional power worldwide that was to mark the middle and later years of the century.

It is not clear, however, and in the third place, whether so dramatic an extension of papal power could have been so successfully achieved without the sharp reaction to revolutionary turmoil and the renewed longing for order that had begun to set in even before the dawn of the era of Restoration.[57] Still less could it have been achieved without the renewed sense of mystery, heightened responsiveness to the beauty of holiness, recovered feeling for the depth and richness of community life, and mounting enthusiasm for the medieval 'age of faith'—all of which were part and parcel of that great shift in sensibilities that we today associate with the Romantic movement. But such developments did not make their presence felt overnight. Only in retrospect can the first beginnings of the historic transformation of the stature of the pope and of the prerogatives routinely attaching to his office be detected during the Napoleonic and Restoration eras. And that despite the fact that it was the circumstances of those years that called forth from an unexpected quarter the book that was subsequently to be labelled as the very charter of ultramontanism.

The author was Joseph de Maistre, in 1819 when the book appeared ambassador of the King of Sardinia to the Tsar's court at St Petersburg, and since described, engagingly enough though with varying degrees of accuracy, as 'more theologian than Christian, more jurist than theologian', as 'Praetorian of the Vatican', as literary colonel of the papal Zouaves, as 'prophet of the past, historian of the future', and presented by Isaiah Berlin, in a characteristically lively essay, as one of those who were in some measure 'Catholic before they were Christians', and as a man whose

---

[56] Chadwick, *Popes and European Revolution*, 487–94.

[57] Evident in the political writings that Louis Bonald published right at the start of the century. But Bonald, with Joseph de Maistre and the abbé de Lammenais one of 'le fameux triumvirat catholique' (thus C. Latreille, *Joseph de Maistre et la papauté* (Paris: Hachette, 1906), 260), while stressing the centrality of authority, focused more generally on the authority of the Church and only came to ultramontane ideas later on under the influence of de Maistre. See Congar, 'L'Ecclésiologie de la Révolution Française', in Nédoncelle *et al.*, *L'Ecclésiologie*, 77–114 (at 77–81).

thinking was fraught with dark intimations of the Fascist future.[58] The book was *Du pape*, which was to be followed in 1821, and after his death, by a related treatise: *De l'Église Gallicane dans son rapport avec le Saint-Siège*.[59]

Although it evoked torrents of praise and blame during the first half of the nineteenth century,[60] *Du pape* has not drawn in subsequent years the sort of attention that other of De Maistre's writings have; nor has it been submerged in the ocean of commentary to which those other writings gave rise. From its pages can be drawn no picturesque or violent passages comparable to his oft-cited evocations of (what he called) the 'prescriptive fury' of the natural world or the 'inexplicable being' of the executioner.[61] But, that said, it does not lack the stylistic brilliance so evident in those other works, and it is written with a forceful clarity as elegant as it is (sometimes) brutal. Nor does it fail to witness to the great transformation the revolutionary experience had wrought in his own thinking and sensibilities, erasing the marginal liberalism and Gallican sympathies of his youth and turning him, as Berlin puts it, into

a ferocious critic of every form of constitutionalism and liberalism, an ultramontane legitimist, a believer in the divinity of authority and power, . . . an unyielding adversary of all that *lumières* of the eighteenth century had stood for—rationalism, individualism, liberal compromise and secular enlightenment. His world had been shattered by the satanic forces of atheistical reason and could be rebuilt only by cutting off the heads of the hydra of the revolution in all its multiple disguises. Two worlds had met in mortal combat. He had chosen his side and meant to give no quarter.[62]

No quarter, certainly, is extended in either of these books to the 1682 Declaration of the Gallican Clergy, to the endorsement of the Constance decree *Haec sancta* embedded in the second of its articles, or to the sympathetic Gallican theologians who, echoing the so-called 'maxims of Paris'

[58] P. R. Rohden, *Joseph de Maistre als politischer Theoretiker* (Munich: Verlag der Münchner Drucke, 1929), 90, cited from R. A. Lebrun, *Throne and Altar* (Ottawa: University of Ottawa Press, 1965), 117; Isaiah Berlin, 'Joseph de Maistre and the Origins of Fascism', in Berlin, *The Crooked Timber of Humanity* (New York: Alfred A. Knopf, 1991), 91–174 (see 94 and 170); C. J. Gignoux made 'Prophet of the past, historian of the future', the subtitle of his book, *Joseph de Maistre: Prophète du passé, historien d'avenir* (Paris: Nouvelles Éditions Latines, 1963).

[59] For background, context, and commentary on these books and on their reception, see Latreille, *Joseph de Maistre*. Shorter discussions in Gignoux, *Joseph de Maistre*, 180–99, and Lebrun, *Throne and Altar*, 122–54. For recent interpretations of de Maistre's thought see the essays gathered in R. A. Lebrun, ed., *Joseph de Maistre's Life, Thought, and Influence* (Montreal and Kingston: McGill-Queen's University Press, 2001).

[60] For which, see Latreille, *Joseph de Maistre*, 239–354.

[61] Berlin, 'Joseph de Maistre', in *Crooked Timber of Humanity*, 111–12, 116–18.

[62] Ibid. 105–6.

and exhibiting a wholly 'deplorable blindness', had committed themselves to supporting nothing other than 'the insupportable'.[63] Even Bossuet, whose 'great genius' and 'illustrious shade' De Maistre dutifully invokes but whom he handles, it must be remarked, with a species of dismissive condescension no less real for being quite so deferential—even Bossuet was capable of going awry, as of course he did when he endorsed that unfortunate decree *Haec sancta*. Ignorant of the fact that the final version of that decree, approved by Constance at its fifth general session, was more sweeping and more universal in its claims than the earlier version voted at the fourth session,[64] it is on the latter that De Maistre concentrates his formidable ire.

Its claim that the council is superior in authority to the pope is nothing less, he insists, than 'evidently ridiculous' and 'radically void'.[65] The very thought that the episcopal body acting apart from the pope and even in opposition to him could make laws limiting him in the exercise of his office is nothing other than an insult to 'sane theology and sane logic'.[66] In advancing such a claim Constance was simply perpetrating what the English are prone to calling a 'non-sense'—as, for that matter, were such other 'headless' bodies as the Long Parliament in England or the Constituent Assembly and its unfortunate successor bodies in France when they all advanced their comparably illegitimate claims. Ecumenical councils being no more than a periodic or intermittent presence in the life of the Church, they can hardly be bearers of sovereign power or of the prerogative of infallibility.[67] All they can be is 'the parliament or estates-general of Christendom, assembled by the authority and under the presidency of the sovereign', and, without his authority, possessing, therefore, not even a power of co-legislating.[68] Independently of the pope there cannot even be a general council, and to speak of the latter as being above the pope makes, then, no more sense than to speak of the Westminster Parliament as being above the king of England.[69] And should anyone claim that no such comparison can properly be made between general councils in the Church and parliaments or estates-general in the secular political world, let that claim be recognized for the sophistry it is—for 'general councils, are they not ecclesiastical estates-general, and estates general, are they not civil ecumenical councils?'[70]

---

[63] Maistre, *Du pape, Diss. prélim*, and bk. 1, ch. 12, ed. Lovie and Chétail, 22 and 85; idem, *L'Église Gallicane*, bk. 2, 145.

[64] For the differences in question see above, Ch. 2.

[65] Maistre, *Du pape*, bk. 1, ch. 12, ed. Lovie and Chétail, 84.

[66] Ibid., bk. 1, ch. 11, p. 82.   [67] Ibid., and bk. 1, ch. 3, p. 37.

[68] Ibid., bk. 1, ch. 3, p. 36.   [69] Ibid., bk. 1, ch. 3, p. 36; ch. 12, pp. 82–5.

[70] Ibid., bk. 1, ch. 4, p. 42.

And so on. De Maistre's actual knowledge of conciliar history, of the 'maxims of Paris', of the Gallican tradition in general, and of Bossuet's views in particular was really quite deficient—very much, indeed, a second-hand, arms-length affair.[71] As a result, the historical obstacles one would have thought that Bossuet's voluminously informed *Defence of the Declaration of the Gallican Clergy* might have posed for him had he bothered to read it, or, at least, to read it with any degree of attention, appear to have given him no pause at all. Instead, he disposed of any such putative obstacle briskly and handily by simply questioning the very fact of Bossuet's authorship of that work, boldly insisting, in the teeth of every evidence to the contrary, that 'in a very real sense' the work is not really his.[72] QED! In any case, and certainly where constitutions, institutions, and even religious dogmas were concerned, historical inquiry into origins was, he thought, a poor guide to understanding in that it failed to take into account the insensible evolution or development of such things across the fullness of time. One would search the scriptures and Church fathers alike in vain, he felt, for any sort of 'constitutional charter of the Church'. The papal monarchy and doctrine of papal infallibility serve to illustrate that crucial point. 'Neither theology, nor history suffice to prove these magnificent privileges of the see of Peter.'[73] De Maistre's central appeal, accordingly, is neither to history nor to experience but rather to authority. As Berlin puts it with reference to his characteristic mode of argument, what is involved is a matter of 'pure dogma used as a battering ram'. His 'ultimate principles and premises nothing can shake' and his 'considerable ingenuity and intellectual power are devoted [instead] to making the facts fit his preconceived notions'.[74]

Those notions are clear, straightforward, and firm. As a man who chose to call himself a 'severe apostle of unity and authority',[75] his focus

[71] For the inadequacy of de Maistre's sources and the inexact and dishevelled way in which he deployed them, see Latreille, *Joseph de Maistre*, 40–95. The book, he rightly observes, is the work of a thinker rather than that of a scholar (*érudit*).

[72] Maistre, *L'Église Gallicane*, bk. 2, ch. 9, p. 171.

[73] The words are those of Latreille, *Joseph de Maistre*, 205, whose discussion (202–8) of the notion of doctrinal development I follow here. As he correctly notes (206 n. 2), in this respect, Cardinal Newman acknowledged de Maistre (as also, perhaps, Johann Adams Möhler) among his precursors, while, in an oblique way, revealing that he may not actually have *read* those two authors. See J. H. Newman, *An Essay on the Development of Christian Doctrine* (London: Longmans, Green & Co., 1885), 29. Cf. O. Chadwick, *From Bossuet to Newman* (Cambridge: CUP, 1987), 111–228.

[74] Berlin, 'Joseph de Maistre', in *Crooked Timber of Humanity*, 162–3.

[75] J. C. Murray, 'The Political Thought of Joseph de Maistre', *Review of Politics*, 11 (1949), 72.

throughout is on monarchy, sovereignty, infallibility. The truths of theology being nothing other, he says, than 'general truths manifested and divinized in the religious sphere',[76] what is true of any conceivable political society has to be true also of the Church universal. That church, then, must of necessity be a monarchy, and the sovereign pontiff the fixed Copernican point around which the whole vast cosmos of Christendom ceaselessly revolves.[77] All real government being by definition absolute, that government exists no more if it concedes even a possibility of dissent from its edicts.[78] No council, then, without the pope. No appeal from pope to council. No council, accordingly, above the pope.[79] Absolute and sovereign, the pope reigns supreme over a Church whose very being is contingent on his will.[80] And, if sovereign, then of course infallible, too. Sovereignty and infallibility, he insists, are 'perfect synonyms'. 'In virtue alone of social laws, all sovereignty is infallible in nature.' And lacking that crucial prerogative, a government is really no government at all.[81]

The immediate response to De Maistre's *Du pape* was decidedly cool, and to the abbé de Lammenais he confessed to being 'completely disheartened' by its discouraging nature. The Vatican itself evinced at first a chill reserve to a work of ecclesiology so disappointingly untheological in its characteristic mode of reasoning and so adamantly political in the spirit which informed it.[82] But initial reactions notwithstanding, all of that was eventually to change. And the fact that the book was to go through no less than forty editions during the course of the nineteenth century is, perhaps, at once the cause and consequence of that change.[83] As early as 1822, when the work was reissued in German translation, while the liberals of the Tübingen theological faculty excoriated it, it was received quite warmly by their more conservative colleagues at Mainz, themselves bell-wethers of the growing strength among theologians of unmistakably ultramontane sympathies.[84] Admittedly, the process of change was quite gradual, especially so in Germany and Austria, where there was no figure quite like the

---

[76] Maistre, *Du pape*, bk. 1, ch. 1, ed. Lovie and Chétail, 27.

[77] Ibid., *Discours prélim*, 24: 'le christianisme repose entièrement sur le Souverain Pontife'. Similarly, ibid., bk. 1, ch. 1, pp. 28–30; ch. 6, p. 55.

[78] Ibid., bk. 1, ch. 1, ed. Lovie and Chétail, 27–8.   [79] Ibid. 28; ch. 3, pp. 36–7.

[80] Ibid., *Discours prélim*, ed. Lovie and Chétail, 24.

[81] Ibid., *Discours prélim*, 7–8, bk. 1, ch. 1, 27–8.

[82] Murray, 'Political Thought', 44 and 81.

[83] Lebrun, Introduction to Joseph de Maistre, *The Pope* (New York: Howard Fertig, 1975), p. xv.

[84] For the contrast between the two schools and their respective journals (the *Tübinger Theologische Quartalschrift* and the *Katholik* of Mainz), see Schneider, *Konziliarismus*, 103–17.

abbé de Lammenais who in France proved himself capable of popularizing ultramontane tenets even among the younger clergy.[85] But it was real enough, and it finds a reflection in the complex evolution evident in the ecclesiological views of Johan Adam Möhler (d. 1838), the leading luminary of the Tübingen School and one of the most distinguished of nineteenth-century Catholic theologians.[86]

In his early courses on canon law Möhler had openly defended conciliarist and Gallican views, in so doing calling upon the authority of d'Ailly, Gerson, and John of Segovia. If his famous work, *Die Einheit der Kirche oder das Prinzip der Katholicismus* (1825) was not written explicitly as a reply to De Maistre, it still reads very much as an essentially episcopalist rebuttal of the latter's high papalist views, a blunt rejection of his attempt to comprehend the essence of the Church via the deployment of secular political categories, an echoing instead of the Febronian characterization of the pope as its *centrum unitatis*, and an affirmation (not without continuing reference to the fifteenth-century councils) of the priority of the episcopal body as a whole to any claims made for the papal authority alone. As time went on, however, and this is evident especially in the fourth and fifth editions of his great *Symbolik* (1835 and 1838), Möhler came to think of the Church less and less in juridical terms of any sort, whether conciliarist or papalist, and more and more in Romantic 'organic' terms, as a community infused with the energy of the Holy Spirit, one in which the relationship of papacy and episcopacy was understood dialectically rather than being grasped in destructively oppositional fashion.

On a broader scale, moreover, a parallel if by no means identical evolution is evident in the shifting way in which church historians came to understand the history of the fifteenth-century general councils. And, in this connection, by dint of examining several extensive treatments of the history of Constance written across the course of the century prior to the assembly in 1870 of the First Vatican Council, Hans Schneider has held up a

---

[85] 'It was to be the Abbé de Lammenais who was to achieve the conversion of the French clergy to ultramontanism'—thus Roger Aubert, in Aubert *et al.*, *The Church between Revolution and Restoration* (New York: Crossroad, 1980), 104–15 (at 110). See also idem, 'La Géographie écclesiologique au XIXe siècle', in Nédoncelle *et al.*, *L'Ecclésiologie*, 11–15 (at 19–20). Sieben, *Katholische Konzilsidee*, 61–77, traces the progressive decline in the authority accorded to *Haec sancta* in Germany during the first half of the 19th cent.

[86] Following here J. R. Geiselmann, 'Les Variations de la définition de l'Église chez John Adam Möhler, particulièrement en ce qui concerne le relation entre l'Episcopat et le Primat', in Nédoncelle *et al.*, *L'Ecclésiologie*, 141–95. Cf. Aubert, 'La Géographie ecclésiologique au XIXe siècle', ibid. 25–9; Schneider, *Konziliarismus*, esp. 111–15, 131–5, Sieben, *Katholische Konzilsidee*, 62–4.

helpful mirror in which changes in the contemporary ecclesiological consciousness can readily be observed.[87]

His focus on the writing of Church history is more than appropriate. With the suppression of the Jesuit order in 1773 and the dismantling in the Catholic universities and other *Hochschule* of the old Jesuit *Ratio studiorum*,[88] Church history as a discipline had begun to find in the Catholic world the place in the intellectual sun it had long since come to enjoy at the evangelical universities. And when finally it did so, it is hardly surprising, during the Josephinist era, that it should characteristically have portrayed the fifteenth-century councils, the decrees *Haec sancta* and *Frequens*, the deposition of the popes, and the ending of the Great Schism all in a very positive light.[89] More than fifty years later, Ignaz Heinrich Freiherr von Wessenberg (d. 1860) was to write in a similarly episcopalist vein, discerning a close connection between the conciliar limitation of papal power and the effecting of Church reform, and emphasizing the need for a general recognition of the conciliarist superiority teaching embedded in *Haec sancta*, a full translation of which he provided. By that time, however, such views had ceased to be fashionable even at Tübingen, where Carl Joseph Hefele (d. 1893), Möhler's successor as professor of Church history, when reviewing Wessenberg's book in 1841, took strong exception to some of his claims.[90] When he himself came later to write his own great history of the councils, Hefele took a very different view of Constance, its actions, and its decrees than had predecessors like Royko and Wessenberg. *Haec sancta*, for him, was no enduring doctrinal or disciplinary norm but, rather, an extraordinary measure precipitated by the crisis of the time. When the decree was passed Constance, lacking a papal head, was not (yet) a legitimate general council. *Haec sancta* was later to be approved neither by Martin V nor Eugenius IV. And the action which it underpinned—the deposition of John XXIII—was an action taken, not against a legitimate pope but against a merely doubtful claimant to the papal office. And so on.[91]

---

[87] Schneider, *Konziliarismus*, 80–8, 148–65.

[88] And, along with it, a certain indifference to historical studies.

[89] Thus K. Royko, author of three textbooks in Church history and of a *Geschichte der grossen allgemeinen Kirchen versammlung zu Kostnitz* (Prague, 1784–5) portrayed Constance as an ecumenical council when it deposed John XXIII. The latter he portrayed as no less legitimate as a pope than was the superiority decree on which his deposition was based and which Martin V was to confirm. For which, see Schneider, *Konziliarismus*, 148–57.

[90] Schneider, *Konziliarismus*, 151–4. For the importance of Wessenberg's role—he refers to him as 'doubtless the most defamed and execrated of the Aufklärung Catholics'—see Swidler, *Aufklärung Catholicism*, 29.

[91] Hefele, and Hergenröther, *Conciliengeschichte*; Hefele, *Histoire des conciles*. In both cases the pertinent vols. are i and vii. Schneider, *Konziliarismus*, 161–5.

This shift in stance is the more striking in that Hefele, who was to emerge at Vatican I as a prominent member of the anti-infallibilist minority, was himself no ultramontane and certainly no sympathizer with the ideas of De Maistre. In other circles, however, and as the century wore on, the impact of those very ideas was to make itself evident, and unambiguously so.[92] In 1868, the Jesuit paper *Civiltà cattolica*, which, along with Louis Veuillot's *L'Univers* in France, had become one of the house-organs of the pro-infallibilist camp, carried a revealing article by one of its Jesuit editors, the neo-Thomist philosopher, Matteo Liberatore. In it, having traced back the contemporary collapse of order to the primordial ecclesiological Fall that had taken place in the fourteenth and fifteenth centuries when the conciliarists had moved to place limits on papal power, he insisted that the 'restoration of the principle of authority' was the necessary prerequisite for the salvation of society at large. The sole route to that happy outcome, he went on to argue, was the restoration to its fullness of power of that 'principal authority, the rule and type of every other authority on earth', namely, the papacy itself. And if that process of restoration were indeed to begin, then papal infallibility simply *had* to be defined.[93]

Here, as more generally in so many authors of the Vatican I era, the impact of De Maistre's 'metaphysics of sovereignty' and his understanding of infallibility as essentially final authority and the power of sovereign decision is evident. In such a view, the age-old understanding of the Church's magisterial authority as involving the identifying and witnessing to the truth of what had been handed down by immemorial tradition was, in effect, marginalized. In the fourteenth century, Pope John XXII had viewed the notion of papal infallibility as one incompatible with the traditional doctrine of papal sovereignty in that it would bind popes to the pronouncements of their predecessors.[94] But now, five centuries later, and by

---

[92] For this shift in ecclesiological posture, see especially the lengthy essays contributed by Aubert, 'La Géographie ecclésiologique au XIXe siècle', and Congar, 'L'Ecclésiologie de la Révolution Française', in Nédoncelle *et al.*, *L'Ecclésiologie*, 11–55, 77–114.

[93] Cited by Schatz, *Papal Primacy*, 149, from *Civiltà cattolica*, 19 (1868), ser. 7, iii. 528–30. Sieben, *Katholische Konzilsidee*, 133–60, contains a useful discussion of the role which *Civiltà cattolica* played at this time. There is an interesting discussion of Liberatore's philosophical development in J. Inglis, *Spheres of Philosophical Inquiry* (Leiden: E. J. Brill, 1998), esp. 74–8.

[94] When that doughty canonist first encountered the doctrine in 1326, although he did not meet it head on, he did contrive to brush it aside as a 'pestiferous doctrine'—see the bull *Quia quorundam*, *Extravagantes Joann XXII*, tit. 14, c. 5; in *Corpus Juris Canonci*, ed. Friedberg, ii. 1230. I follow here Brian Tierney's claim that the doctrine of papal infallibility was designed, at least in its late medieval inception, 'to limit the power of future popes, not to loose them from all restraints'. See his *Origins of Papal Infallibility*, 130. Cf. Oakley, *Western Church*, 148–57.

one of the ironies in which the history of ideas abounds, infallibility was coming to be aligned with sovereignty and the emphasis placed on conclusive 'decision' or solemn 'definition', with no ambiguity to be allowed concerning the precise (and papal) locus of the crucial decision-making authority.[95]

De Maistre's views, then, certainly left their imprint on subsequent ecclesiological thinking. None the less, they constituted but one (admittedly prominent) strand in the complex set of intersecting developments that came gradually to rally so many bishops, canonists, theologians, lower clergy, and ordinary members of the faithful around the banner of centralized papal authority, and that were to eventuate in the triumph of a version of ultramontanism at the First Vatican Council. Absent the fuller account that cannot be given here,[96] two things should be noted about that broad set of developments. First, that it grew as much from the bottom-up as from the top-down. In a letter written in 1856, Alexis de Tocqueville himself commented on that fact. 'The pope', he said, 'is driven more by the faithful to become absolute ruler of the Church than they are impelled by him to submit to his rule. Rome's attitude is more an effect than a cause.'[97] And that was especially the case before 1848. Second, that in so far as the papacy itself came eventually to drive the whole process, one should not underestimate the importance of the fact that the man who was elected pope in 1831, and who took the title of Gregory XVI, was none other than the Camaldolese monk, Fra Mauro Cappellari, who in 1799 and at a very dark moment for the papacy had uttered a great rallying cry of resistance to the satanic forces unleashed by the French Revolution. In his *Trionfo*

[95] See Pottmeyer, *Unfehlbarkeit und Souveranität*, esp. 61–73, 352–4. Useful synoptic statement in Hermann Josef Pottmeyer, '"Auctoritas suprema ideoque infallibilis." Das Missverständnis der päpstlichen Unfehlbarkeit als Souveränität und seine historischen Bedingungen', in G. Schwaiger, ed., *Konzil und Papst* (Munich: F. Schöningh, 1975), 503–20 (esp. 516–20). The alignment of infallibility with sovereignty had become by 1870 so widespread as to be taken for granted even by so vigorous an opponent of the definition of papal infallibility as Henri Maret, dean of the Parisian theology faculty. In his *Du concile général*, ii. 62–3, alluding to de Maistre, he affirms that 'dans la société spirituelle ... l'infaillibilité ... est un attribut nécessaire de la souveraineté; elle est un de ces caractères essentials'. He then adds: 'il soit que, dans l'Église et pour l'Église, la question de l'infaillibilité est identique à celle de la souveraineté. Le pouvoir infaillible est le vrai pouvoir souverain.' And that position he reaffirmed in his later response to his critics, *Le Pape et les évêques* (Paris: Henri Plon, 1869), 8. For Maret's general argument, see below, pp. 209–15.

[96] For a good, recent narrative encompassing these developments, see O. Chadwick. *A History of the Popes: 1830–1914* (Oxford: Clarendon Press, 1998), 1–214. Also R. Aubert, *Le Pontificat de Pie IX* (Paris: Bloud & Gay, 1952); idem, in Aubert et al., *The Church in the Age of Liberalism*, tr. P. Becker (New York: Crossroad, 1981), 304–30.

[97] I cite this from Schatz, *Papal Primacy*, 151.

della Santa Sede he had pictured 'a papal church whose unchangeability enabled it to stand firm against the storm of changing times and turn back the attacks of all innovators'. Like De Maistre a few years later, he had aligned 'papal infallibility with papal sovereignty', and had advanced the twin notions that 'the pope is infallible "independently of the Church" and that the Church is dependent only on the pope, not the pope on the Church'.[98] Prophetic enough of things to come. During the thirty years since its publication the book had been read almost as little as it is read today. But with Cappellari's ascent to the papal throne it was soon to be translated into four languages, and the principles it enunciated were to set the tone for a fifteen-year pontificate that can be seen in retrospect to have constituted 'a decisive phase in the progress of ultramontanism'.[99]

HENRI MARET, VATICAN I, AND THE DEMISE OF THE CONCILIARIST TRADITION

By 1789, as they spread steadily across Europe, Gallican and Febronian versions of the old tradition of conciliarist constitutionalism in the Church had seemed to carry the very future in their bones. By 1848, however, those who still advocated even a moderate version of that position had found themselves reduced to an increasingly beleaguered minority. And after 1848, as Rome began to place itself unambiguously in the leadership of the ultramontane tendency and to launch a systematic and efficient campaign to weed out the last vestiges of anything smacking of Gallicanism or Febronianism,[100] such constitutionalists were to find themselves pressed

[98] Ibid. 144.
[99] R. Aubert in Aubert *et al.*, *The Church in the Age of Liberalism*, 304.
[100] A campaign that may be said to have reached its peak in 1870 during the Vatican Council, when Pius IX himself summoned and rebuked Cardinal Guidi, the Dominican archbishop of Bologna, who, speaking for a group of Dominican theologians, had argued in conciliar debate that 'if anyone says that the Pope when he speaks does so by his own will independent of the Church, that separately and not with the counsel of the bishops who show the tradition of their churches, let him be anathema'. Words which a furious pope denounced (famously) as erroneous 'because I, I am tradition. I, I am the Church!' See Chadwick, *History of Popes*, 210–11. Many have doubted that this celebrated scene played out in precisely that way and that Pius IX actually uttered those startling words. But they have done so, it now seems clear, without justification. K. Schatz, *Vaticanum I* (Paderborn: F. Schöningh, 1993–4), iii, app. I, 323–33, has weighed the evidence carefully and concluded (iii. 332) 'Dass die Szene sich im wesentlichen so abgespielt hat, dürfte jetzt kaum mehr in Frage stehen.' Similarly, 'dass der Ausdruck "La tradizione sono Io" in dieser oder geringfügig abgewandelter Form darbei gefallen ist, kann also historisch gesichert gelten.'

very hard indeed. So hard, in effect, and with so notable a lack of restraint, as to stimulate among them an anguished negative reaction.

That was certainly true in Germany where in 1869 Ignaz von Döllinger, the leading liberal church historian of the day, was nudged finally into a posture of outright (if anonymous) resistance. Publicized in the notorious 'Janus' articles, that resistance encompassed, among other things, a firm commitment to the conciliarist constitutional vision embedded in the Constance decree *Haec sancta* and a passionate insistence on its faithfulness to the ancient communitarian and collegial understanding of the Church's nature.[101] France, too, saw a comparably negative reaction among the liberals to mounting Vatican intrusion into the life of the French church. That interference had reached truly dramatic proportions when, between 1850 and 1852, Rome placed on the Index of Prohibited Books several textbooks in theology and canonistics which the French bishops had themselves approved for use in the seminaries, and had done so in part because those books had seen fit to recognize as a 'free opinion' the positions endorsed in the Gallican articles of 1682. But in France that reaction took a somewhat more open and organized form than it did in Germany, leading a cluster of bishops to dig in anew, ideologically speaking, along neo-Gallican lines.[102] Some of those involved, including Georges Darboy, archbishop of Paris, were later to figure prominently as leaders of the anti-infallibilist minority at the Vatican Council. And one of them, after more than a decade of study, was to publish in 1869 a book which has been described both as 'the swan song of Gallicanism' and as the first French work in ecclesiology to count since the era of Lammenais.[103] That book, though translated almost immediately into German and Italian, was not well understood at the time. It tended to be dismissed half-read as no more than a tired Gallican manifesto and, at least until the era

---

[101] 'Janus', The Pope and the Council', §§ XXII–XXVII, pp. 292–346. Döllinger is not always accurate in his rendition of the views of those he discusses. Thus, having incorrectly attributed to Torquemada the invention or convenient 'discovery' of the old canonistic notion that a pope who lapsed into heresy ceased *ipso facto* to be pope; he goes on also to speak inaccurately of 'Cajetan's hypothesis of an heretical Pope being deposed *ipso facto* by the judgment of God.' For Cajetan's true position, see above, Chs. 2 and 3.

[102] Sieben, *Katholische Konzilsidee im 19. und 20. Jahrhundert*, 80–1; R. Aubert in Aubert et al., *The Church in the Age of Liberalism*, 305–6; idem, *Le Pontificat de pie IX*, 262–78, 305–10. See also J.-R. Palanque, *Catholiques Libéraux et Gallicans en France* (Aix-en-Provence: Ophrys, 1962), esp. 21–32, 61–103; C. Bressolette, 'Ultramontanisme et gallicanisme', *Freiburger Zeitschrift für Philosophie und Theologie*, 38 (1991), 3–25.

[103] Thus Aubert, 'La Geographie ecclésiologique', in Nédoncelle et al., *L'Ecclésiologie*, 49–50.

of Vatican II, was well-nigh forgotten.[104] Historically speaking, however, it warrants close attention.

Its author was Henri Maret (1805–84), a distinguished and widely respected scholar who was destined to be the last dean of the theology faculty at the Sorbonne. Because of his politically liberal and ecclesiastically Gallican sympathies, Pius IX had refused to approve his appointment as bishop of Vannes, but had conceded to him the titular bishopric of Sura *in partibus infidelium*. And, by virtue of that title, he was later able to participate as a voting member in the deliberations of the First Vatican Council. The book was a large, two-volume work submitted as a memorandum to the upcoming council and entitled *Du concile général et de la paix religieuse*. Its tone was irenic, serenely lucid, calmly generous, persistently seeking—as he himself insisted[105]—a viable middle ground between the Gallican orthodoxy of the past and the extreme ultramontanism of the present, and conveying a genuine desire to accommodate some at least of the aspirations common to the many Catholics of his day who had come to pin their hopes on the sort of religious leadership currently emanating from Rome. Its mode of argument derived less from the older world of scholastic disputation and more from the type of historically grounded reasoning favoured by Bossuet and Febronius. It was a mode of argument, however supple, that was not always informed by the most recent findings of German 'scientific' historical scholarship, and, perhaps because of that,

---

[104] It is true that Thysman's fine article, 'Le Gallicanisme de Mgr. Maret et l'influence de Bossuet', *Revue d'histoire ecclésiastique*, 52 (1957), 401–65, predated that era, but in the preface to his book, written in 1919 but published for the first time in 1962, Palanque notes (p. vii) that it was the convocation of Vatican II that led him to consider publication. And the presence of concerns typical of Vatican II are at times so strong in Bressolette, *Le Pouvoir dans la société el dans l'église: L'Ecclésiologie politique du Monseigneur Maret* (Paris: Éditions du Cerf, 1984), as to incline him to reduce Maret's unambiguously conciliarist commitment to something more directly cognate to the modern doctrine of episcopal collegiality (see esp. 129–31). Sieben, *Katholische Konzilsidee*, devotes a full chapter (72–100) to Maret.

[105] Maret states in a passage from an unprinted autobiographical manuscript which Bressolette, *Le Pouvoir*, prints at 134: 'L'esprit exclusif et violent de l'école ultra-catholique, les excès de la centralisation, l'incomparabilité apparente que cette école et cette direction élevaient entre l'Église et la société moderne, contribuèrent beaucoup à m'affermir dans mes convictions du caractère modéré de la monarchie pontificale. Je fus peu à peu induit à une doctrine de milieu entre le gallicanisme orthodoxe et l'ultramontanisme extreme ou je croyais conserver tout ce qu'il y avait de vrai dans les deux systèmes.' A. Riccardi prints the same passage in his book on Maret, *Neogallicanismo e cattolicismo borghese* (Bologna: Il Mulino, 1976) at 81–2. Writing later on (1869) in his *Le Pape et les évêques*, 4, Maret was to note (somewhat plaintively, it may be) that ultramontanism had by that time gained such an ascendancy that 'notre livre [i.e., his *Le concile général*], bien qu'il porte le caratère de la modération et de la conciliation devait être en butte à ses plus violentes attaques'.

Döllinger was to characterize the book, somewhat condescendingly, as 'a companion piece to Bossuet's *Defensio*'.[106]

Dependent on Bossuet in many ways, of course, it was. During the decade prior to the publication of the book Maret had made a systematic study of the *Defensio* on which he often relied as a guide to the sources, and he had certainly absorbed much of Bossuet's spirit. But a close reading reveals that he usually pursued his historical investigations beyond the witness of Bossuet, reaching back directly to the sources and deploying them sometimes more accurately and effectively than had Bossuet himself.[107] Moreover, Maret's characteristically Gallican reverence for Bossuet and the shared moderation of their conciliarism notwithstanding, there are clear differences between the forms of Gallicanism the two men espouse.

In the first place, being himself a staunch advocate of divine-right royalism, much of Bossuet's *Defensio* had been devoted to a vindication of the first of the four Gallican articles and, therefore, to an analysis of the relationship between the two powers, temporal and spiritual.[108] Of those sections of Bossuet's work Maret made little use. Although he had hoped to add a third volume devoted to such matters he never did so, and the book he actually produced focused exclusively on the Church's internal constitution.[109] In the second place, the goal of reforming the Church in head and members (starting, in effect, with the head), the conviction that the regular assembly of general councils was the constitutional instrumentality essential to the achievement of that goal, and the emphasis, therefore, on the continuing validity and pertinence of the Constance decree *Frequens*—in this combination of the strict conciliar theory with the reforming strand in conciliarist thinking, he stood somewhat closer in spirit to the great conciliarists of the fifteenth century than he did to his more immediate Gallican forebears.[110] The same is true also, and in the third place, of the degree to which his can appropriately be called a 'political

---

[106] It was after all, he pointed out, a product merely of French, not of German 'scientific' scholarship. See Schneider, *Konziliarismus*, 180–1 nn. 115 and 116.

[107] As Thysman's careful comparison makes clear. See esp. 'Le Gallicanisme', 411–30.

[108] See above, Ch. 4.

[109] Bressolette, *Le Pouvoir*, 18–19; Thysman, 'Le Gallicanisme', 404 n. 3. Some sense of the direction such an additional volume might have taken can be gleaned from the record of his teaching at Paris. See Henri Maret, *L'Église et l'état*, ed. C. Bressolette (Paris: G. Beauchesne, 1979).

[110] Palanque, *Catholiques*, 31; Bressolette, *Le Pouvoir*, 94, 101–2. From 1848 onwards, Maret had called for the assembly of a general council to pursue the work of reform. In 1869 he went on to propose the application of *Frequens* in order to ensure the periodicity of councils. See his *Du concile general*, ii. 389–412.

ecclesiology'.[111] Though he makes the ecclesiologist's usual noises to the
effect that the Church is a society possessed of a constitution that is
sui generis, its mode of governance not to be assimilated in judgement to
that of any merely human government, and about the concomitant danger
of pushing too far analogies with the secular polity,[112] none the less he parts
company again with Bossuet (and, for that matter, with Febronius, too) in
the willingness to deploy such analogies—which he shares, of course, with
his fifteenth-, sixteenth-, and seventeenth-century predecessors.

He does so with a notable lack of diffidence. The Church, after all, does
not endure in some sort of lonely isolation. It is embedded in human society at large and a process of reciprocal influence has to be acknowledged as
inevitable. Analogies, accordingly, can be helpful, and 'the political analogy
which can best enable us to grasp the relationship of papacy and episcopate
is that of constitutional monarchy, the ideal of the liberals'. For, without
question, it helps us better understand how it is that 'the bishop can at the
same time be submitted to the pope and [yet, with him] a member of the
sovereign'.[113] Moved by the conviction that, for the human person created
in the image and likeness of his divine maker, liberty could be nothing less
than a God-given right which the Church must herself view necessarily as
sacred, Maret was moved also and accordingly by a deep sympathy with the
revolutionary aspirations of 1789 (if not the revolutionary excesses of 1793).
He was moved also by the serene assumption that the relationship of the
two spheres, temporal and spiritual, should properly be one of harmony
and analogy. Both spheres, he thought, should be infused by the sort of
'wise liberalism' that led him, already in the years after 1848 and long before
the convocation of Vatican I, to proclaim also the need for a general council to reform the internal life and government of the Church.[114]

In conscious opposition, then, to De Maistre, Maret sought to identify
in the Church's constitution a liberal element that could open the way to

---

[111] Bressolette, *Le Pouvoir*, 98–112, 133, makes a good case for so doing.

[112] Maret, *Du concile general*, i. 541; ii. 38, 283. Similarly, ii. 259–60, where he claims that
Richer's (alleged) attack on the authority of pope and bishops stemmed from his assimila-
tion of the Church to 'the image of political society'. Cf. Bressolette, *Le Pouvoir*, 111; Thysman,
'Le Gallicanisme', 401.

[113] *Du concile général*, ii. 283. Cf. i. 541. Bressolette, *Le Pouvoir*, 107.

[114] Bressolette, *Le Pouvoir*, 135, citing a letter which Maret wrote in 1859 to Napoleon III,
and in which, having made the case that the search for conciliation in all relations between
Christianity and modern civilization called for far-reaching reform in ecclesiastical governance, he went on to argue (Bressolette's précis): 'Une vision politique de l'évolution dé-
mocratique de la société moderne commande l'insistance sur le restauration des libertés
canoniques des synodes et conciles, et sur le rétablissement des droits de l'aristocratie épis-
copale par rapport à la monarchie papale.'

his longed-for 'reconciliation of the Church with the modern notion of freedom'.[115] Noting the presence in the Church's constitution of a 'democratic' element in that any member of the faithful could be called to the episcopal state and that it was the original practice of Christian communities to elect their bishops, he insists, none the less, that democracy cannot claim sovereignty in the Church. But nor does that sovereignty reside in any form of absolute monarchy. It belongs, instead, to monarchy tempered with aristocracy (in one place he calls it 'a monarchy essentially aristocratic and deliberative'), in effect, what is sometimes called a mixed government, one framed along the same lines as 'constitutional and representative monarchy' in the world of secular regimes.[116]

That much can be said, Maret believes, even without having determined the precise relationship between pope and bishops. But as soon as one attempts to make that determination, one comes up against the fact that two long-standing schools of thought compete for one's allegiance. The first is the Italian school, which he describes as 'celebrated and worthy', and its great representative is Bellarmine. 'In the system of this school,' he says, 'the pope possesses a monarchical power that is pure, indivisible, absolute and unlimited.' To that power, notwithstanding rhetorical gestures to the contrary, no counter-weight is conceded—other than that furnished by 'the Christian virtues' and 'the sacred doctrines of the faith'.[117] The competing school, that of Paris, with Bossuet 'the incomparable doctor' as its great representative, asserts to the contrary that, while the pope is indeed the monarch of the Church, that monarchy is 'truly and efficaciously tempered by [the] aristocracy' of the bishops. For the bishops are not merely vicars or advisers to the pope, but, by divine right, co-judges and legislators with him, constituting in union with him 'the ecclesiastical sovereignty'.[118]

One has to decide between these competing schools, and to do so (he says) one has to put them to the test of scripture and tradition. So far as the scriptures are concerned, the celebrated cluster of texts (notably Matthew 16 and 18) which together constitute what he calls (and *pace* De Maistre) the very 'constitutional charter' of the Church, certainly seem to suggest

---

[115] Sieben, *Katholische Konzilsidee*, 100. As Maret himself wrote in an autobiographical statement that remains unpublished: 'J'avais consacré ma vie à la conciliation de la foi et de l'Église avec tout ce qu'il y a vrai et de légitime dans la science et dans la société moderne. Le caractère tempéré de la monarchie pontificale me parut très propre à devenir un premier moyen de conciliation. Cette conciliation demandait bien des réformes dans l'Église.' The extract is printed by Bressolette and Riccardi. See above, n. 105.

[116] Maret, *Du concile général*, i. 117–19, 129–30, 536–41.

[117] Ibid. i. 129–30.   [118] Ibid. i. 131.

that the sovereign power was given, not to Peter alone, but to the 'collective unity' of Peter and the other apostles, and to exclude from the government of the Church therefore any sort of 'pure, absolute and indivisible monarchy'.[119] But it is to the acts of the general councils down through history that one must turn for the 'authentic commentary' on and 'legitimate interpretation' of that fundamental scriptural 'constitutional charter'.[120] To that 'authentic commentary', then, he wastes no time in turning, conducting a careful and detailed canvass of the history of the general councils from Nicaea to Trent, devoting particular attention to the fifteenth-century councils from Pisa to Florence and more space to Constance than to any other general council, Trent itself not excluded. This last is no accident since, he says, on the conflicted issue of the pope–bishop relationship the decrees emanating from Constance and Florence are 'the most weighty and celebrated'. And, in so saying, he makes it clear that he has in mind the Constance decrees *Haec sancta* and *Frequens* and the Florentine decree *Laetentur coeli*, the first conciliar definition of the Roman pontiff's primacy.[121]

What, then, does he conclude? First, that notwithstanding the 'legitimate subordination of bishops to pope', scripture, tradition, and conciliar history alike preclude the attribution to the pontiff of any 'pure, indivisible and absolute monarchy'.[122] At the same time, they also preclude the opposite extreme—namely, the attribution to the general council of any 'absolute and unlimited superiority over the pope'. But, then, he correctly reminds us, and contrary to ultramontane claims, neither the fathers assembled at Constance who framed *Haec sancta* nor the French clergy who approved the Gallican declaration of 1682 advanced so extreme a position. And that is above all true of the 'great bishop, Bossuet himself'.[123] What instead emerged from Constance (itself a legitimate council ecumenical in nature right from the time of its first assembly[124]) was the mediating position expressed quintessentially in *Haec sancta*. Invoking, somewhat anachronistically, the criteria which Melchior Cano (d. 1560) in the sixteenth century had stipulated if one were to classify a conciliar enactment as a

---

[119] Ibid. i. 136–42.　　　　　　　　　　　　　　　　[120] Ibid. i. 142.

[121] Ibid. i. 379: 'Les décrets émanés de Constance et de Florence sont ce qu'il y a de plus grave et de plus célèbre sur cette matière tant disputée.' Maret devotes the whole of books 2 and 3 of the work (i. 145–504) to this task. The discussion of Constance alone runs from i. 386 to 432.

[122] Ibid. i. 337–8; where he notes, too, that 'certes, s'il y a quelque chose de clair, de certain dans l'histoire de ces neufs siècles que nous venons d'étudier, c'est que le Pape avec les évêques est plus grand, plus respecté, plus obéi, que lorsqu'il est seul'.

[123] Ibid. i. 342, 417–19.　　　　　　　　　　　　[124] Ibid. i. 386–405.

dogmatic definition, Maret, while conceding that the decree did indeed 'touch on matters of faith' and pertained to 'the domain of faith', nevertheless concluded that it did not proclaim 'a dogma of faith, rigorously defined'. Instead, it should properly be viewed as a 'constitutional law' having for its object the regulation of the use of ecclesiastical power, and one that was worthy of the 'most profound respect'.[125] Recognized in practice by successive popes from John XXIII and Martin V onwards, reaffirmed more than once by the Council of Basel and in no way qualified by the ecclesiological decrees of Florence and Lateran V,[126] it was a decree that simply stated 'more clearly and solemnly' than heretofore what had, in fact, been 'the constant and universal law of the Church', grounded in scripture itself, affirmed by fifteen centuries of tradition, and of continuing validity 'right down to the present'.[127] In accordance with the position it stated, the Church's constitution was to be viewed as a mixed one, a 'monarchy . . . essentially aristocratic and deliberative', one in which the pope, while possessing by divine authority the plenitude of power, was no pure absolute and unlimited monarch but a ruler who, in the exercise of that power, was limited by the aristocratic element constituted by the bishops themselves—'true princes', he added, possessing by divine right a share in the Church's sovereign power.[128] That power they were to wield in general councils regularly assembled, as *Frequens* had stipulated, working to reform the abuses that centuries of over-centralization had spawned, and forming a permanent part of the Church's constitutional machinery. And, as *Haec sancta* had specified, in certain extraordinary cases—schism, matters pertaining to the faith, and reform in head and members—the bishops assembled in council, acting alone or in opposition to the pope (and not simply a pope of doubtful legitimacy) could, by a determinative and not merely declaratory judgement, stand in judgement over him, punish him, and, if need be, proceed to depose him.[129]

[125] *Du concile général*, i. 408–12. Cf. the discussion above, Ch. 2. In classifying *Haec sancta* as a constitutional law Brian Tierney comes very close to Maret's position, but, unlike Maret, qualifies the import of the decree in relation to a pope of unquestioned legitimacy.

[126] In relation to Lateran V and its alleged abrogation of *Haec sancta* via the bull *Pastor aeternus*, Maret emphasizes the fact that even papalists like Bellarmine and Muzzarelli conceded that council to have been of doubtful ecumenicity. Similarly, he endorses the related point made by Bossuet and Tournély to the effect that *Pastor aeternus* was concerned with a different issue and that the glancing and rather general words some had interpreted as an abrogation of *Haec sancta* were merely incidental to the bull and susceptible of a different and more restricted reading. See *Du concile général*, i. 493–8. Cf. Oakley, 'Conciliarism at the Fifth Lateran Council?', 461–3, for the point at issue.

[127] *Du concile général*, i. 387–504. The words quoted appear at 425.   [128] Ibid. i. 536–41.

[129] See esp. ibid. i. 379–468, 530–43. Similarly, Maret, *Le Pape et les évêques*, 80.

All in all, an impressively robust reaffirmation of the age-old tradition of conciliarist constitutionalism in the Latin Church, and in which the conciliarists of the classical era, half a millennium earlier, would certainly have recognized the broad contours of their own ecclesiology. To that tradition, moreover, Maret did not hesitate to recur while participating in the debates at the First Vatican Council. Nor, though we hear little about it nowadays, was he alone in so doing. Darboy, archbishop of Paris, Strossmayer, bishop of Djakove, Vérot, bishop of St Augustine, Florida (but trained in France at Saint-Sulpice)—all of them strove to call attention to the legacy of Constance. They were forced to do so, however, in the teeth of vociferously impatient objections from the floor,[130] and when Vérot tried to read aloud and into the record the text of *Haec sancta* he was interrupted by shouts of 'Non! Non!'[131]

Before the year was out, of course, and its antiquity notwithstanding, Maret's position was to be doomed, thrust into the outer darkness of heterodoxy by *Pastor aeternus*, the First Vatican Council's historic decree on the primacy of jurisdiction and infallibility of the pope. Or so the pertinent curial officials clearly concluded. If Lord Acton as a layman was able to avoid any forthright endorsement of the council's teaching on infallibility against which he had fought so vigorously, clerics like Döllinger and Maret were permitted very little room for manœuvre. Refusing to submit, the former was accordingly excommunicated. And the latter was to find that his earnest attempts to identify some fugitive common ground between his own form of neo-Gallicanism and the ecclesiology which informed *Pastor aeternus* were unacceptable at Rome. In August 1871, then, though without specifying what it was, precisely, that he had in mind, he publicly disavowed 'whatever in his book and in his *Defense* is opposed to the Council's definition'.[132]

---

[130] Though not necessarily from the council presidents who, while doubtless upset with Bishop Strossmayer's invocation of the Constance decree *Frequens* mandating the regular assembly of general councils, and while certainly interrupting Maret and betraying a measure of irritation with the irrepressible Vérot, nevertheless proved themselves to be reasonably judicious. The assembled bishops, however, frequently fell short of that standard. Only Maret's deafness appears to have spared him the knowledge that while he was speaking voices were raised shouting 'haereticus est, . . . taceat . . . nolumus audire amplius'. For the speech itself, see Mansi, *Sacrorum conciliorum collectio*, lii. 429–41. Cf. Riccardi, *Neogallicanismo*, 270–4; Schatz, *Vaticanum I*, iii, app. III, 323–7; 'Quirinus', *Letters*, i. 97 (letter 4).

[131] Schneider, *Konziliarismus*, 185–8. For Vérot's rather blunt speech, not only evoking dist. 40, c. 6, of Gratian's *Decretum* (on the judgement of heretical popes) and the fact that the proposed teaching on papal infallibility was not held at the time of the Council of Constance, see Mansi, *Sacrorum conciliorum collectio*, lii. 955–66. He concluded the speech, which had been punctuated by 'risus', 'murmur', 'dissensus', and shouts of 'hora tarda est', with the wry comment: 'Doleo quod vobis tam molestus fuerim.'

[132] Palanque, *Catholiques*, 179–80. Cf. Schatz, *Vaticanum I*, iii. 293–4.

With that outcome, and the rapid descent into oblivion of the storied Gallican past, the great constitutional struggle of half a millennium and more, it seemed, had now reached its term.[133] During the waning years of the century, with the older members of the conciliar minority departing the scene and Acton withdrawn now into his historical labours at Cambridge, while distant echoes of desultory skirmishes far away on the very margins of the ecclesiological battlefield came eventually to be heard,[134] a great silence continued to brood over what had, until recently, constituted the very centre of the line. And the solitary horseman to be observed picking his confident way through the poignant litter and lonely detritus of battle turns out, on closer inspection, to be none other than the resilient ghost of Bellarmine.

As a result, and startling enough though it may well be, the fact remains that if one aspires to identify any unambiguously enduring contribution made to the shaping of European history by the age-old tradition of conciliarist constitutionalism, one has to turn from the enclosed and sometimes claustrophobic realm of ecclesiological strife which has been our concern up to now to the larger (if no less conflicted) world of secular political thinking.

---

[133] What Maret, *Le Pape et les évêques*, 2, characterized as 'une de plus difficiles controverses qui aient jamais été agitées dans l'Église'.

[134] In the years after Vatican I controversy surfaced on at least two significant issues relating to the role and status of general councils, but their connection with the older Roman–Gallican disputes, while not entirely lacking, was in both cases indirect. The first issue, very much an intra-theological debate, rumbled on for the better part of a century and led eventually into the deliberations preceding the Second Vatican Council's framing of the doctrine of episcopal collegiality. It concerned the question, left unresolved by Vatican I, as to whether there were one or two bearers of infallibility in the Church—simply the pope, or the pope, on the one hand, and the council united with the pope on the other. The second question, which surfaced immediately after Vatican I and fizzled out in the early years of the 20th century, pitted ecclesiastical historians against dogmatic theologians. It concerned the councils of the ancient Church in which the Roman emperors had played so dominant a role, and focused on the question of the degree to which the popes of the day had actually exercised the (later) papal prerogatives of convoking general councils, presiding over them, and confirming their decrees. For these controversies, see Sieben, *Katholische Konzilsidee*, 186–214, 229–43.

6

Democritus's Dreame:*
Conciliarism in the History
of Political Thought

[W]hat is of [the power of ecclesiastical] jurisdiction is not supernatural and outside the ordinary operations of human affairs. For it
is not beyond the ordinary condition of man that some men should
have jurisdiction over others, for that is in a certain way natural . . .
So then, just as jurisdiction is conferred by consent of men, so
contrariwise may it be taken away by consent.

(John of Paris, 1301–2[1])

The mystical body of the Church has this power [of assembling itself
in general council] not only by the authority of Christ, but also by the
common natural law. This is clear because any natural body naturally resists its own division and partition, and, if it is an animate
body, naturally summons up its members and all its powers in order
to preserve its own unity and to ward off its division—and, in a like
way, [so, too] any civil body, or civil community, or rightly ordained
polity.

(Pierre d'Ailly, 1409[2])

Suppose that power over the whole Church had been conferred on
the pope in such away that, although he exercised it to the Church's
destruction and not its edification, . . . nevertheless, he could not be
punished by the whole Church. From this it would follow . . . that the
ecclesiastical polity was not as well ordered as the civil polity, because
it would be against the good ordering of the civil polity not to be able

---

* John Maxwell, *Sacro-sancta Regum Majestas: Or, The Sacred and Royal Prerogatives of
Christian Kings* (Oxford, 1646), 104.

[1] John of Paris, *Tractatus de potestate regia et papali*, c. 25; ed. Bleienstein, 209; tr. Watt, 252.

[2] Pierre d'Ailly, *Propositiones utiles*, Martène and Durand, *Veterum Scriptorum et Monumentorum*, vii. 910.

to remove a member whose conduct might result in the destruction of the whole.

(Jacques Almain, 1512[3])

The Holy Church is not like the Republic of Venice, or of Genoa, or of some other city... [where] it can be said that the Republic is above the Prince. Nor is it like a worldly kingdom in which the people transfers its own authority to the monarch . . . For the Church of Christ is a most perfect kingdom and an absolute monarchy which neither depends on the people nor has from it its origin, but depends on the divine will alone.

(Robert, Cardinal Bellarmine, 1606[4])

Ecumenical councils, are they not ecclesiastical estates-general, and estates-general, are they not civil ecumenical councils?

(Joseph de Maistre, 1819[5])

If by ecclesiology one means the brand of theology devoted to the self-reflection of the Church on its own nature, then I believe it accurate to say that contemporary Roman Catholic ecclesiologists are apt to betray a measure of uneasiness about the propriety of admitting into their subdisciplinary discourse such arguments concerning the nature and structure of the Church as are based upon, or make central use of, analogies drawn from secular political entities. That uneasiness is perfectly understandable. It stems in no little part from their own firm reappropriation in recent years of pre-scholastic, patristic modes of thought, with their characteristic emphasis on the Church's interior reality as a *communio* or mystical community of salvation grounded in or manifested by its sacramental life. But I am inclined to think that it stems also, at least in some degree, from a shift over the past two decades in the attention of ecclesiologists away from the more exterior, institutional aspects of their field and towards its more fundamental—or, at least, more abstract and theoretical—dimensions. And it is tempting to speculate that the shift at Rome during that period into an unambiguously Themidorian mood may have rendered somewhat less than appealing as a career subspecialty the more concrete, institutional, or constitutional aspects of ecclesiological work. Certainly, on the latter (perhaps ungenerous) note, there come

---

[3] Jacques Almain, *Tractatus de auctoritate ecclesiae*, in Gerson, *Opera omnia*, ed. Dupin, ii. 991.

[4] Robert, Cardinal Bellarmine, *Risposta . . . ad un libretto . . . di Gio. Gersone*, printed in Bellarmine, *Risposta del Card. Bellarmine a due libretti*, 75–6.

[5] Maistre, *Du pape*, ch. 4, ed. Lovie and Chétail, 42.

irresistibly to mind from the late fourteenth century the words of a Parisian theologian, Jean Courtecuisse (Johannes Breviscoxe). After ruminating provocatively in one of his academic writings about the source of some aspects of the papal power of coercive jurisdiction, he wryly noted (tongue firmly in scholastic cheek): 'But this I do not *assert*. For it is perilous to speak of this matter—more perilous, perhaps, than to speak of the Trinity, or the Incarnation of Jesus Christ, our Saviour.'[6]

Such late twentieth-century preoccupations, however, should not be permitted to screen from us the fact (clearly reflected in the several epigraphs to this chapter) that for 700 years and more arguments based on secular political analogies, or arguments simply assuming something of a constitutional overlap between political and ecclesiastical modes of governance, served as a mainstay of ecclesiological discourse, whether highpapalist or constitutionalist. Hardly surprising, of course, given the marked degree to which in the Middle Ages secular and religious were intertwined, and ecclesiology and secular constitutional thinking, whether more absolutist or constitutionalist, constantly influenced one another. So much so, indeed, that 'the juridical culture of the twelfth century—the works of Roman and canon lawyers, especially those of the canonists where religious and secular ideas most obviously intersected—formed a kind of seedbed from which grew the whole tangled forest of early modern constitutional thought'.[7]

Certainly, already by the thirteenth century people had begun to think of the visible Church as a kingdom (*regnum ecclesiasticum*), and in some cases to assimilate it to the *imperium* and to speak of the pope as 'the true emperor' (thus the theologian, Augustinus Triumphus), or even 'the celestial emperor', a figure to whom could properly be applied such celebrated Roman legal tags as 'what pleases the prince has the force of law' (*quod principi placuit legis vigorem habet*) or 'the prince is freed from the law' (*princeps legibus solutus est*).[8] Among theorists of high-papalist disposition, indeed, the portrayal of the pope as a sort of quasi-absolute

---

[6] Breviscoxe, *Tractatus de fide et ecclesia, Roman Pontifice et concilio generali,* in Gerson, *Opera omnia,* ed. Dupin, i. 882. Cf. Oakley, 'The "Tractatus De Fide et Ecclesia" of Breviscoxe'. For some sense of the range of current Roman Catholic ecclesiological work, see A. Dulles and P. Granfield, *The Theology of the Church* (New York: Papalist Press, 1999).

[7] Thus B. Tierney, *Religion, Law, and the Growth of Constitutional Thought* (Cambridge: CUP, 1982), 1. For the mutual interpenetration of the two laws, canon and civil, until they formed a *jus commune,* a 'single intellectual system', see also K. Pennington, *The Prince and the Law 1200–1600* (Berkeley: University of California Press, 1993) and idem, *Pope and Bishops* (Philadelphia: University of Pennsylvania Press, 1984).

[8] E. Kantorowicz, *The King's Two Bodies* (Princeton: Princeton University Press, 1957), 202 n. 28; Ullmann, *Medieval Papalism,* 154 ff.

monarch was so much of a cliché, at least from the time of James of
Viterbo in the early fourteenth to Joseph de Maistre in the early nineteenth
century and beyond, as to lend at least a patina of credibility to Thomas
Hobbes's celebrated description of the papacy as 'no other than the *ghost*
of the deceased *Roman empire*, sitting crowned on the grave thereof'—an
observation no less illuminating in its fundamental perception for being
derisive in its conscious intent.[9] And if James of Viterbo produced in his
De regimine christiano what has been described as 'the most ancient treatise on the Church', and certainly the first to treat the Church consistently as a kingdom with the pope as its king, five centuries later Joseph
de Maistre, who had certainly never read him, was to push that same
ecclesiastio-political regalism to its logical conclusion, assimilating
infallibility to sovereignty and viewing it as an attribute of any power that
was truly monarchical.[10] 'Hence', as the German church historian Ignaz
von Döllinger wrote in 1869 in the celebrated 'Janus' papers, 'the profound
hatred, at the bottom of the soul of every genuine ultramontane of free
institutions and the whole constitutional system'.[11]

    Much the same was true of the constitutionalist side of the coin. Some
fluctuations did occur in that thinkers like Bishop Bossuet in the seventeenth century and Febronius in the eighteenth, responsive as they were to
pre-scholastic and patristic modes of thought, betrayed considerable uneasiness about the importation into ecclesiological discourse of arguments and analogies drawn from the world of secular politics.[12] But in this
they were the exception rather than the norm. To most conciliarist sympathizers, from John of Paris at the start of the fourteenth century to
Henri Maret, dean of the Sorbonne theology faculty in 1869 on the very eve
of the First Vatican Council, such reservations simply do not seem to have
bulked very large. And that was particularly true of the so-called 'divines
of Paris', from Pierre d'Ailly and Jean Gerson in the fifteenth century, via
Jacques Almain and John Mair in the sixteenth, to Edmond Richer in the
seventeenth. All of these men, in effect, as John Neville Figgis pointed out

---

    [9] Hobbes, *Leviathan*, pt. 4, ch. 47; ed. M. Oakeshott (Oxford: Basil Blackwell, 1946), 457.
    [10] Ed. Arquillière, *Le Plus Ancien Traité de l'eglise*. For De Maistre, see above, Ch. 5.
    [11] Having just observed that 'Church and State are like two parallel streams, one flow-
ing north and the other south. The modern civil Constitutions, and the efforts for self-
government and the limitation of arbitrary royal power, are in the strongest contradiction to
Ultramontanism, the very kernel and ruling principle of which is the consolidation of
absolutism in the Church. But State and Church are intimately related; they act and react on
one another, and it is inevitable that the political views and tendencies of a nation should
sooner or later influence it in Church matters, too.' See 'Janus', *Pope and Council*, 21–2.
    [12] See above, Chs. 4 and 5.

long ago, simply *assumed* that 'arguments applicable to government in general could not be inapplicable to the Church'.[13]

Concede that point, of course, and it becomes easier to concede also that the movement of ideas and traffic in analogies may not have been unidirectional but, rather, reciprocal, and that historians of political thought, reluctant in this though some of them may be, might do well to keep a weather-eye cocked for the shaping impact on modes of thinking about the secular polity of ideas that had their origin in the alien intricacies of ecclesiological discourse. It has long been customary to recognize that fact in relation to the ideology of absolute monarchy and to the notion of sovereignty itself. And in one of the reports from the First Vatican Council which Döllinger, using (and reshaping) materials sent to him by Lord Acton, put together as letters and had printed in 1870, in the *Augsburger Allgemeine Zeitung* under the pseudonym of 'Quirinus', he noted that that fact had come to seem so self-evident in his own day as to lead Giacomo Margotti (d. 1887), writing in the uncompromisingly papalist journal *Unità cattolica* which he himself had founded in 1863, to tout 'the wholesome political fruits [to be] looked for from the [definition of] the dogma of infallibility'. From 'the bright example set by the bishops in their submission to an infallible pope', Margotti had intimated, 'the nations will learn to submit as children to their sovereigns, [and] the kingdom of unrighteousness will pass away'. '[A]bsolutism in the Church will lead to Absolutism in the State.' Anyone tempted to be sceptical about that happy prospect, he added, should be mindful of the fact that 'Gallicanism, which demanded fixed guarantees against papal decisions . . . paved the way for constitutionalism and parliamentarism; for after a pope whose decrees *ex cathedra* are not irreformable, [came] a king limited by the Constitution, and then the era of parliamentary revolutions and political storms [was] introduced.'[14]

If, in hindsight, there is a slightly hallucinatory quality to Margotti's *prospective* claim, that should not blind us to the fact that, buried somewhere in his wildly exaggerated *retrospective* assumption about the impact of Gallican ideas on secular political and constitutional thinking, may lie a nugget of historical truth significant enough to warrant the effort of archaeological exploration in the political thinking of centuries preceding in order to retrieve it for examination and analysis.

---

[13] Figgis, *Political Thought*, 47. For d'Ailly and Gerson, see above, Ch. 2; for Almain and Mair, Ch. 3; for Richer, Ch. 4.

[14] 'Quirinus', *Letters from Rome*, ii. 778 n. 1 (appended to Letter 66).

THE ARGUMENT OF FIGGIS

Happily, the pursuit of that effort of retrieval has been facilitated by the fact that distinguished forerunners long ago prepared the way by laying down a preparatory barrage of pertinent claims. If some of those claims were blatantly propagandistic in intent, others were soberly historical in nature. From among those who advanced the former, let me adduce the royalist divine John Maxwell, Anglican bishop of Tuam, writing in 1644 during the turmoil of Civil War; from those who advanced the latter, John Neville Figgis, writing in the opening years of the twentieth century. As for Maxwell, he confessed, rather engagingly, that

I think, or fansie at least, that this opinion that Sovereignitie is seated in the Communitie, every individuall having its share, which by derivation from all and everyone, is concentrated in the Person of the King, is not unlike that dreame of Democritus and other Philosophers, who fancied to themselves that the whole *Universe* was composed and *diversified by a casual* concourse, of what I know not, fantastical and imaginerie *Atoms*.[15]

And he spoke thus at the end of a long and powerful attack on those 'Jesuits and Puritans', who, 'to depress Kinges averre, that all power is originally, radically and formally inherent in the People or Communitie, and from thence is derived to the Kinge'. That deplorable idea these Puritans ('Rabbies', he calls them) did not draw from 'the sound Protestants of the Reformed Churches' but from such monarchomachs of the previous century as Boucher, Rossaeus, and Hotman, and they, in turn, had 'borrowed' it (or so he charged) from 'the polluted cisterns' of 'the Sorbonistes and others of that kinde' (i.e. the scholastic theologians of Paris). And, in making that charge, he cites the writings of John of Paris, Jean Gerson, and Jacques Almain. These were men who, he says,

to oppose the Pope, his infallibilitie in judgement, his unlimited power, and to subject him to a Councell, did dispute themselves almost out of breath, to prove that *potestas spiritualis summa* was by Christ first and immediately given *unitati*, or *communitati fidelium*, that so the power might never perish, the truth might ever be preserved, and that howsoever for the time it was virtually in the Pope, yet he had it onely from the communitie of the faithfull *communicatively*, and in the case of defailance, in them it was *suppletive*; and in the case that the power of the Church was abused to heresie or tyrannie, the Pope was deposable (not only censurable) by a Councell. This question was acutely disputed before, about and after the Councell of Constance.[16]

---

[15] Maxwell, *Sacro-sancta*, 104.   [16] Ibid. 6, 12, 14–16.

Statements such as that were, of course, grist to the mill of a historian like Figgis who, following up on suggestions made a few years earlier by Otto von Gierke and by his own teacher at Cambridge, Lord Acton,[17] went on in one of his Birkbeck lectures to urge very forcefully the significance of the role he believed the conciliar movement to have played in the history of European political thought. That it should be cast in such a role at all is not, of course, to be taken for granted. Conciliar theory was, after all, an ecclesiological doctrine. If it was indeed a form of constitutionalism, it was *ecclesiastical* constitutionalism that was involved and, *pace* the assertions of such as Maxwell, its claim to a place in the history of political thought is by no means self-evident. But on this matter Figgis's opinion was characteristically robust, 'Probably the most revolutionary official document in the history of the world', he said, 'is the decree of the Council of Constance [*Haec sancta*] asserting its superiority to the Pope, and striving to turn into a tepid constitutionalism the Divine authority of a thousand years. The [conciliar] movement is the culmination of medieval constitutionalism. It forms the watershed between the medieval and the modern world.'[18] And why is this so? Because, in the first place, the scandal of the Great Schism had the effect of turning attention from the familiar dispute between the two powers, temporal and spiritual, and focusing it upon the nature of the Church itself. Because, in the second, '[s]peculation on the possible power of the Council as the true depository of sovereignty within the Church drove the [conciliar] thinkers to treat the Church definitively as one of a class, political societies'. Because, in the third, the conciliar thinkers of Constance

appear to have discerned more clearly than their predecessors the meaning of the constitutional experiments which the last two centuries had seen in considerable profusion, to have thought out the principles that underlay them, and based them upon reasoning that applied to all political societies; to have discerned that arguments applicable to governments in general could not be inapplicable to the Church. In a word, they raised the constitutionalism of the past three centuries to

---

[17] O. Gierke, *Political Theories of the Middle Age*, ed. and tr. F. W. Maitland (Cambridge: CUP, 1900), 49–58. Acton, *Lectures on the French Revolution*, ed. J. N. Figgis and R. V. Laurence (London: Macmillan & Co., 1910), 17, was clearly struck, as was Gierke, by the pertinence of 'the whig principles' embedded in conciliar theory to the history of *secular* political thought. The lectures were delivered at Cambridge in the 1890s. Burns, *Lordship, Kingship, and Empire*, 10 n. 14, notes that Acton's position on the matter had shifted somewhat over the previous forty years and that, earlier on, he had been 'unimpressed by Gerson's attempt to apply the principles of the secular polity to the Church'. Cf. Acton, *The History of Freedom and Other Essays*, ed. J. N. Figgis and R. V. Laurence (London: Macmillan & Co., 1907), 191–2.

[18] Figgis, *Political Thought*, 41.

a higher power, expressed it in a more universal form, and justified it on grounds of reason, policy, and Scripture.[19]

According, then, to Figgis, the conciliar movement was to be regarded as 'having helped forward modern constitutional tendencies'. Why? Because it stripped 'the arguments for constitutional government . . . of all elements of the provincialism, which might have clung to them had they been concerned only with the internal arrangements of the national States'. Conciliar theorists expressed their principles 'in a form in which they could readily be applied to politics', and so applied they were. 'Even [sixteenth-century] Huguenot writers like Du Plessis Mornay', said Figgis,

> were not ashamed of using the doctrine of the Council's superiority over the Pope to prove their own doctrine of the supremacy of the estates over the king . . . Emperors might be the fathers of the Council [of Constance] and kings its nursing mothers, but the child they nursed was Constitutionalism, and its far off legacy to our own day was the Glorious Revolution [of 1688].[20]

Three main claims, then, are made in this argument, claims that I will distinguish one from another and take up separately. The first is that the source of fourteenth- and fifteenth-century conciliar theory is to be found in the secular constitutional experiments of the previous centuries. The second is that conciliar theory exerted a demonstrable influence on the constitutionalists and resistance theorists of the sixteenth and seventeenth centuries. The third is that it did so (and herein lies its historical significance) because of the precision with which it discerned the theoretical principles underlying medieval constitutionalism, the universality with which it formulated those principles, and the clarity and force with which it restated them. And to say that is to say also that conciliar theory was not only an ecclesiological but also a political theory.

Although he had clearly read widely in the pertinent sources, the actual evidence that Figgis adduced in support of his assertions was really, in fact, quite scanty. But that did not prevent his claims being received enthusiastically in the inter-war years (and without benefit of further investigation) by a series of widely read historians of political thought—from H. J. Laski (his pupil) to R. G. Gettell, R. H. Murray, C. H. McIlwain, and George H. Sabine.[21] But interest in conciliar *theory*, at least, languished somewhat in

---

[19] Figgis, *Political Thought*, 47.   [20] Ibid. 46–8, 63.
[21] Laski, 'Political Theory in the Later Middle Ages', in H. M. Gwatkin *et al.*, eds., *The Cambridge Medieval History* (Cambridge: CUP, 1911–36), viii. 838; R. G. Gettell, *History of Political Thought* (New York and London: Century & Co., 1924), 133–5; Murray, *The History*

the years after Figgis wrote, and it was only after the Second World War that concern with the subject began to quicken again. And when it did, as we have already seen in an earlier chapter,[22] the validity of his first claim—which concerned the influence on ecclesiology of secular constitutional experiments in the national monarchies of the thirteenth and fourteenth centuries—was brought into question, and the roots of conciliar theory found to be thrust deep into the soil of earlier canonistic thinking, back as far, indeed, as the Decretist commentaries of the twelfth century in which religious ideas and ideas drawn from the newly revived Roman law had come to be inextricably intertwined with fruitful consequences for later constitutional developments, secular no less than ecclesiastical.

THE CONCILIAR LEGACY TO SIXTEENTH- AND SEVENTEENTH-CENTURY POLITICAL THOUGHT: SCOTLAND, FRANCE, ENGLAND

If Figgis's first claim has proved to be off the mark, it has become increasingly clear that his second claim—that pertaining to the subsequent impact of conciliar theory on the resistance theories of the sixteenth and seventeenth centuries—was very much on target. It is true, of course, and in striking contrast with the history of the conciliarist *ecclesiology*, that interest in this particular issue has been almost exclusively an Anglophone concern.[23] That fact duly acknowledged it remains the case that in the years after the Second World War when, in conciliar studies at large, attention began to shift from matters diplomatic and political to ecclesiological and doctrinal issues, Figgis's claim began to draw renewed support from a whole series of scholars with interests in late medieval and early modern political thought.[24] And with the publication in 1978 of Quentin

of Political Science (New York: D. Appleton & Co., 1930), 101; McIlwain, *The Growth of Political Thought* (New York: Macmillan Co., 1932), 348 n. 2; G. H. Sabine, *A History of Political Theory* (New York: Henry Holt & Co., 1956), 326–7.

[22] See above, Ch. 2.

[23] Otto Gierke stands out as an important exception to that generalization. Also, more recently, Juan Beneyto Perez, *Historia de las doctrinas políticas* (Madrid: Arguilar, 1964), 161–4. Much of the material in the middle section of this chapter is drawn from Oakley, 'Anxieties of Influence', 60–110 (at 87–108), where the argument is developed in more detailed fashion and at somewhat greater length.

[24] Rueger, 'Gerson, the Conciliar Movement', 467–80; A. J. Black, 'The Conciliar Movement', in Burns, ed., *Cambridge History of Political Thought c.330–c.1450* (Cambridge: CUP, 1988), 573–87 (esp. 586–7); idem, *Political Thought in Europe: 1250–1450* (Cambridge: CUP, 1992), 169–78; Burns, 'Conciliarist Tradition in Scotland', idem, *Lordship, Kingship, and Empire*, 10–12; Oakley, 'From Constance to 1688'; idem, 'Figgis, Constance, and the Divines of Paris'; idem, 'Natural Law'.

Skinner's *Foundations of Modern Political Thought*, with its informed and forceful acknowledgement of the importance of the contribution which the conciliar theorists had made to the shaping of early modern political thinking,[25] that point of view was now poised on the edge of being 'mainstreamed' among historians of political thought at large.

In order, of course, to be indebted to the views of the fifteenth- and sixteenth-century conciliarists, resistance theorists and constitutionalists of the seventeenth century had to have access, direct or indirect, to such views. If historians might once have had reason to be doubtful on that score, such doubts must surely have been laid to rest by the research findings of the past forty years which have made it abundantly clear that for such theorists access to the views of their conciliarist predecessors can have presented no problem at all.[26] The less so, indeed, in that the resistance theorists of the sixteenth century, whose own authority was to be invoked by their English parliamentary successors in the following century, themselves provided an additional (if indirect) mode of access to conciliarist ideas, along with the example of their application to the world of secular politics. That was clear enough in the case of the Calvinists among those sixteenth-century theorists. It was almost as clear in the case of the Jesuit, Juan de Mariana, who, in the context of discussing whether or not the commonwealth possessed greater power than did the king, alluded (somewhat uneasily, perhaps) to the analogy of conciliar superiority—a move that did not escape, later on, the sharp, if approving, eye of the English Puritan parliamentarian, William Prynne.[27] And if there is no mention of conciliarism in the tracts of Rossaeus or Boucher, the leading resistance theorists of the French Catholic League, one should recognize that their alignment with Rome gave them every incentive to conceal any indebtedness of that sort if it did, indeed, exist.[28]

Whatever the case, the silence of those Catholic monarchomachs on this particular matter was not to carry much weight with John Maxwell when, half a century later, he came to attack the allegedly populist or

---

[25] Skinner, *Foundations of Modern Political Thought*, 2; idem, 'The Origins of the Calvinist Theory of Revolution', in Malament, *After the Reformation*, 309–30.

[26] See above, Chs. 2, 3, and 4.

[27] Mariana, *De rege et Regis institutione*, lib. I, c. 8, pp. 72–4. Prynne, *The Soveraigne Power of Parliaments and Kingdoms*, 68.

[28] In the works of Rainolds (Rossaeus), *De justa reipublicae Christianae* (1590), and Boucher, *De justa Henrici Tertii abdicatione* (1596), students of conciliar theory are likely to encounter much that may strike them as familiar, but no grounds for asserting anything other than interesting parallelisms. Cf. F. J. Baumgartner, *Radical Reactionaries* (Geneva: Droz, 1975).

democratic ideas of Jesuit and Puritan. I have drawn attention to Maxwell more because of his vituperative *esprit* than because there was anything really unusual about his attempt to discredit the notion of popular sovereignty and to undercut the parliamentary advocacy of a right of legitimate resistance against tyranny by linking them so damagingly with popery. 'Jesuit' had become a useful 'snarl-word' long before the end of the Elizabethan era,[29] and the coupling of Jesuit and Puritan as bedfellows in sedition had become a cliché by the time James I lent it his own royal authority when in 1609 he dubbed Jesuits as 'nothing other than *Puritan—papists*'.[30] Even before the Gunpowder Plot of 1605 the 'Romishe schooles' had come to be viewed, in Thomas Morton's words, as 'seminaries of rebellion'.[31] But, as we have already seen,[32] the great Europe-wide ideological controversy pivoting on the English Oath of Allegiance dispute from 1606 onwards helped stimulate in England a marked quickening of interest in conciliar theory and in the dramatic actions taken two centuries earlier by the Councils of Pisa, Constance, and Basel.

As a result, one begins to encounter expressions of alarm from staunch royalists focused now specifically on the unhappy availability of the conciliar precedent of the trial and deposition of popes to those benighted contemporaries who wished to legitimate a right of resistance against temporal rulers. Thus David Owen, writing in 1610 his *Herod and Pilate Reconciled*, argued that the 'politicke divines' of the day had 'learned their errour, of the *power of States—men over Kings*', thereby investing 'the people and nobles with the power over kings, to dispose of their kingdoms', from such papistical schoolmen as John of Paris, Jacques Almain, and Marsiglio of Padua. And he went on to berate the Calvinist leaders Theodore Beza and Lambert Daneau for having endorsed the idea that 'as a generall councell is above the Pope, so the Kingdome or the Peeres of the Land, are above the King'.[33] In committing themselves to that position, Beza and Daneau, far from being alone, had been at one with most of the leading Protestant advocates of resistance theory in the latter half of the sixteenth century—from John Ponet, exiled bishop of Winchester, writing his *Short Treatise of Politicke Power* in 1556 during the reign of Mary Tudor, to George Buchanan, writing his *De jure Regni apud Scotos* in 1567, to the Huguenot authors of the *Vindiciae contra tyrannos* and the *Discours*

[29] Clancy, *Papist Pamphleteers*, 88.
[30] *A Premonition to all most Mightie Monarchies*, in *Political Works of James I*, ed. McIlwain, 126.
[31] Morton, *An Exact Discoverie* (1605), 1. [32] See above, Ch. 4.
[33] Owen, *Herod and Pilate Reconciled* (1610), 43–6, 48, 50–1.

politique who produced their statements during the French Religious Wars and in the anguished aftermath of the St Bartholomew's Day massacre.[34] All of these authors—and Ponet, Buchanan, and Du Plessis Mornay at considerable length—had adduced conciliar theory and practice in order to argue (in the words of the *Vindiciae*) that if the general council can depose the pope, who regards himself 'as much in dignity above the Emperour as the Sun is above the Moon', 'who then will make any doubt or question, that the general assembly of the Estates of any Kingdom, who are the representative body thereof, many not only degrade and disthronize a Tyrant, but also disthronize and dispose a king, whose weakness and folly is hurtful or pernicious to the State'.[35]

It is not surprising, then, that four years after the appearance of Owen's book, and in the process of writing against Cardinal Bellarmine a truly enormous treatise on the pope's power in matters temporal (one punctuated with quotations from such conciliarists as John of Paris, Pierre d'Ailly, Jean Gerson, Dietrich of Niem, Francesco Zabarella, Nicholas of Cusa, Panormitanus, Aeneas Sylvius Piccolomini, Jacques Almain, and John Mair)—it is not surprising that John Buckeridge, bishop of Ely, felt it necessary to challenge the very pertinence of the conciliar analogy to matters political by insisting that according to 'many theologians of great name . . . the ecumenical council is said to have *greater* authority over a pope than the people is said to have over a prince' (emphasis mine). For whereas the pope's position is founded in grace, the king's is founded in nature. And whereas the pope can be called before a tribunal by which he can 'without doubt' be deposed, 'no one', the people being inferior to him, 'can judge, punish or depose a king'.[36]

Similarly, thirty years later, during the first Civil War, John Bramhall, subsequently archbishop of Armagh and tenacious adversary of Thomas Hobbes, reacting as had Owen to Beza's invocation of the conciliar analogy, made a similar attempt to neutralize its force by conceding the council's power of deposition while at the same time noting that, pertaining as

---

[34] Ponet, *A Shorte Treatise*, [102]–[106]; cf. [60]. Buchanan, *De jure regni apud Scotos*, in *Opera omnia*, ed. Ruddiman, i. 8, 30, 36. 'Junius Brutus', *Vindiciae contra tyrannos*, 173–4; Anon., *Discours politique*, in S. Goulart, ed., *Mémoires de l'Estat de France* (Meidelbourg, 1576), iii. fos. 147^b–213^b (at 209^b–210^b).

[35] This passage I cite from the 17th-cent. English translation, itself testimony to the appeal of the work: *Vindiciae contra tyrannos . . . Being a Treatise Written in English and French by Junius Brutus* (1689), 142. For a more extensive discussion of the 16th-cent. phase in the influence of conciliarist views on Calvinist resistance theory, see Oakley, 'On the Road from Constance to 1688'.

[36] J. Buckeridge, *De potestate papae* (London, 1614), 675–6 (citing William Barclay); cf. 677–86.

it did to the pope, it pertained also to an elected rather than a hereditary ruler and that it was 'grounded in a known [canon] law'. In comparison, he insisted, ['t]he king's crown sits closer, the Council's power is greater, the like law is wanting'.[37] And around the same time another royalist, Henry Ferne, later to become bishop of Chester, accusing his parliamentary opponents of Jesuitical practice and of borrowing their arguments from 'the *Romane* Schools', derided them for harbouring silent thoughts of parliamentary infallibility and for being willing to attribute a binding force to the decrees of a parliament acting in the absence of the king on the grounds that '[s]*uch a power of binding has a generall Councell* [of the Church] *to its decisions, and why should a Civill Generall Councell of England* [i.e. the Parliament] *have lesse power in it?*'[38]

Such royalist counter-attacks were launched, however, in vain. Even after the Oath of Allegiance controversy and affiliated disputes had died down, familiarity in England with the conciliarist literature and with the action of the fifteenth-century councils in judging and deposing popes was such that when in April/May 1628 'parliamentary proceedings came [for the first time in that era] to be dominated by a contest between King and Commons about the nature and limits of supreme authority', it was perfectly natural for Sir Dudley Digges (the elder) to reach in debate for a comparison between their own concerns and those of their conciliarist predecessors. Just as the fathers assembled at the Council of Basel, he said, had debated 'whether the Pope be above the church or the church above the Pope, so now is there a doubt whether the law be above the King or the King above the law'.[39] If the successive editions of Foxe's *Book of Martyrs*, with its lengthy extracts from Aeneas Sylvius Piccolomini's (conciliarist) *De gestis concilii Basiliensis* can only have reinforced that familiarity, the English translation of the *Vindiciae* (from which I quoted earlier and which appeared and reappeared in 1622, 1631, 1648, and 1689), and the reissues in 1639 and 1642 of Ponet's *Shorte Treatise of Politicke Power* served

[37] Bramhall, *Serpent—Salve* in *The Works of the Most Reverend Father in God, John Bramhall, D.D.*, ed. A.W.H. (Oxford: J. H. Parker, 1842–5), iii. 316.

[38] Ferne, *The Resolving of Conscience* (Oxford, 1643), sig. A 3; idem, *Conscience Satisfied* (Oxford, 1643), 38–9.

[39] For the passage in question, see R. C. Johnson *et al.*, eds., *Commons Debates 1628* (New Haven and London: Yale University Press, 1972–83), iii. 102 (26 Apr. 1628). 'The discourse of the Council of Basel' to which Digges refers is, or so the editors conclude, Aeneas Sylvius Piccolomini's conciliarist *De gestis concilii Basiliensis commentariarum*, and they refer us to the latter's rendition of the celebrated speech which the bishop of Burgos delivered in 1431. For which, see above, Chs. 3 and 4, and, below, p. 248. Cf. C. Russell, *Parliaments and English Politics* (Oxford: Clarendon Press, 1979), 354.

to draw attention to the pertinence of the conciliar precedent to the constitutional dilemma with which the mid-century parliamentarians were now confronted.[40] So, too, did the continued circulation of Buchanan's *De jure regni apud Scotos*, the persistent notoriety of which is evidenced by its targeting for governmental condemnation in 1584, 1660, 1664, and 1688 and by its inclusion among a list of works which the University of Oxford condemned as subversive in 1683.[41]

Thus the irrepressible, robust parliamentarian, William Prynne, who made extensive use of the arguments of Ponet, the *Vindiciae*, Buchanan, and the latter's old teacher, the conciliarist John Mair, repeatedly invoked the example of conciliar jurisdictional superiority set by the Councils of Pisa, Constance, and Basel and even by the *conciliabulum* of Pisa in 1511.[42] He also quoted, and at length, Aeneas Sylvius's rendition of a speech delivered in 1431 during the debates at Basel. In that speech the bishop of Burgos, ambassador of the king of Castile, in his attempt to make the case for the superiority of council to pope, had appealed to a secular analogy that he clearly assumed would strike his listeners as unexceptionably commonsensical. 'The Pope', he said,

is in the Church as a King is in his Kingdome, and for a King to be of more authority than his Kingdome, it were too absurd. Ergo. Neither ought the Pope to be above the Church . . . And like as oftentimes Kings, which doe wickedly governe the commonwealthe and express cruelty, are deprived of their Kingdoms; even so it is not to be doubted but that the Bishop of Rome may be deposed by the Church, that is to say, by the generall Councell.[43]

The English translation from which Prynne is citing is the one printed in Foxe's *Book of Martyrs*,[44] and its appeal to English parliamentarians (at a time when belief in the subordination of king to kingdom had long since lost its status as a matter of simple common sense) is reflected in the fact that the same lengthy quotation drawn from the same source had been prominently featured a year earlier in William Bridge's rebuttal of one of Henry Ferne's royalist tracts. Bridge had also made considerable use of the conciliarist writings of Jacques Almain, and the latter's authority is further invoked, along with that of Ockham, Gerson, and Mair, in Samuel

[40] See Laski, ed., *A Defence of Liberty Against Tyrants* (London: B. Franklin, 1924), introduction, 59–60; W. S. Hudson, *John Ponet* (Chicago: University of Chicago Press, 1942), 209–10.

[41] See Oakley 'From Constance to 1688', 11 and n. 50.

[42] Prynne, *The Soveraigne Power of Parliaments and Kingdoms*, 5–7, 9, 20, 23, 31, 68, 73, 122, 136, 144–5; *Appendix*, 100–12, 161.

[43] Ibid. 6.   [44] Foxe, *Actes and Monuments*, ed. Cattley, iii. 611–12. See above, Ch. 3.

Rutherford's *Lex, Rex*, a work written in 1644 by way of response to Maxwell's *Sacro-sancta regum majestas*.[45]

Clearly, then, Figgis was correct in his claim that conciliar theory exerted a demonstrable influence upon the constitutional and resistance theorists of the sixteenth and seventeenth centuries. If, after the onset of the Reformation, the Catholics among them were rarely explicit enough on the matter to warrant anything more than the cautious mention of parallels and similarities, with the Protestants we are on firmer ground. As Quentin Skinner has rightly observed in relation to one strand in the sixteenth-century phase of the story, 'when the Calvinist George Buchanan stated for the first time on behalf of the Reformed Churches a fully secularized and populist theory of political resistance, he was largely restating a position already attained by the Catholic John Mair in his teaching at the Sorbonne half a century before'.[46] And as Zofia Rueger put it in relation specifically to seventeenth-century England, 'the conciliar precedent was deemed of sufficient importance and relevance to be invoked frequently enough to force the Royalist writers into a polemic', forming, as a result, 'a distinct strand of the controversy over the right of resistance in the years 1642–1644'.[47] Scholars will doubtless disagree about how substantial in individual cases this conciliar legacy was, but they will certainly not be warranted in ignoring it, still less in questioning its existence. What they may do, however, and properly so, is to ask why this conciliar legacy should be thought of as significant, noteworthy, possessed of a measure of explanatory power. And that brings us, of course, to Figgis's third and most important claim, which concerned the very status and significance of conciliar theory in the history of political thought.

THE NATURE AND SIGNIFICANCE OF THE CONCILIAR LEGACY TO POLITICAL THOUGHT

In this connection, it will be recalled, Figgis asserted that conciliar theory lent itself to the use it subsequently received precisely because of its intrinsic nature, because of the universality and force with which it advanced what was not only an ecclesiological option but, beyond that, a political

[45] W. Bridge, *The Wounded Conscience Cured* (London, 1642), 2, 7–8; also his *The Truths of the Times Vindicated* (London, 1643), 2–7, 49; Rutherford, *Lex, Rex: The Law and the Prince* (London, 1644), 50, 418, 449.

[46] Quentin Skinner, 'The Origins of the Calvinist Doctrine of Resistance', in Malament, *After the Reformation*, 325.

[47] Rueger, 'Gerson, the Conciliar Movement', 325.

theory. And we have to acknowledge the degree to which ignorance of Figgis's claims or agnosticism and even outright scepticism about their validity have persisted among historians. Some—for instance, Pierre Mesnard, R. W. and A. J. Carlyle, J. W. Allen, Christopher Morris, and, more recently, Julian Franklin—if they betray any consciousness at all of conciliar thinking, appear to have regarded it, in its sixteenth- no less than its fifteenth-century expression, as irrelevant, strictly speaking, for the history of political thought.[48] Others—Walter Ullmann, J. B. Morrall, and, more recently, Cary Nederman—have expressed reservations (though not necessarily with express reference to Figgis) about the failure of conciliarists to translate theory into practice, about the coherence and universality of their theoretical position itself, and about the degree to which the early modern constitutionalists who appealed to it in support of their own claims may have done so selectively and anachronistically, without a historically accurate understanding of the position itself.

Thus, more than thirty years ago, while conceding that conciliarism was 'undoubtedly' a 'political doctrine', that it was a 'ruthless' application of what he called 'the ascending theory of government' (that is, popular sovereignty) to the one body 'which at first sight would have seemed immune' to it, Ullmann expressed grave doubts about the degree to which the conciliarists had really acted on their principles. By their deeds, he implied, ye shall know them. The old Romano-canonical principle 'what touches all, by all should be approved' was a persuasive political slogan, but one missed its appearance in practice. Constance and Basel were 'as heretofore' merely 'ecclesiastical assemblies' dominated, moreover, by the higher clergy. 'The lower clergy and the educated layman', he argues, 'were . . . knocking at the gate, and were refused entry.' 'Laymen indeed could submit memoranda, reports, make speeches and take part in the council's debates, but they were not allowed to vote except in so far as they were delegates of Kings who were not of course merely laymen; in so far the old theocratic-descending point of view was applied once again.'[49] Or as

---

[48] P. Mesnard, *L'Essor de la philosophie politique au XVIe siècle* (Paris: Ancienne Librairie Furme; 1936); Allen, *History of Political Thought*; idem, *Political Thought in England*; R. W. and A. J. Carlyle, *A History of Political Thought in the West* (Edinburgh and London: William Blackwell & Sons, 1903–36), vi. 163–7, and 247, where A. J. Carlyle *contrasts* 'the ecclesiastical questions of the relation between the Pope and the General Council', which he excludes from consideration, with the remarks of the conciliarists concerning properly 'political principles'; Julian A. Franklin, review of Skinner, *Foundations of Political Thought*, in *Political Theory*, 7 (1979), 552–8 (at 557–8).

[49] Ullmann, *Principles*, 288–315; idem, *History of Political Thought*, 219–25, 313–14. For an earlier and fuller analysis of these and J. B. Morrall's affiliated claims, though not those

J. B. Morrall had put it when expressing similar sentiments a few years earlier, the early fifteenth-century conciliar thinkers 'were all strict believers in clerical monopoly of church government', and the conciliar theory itself was 'still inseparably wedded to the orthodox hierarchical conception of authority as coming from above rather than below'. As a result, 'all the ingenuity of thinkers even of Gerson's caliber could not give the representative principle, based essentially on delegation from below, its full expression'.[50]

To such an assessment of the fifteenth-century councils it would be easy enough to take exception. At Basel, voting rights were extended in unprecedented degree to members of the lower clergy and it is implausible to dismiss the grant of a vote to lay ambassadors simply as an acknowledgement of the allegedly clerical status of their royal or princely masters. But Ullmann's remarks and those of Morrall were addressed to the theoretical formulations of the conciliarists and not merely to their alleged failure to translate theory into practice. That lag in practice, they implied, was but the reflection of the internal incoherence of the theory itself. The conciliarists were unable fully to escape the gravitational pull of 'the old theocratic-descending point of view'. What they did, Ullmann claimed, 'was to refurbish the old episcopalist system under the cover of a progressive movement: stripped of its inessential paraphernalia, conciliarism was a late-medieval revival of episcopalism'.[51] That being so, and given what Morrall called 'the ambiguity inherent in the whole conciliar position',[52] its place likewise in the history of political thought can only be an ambiguous one. The eagerness of the early modern constitutionalists and resistance theorists to evoke the conciliar precedent should not encourage us to overlook that fact. Conciliarist ideas may well have influenced such theorists but the latter, Ullmann insisted, did not swallow their conciliarism whole. Instead, they selected from among the conciliar materials handed down to them and chose to emphasize 'only one strand of conciliarist thought'.[53] And even then, if a forceful argument advanced by Nederman

---

advanced later by Cary J. Nederman, see Oakley, 'Figgis, Constance and the Divines of Paris', 376–86. For the background to Ullmann's treatment of conciliar thinking in particular and medieval constitutionalism in general, and for the distorting nature of the distinction he persistently deploys between the 'ascending' and 'descending' theories of government, see Oakley, 'Celestial Hierarchies Revisited'.

[50] Morrall, *Political Thought*, 126–7.
[51] Ullmann, *Principles*, 314; idem, *History of Political Thought*, 223–5.
[52] Morrall, *Political Thought*, 128.
[53] Quoting here Ullmann's review of Oakley, *The Political Thought of Pierre d'Ailly*, in *Renaissance News*, 18 (1965), 305–7.

is correct, they read those selected materials anachronistically, reinterpreting them, 'selectively and in accordance with their own particular problems and assumptions'.[54]

Clearly, the issues these criticisms raise are exceedingly intricate. Impinging directly on Figgis's third influence claim, they render the assessment of its validity a rather more complicated affair than that of the two preceding. Complex and taxing, it may be, but not impossible. And I would suggest that it can best be approached by posing four questions.

First, did the restriction on voting rights at the fifteenth-century councils really witness to some fundamental ambiguity in conciliar theory itself, signalling that what the conciliarists were engaged in—their invocation of the corporational representative principle notwithstanding—was nothing more, in essence, than a 'revival of episcopalism'? Secondly, what aspects of conciliar theorizing and practice were the seventeenth-century parliamentarians, or, for that matter, their sixteenth-century monarchomach predecessors, invoking? Thirdly, why was it, after all, if the conciliar precedent was so unhelpfully ambiguous, that they insisted on flourishing it, knowing (as they had to) that it could expose them also to the damaging charge of crypto-popery? Fourthly, in evoking the conciliar experience and exploiting the ideas of the conciliarists, was their understanding historically accurate, or were they reading those theorists anachronistically, reinterpreting their thinking 'selectively' through the distorting lens interposed by their own later 'problems and assumptions'? I will address each of these questions in turn.

First, and as I have been at pains to emphasize,[55] conciliarist theorizing was far from possessing any sort of monolithic unity. Even if we limit ourselves to the Parisian conciliarists whose names crop up so frequently in the works of the seventeenth-century English controversialists, we will encounter important shades of difference in their respective positions. The matter of voting rights affords a good illustration of that fact. Thus whereas Mair does not discuss voting rights and makes no mention of lay

---

[54] An allegation made with specific reference to the use made of Gerson's ideas but as part of a sweeping dismissal of the pertinence to the shaping of early modern constitutionalism of conciliar theory in particular and medieval ecclesiology in general. See Nederman, 'Conciliarism and Constitutionalism', *History of European Ideas*, 12 (1990), 189–209 (at 189–92); for a rebuttal, Oakley, 'Nederman, Gerson, Conciliar Theory and Constitutionalism: *Sed Contra*', *History of Political Thought*, 16 (1995), 1–19; and, for what I myself may be forgiven for viewing as an unconvincing response, Nederman, 'Constitutionalism—Medieval and Modern: Against Neo-Figgisite Orthodoxy (Again)', *History of Political Thought*, 17 (1996), 179–94.

[55] See above, Ch. 2.

representation in general councils,[56] d'Ailly, Gerson, and Almain do both. But while Gerson insists that the right to vote be enjoyed by the lower clergy as well as by the bishops and that no member of the faithful be refused a hearing, he is willing to see the laity restricted to a merely consultative or advisory capacity—though it is important to note that he sees nothing permanent or necessary about such a restriction.[57] Almain follows him faithfully in this,[58] but d'Ailly is a good deal more forthcoming. Though the unlearned and those of the lowest ranks are not specifically summoned to the council, no Catholic, he insists, should be excluded. Nor should kings, princes, or their representatives be denied a vote (*determinatio conclusiva; vox definitiva*) any more than should doctors of theology or of canon or civil law, for they are all men with authority over the people.[59]

The selective procedures suggested here are by no means democratic, but it would surely be anachronistic to expect them to be so. If that is what Morrall means when he speaks of giving the representative principle its 'full expression' (and his comparison with the make-up of the House of Commons prior to the Great Reform Bill on 1832 suggests that it is),[60] then the conciliar theorists undoubtedly fall short of the mark. But then, so too, of course, would the Estates in sixteenth-century France and the

[56] He defines a general council as follows: 'A council . . . is a congregation [of representatives] drawn from every hierarchical rank whose concern it is, summoned by those to whom that duty pertains, to deal according to the common intention with matters concerning the general welfare of Christendom.' Mair, *Disputatio de auctoritate concilii*, in Gerson, *Opera omnia*, ed. Dupin, ii. 1132.

[57] Just as in some periods, he says, prelates have been elected by the whole people and clergy and in others by the clergy alone, similarly the council, if it so desires, is at liberty to extend or restrict the vote in accordance with the needs of the times—Jean Gerson, *De potestate ecclesiastica*, in Glorieux, vi. 241–2; cf. his *Sermo*: '*Ambulate dum lucem habetis*', ibid. v. 44.

[58] Jacques Almain, *Tractatus de auctoritate ecclesiae*, in Gerson, *Opera omnia*, ed. Dupin, ii. 1011–12; idem, *Expositio . . . de potestate ecclesiastica et laica*, ibid. 1067; and idem, *Quaestio resumptiva . . . de dominio naturali, civili et ecclesiastico*, ibid. 973.

[59] Pierre d'Ailly, *Oratio de officio imperatoris*, in Gerson, *Opera omnia*, ed. Dupin, ii. 921, and *Disputatio de jure suffragii quibus competat*, in H. von der Hardt, *Rerum concilii oecumenici* (Leipzig, 1679–1700), ii. 225–7; cf. d'Ailly, *Tractatus de ecclesiastica potestate*, in Gerson, *Opera omnia*, ed. Dupin, ii. 941. This, it should be noted, marked a break with his earlier (1403) advocacy of the position that the 'definitive authority in a council belonged to the bishops alone'. See his *Tractatus de materia concilii generalis*, ed. Oakley, in *Political Thought of d'Ailly*, appendix III, pp. 244–345 (at 268, 272–3); cf. my comment, ibid. 152–4.

[60] See Morrall, *Political Thought*, 128–9, where he comments that for Gerson 'the presence of the laity is not necessary for they are represented in the Council by the clergy; the argument is reminiscent of the theory of "virtual" representation in the pre-1832 British House of Commons as put forward by those who opposed the reform of that institution'. For a succinct analysis of the complex notion of representation involved in conciliar thinking, see Tierney, 'The Idea of Representation'.

Parliament in seventeenth-century England. As d'Ailly put it, 'what touches all must be approved by all, or at least by many and the more notable ones'. An aristocratic principle of selection is clearly at work, but the important thing to recognize is that it is not predicated upon the possession of powers of a hierarchical nature. That is the factor fundamental to any strictly episcopalist position, but clearly not the one d'Ailly has in mind, for, after the assembly of Constance, he pointedly insisted that doctors of theology or of either of the two laws had greater authority over the Christian people and, therefore, a better claim to the vote than ignorant or merely titular bishops or archbishops.[61]

Secondly, and as I have argued,[62] during the late sixteenth and much of the seventeenth century English people had become better acquainted with the history of the fifteenth-century councils and the writings of the conciliarists than at *any* previous time—the fifteenth century not excluded. And while in general they invoked that history and those writings for a variety of purposes, the parliamentarians among them were markedly selective in what they drew from such sources. Surprisingly, perhaps, they did not seek to exploit the quasi-oligarchic strand (with its evocation of the idea of mixed government) that had been present already in the ecclesiology of John of Paris, had found some resonance in Gerson's conciliar thought, and had been so prominent a feature of the conciliarism of d'Ailly, Zabarella, and Nicholas of Cusa.[63] Instead, they focused almost exclusively on the precedent established by the central conciliar assertion of the ultimate jurisdictional superiority to the pope of the general council acting as representative of the universal church, and on the historic vindication of that superiority by the conciliar judgement and deposition of popes at Pisa, Constance, and Basel.[64] And that fact, that selectivity, speaks to our third question.

Neither the English, French, and Scottish resistance theorists of the sixteenth century nor the English parliamentarians of the seventeenth appear to have found anything at all ambiguous about the central strand of conciliar thinking upon which they placed so much emphasis. Nor did the

---

[61] Pierre d'Ailly, *Disputatio de jure suffragii quibus competat*, in Hardt, *Rerum*, ii. 225–7.

[62] See above, Ch. 4.

[63] For which, see above, Ch. 2.

[64] Cf. Rueger, 'Gerson, the Conciliar Movement', 483: '[T]he conciliar assertion of supremacy and the conciliar deposition of the Pope appeared to offer a unique example of a seemingly successful application of the universal medieval principle [i.e. the right of resistance to a ruler turned tyrant] to the only form of medieval monarchy which was founded exclusively on divine right and excluded the idea of consent—the Papacy. At least this is what to Buchanan seemed to be the chief lesson of the Conciliar Movement.'

French Huguenots appear to have lost any sleep over their indebtedness to scholastic predecessors for their revolutionary ideas. Quite the contrary, in fact. If Skinner is correct, they may even have seen it as a distinct advantage. For it helped them in their attempt 'to neutralize as far as possible the hostile Catholic majority by showing them the extent to which revolutionary political actions could be legitimated in terms of impeccably Catholic beliefs'.[65] That was far from being the case, of course, with their seventeenth-century English successors. 'In Stuart England there was much political capital to be made from convicting one's opponents of popery',[66] and the sensitivity of the parliamentarians to the charge of crypto-popery and even more of Jesuitry is reflected in their anxious attempts to deflect its force. In relation to the despised doctrine of popular sovereignty Maxwell had charged that 'Puritan and Jesuite in this, not only consent and concurre, but like *Herod* and *Pilate* are reconciled to crucify the Lord's anointed.'[67] To that Rutherford retorted that Maxwell, having taken 'unlearned paines, to prove that Gerson, Occam, Jac[obus] de Almaine, Parisian Doctors maintained these same grounds anent the peoples power over Kings in the case of Tyranny [as did the Jesuits]', had by so doing given 'himselfe the lye' and inadvertently demonstrated that 'we have not this Doctrine from Jesuites'.[68] But if not from Jesuits, clearly still from papists. And that charge Bridge was forced to shrug off with the rejoinder that 'Reason is good wherever we finde it; neither would *Abraham* refuse the use of the Well because Abimalech's men had used it, no more will we refuse good reason, because Papists have used it.'[69]

A reasonably robust stance it may be, but it does invite one to inquire into the nature of that 'good reason'. And here it is important to emphasize the degree to which the seventeenth-century opponents of absolutism in England confronted a new orthodoxy that had begun to establish itself, especially among Anglican churchmen, long before the end of the Elizabethan era. Johan Sommerville has argued that, when Richard Hooker in the 1590s had evoked the commonplace idea that the royal authority flowed by natural law from the consent of the realm, 'such ideas were [in fact] already . . . going out of vogue among the higher clergy'.[70] A new 'divine-right' orthodoxy had begun to develop which, despite that perhaps misleading label, continued the practice of grounding governmental

---

[65] Skinner, 'The Origins of the Calvinist Theory of Revolution', in Malament, *After the Reformation*, 325.

[66] J. Sommerville, *Politics and Ideology in England* (London: Longman, 1986), 46.

[67] Maxwell, *Sacra-sancta*, 3.   [68] Rutherford, *Lex, Rex*, 418.

[69] Bridge, *Truths of the Times*, 49.   [70] Sommerville, *Politics*, 3.

238   *Conciliarism and Political Thought*

authority in the natural law rather than in the revealed word of God.[71] At the same time, however, it inserted a sharp distinction between the *power* of the king, which was seen to be derived solely and directly from God, and his *title*, which might derive from designation by the people. In framing this type of designation theory, Anglican divines had not hesitated to adduce by way of analogy the fact the pope claimed to hold his power immediately from God alone, even though as an individual he owed his title to a human electoral process. Thus William Barrett in 1612, John Buckeridge in 1614, Robert Bolton in 1639—this last insisting against Bellarmine's derivation of royal authority from the community that

the question is not by what meanes, whether by hereditary succession or election, or any other humane forme, a Prince comes into his kingdome, but whether by the ordinance of GOD we ought to obey him when he is established.... [T]he Pope is hoisted into his chaire of pestilence, by the election of the Cardinals or worse meanes, and yet that hinders not our adversaries from holding it a divine ordinance.[72]

This being so, and the opponents of the new orthodoxy in the period leading up to the Civil War having lost, in effect, the ideological initiative, many hesitated to claim in theory for a Parliament increasingly bypassed in practice any unambiguous right of resistance to the king, let alone a right of deposition.[73] Only the more robust among those opponents were willing to push forward into what had now, in the past half-century, become more radical territory and to invoke against the king the inherent power of the community as wielded through its representatives in Parliament. And when they did, secular 'parliamentary theory in the later Middle Ages not having kept abreast of practice' and 'ecclesiastical conciliarism ... [having] ... provided a general theory of constitutions for use by aspiring parliamentarians', it is understandable, as Antony Black has recently asserted, that some among them should 'look back ... on conciliarism as the closest historical precedent for what they were trying to do'.[74] But that brings us to our fourth and final question: were these

[71] Sommerville, *Politics*, 12.

[72] W. Barret, *Jus Regis* (Basel, 1612), 28; Buckeridge, *De potestate papae*, 291; R. Bolton, *Two Sermons* (London, 1639), sermon 1, 16. For a Catholic endorsement of that view, see R. Sheldon, *Certain General Reasons* (London, 1611), 11–12.

[73] See J. H. Franklin, *John Locke and the Theory of Sovereignty* (Cambridge: CUP, 1978), 22–49. Such, indeed, was the hesitancy and confusion in the thinking of the parliamentary leaders on this score that, when the Civil War finally broke out, 'they claimed to be fighting for the corporate whole of king-in-parliament against the erring person of Charles'—thus Tierney, *Religion, Law*, 83.

[74] Or again, 'The poverty of theory about secular parliaments contrasts with the wealth of

parliamentarians (and their sixteenth-century predecessors), as Figgis believed, correct in their judgement about that precedent? Or were they guilty, in effect, of understanding history anachronistically, reading their conciliarist sources in distorted fashion?

Given the range and complexity of the vast ocean of literature that it is customary to label as conciliarist, the question may appear more formidable than it in fact is. Central, after all, to the pertinence and force of the conciliar analogy when evoked by constitutionalists, parliamentarians, and advocates of legitimate resistance against kings turned tyrant was the assumption on which Figgis placed so much emphasis—namely, that the Church was 'one of a class, political societies', and that as a political community it possessed by natural law the ultimate right (as, for that matter, did any natural body) to gather up its resources and exert its inherent power to prevent its own ruin.[75] And although, as we have just seen, they themselves could not on occasion resist the temptation to deploy the papal analogy for their own purposes, central to the response of the royalists was the insistence that the ecclesiastical analogy was invalid, because the papal monarchy was founded in grace not in nature, because it was elective not hereditary, and/or because the general council by virtue of a known canon law possessed a greater authority over a pope than did the estates of any realm over their king.

Now it should be noted that this ideological stand-off is the mirror-image of one that had occurred already during the conciliar epoch itself. Embedded in the conciliarist literature are countless examples and analogies drawn this time from the political arrangements of the *secular* world,[76] invoked, of course, to help elaborate the case for the supreme authority of the general council within the Church. The much-cited speech of the bishop of Burgos at Basel in 1431 simply represents a particularly striking example, and it should be noted that this conciliarist willingness to rely on

ideas about the representative or constitutional role of councils in the late medieval church'—see Black, *Political Thought in Europe*, 166, 169, 178. His whole chapter on parliamentary representation (162–85) is excellent.

[75] See e.g., Bridge, *Wounded Conscience*, 46.

[76] For some representative passages from the Parisian conciliarists see Jean Gerson, *Tractatus de unitate ecclesiae*, in Gerson, *Œuvres complètes*, ed. Glorieux, vi. 137; *Sermo*: 'Prosperum iter faciet*', ibid. v. 478–9; *De auferabilitate . . . papae*, ibid. iii. 301–2; *De potestate ecclesiastica*, ibid. 225, 247–9; Jacques Almain, *Quaestio resumptiva . . . de dominio naturali, civili et ecclesiastico*, in Gerson, *Opera omnia*, ed. Dupin, ii. 970; idem, *Expositio circa decisiones Magistri Guillielmi Occam . . . de potestate ecclesiastica et laica*, ibid. 1024, 1075–6, 1107; idem, *Tractatus de auctoritate ecclesiae*, ibid. 991, 1009. For John Mair, see Oakley, 'From Constance to 1688', 13–19; for Pierre d'Ailly, idem, *Political Thought of d'Ailly*, esp. 52–4; for the conciliarists of Basel, Black, *Monarchy and Community*, 7–52.

secular analogies endured down into the seventeenth century. Thus Mair and Almain in the early sixteenth century, who came close to treating the ecclesiastical and secular polities univocally; thus Sir Thomas More in the 1530s, when he argued that 'counsayles do represent the whole church . . . as a parliament representeth ye hole realme'; thus Edmond Richer in 1606 when, having argued that absolute or despotic monarchy is repugnant to natural and divine law and that the best political regimen is monarchy tempered by aristocracy, he concluded that the universal Church is precisely such a monarchy tempered (via the general council) by an aristocratic component; thus Paolo Sarpi in 1606, when, defending against Bellarmine's aspersions the orthodoxy of Gerson's conciliarist commitments (and following up on other secular political analogies), he noted that it did not follow from God's having 'placed a King to governe a Kingdome' that that king 'is superior to his whole kingdome assembled together'.[77]

Moreover, the conciliarists who had pursued that line of march had usually focused their attention also upon the sector wherein ecclesiastical power is at its closest, in quality if not in purpose, to secular governmental authority. As we have seen,[78] when they spoke of the Church as the *corpus Christi* or *corpus Christi mysticum* those expressions had lost for them the rich sacramental associations present in the earlier patristic usage and had acquired in their place corporative and political associations. Instead of the parallel being drawn with the sacramental body of Christ and *corpus mysticum* being taken to denote the incorporation of the faithful with Christ in a mysterious community of salvation, the analogy was drawn now from natural bodies or bodies in general and the expression taken to denote a 'moral and political [as opposed to real or physical] body'. Further than that, of the traditional categories of ecclesiastical power, it was not the power of order (*potestas ordinis*), the truly sacerdotal power, on which these conciliarists laid their stress. That power, they said, pertained quintessentially to the eucharist, which they designated not as the mystical but as the 'true body of Christ' (*corpus Christi verum*). Their own concern lay rather with jurisdiction (*potestas jurisdictionis*), for that was the power that pertained to the *corpus Christi mysticum*, and especially with its public, coercive, and unambiguously non-sacramental and *political*

---

[77] Sir Thomas More, *The Confutation of Tyndale's Answer*, in *The Complete Works*, ed. Schuster *et al.*, viii/1, 146/15–21; cf. Gogan, *Common Corps*, 290–9. Richer, *Apologia*, 14–20. Sarpi, *Apologia*, ed. Busnelli and Gambarin, iii. 128–9. I cite the English version, *Apology or Apologeticall Answere*, 74–5.
[78] See above, Prologue and Ch. 2.

subdivisions—the *potestas jurisdictionis in foro externo*, which d'Ailly referred to simply as 'the governmental power' (*potestas regiminis*).[79] That was the modality of ecclesiastical power they had in mind when they made their case for the superiority of council over pope. And they grounded that case not simply in scripture, or Church history, or ecclesiastical custom, or canon law (though of course they did all of those things), not simply, that is, in the rights, privileges, customs, and laws proper to the *communitas fidelium*, but also in the mandates of the natural law, the law that pertained to all political bodies and, indeed, to the community of mankind itself.

But, then, not all conciliarists framed the case they made in this particular way. In response to the papal counter-offensive of the 1430s and 1440s designed to portray the Baselian conciliarist ecclesiology as a revolutionary attack on the very principle of monarchical rule, temporal no less than spiritual, it will be recalled[80] that such conciliarists as John of Segovia and Panormitanus had sought to present their own conciliar views in such a way as to suggest, rather, that they were irrelevant, strictly speaking, to matters political. And in that they were to be followed in part by such early sixteenth-century conciliar thinkers as Pierre Cordier in Paris and Giovanni Gozzadini in Italy.[81] Had the later constitutionalists and advocates of the legitimacy of resistance to kings turned tyrant tried to rely on the arguments of those conciliarists, then, they would indeed have been forced to place their emphasis on what was only one facet of an exceedingly complex and perhaps ambiguous position. Whether, in invoking the conciliar analogy, they were or were not guilty of an anachronistic reading of the conciliar past and to conciliar texts depends, in effect, on the particular past they had in mind and on the specific strain of conciliarism that informed their understanding of what was at stake in the fifteenth-century conciliar experience.

So far as the monarchomachs of the sixteenth century are concerned, for they refrained from citing individual conciliar thinkers, the question is not readily susceptible of answer—though his teacher, John Mair, had clearly had a hand in shaping Buchanan's political thinking and *may* have had some impact also on that of Ponet.[82] But with their seventeenth-century English successors we are on much firmer ground. The range of proto-conciliarist and conciliarist literature cited by the English writers of the late sixteenth and seventeenth centuries is admittedly quite broad.

---

[79] Pierre d'Ailly, *Utrum Petri ecclesia lege reguletur*, in Gerson, *Opera omnia*, ed. Dupin, i. 667–8.
[80] See above, Ch. 2.   [81] See Oakley, 'Natural Law', 801–5.
[82] See Oakley, 'From Constance to 1688', 11–31; Hudson, *John Ponet*, 171–2.

Despite Foxe's inclusion, via his translation of Aeneas Sylvius Piccolomini, of one of John of Sergovia's speeches in his *Book of Martyrs*, I believe I have come across only a single reference to Segovia in the seventeenth-century writers, and references to Marsiglio of Padua, though by no means lacking, do not appear with great frequency. One hears much more of Aeneas Sylvius, Dietrich of Niem, William of Ockham, Nicholas of Cusa, Panormitanus, and Francesco Zabarella. But it is the members of the 'School of Sorbonne' who top the list, from John of Paris, via d'Ailly and Gerson, to Almain and Mair. It is almost exclusively from these latter conciliarists, the so-called 'Sorbonnists' or 'divines of Paris', whose works Richer had recently made conveniently available, that the mid-century parliamentarians are accused by their royalist opponents of having drawn their benighted ideas. And it is upon the authority of those particular conciliarists that they themselves do in fact rely.

That being so, there was nothing anachronistic about their conviction that the fifteenth-century conciliar experience represented a valuable historical precedent that could help advance the case for legitimate resistance that they themselves were struggling to make. Figgis may have been off the mark in his unargued assumption that conciliar theory had simply sprung form a transfer into the ecclesiological realm of lessons drawn from such secular constitutionalist experiments as the deposition of Richard II, king of England. But he was right, none the less, in his claim that the Parisian conciliarists had given a notably universal expression to the principles underlying medieval constitutionalist aspirations at large—themselves, as we have seen, the outgrowth of that twelfth-century Romano-canonical seedbed in which the secular and the religious had interpenetrated with such fruitful results. And he was right, too, in his claim that the notably universal expression was destined to take on a heightened significance in a later era when absolute or quasi-absolute monarchy was coming to be regarded as the only civilized form of government, when representative assemblies in much of Europe had entered upon a period of decline, and when such traditional medieval limitations on monarchical power were coming to be dismissed as 'inefficient clogs upon the wheels of government, not merely wrong but stupid'.[83] And, long in its reach though Figgis's claim undoubtedly was, it is now time to suggest that it was even longer than he himself realized. For, as has recently became clear, it extended, in effect, all the way down to the onset of the French Revolution itself.

[83] Figgis, *Political Thought*, 60–1.

FROM CONSTANCE TO 1789?

If one shifts the focus of attention from the first half of the seventeenth century in England back to the same period in France, and if one focuses in particular on Edmond Richer's defence of conciliarist views against the onslaughts of Cajetan and Bellarmine,[84] one finds that in the clarity of his affirmation that the Church was indeed to be understood very much as 'one of a class, political societies', Richer remained faithful to the guiding intuition of his Parisian predecessors all the way back to the fourteenth century. That fact, it must now be added, is by no means to be taken for granted. It is easy enough to recognize that Richer's understanding of the ecclesiastical polity is diametrically opposed to that of Cajetan and Bellarmine. But it is almost as easy to miss the fact, his reference to the highly unusual elective kingship of Poland notwithstanding,[85] that his view of the secular polity is equally at odds with theirs—always assuming, that is, that the secular polity one has in mind is that of France, and the particular kingship that of this Most Christian Majesty. If that is indeed the case, then his position overall is almost the mirror-image of Cajetan's. For the latter, the Church, in which the supreme power of the papal monarch is conferred upon him directly by Christ, was to be *contrasted* with the secular polity in which (as he was perfectly willing to concede) the governmental power 'is devolved to one or more by the [whole] community'.[86] For Richer, on the other hand, the reverse is true. For him, and in this he has much in common with the English divines Buckeridge and Bramhall, it is rather the ecclesiastical power which resides in the community. The king of France, on the other hand, he portrays as no merely ministerial figure but as a sacral monarch, the representative of God to his people, by virtue of his legitimating inheritance divinely endowed with special graces.[87] Unlike some of the conciliarists of the Basel era, however, and his own intense royalism notwithstanding, he made no effort to frame his conciliarist commitments in such a way as to render them less relevant or even

---

[84] See above, Ch. 4. [85] Richer, *Defensio*, lib. III, qu. 1, p. 312.
[86] Cajetan, *Apologia*, c. 1, ed. Pollet, 205; Burns and Izbicki, *Conciliarism and Papalism*, 203.
[87] For Richer's vision of the *French* kingship, see Monique Cottret, 'Edmond Richer (1559–1631): Le Politique et le sacré', in H. Méchoulan, ed., *L'État Baroque* (Paris: Librairie Philosophique J. Vrin, 1985), 161–77, where she portrays him as 'défenseur de la monarchie absolue et gallicane' (170) and as being, in his political thinking, in direct contradiction with the views of the 18th-cent. *richéristes* who 'sur le plan politique . . . bâtiront un système fondé sur la démocratie à l'image du gouvernement de l'Église primitive' (167). For the 17th-cent. 'redivinization' of the French kingship, see Kley, *Religious Origins*, esp. 32–49.

irrelevant to matters political.[88] Quite the contrary, indeed, and we should recognize that a considerable historical significance attaches to that fact. It meant, in effect, that Richer did nothing to conceal, blunt, or deflect the obviously constitutionalist implications for secular political life of the conciliarist teachings handed down by John of Paris, d'Ailly, Gerson, Almain, and Mair. He himself had already done much (and was in the future to do still more) to make the writings of those great Parisian predecessors readily available to his contemporaries, thereby projecting their teachings forward into the great ideological conflicts, Gallican and Jansenist, of seventeenth- and eighteenth-century France. His name, certainly, came to be closely associated with theirs. For many Frenchmen in the eighteenth century his publicistic writings served, indeed, as the central conduit through which the old Parisian conciliarist teaching came to be known and made available for renewed service, as Jansenists and quasi-Jansenists in the wake of the condemnatory papal constitution *Unigenitus* (1713) appropriated Gallican ideas for use in their own anti-papal and anti-royal causes.[89]

Unfair, then, to the precise lineaments of Richer's own thinking though it may have been, it is not altogether surprising that, when defending the royalist cause in 1754 against the 'judicial Jansenists' connected with the Parlement of Paris, Abbé Bertrand Capmartin de Chaupy should have tried to finger Richer as the villain originally responsible for having introduced into France what he viewed as the alien and deplorable notion that whatever 'power governed society belonged to that society, which retained its property while delegating [to the ruler] only the exercise'. Confronting opposition from the temporal as well as the spiritual authorities, the Jansenists, he alleged, had appropriated that deplorable notion; it had come to be applied to the French state itself and 'the Parlement let itself be carried away by the torrent'.[90] Nor was that accusation merely the expression of an isolated sentiment.[91] It reflected much the same fearful apprehension of the broader constitutionalist implications of the

---

[88] See above, Ch. 2.

[89] For the development of Jansenism and the lead-in to *Unigenitus*, see Louis Cognet in Müller *et al., Age of Absolutism*, 24–57. For Jansenist and quasi-Jansenist resistance to papal condemnation and royal persecution and the role it played in the development of 'patriot constitutionalism' in France, see Kley, *Religious Origins*, esp. 70–136, 159–74, 236–48.

[90] Abbé Bertrand Capmartin de Chaupy, *Observations sur le refus que fut le Châtelet de reconnaître la Chambre royal* (France, 1754), 196–8—cited from Kley, *Religious Origins*, 226–7.

[91] Kley, *Religious Origins*, 227, 365, refers also to the similar views of Pierre-François Lafitau, bishop of Sisteran, and those, later on, of Augustin Barruel who, he says, 'established a sort of diabolical "genealogy" of ideas that went from Jean de Paris to Jan Hus to Martin Luther to Thomas Müntzer to Edmond Richer, culminating in the philosophes, the French Revolution and the casuists of the Civil Constitution of the Clergy'.

conciliarist position as that which the papal propagandists of the 1430s and 1440s had tried to exploit in order to frighten the monarchs of Europe into aligning themselves with Eugenius IV.[92] Or again, that Pope Innocent XI himself made use of during his great dispute with Louis XIV in the 1680s, when he needled the French ambassador by pointing out to him that 'if councils were superior to the pope whose power comes from God, then the Estates General would have leave to press the same claim against kings'.[93]

But, then, it was not only the royalist opponents of the conciliarist ecclesiology who came to be aware of such constitutionalist implications for the world of secular politics. That was no more true in the France of the eighteenth century than it had been in the France of the sixteenth century—or, for that matter, the Scotland and England of the sixteenth and seventeenth centuries. Focusing on the complex interplay of 'competitive Catholicisms', Jansenist and 'devout', in eighteenth-century France, and, mounting a powerful case for 'the religious, indeed Catholic, origins of the undoing of absolutism and especially . . . the Jansenist Catholic provenance of notions of political liberty in eighteenth-century France'.[94] Dale Van Kley has recently drawn attention to the persistent proclivity of eighteenth-century French critics of monarchical policy to invoke the conciliarist constitutionalism of Richer, Gerson, and the other 'old theologians of Paris' and to exploit its implications not only for the governance of the universal Church but also, as had their sixteenth-century predecessors, for that of the French kingdom itself. That was particularly true of those of Jansenist sympathies who, battered by repeated papal condemnations, and especially by *Unigenitus*, had themselves appropriated the conciliar ecclesiology. In true conciliarist fashion, they appealed in 1712 and 1719 from the judgement of the pope to that of a future general council and, by their stubborn refusal after 1720 to withdraw those appeals, 'sustained the conciliarist tradition in eighteenth-century France and perpetuated it as part of public discourse'.[95] And it was true quintessentially, or so Van Kley argues, of those 'judicial Jansenists' affiliated in one way or another with the Parlement of Paris. For that body, having come to function as the defender *par excellence* of the Gallican tradition,

[92] See above, Chs. 1 and 2.

[93] See Kley, *Religious Origins*, 37. Cf. Martimort, *Le Gallicanisme de Bossuet*, 544. For the context, see above, Ch. 4.

[94] Kley, *Religious Origins*, 373, where he adds that 'in playing this role, Jansenism, while remaining discernibly Catholic, transmitted a part of the Protestant monarchomach heritage to the eighteenth century'.

[95] Kley, 'Estates General', 1–52 (at 21).

something of a 'symbiosis' developed between the conciliarist tradition, 'parliamentary constitutionalism', and Jansenism.[96]

Thus, writing in the immediate aftermath of *Unigenitus*, the Oratorian, Vivien de la Borde, and Nicolas Le Gros, canon of Rheims, both turned to conciliar history and the teaching of the conciliarists in order to make their oppositional case. *Unigenitus*, De la Borde argued, made even clearer than heretofore the essential fallibility of the pope, proclaimed long since 'by the councils of Constance and Basel, [but] obscured by the haughty (*orgueilleuse*) pretensions of the Roman court'. It is in 'the whole body of the nation or society of men that we call the Catholic Church' that 'the law of the faith subsists essentially as a public law', and it is the task of the bishops 'assembled in the most holy councils' and 'representing the universal Church' to reflect the confession of the faithful and, as it were, to 'speak' that law. Such, he added, had always been 'the constant doctrine of our Church of France'.[97]

In two works published a little later, Nicolas Le Gros went further. Evoking the authority of the ecumenical councils, echoing *Haec sancta* and the great deeds of Constance and Basel, and appealing repeatedly to an impressive array of conciliar thinkers from d'Ailly, Gerson, and Nicholas of Cusa to Almain, Mair, and Richer, he lamented the way in which *Unigenitus*, by its pretensions to papal infallibility, had undercut the need for and the authority of general councils.[98] And yet, in matters of faith there is no infallible judge other than the universal Church itself and the general council which represents it and which 'the theologians of Paris' have been at pains to teach, is above the pope, possesses an authority superior to his, can annul his judgements, and can also, if need be, depose him.[99] For, as those theologians have also taught, while the 'use' or strictly 'ministerial' exercise of the ecclesiastical power is conceded to individual ecclesiastical officials, the pope himself included, 'the proprietary possession of power', or power 'taken in itself', resides ultimately in the whole body of the Church alone.[100]

A similar deployment of the conciliarist ecclesiology, replete with references to Constance, Basel, *Haec sancta*, and *Frequens*, along with an

---

[96] Kley, 'Estates General', 22–4.

[97] Borde, *Du témoignage de la verité*, 82, 88, 93–4, 127. Cf. Kley's commentary in his *Religious Origins*, esp. 77–85.

[98] Le Gros, *De renversement des libertez*, i. 115, 121–2. Cf. Kley's commentary in his *Religious Origins*, esp. 77–85, 89–91.

[99] Le Gros, *De renversement des libertez*, i. 122–35, 346–9, 388–9, 434; idem, *Memoire sur les droits du second ordre*, 8–9, 31, 45, 69.

[100] Le Gros, *De renversement des libertez*, i. 317, 340.

invocation of the authority of the old Parisian theologians from Gerson to Richer and of the familiar distinction between the ministerial and delegated exercise of ecclesiastical power by church officers and the possession of the fullness of that power by the body of the Church itself, is to be found in the *Apologie* which the 'judicial Jansenists' Claude Mey and Gabriel-Nicholas Maultrot published in 1753; and in even more marked degree, in the *Maximes du droit publique François* which they and others published in 1772.[101] Described by Van Kley as a sort of 'bible of the French legal community' and, again as a 'massive summa of patriot constitutionalism',[102] the *Maximes* were presumably the route whereby ideas associated with the conciliarist ecclesiology found their way into such pamphlets of the immediately pre-revolutionary era as those of Guillaume Saige and Joseph-Antoine Hédouin de Pons-Ludon.[103]

All of these authors, moreover, in much the same way as the sixteenth-century monarchomachs in France and Scotland or their seventeenth-century successors in England, pressed the conciliar analogy of the superiority of council to pope into service in order to make their own oppositional case subordinating the authority of the king to that of the nation. They did so to make the particular point—and especially so on the very eve of the Revolution—that the longed-for Estates General (in this like the Council of Pisa in 1409) could be assembled even in the absence of a royal summons and even in defiance of the royal will.[104] They did so, too, in order to make the more fundamental point that sovereignty resided in the whole body of the kingdom and that the power which the king exercised via delegation from that kingdom was both limited and revocable.[105]

In the context of such a familiar argumentative tactic, perhaps it should

---

[101] [Mey and Maultrot], *Apologie des jugements rendus en France*, esp. i. 40–2, 56, 219–20, 231–2, 287; ii. 20–1, 86–91, 94–5. [Mey *et al.*], *Maximes du droit public François*, esp. i. 267–9 (where, among others, he cites Jacques Almain and John Mair; ii. 151–61, where he cites John of Paris, Pierre d'Ailly, Aeneas Sylvius Piccolomini's pro-conciliarist *Commentarius de gestis Basiliensis Concilii*, Almain, and Mair. Also the 'Dissertation sur le droit de convoquer les Etats-généraux', 17 (attached as a separately paginated appendix to that second volume). Cf. Kley's commentary in his *Religious Origins*, esp. 195–203.

[102] Kley, 'Estates General', 12; idem, *Religious Origins*, 257.

[103] G. Saige, *Catéchisme du citoyen* (1788), esp. 55–9, 72–6; [idem], *Code National, ou Manuel François* (1789), esp. 66–7, 89–90. Hédouin du Pons-Ludon, *Lettre d'un patriote* (1789), 3. For other pamphlets of the period also invoking the conciliar ecclesiology, see Kley, 'Estates General', 10–18; idem, *Religious Origins*, 315–16.

[104] Thus e.g. Saige, *Code National*, 55, 66–7, 89–90; also 'Dissertation sur le droit de convoquer les Etats-généraux', 17 (appended to Mey *et al.*, *Maximes du droit public françois*, 1).

[105] Thus e.g. Le Gros, *De renversement des libertez*, i. 344–5; [Mey and Maultrot], *Apologie*, ii. 129–30; [Mey *et al.*], *Maximes du droit public*, i. 269–70, ii. 154–60; Saige, *Catéchisme du citoyen*, 57, 63–4, 72–3.

come as no surprise to find embedded in the *Maximes*[106] a translation of Aeneas Sylvius Piccolomini's rendition of the celebrated speech which the bishop of Burgos had made at the Council of Basel, drawing the analogy between kingdom and Church and concluding for the subordination alike of king to kingdom and pope to Church as well as for the power of both kingdom and Church to correct and depose their respective rulers should the latter lapse into tyranny. Thus, that familiar speech, which in the sixteenth-century Foxe had translated into English and Richard Hooker had invoked, and which had been prominent enough in seventeenth-century parliamentary discourse to be alluded to in a House of Commons debate,[107] was now, a century and more later and no less than three centuries after its original delivery, put to comparable use in French constitutionalist discourse. Moreover, that Mey, Maultrot, and the other 'patriot constitutionalists' relied less in their Gallican moments on the 1682 episcopalist Declaration of the Gallican Clergy than on the older Parisian conciliarists, all of whom were accustomed to treat the Church very much as a political society,[108] undoubtedly eased the way to their appropriation of the conciliarist ecclesiology for secular political purposes, just as the reliance on those particular conciliarists had similarly made it possible for their seventeenth-century parliamentary predecessors in England to make what had been essentially the same move.

'Grace does not destroy nature but *consecrates* it', said De la Borde in a revealingly amended version of the old Thomist dictum that 'grace does not destroy nature but completes (or perfects) it'.[109] And from his *Du témoignage de la vérité chez l'église*, published in 1714, to Hédouin's *Lettre d'un patriote à son ami*, published in 1789, any differences in nature between the structure of government in the secular polity and that in the universal Church are insistently minimized. There is an 'exact comparison', we are told, between 'the nature of the Estates General' and that of 'the ecumenical council'.[110] In the 'nation that we call the Catholic Church', 'the law of the faith' subsists essentially 'as a public law . . . in the entire body'. As a 'human society founded by God', it necessarily possesses all the attributes and instrumentalities that every nation has.[111] In it the spiritual

---

[106] [Mey *et al.*], *Maximes du droit public*, ii. 161.   [107] See above, p. 229.

[108] As Kley, *Religious Origins*, 196, properly emphasizes.

[109] Borde, *Du témoignage de la vérité*, 148: 'La grace ne détruit pas la nature, mais la *consacre*' (italics mine). Unlike the traditional version—*Gratia non tollit naturam, sed perficit*—De la Borde's formulation suggests that nothing was lacking in nature; it did not need grace to be complete.

[110] Hédouin du Pons-Ludon, *Lettre d'un patriote à ses amis*, 3—a sentiment in which de Maistre, writing from a very different point of view, would concur. See above, Ch. 5.

[111] Borde, *Du témoignage de la vérité*, 82, 144.

authority resides very much as does the temporal authority in a republic.[112] In its 'external form', indeed, the Church is 'a true republic', where 'the laws alone reign' and 'the sovereign authority resides in the general will'.[113] And so on. The analogy being so confidently and insistently drawn, it would seem that the pertinence of the fifteenth-century conciliar experience to the constitutionalist aspirations of the judicial Jansenists and patriot constitutionalists of the eighteenth century could hardly have been any more readily apparent.

To suggest, of course, that there was anything like a direct route from Constance to 1789 would be an even greater exaggeration than that indulged by H. J. Laski in 1936 when, thinking of the use that English parliamentarians had made of conciliarist ideas in the seventeenth century, he boldly proclaimed that 'the road from Constance to [The Glorious Revolution of] 1688 is a direct one'.[114] But if the scholarship of the past half-century has clearly put beyond question the fact that such a path did indeed exist from Constance to at least 1644, it would now appear to be the case that there was also something of a parallel track in France, one that wound its tortuous way through the thickets of eighteenth-century Gallican and Jansenist religio-political debate all the way down to the years immediately prior to the Revolution itself. Ironically enough, the tradition of conciliarist constitutionalism which was destined ultimately to vanish almost without trace from the ecclesiological arena in which it had been spawned, succeeded nevertheless, and before departing the scene, in leaving an enduring imprint of no little significance on the lineaments of secular political and constitutional thinking. It turns out, then, that there may have been something prophetic about the point John Ponet had made so forcefully, some two centuries earlier, when writing from bitter exile during the reign of Mary Tudor, and referring to the conciliar experience of the previous century and to the 'lawe of nature to depose and punish wicked governours' which 'hath not only been revived and exercised in political matters, but also in the church', he boldly proclaimed that 'by this lawe [of nature] and arguments of the Canonistes and example of deprivacion of a Pope are all clokes (wherewith Popes, Bishoppes, priests, Kaisers and Kings use to defend their iniguitie) utterly taken away'.[115]

[112] Le Gros, *De renversement des liberty*, i. 344.
[113] Saige, *Catechisme du citoyen*, 57, 72, 76–7.
[114] Harold J. Laski, 'Political Theory in the Later Middle Ages', in Gwatkin *et al.*, *Cambridge Medieval History*, viii. 638.
[115] Ponet, *Shorte Treatise of Politicke Power*, in Hudson, *John Ponet*, [105].

Epilogue: Unfinished Business,
Trailing Ends

God's handwriting exists in history independently of the Church,
and no ecclesiastical exigency can alter a fact.

(Lord Acton[1])

[H]istory, and antiquity, and facts . . . of the past vanish before the
presence of an order of facts which are divine—namely, the unity,
perpetuity, infallibility of the Church of God.

(Henry, Cardinal Manning[2])

I, I am Tradition, I, I am the Church.

(Pope Pius IX[3])

That the First Vatican Council's twin definitions of papal infallibility and
papal primacy of jurisdiction introduced something of a break or discontinuity into the course of Church history is not in doubt. No sooner was
the council over, however, than disagreement began to surface about just
how sharp or menacing that discontinuity actually was. For Ignaz von
Döllinger (as for so many of the leading German church historians) it constituted so great a caesura as to preclude his acquiescing in the binding
force of the council's decrees. His excommunication, therefore, was inevitable, and the adoption of his viewpoint by those who came together
in what was to be known as the Old Catholic Church doomed that body in
Roman Catholic eyes to schismatic status.[4] But for most Catholics at the
time, and the historians no less than the theologians and canonists, the

---

[1] Acton, *History of Freedom*, 473.
[2] H. E. Manning, *The Temporal Mission of the Holy Ghost* (London, 1865), 204.
[3] For this (it now seems authentic) exclamation of Pius IX, see Schatz, *Vaticanum I*, iii.
app. 1: 312–22 (at 314); Chadwick, *History of the Popes*, 250.
[4] Writing in the 1960s, the Old Catholic bishop Urs Küry, *Die Altkatholische Kirche*
(Stuttgart: Evangelisches Verlagwerk, 1966), 29, was at pains to note that the Constance decrees *Haec sancta* and *Frequens* possessed the validity of articles of faith. In what follows I
draw largely on Schneider, *Konziliarismus*, 214–339 (to whom I owe my acquaintance with
Küry's book); Sieben, *Katholische Konzilsidee im 19. und 20. Jahrhundert*, 186–277; Oakley,
Council over Pope?, 105–90, and the literature referred to therein.

element of discontinuity does not seem to have loomed all that large. For them, in effect, Manning's claim during the run-up to the council that 'Ultramontanism is Catholic Christianity'[5] appeared simply to have been vindicated. On matters ecclesiological, what, during the long centuries of Roman–Gallican strife, had been the *opinio communis* of the Roman theological school alone had now become the *opinio communis* of Catholic theologians and historians in general, and, in its broad outlines, it coincided with the position which Bellarmine had staked out long ago.[6] In the standard ecclesiological treatises, then, Constance and Basel were brushed to one side, *Haec sancta* and *Frequens* (if mentioned at all) fell victim to theological and legal redundancy, and the neuralgic issue over which Catholic theologians of the rival Roman and Gallican schools had fought so bitterly and for so very long ceased now to be of compelling interest, a matter ripe, in fact, for incipient consignment to the dust-heap of history.

Eloquent testimony to that fact is what appears, in the first decade of the twentieth century, to have been a total absence from the intense debates surrounding the modernist crisis of any echo of the fifteenth-century conciliar past, let alone any explicit invocation of the conciliarist ecclesiology itself. The more surprising in that those debates came increasingly to focus on the problem of ecclesiastical authority and its exceedingly heavy-handed exercise by the Roman curia. Among the modernists (or those who sympathized with their cause), not even the redoubtable Maude Petre, proud descendant of the eighteenth-century recusant leader, Sir Charles Petre, and staunch latter-day admirer of the 'Old' or 'Cisalpine' or 'Anglo-Gallican' Catholicism which Petre and his fellow members in the Cisalpine Club had espoused—not even Maude Petre in the anguish of her own state of quasi-excommunication seems to have thought of turning for relief to the tradition of conciliarist constitutionalism with which her beloved ancestor and his colleagues had so clearly sympathized.[7]

---

[5] J. Pereiro, *Cardinal Manning* (Oxford: OUP, 1964), 255.

[6] Sieben, *Katholische Konzilsidee*, 188, speaking specifically of papal convocation as a necessary prerequisite for the legitimacy of a general council; cf. Schneider, *Konziliarismus*, 206.

[7] For the 18th-cent. recusant 'Cisalpines' or 'Anglo-Gallicans', see above, Ch. 4. And for Maude Petre, see C. F. Crews, *English Catholic Modernism* (Notre Dame, Ind.: University of Notre Dame Press, 1984). For the modernists in general, see O'Connell, *Critics on Trial*, and for the centrality of the question of authority to the modernist crisis, L. R. Kurtz, *The Politics of Heresy* (Berkeley: University of California Press, 1986), esp. 107, 144, 165–6, 187. Cf. Schneider, *Konziliarismus*, 237–8. Noting that, although the modernists mounted no express or fundamental attack on the dogmas of 1870, he comments: 'Doch wurde die Stellung des Papstes indirekt stark in Frage gestellt und durch neutestamentliche und Kirchengeschichtliche Forschungen historisch relativiert. An den Konstanzer Dekreten und dem Konziliarismus zeigten sich die Modernisten jedoch nicht interessiert.'

Apart from a moment of controversy in the 1960s, which quickly proved, as we shall see, to be evanescent, the century and more stretching from the First Vatican Council to the present, then, has not been distinguished in theological (or reformist) circles by much interest in the conciliarist tradition—certainly not by any sustained effort to confront it or to explore the possibility that it might still convey something of value conducive to a deeper understanding of the nature and constitutional status of the universal Church.[8] And that despite the fact that these were years marked by a great deal of ferment and creativity in Roman Catholic ecclesiology at large. But the process of clarification, enrichment, and development characteristic of some sectors of that branch of theology has not extended to the unresolved issues pertaining to the conciliarist tradition. There confusion and disarray continue to be the order of the day, and, with them, the growth of a worrying gap between the high-papalist ecclesiological vision endorsed by Vatican I (and, if modified, not dislodged by Vatican II) and the direction in which historical investigation has come more and more insistently to point.

For the better part of a century after Vatican I historically minded theologians and even church historians themselves found it possible to ignore or to bracket the problem, though they paid a certain intellectual price for so doing. The price in question was their willingness in the last resort to invoke doctrinal and canonistic rather than truly historical criteria of judgement when it came to assessing the import of the conciliar epoch and the ecumenical status of the Council of Constance at the moment in which it promulgated *Haec sancta*. That is marginally evident even in the position endorsed in 1946 by Yves Congar, later to be viewed as one of the great 'liberal' theologians at Vatican II,[9] and it determined in unambiguous fashion the stance adopted in the mid-1960s by Joseph Gill, the leading expert on the Council of Florence.[10] Drawing conclusions from the fact that the Council of Pisa 'was not numbered in the list of general councils generally recognized by the Church' and that Gregory XII 'in the general opinion of today was in fact the genuine pope', he was content simply to label John XXIII as an 'anti-pope' and to dismiss *Haec sancta* in traditional Roman fashion as the work of an assembly that was not a legitimate general council prior to its reconvocation by Gregory XII.[11]

---

[8] On which, see above Prologue.

[9] Schneider, *Konziliarismus*, 224, draws attention to this fact.

[10] At that time professor at the Pontifical Oriental Institute at Rome.

[11] J. Gill, 'The Fifth Session of the Council of Constance', *Heythrop Journal*, 5 (1964), 131–43. He later returned to the topic in a more general statement that betrayed no change in his

Clear enough that may well be, but (as we have seen) less robust a position and more exposed to attack than one might be tempted to think. A quick perusal of some of the pertinent articles contributed to the standard twentieth-century Catholic encyclopaedias gives a revealing glimpse of the formidable and somewhat startling penumbra of uncertainty, confusion, and disarray which detracts, willy-nilly, from the confident clarity of such affirmations. Having dwelt on this matter elsewhere,[12] I can limit myself here to a few illustrations. Thus whereas in 1908 in the *Catholic Encyclopedia*'s article on the Council of Pisa (1809) Louis Salembier, who knew the territory well, concluded in gingerly fashion that 'perhaps it is wise to say with Bellarmine that the [Pisan] assembly was a general council that was neither approved nor disapproved', the article on 'Councils, General' in the same work simply omitted Pisa from the list of ecumenical councils (as, indeed did the *New Catholic Encyclopedia* published half a century later), declared Constance to be legitimate only after 'Gregory XII had formally convoked it', and Basel only to 'the end of the twenty-fifth session'.[13] In 1911, moreover, the article on 'Conciles' in the *Dictionnaire de théologie catholique*, opting for more radical surgery, simply excised Pisa, Constance, and Basel from its list of ecumenical councils which jumped, therefore, from Vienne in 1311–12 to Florence in 1439–45.[14] A particularly bold exercise in the politics of oblivion!

More recent listings and articles have not really succeeded in dispersing that sort of incoherence and confusion, and it is compounded by a similar element of disarray in the varying judgements expressed concerning the legitimacy of the rival lines of contending popes during the period of the Great Schism. So that, for example, in a single work, the second edition of the *Lexikon für Theologie und Kirche*, while in one place it is affirmed that no certain decision can be reached on the legitimacy of the Avignonese popes but that a strong case can be made for the legitimacy of the Pisan pontiffs, in another Clement VII, Benedict XIII, and Alexander V are all labelled as 'antipopes', and in yet another John XXIII is oddly designated as 'Konzilspapst'.[15] Even more surprising is the development that has taken

position: 'Il decreto *Haec sancta synodus* del concilio di Costanza', *Rivista di storia della Chiesa in Italia*, 12 (1967), 123–30. Cf. the remarks in Oakley, *Council over Pope?*, 111–13, and in Tierney, 'Hermeneutics and History', 357–9.

[12] See Oakley, *Council over Pope?*, 122–7.

[13] See *Catholic Encyclopedia*, s.v. 'Councils, General'; *New Catholic Encyclopedia*, s.v. 'Constance, Council of', and 'Councils, General (History of)'. In contrast, Alberigo and Tanner, *Decrees*, i. 402–51, which carries the *imprimatur*, prints all the decrees of Constance, including *Haec sancta*. At the same time, however, it excludes the Council of Pisa.

[14] *Dict. de théol. cath.*, s.v. 'Conciles'.

[15] *Lexikon für Theologie und Kirche*, 2nd edn., s.v. 'Papstliste', 'Alexander V', 'Benedikt XIII', 'Clemens VII', 'Johannes XXIII'.

place over the course of the last century in the views expressed on the question of legitimacy, surprising because it runs directly counter to the growing tendency among historians to regard the whole question of the legitimacy of the Roman and Avignonese lines of popes as one that simply cannot be settled *historically*.[16] Thus whereas at the start of the century there was a disposition to view the Pisan pontiffs as legitimate popes, from mid-century onwards what K. A. Fink has called the 'curialist opinion', which in the nineteenth century had come to classify the Roman line as the legitimate one and the Avignonese as illegitimate, now began as a matter of course to downgrade the Pisan popes to the latter status. In 1947 a new list of popes was published in the *Annuario Pontificio* categorizing the Pisan popes as anti-popes and replacing the previous list (published annually from 1913 to 1946) which had treated them as legitimate. The new list was the work of Angelo Mercati, prefect of the Vatican Archives, and though he made no bones about the fact that his judgement concerning the legitimacy of the popes during the period of the Great Schism was based, not on historical grounds alone but on canonistic and theological criteria as well,[17] historians do not in general seem to have been disposed to question that judgement. It was swiftly mainstreamed, therefore, in histories and listings published under Catholic and non-Catholic auspices alike, from the *Enciclopedia Cattolica* in 1949 and 1952 to the *Oxford Dictionary of the Popes* (1986), the *New Encyclopedia Britannica* (1991), and Eamon Duffy's recent history of the popes (1997).[18]

---

[16] A tendency reflected in at least one of the articles in the 2nd edn. of the *Lexikon für Theologie and Kirche*, s.v. 'Papstliste' (by Remigius Bäumer). In contrast, the 3rd edn. of the *Lexikon*, published between 1993 and 2001, maintains both in its general list of popes and in the entries for individual Roman, Avignonese and Pisan popes a studious impartiality, simply identifying them by their respective 'obediences'.

[17] *Annuario Pontificio* (1947); A. Mercati, 'The New List of Popes', *Mediaeval Studies*, 9 (1947), 71–80. Cf. for commentary, Fink, 'Zur Beurteilung', 335–7; Oakley, *Council over Pope?*, 124–6.

[18] *Enciclopedia cattolica*, s.v. 'Papa' and 'Antipapi' (and they are all listed as *antipapi autentici* as opposed to *antipapi dubbi*); J. N. D. Kelly, *Oxford Dictionary of the Popes* (Oxford and New York: OUP, 1986); M. Eliade, ed., *The Encylopedia of Religion* (New York and London: Macmillan, 1987), p. xi; s.v. 'Papacy'; *The New Encyclopedia Britannica*, Micropedia ix. 123, s.v. 'Popes and Antipopes'; M. Glazier and M. K. Hellwig, eds., *The Modern Catholic Encyclopedia* (Collegeville, Minn.: Liturgical Press, 1994), 681–3, s.v. 'Popes and Antipopes, Chronological List of'; R. P. McBrien, ed., *The Harper Collins Encyclopedia of Catholicism* (San Francisco: Harper, 1995), 1013–33, s.v. 'List of Popes'; P. G. Maxwell-Stuart, *Chronicle of the Popes* (New York: Thames & Hudson, 1997); R. P. McBrien, ed., *Lives of the Popes* (San Francisco: Harper San Francisco, 1997); E. Duffy, *Saints and Sinners* (New Haven and London: Yale University Press, 1997), app. A, 293–9. Duffy comments (127) that '[i]n the long perspective of history, the Roman Catholic Church has accepted that the "real" popes were Urban and . . . [his] successors. At the time, however, and throughout the thirty-nine years

The fact of the matter is, as Fink pointed out, that 'the list of popes in the *Annuario Pontificio* can to some extent be regarded as an official pro- nouncement',[19] and the tendency of historians (not only Catholic histor- ians) simply to accept its downgrading of the Pisan pontiffs to the status of 'antipopes' is a striking example of the difficulty they have experienced in viewing such critical questions pertaining to the conciliar epoch in terms that are fully historical. This was all the more striking, indeed, since the twentieth century witnessed a marked quickening in the pace of historical research focusing on conciliarism and the fifteenth-century councils, the accumulating results of which came to point increasingly in a direction very much at odds with the 'curialist opinion'.[20] A central feature of that research effort was the intense commitment to the recovery and publica- tion of the pertinent source materials which Heinrich Finke pursued for more than forty years. That effort culminated in 1928 with the publication of his four-volume *Acta Concilii Constantiensis*, which, it has rightly been said, 'put on a new footing research into the Council of Constance'.[21]

It is not surprising, then, that it was a former student and editorial col- laborator of Finke's, Johannes Hollnsteiner, who responded influentially in the 1920s to the more highly nuanced (and less polemically determined) historical understanding of the conciliar epoch that was now taking shape. He did so by reviving and putting to new use an interpretative approach

during which the Schism persisted, this sort of clarity was hard to come by.' But, then, *his- torically* speaking, it still is. Thus, e.g. Cross and Livingstone, eds., *The Oxford History of the Christian Church*, 3rd edn. (Oxford: OUP, 1993), 1785–6, lists all the popes of the Avignonese and Pisan lines as anti-popes. At the same time, however, its entry for Alexander V (38) describes him as 'Pope', while its entry for John XXIII (885), listing him as an anti-pope, explains that fact by noting 'that the validity of his election has been contested as being simoniacal'.

[19] More official, interestingly enough, than the statement of a pope. Fink, 'Zur Beurteilung', 335–6, continues by noting that when in 1958 Pope John XXIII chose his title he announced that the name John had been borne by twenty-two papal predecessors '*extra le- gitimitatis discussiones*'—by that qualification making it clear that he himself was passing no judgement on the legitimacy of the Pisan line. But this clearly did not accord with curial opinion or the mandates of the *Annuario Pontificio*, and in the later official version of the speech in the *Acta Apostolicae Sedis* the words *extra legitimitatis discussiones* are omitted.

[20] In its earlier phases (about 1890–1930) this investigative effort focused on the onset of the schism, the rise of conciliar theory, the views of some of the leading conciliarists, and the course of events at the Council of Constance. Prominent among the historians involved were August Kneer, H.-X. Arquillière, Franz Bliemetzrieder, and, above all, Heinrich Finke. See Schneider, *Konziliarismus*, 226–8. As we have seen and as Schneider's own bibliography makes clear, in its subsequent phases this investigative effort has succeeded in generating a truly enormous body of specialized scholarly literature.

[21] Thus Schneider, *Konziliarismus*, 227, who notes also (n. 94) that Finke supervised no less than forty dissertations on the era of the Great Schism and on the general councils of the 15th cent.

that derived ultimately from one of Torquemada's subsidiary arguments and that, over the centuries, had been evoked periodically by papalists in order to blunt the force of the conciliarist and Gallican ascription of an enduring validity to the Constance superiority decree, *Haec sancta*.[22] That approach, sometimes labelled as the 'emergency theory' (*Notstandtheorie*), has taken more than one form. All of them pivot, however, on a willingness fully to recognize the gravity of the crisis confronting the churchmen assembled in 1415 at Constance, as well as the concomitant (and quite genuine) need they felt, after more than thirty years of scandalous confusion and disarray, to do something about the schism. Rather than brushing *Haec sancta* to one side in traditional fashion as the ephemeral product of a would-be or illegitimate general council, it treated the decree, then, as the understandable and historically significant response of concerned churchmen to a supremely difficult situation—in effect, as an emergency measure possessed of a certain validity, though one strictly limited in scope and time to the crisis conditions then prevailing.

For earlier controversialists of papalist bent the very existence of *Haec sancta* had loomed large as a potential threat to the absoluteness of papal authority. For them, accordingly, the classification of that decree as nothing more than a time-bound emergency measure had afforded a reasonably persuasive way of coping with that threat. For Hollnsteiner, however, and for the numerous historians who later followed his lead (among them, as we have seen, Jedin and Brandmüller during the Vatican II era),[23] its appeal was different in nature. They were heirs, after all, to a maturing conciliar historiography that was serving progressively to render the course of events at Constance more readily comprehensible. It was serving also, moreover, to bring the leading conciliarists into focus, not as the dangerously radical followers of Marsiglio of Padua and William of Ockham Torquemada had made them out to be, but rather as responsible and fairly moderate churchmen whose conciliar views stemmed from a perfectly orthodox tradition of canonistic thinking. Such historians, as a result, had to cope with a growing tension between their Catholic embrace of the ecclesiological vision endorsed by Vatican I and the position with which their historical commitments now contrived adamantly to align them. That being so, the great appeal for them of the emergency theory was that it held out the hope, at least, of being able to adhere fully to their commitments as historians without being propelled thereby into some sort of doctrinal

---

[22] Hollnsteiner, 'Konstanzer Konzil', 240–56. Cf. Frencken, 'Erforschung', 359–89 (*Exkurs*; *Hollnsteiners Notstandstheorie*).

[23] See above, Ch. 2.

collision with the exacting teaching of Vatican I on the nature and reach of the papal authority.[24]

For many, perhaps most, that hope seems to have been realized. But not for all. Returning to the issue in 1965, and amid the ecclesiological ferment stimulated by Vatican II, Jedin himself conceded the difficulties that the very wording of *Haec sancta* posed for his own earlier attempt to interpret it as a time-bound emergency measure of limited applicability.[25] And, as early as 1946, Karl August Fink, then emerging as the leading authority on the Council of Constance,[26] had begun to distance himself from his own earlier endorsement of a version of that emergency theory. By 1962, accordingly, he had come to conclude, given the circumstances now known to have surrounded the contested election of 1378, that contemporaries were in a state of 'invincible ignorance' concerning which of the two rival claimants was the true pope. Further than that, he had also come to the conclusion that Pisa was a legitimate general council, that of the three papal obediences ensuing, the Pisan was seen at the time to possess the greatest legitimacy, that Constance could claim ecumenicity right from the moment of its first assembly, and that, under the conditions then prevailing, the question of any papal approbation of its decrees had to fall victim to redundancy.[27]

In all of this, Fink was careful to confine himself to judgements that were historical in nature. He neither explored the theological implications of the Constance decrees nor dwelt on any implications they might have for the interpretation of the dogmatic declarations of Vatican I. Nor at first did the Belgian Benedictine Paul de Vooght when, in 1960, and moving along a similar historiographical trajectory, he argued that *Haec sancta* fulfilled all the requirements (including the possession of papal approbation) necessary to make it a dogmatic decree, but at the same time stopped short of drawing the (theological?) conclusion that it had to be viewed, therefore, as dogmatically valid.[28] He was, however, the first to have questioned once more, if on historical grounds, the ease with which *Haec sancta* was being brushed to one side as invalid. And as he developed and refined his case (by 1965 drawing the obvious conclusion from his own historical arguments and declaring the decree to be valid as dogma), his work

---

[24] Schneider, *Konziliarismus*, 234–55. [25] Jedin, *Bischöfliches Konzil*, 38.

[26] See Schneider, *Konziliarismus*, 239–42.

[27] Fink, 'Papsttum und Kirchenreform', 110–22 (esp. 112–13); 'Zur Beurteilung', 335–43.

[28] Instead, he contented himself with noting the relevance of the whole matter to the strict limitations imposed by Vatican I on the exercise of papal infallibility. See Paul de Vooght, 'Le Conciliarisme', in Botte *et al.*, *Le Concile et les conciles*, 143–81.

elicited from Gill the gloomy assertion that 'the principle of superiority of
council over pope, forgotten [!] and denied in the intervening centuries
[since Constance] is being revived'.[29]

By that time, however, the Swiss theologian, Hans Küng, who played so
prominent a role in the debates surrounding Vatican II and its troubled
aftermath, had entered the lists. Pointing out in his *Strukturen der Kirche*
(1962), and in appropriately Gersonian fashion, that 'the (traditionally
understood) legitimacy of Martin V and all other subsequent popes up to
the present day depends on the legitimacy of the Council of Constance
and its procedure in the question of the popes', and noting that modern
theologians, none the less, have not shrunk 'from pointing out the non-
binding character of the Constance decrees, often with quite extraordinary, ostensibly historical, arguments', Küng went on to summarize the
findings of 'the most recent research in Church history', including especially the work of Fink, Tierney, and De Vooght.[30] Among those findings
he included (and endorsed) the evidence in favour of Martin V's general
endorsement of the Constance decrees, though he emphasized that what
was involved was not 'a formal papal approbation'. Such an approbation
Constance had expected 'as little as had the ecumenical councils of Christian antiquity'. And that, he added, 'says as little against the binding character of the decrees of the old councils as it does against the binding
character of the decrees of Constance'.

Thus, if Küng was less concerned than was De Vooght with the question
of papal approbation (and argued, in fact, that it was not 'to be posed
anachronistically'), he was even more insistent that 'the binding character
of the decrees of Constance is not to be evaded'.[31] *Haec sancta* and *Frequens* were not 'something accidental or external, thrust on the Church
from the outside' but 'a logical culmination of ideas that were embedded

---

[29] Gill, 'Fifth Session', 131. Paul de Vooght developed his position and disseminated it from
1960 to 1971 in a series of articles and a book. See his 'Le Conciliarisme', in Botte *et al.*, *Le Concile et les conciles*, 143–81; 'Le conciliarisme aux conciles de Constance et de Bâle (Compléments et precisions)', 61–75; 'Le concile oecuménique de Constance et le conciliarisme',
57–86; 'Le Cardinal Cesarini et le Concile de Constance', in Franzen and Müller, *Konzil von
Konstanz*, 357–81; *Les Pouvoirs du concile*; 'Les Controverses'; 'The Results of Recent Historical Research on Conciliarism', in H. Küng, ed., *Papal Ministry in the Church* (New York:
Herder & Herder, 1971), 148–57.

[30] Küng, *Strukturen der Kirche* (1962); translated (somewhat unevenly if quite quickly) as
Structures of the Church, the version to which my page references are given. See ch. 7, and
esp. 268–319, the words cited above occurring at 270–1. While acknowledging the centrality
of the contributions made by Fink and de Vooght, he also emphasizes (in my view rightly)
the importance of the interpetation Hübler had advanced a century earlier in his *Die Constanzer Reformation*.

[31] Küng, *Structures of the Church*, 271, 277–8, 284.

in the law and doctrine of the Church itself'.[32] What was defined, he said, was not a 'conciliar parliamentarianism' or 'radical conciliarism' in accordance with which 'the regular lawful administration of the Church should be transferred from the pope to the Council and the pope reduced to a subordinate executive organ of the conciliar parliament'. Instead,

what was *defined* was a distinct kind of superiority of the council (along the lines of at least moderate 'conciliar theory'), according to which an ecumenical council has the function of a 'control authority,' not only in connection with the emergency situation of that time but also for the future on the premise that a possible future pope might again lapse into heresy, schism or the like.

His conclusion? That 'the Church might have been able to avoid many misfortunes after the Council of Constance had the fundamental position of the Constance Council—papal primacy and a definite "conciliar control" been upheld'.[33]

When Küng's book appeared, De Vooght commented, and with justice, that no contemporary theologian had before admitted the validity of the Constance definition of the jurisdictional superiority under certain circumstances of council to pope. 'It is without doubt the first time in contemporary Catholic theology that a theologian has loyally accepted these incontestable historical data and tried to interpret them.'[34] He himself was later to insist that 'there is no opposition between Vatican I and the Council of Constance',[35] and Küng (in common with Cardinal König of Vienna) appears to have thought likewise.[36] Others, however, were not so sure. In 1965 Helmut Riedlinger contributed a sobering series of hermeneutical reflections on the matter that left little doubt about the dimensions of the interpretative challenge confronting anyone who

---

[32] Ibid. 301–302; citing the words of Tierney, *Foundations*, 13. [33] Ibid. 284–5.

[34] Vooght, 'Le Conciliarisme aux conciles de Constance et de Bâle (Compléments et précisions)', 74–5.

[35] Vooght, 'Les Controverses', 73.

[36] At least, as subsequent commentators have noted, he moved to eliminate the possibility of such opposition by interpreting *Haec sancta* restrictively and, in effect, by subordinating the conciliarist ecclesiology to that of Vatican I. See Küng, *Structures of the Church*, 284–319. Critical commentary in Oakley, *Council over Pope?*, 135–41 (accusing him of 'deductive timidity!'), and Schneider, *Konziliarismus*, 263–4 (chiding him and de Vooght in somewhat more gentle fashion). While Vatican II was still in progress, and moved, perhaps, by the case Küng had made, Cardinal König of Vienna suggested in 1964 that it was up to the council to effect some sort of synthesis of (or comparison between) the positions hammered out by Constance and Vatican I. See Franz König, 'Die Konzilsidee von Konstanz bis Vaticanum II', in *Konzil der Einheit: 550. Jahrfeier des Konzils zu Konstanz* (Karlsruhe: Badenia Verlag, 1964), 15–30 (at 28–30). Of course, the engine of reform stalled at a point far short of that intriguing possibility.

believed *Haec sancta* to possess doctrinal validity and wished accordingly
to harmonize it with the ecclesiology of Vatican I.[37] Before the decade was
out, moreover, although a great deal of attention had come to be focused
on Constance and its decrees, most of it was the work of historians rather
than theologians, and many of those historians (sometimes with anxious
sidelong glances at Vatican I), while responding as best they could to the
emerging historical consensus on the conciliar epoch, had struggled to
avoid conceding any dogmatic or enduring validity to *Haec sancta*.[38]

So far as the theologians themselves were concerned, none at that time
appears to have felt moved to engage the issue further. Nor, in subsequent
years, do more than a handful appear to have been so moved. One reason
for that may have been the fact that 1970–2 saw the publication of two challenging books focusing specifically on the issue of papal infallibility—the
first a work of theological analysis by Küng, the second a historical study
of origins by Tierney.[39] With that highly significant publishing event, and
the great clamour of controversy and criticism that ensued, attention
came to veer away from the earlier concern with matters pertaining to the
papal primacy of jurisdiction and to be drawn instead into the magnetic
field exerted by the infallibility question. Moreover, while the controversy
which Küng and Tierney had initiated on that latter question did not
quickly dissipate and was destined to enjoy an enduring half-life in subsequent theological discussion,[40] the memory of the earlier round of controversy focusing on the status of *Haec sancta* (and, therefore, on the reach of
the papal primacy of jurisdiction), often appears, at least so far as the ecclesiologists are concerned, to have vanished almost without trace.

A considerable irony attaches to that fact. Speaking of the way in which
things have developed in the century and more since the First Vatican

[37] Helmut Riedlinger, 'Hermeneutische Überlegungen zu den Konstanzer Dekreten', in
Franzen and Müller, *Konzil von Konstanz*, 214–38. While the formidable nature of the challenge is clearly set forth, Riedlinger offers no solutions to it and one finishes reading the essay
feeling somewhat as if one has been skilfully guided through an advanced exercise in
hermeneutical handwringing.

[38] For the body of literature involved, see above, Ch. 2 n. 74.

[39] Küng,*Unfehlbar?*; Tierney, *Origins of Papal Infallibility*. For some sharp exchanges of
viewpoints on the claims advanced by these two books see, in relation to the former, Sieben,
Katholische Konzilsidee, 386–407. And, in relation to the latter, see Bäumer, 'Um die Anfänge
der papstlichen Unfehlbarkeitslehre', 441–50; Tierney's rejoinder (and Bäumer's reply), 'On
the History of Papal Infallibility', 185–94; A. M. Stickler, 'Papal Infallibility: A Thirteenth-
Century Invention', *Catholic Historical Review*, 60 (1974), 427–41; Tierney, 'Infallibility and
the Medieval Canonists', *Catholic Historical Review*, 61 (1975), 265–73; Stickler, 'Rejoinder to
Professor Tierney', *Catholic Historical Review*, 61 (1975), 274–7.

[40] See e.g. the lengthy discussion of the way in which discussion on the matter unfolded up
to 1993 in Sieben, *Katholische Konzilsidee*, 386–407.

Council, Klaus Schatz noted that 'the dogma of infallibility has not . . . [turned out to have had] the significance attributed to it in 1870 by its supporters or opponents'. Instead, and the obsessive preoccupation with that dogma notwithstanding, it is 'the papal primacy of jurisdiction [which] has acquired a greater scope than it actually had in 1870'. As a result, and especially in relation to the nomination of bishops and their selection in such a way as to promote the cause of specific papal policies, 'by the eve of Vatican II Rome ruled the Church in a much stronger fashion and intervened in its life everywhere to a much greater degree than had been the case in 1870'.[41] And, during the past two decades, and despite the summoning of successive episcopal synods and the currency of high-minded talk about episcopal collegiality, that trend towards tighter central control has, if anything, intensified.

That being so, for a Church with a genuinely global presence and the drawbacks attendant upon so marked a degree of centralized monarchical control combined with so small a measure of jurisdictional accountability having become increasingly a matter of frustrated commentary, it is really quite puzzling that the memory of the age-old constitutionalist strand in the Catholic ecclesiological experience appears so thoroughly to have been repressed. One would have thought that ecclesiologists and churchmen of reformist bent might more frequently have found something of value in a constitutionalist tradition (however occluded its memory) that had contrived somehow to endure for more than half a millennium.[42] One would have thought, too, that ecclesiologists might by now have become a little more conscious of the confusion and disarray prevalent in Catholic circles in face of the interpretative challenges posed by the Great Schism, the fifteenth-century councils, and their historic enactments. One would have thought especially that their attention might by now have been caught by the uneasily widening gap between what Fink labelled as 'the curialist position' and the direction in which the historical investigations of the past century have come so persistently to point.

But that has not proved to be the case, and one can only speculate, by way of conclusion, upon the consequences that may well follow from that particular failure to attend to the past. So far as the confidence we are prone to repose in historical knowledge is concerned, ours, it is true, is a more diffident age than was that of Döllinger and Acton, Manning and Maret. Not

---

[41] Schatz, *Papal Primacy*, 167–8, adding 'a systematic policy for the nomination of bishops in the sense of promoting specific trends and especially in the service of positions taken by the magisterium has only manifested itself in our time'.

[42] See above Prologue n. 45.

for us Döllinger's complacently unruffled faith in the ability of the new 'scientific' history to penetrate the opacity of the past. And the cruelties and calamities of twentieth-century life have long since rendered unfashionable any Actonian propensity for detecting the validating finger of God in the stupifying scramble of events. That historians are prone to error we have come to know very well. Perhaps all too well. In retrospect, that is to say, ours may conceivably turn out to have been an age altogether too willing to concede to the empire of the present an unwarranted degree of power over the stubborn confusion of the past. On the repression of memory and the pursuit of the politics of oblivion, after all, recent generations can certainly claim to have written the book. And yet we have also learnt the lesson that such modes of repression are rarely enduringly effective. Institutional counter-memories have proved again and again to have a disconcerting way of resurfacing at the very moment when they are least expected. Sooner or later, then, or so one cannot help thinking, and sooner, it may be, rather than later, Catholic theologians will have to steel their resolve and bring themselves to attend to the particular instance of unfinished business and trailing ends on the longer history of which it has been my purpose in this book to focus. When finally they do so they will doubtless seek to surmount the historical obstacles in their path by appealing either to some version of the admittedly ambivalent notion of 'reception' (whereby the force of a doctrinal position may in some measure be seen to depend on its reception or acceptance by the Church at large)[43] or to one or another theory of doctrinal development. If, on the one hand, they choose to follow the former route, the appeal to reception or non-reception seems destined, if it is to meet the challenge at hand, to take a rather aggressive form.[44] If, on the

[43] While it has had a long (if fluctuating) history, the notion of reception has attained a certain prominence in the years since Vatican II, and especially so in the context of ecumenical dialogue. For two useful overviews that serve to bring out the complexities and difficulties attendant upon the deployment of the notion, see Congar, 'La "Réception"comme réalité ecclésiologique', *Revue des sciences philosophiques et theologiques*, 56 (1972), 369–403; and E. Kilmartin, 'Reception in History', *Journal of Ecumenical Studies*, 21 (1984), 34–54. Cf. Bermejo's use of the notion in relation both to Vatican I and Constance (*Infallibility on Trial*, 105–236, 266–308).

[44] Such as that voiced by Bermejo who (ibid. 219–21), having stressed that, even if we have in mind only Catholics themselves, 'we can no longer speak of a universal and unquestionable reception of Vatican I', insists also that one's view of 'the contemporary reception of the Vatican dogmas cannot be limited to the Catholic Church, which . . . is not, according to Vatican II, simply coterminous with the Church of Christ'. And, he adds, the striking thing about the reception of 'the two dogmas of Vatican I . . . by the Church of Christ at large' is 'the complete, absolute unanimity in the rejection of both these dogmas by 47 percent of Christendom today'. P. Collins, *Papal Power* (London: Fount, 1997), 114–17, would appear to sympathize with this approach.

other hand, they choose the latter, it seems clear that the theory of development invoked will have to be one capable in unusual degree of encompassing, erasing, or transcending a quite radical measure of discontinuity in the history of the Latin or Western Church's self-understanding. And if a De Maistre might not have flinched at such a prospect, surely a Newman would.[45] But the challenge, none the less, remains outstanding and it does not seem destined soon to depart the scene. With what confidence, after all, can one hope to erect a future capable of enduring, if one persists in trying to do so on the foundation of a past that never truly was?

---

[45] Of the seven 'Notes . . . to discriminate healthy developments of an idea from its state of corruption and decay', that Newman identifies, the second is 'Continuity of Principle'. See Newman, *Essay on Development*, 178–85. Cf. Chadwick, *From Bossuet to Newman*, 137–63.

Bibliography

BIBLIOGRAPHIES

On medieval conciliarism and its roots, extensive bibliographical data and commentary may be found in Brian Tierney, *Foundations of the Conciliar Theory: The Contributions of the Medieval Canonists from Gratian to the Great Schism* (Cambridge: Cambridge University Press, 1955), and in the revised edition with discussion of subsequent literature (Leiden: E. J. Brill, 1998); Remigius Bäumer, 'Die Erforschung des Konziliarismus', in Remigius Bäumer (ed.), *Die Entwicklung des Konziliarismus: Werden und Nachwirken der Konziliaren Idee* (Darmstadt: Wissenschaftliche Buchgesellschaft, 1976), 3–50; Giuseppe Alberigo, 'Il movimento conciliare (xiv–xv sec.) nella ricerca storica ricente', *Studi medievali*, 19 (1978), 913–50; idem, *Chiesa conciliare: Identità e significato del conciliarismo* (Brescia: Paideia Editrice, 1981), 340–54; Francis Oakley, 'Natural Law, the *Corpus Mysticum*, and Consent in Conciliar Thought from John of Paris to Matthias Ugonius', *Speculum*, 56 (1981), 786–810. For the enormous outpouring of literature on the Council of Constance itself, see A. Frencken, 'Die Erforschung des Konstanzer Konzils (1414–1418) in den letzten 100 Jahren', *Annuarium Historiae Conciliorum*, 25 (1993), 1–509. Remigius Bäumer, *Nachwirkungen des Konziliaren Gedankens in der Theologie und Kanonistik des frühen 16. Jahrhunderts* (Münster: Aschendorff, 1971), canvasses the scholarly work devoted to the continuing tradition of conciliarist thinking on into the Reformation era, and Hans Schneider, *Das Konziliarismus als Problem der neueren Katholischen Theologie: Die Geschichte des Auslegung der Konstanzer Dekrete von Febronius bis zur Gegenwart* (Berlin and New York: De Gruyter, 1976), does likewise for subsequent centuries down to the twentieth. More recent works can be found listed in the comprehensive classified bibliographies of new scholarship published on a continuing basis in *Revue d'histoire ecclésiastique*.

GENERAL ACCOUNTS

The conciliar movement having gone down to defeat in the mid-fifteenth century, historiographic convention has long dictated that conciliarism itself, at least as any sort of living tradition of thought, likewise petered out. As a result, no general accounts of the tradition really exist for the whole period running from the thirteenth to the nineteenth centuries. The closest approach to such, despite its specific focus on the years running from the late eighteenth to the mid-twentieth centuries is Schneider, cited above. And a quasi-continuous narrative, though episodic in nature and punctuated by considerable gaps, can be constructed from the pertinent chapters in Hermann Josef Sieben, *Die Konzilsidee des lateinischen Mittelalters* (Paderborn: F. Schöningh, 1984); idem, *Die Katholische Konzilsidee von der Reformation bis zur Aufklärung* (Paderborn: F. Schöningh, 1988), and idem, *Katholische Konzilsidee im 19. und 20. Jahrhundert* (Paderborn: F. Schöningh, 1993). For the conciliar background at large, the classic work by C. J. Hefele remains indispensable: *Histoire des conciles d'après les documents originaux*, tr. and ed. H. Leclercq, 11 vols. (Paris: Letourzey et Ané, 1907–51). The most recent shorter accounts are Giuseppe Alberigo (ed.), *Storia dei concilii ecumenici* (Brescia: Queriniana, 1990); Klaus Schatz, *Allgemeine Konzilien: Brennpunkte der Kirchengeschichte* (Paderborn: F. Schöningh, 1997); Norman P. Tanner, *The Councils of the Church: A Short History* (New York: Crossroad, 1999); Christopher M. Bellitto, *The General Councils: A History of the Twenty-One Church Councils from Nicaea to Vatican II* (New York and Matwah, NJ, 2002).

WORKS CITED

Acton, Lord, *The History of Freedom and Other Essays*, ed. J. N. Figgis and R. V. Laurence (London: Macmillan & Co., 1907).
—— *Lectures on the French Revolution*, ed. J. N. Figgis and R. V. Laurence (London: Macmillan & Co., 1910).
Aitken, James M., *The Trial of George Buchanan before the Lisbon Inquisition* (Edinburgh and London: Oliver & Boyd, 1939).
Alberigo, Giuseppe, 'L'ecclesiologia del Concilio di Trente', *Rivista di storia della Chiesa in Italia*, 18 (1964), 221–42.
—— *Cardinalato e collegialità: Studi sull' ecclesiologia tra l'xi e il xiv secolo* (Florence: Vallechi, 1969).
—— *Chiesa conciliare: Identità e significato del conciliarismo* (Brescia: Paideia Editrice, 1981).
—— and Magistretti, Franca, eds., *Constitutionis Dogmaticae Lumen Gentium Synopsis Historica* (Bologna: Instituto per le scienze religiose, 1975).
—— and Tanner, Norman P., eds., *Decrees of the Ecumenical Councils*, 2 vols. (London and Washington, DC: Sheed & Ward and Georgetown University Press, 1990).
Allen, J. W., *A History of Political Thought in the Sixteenth Century* (London: Methuen & Co., 1938).
—— *Political Thought in England: 1603–1660* (London: Methuen & Co., 1938).
Allen, William, Cardinal, *A true, sincere and modest defence of English Catholiques that suffer for their Faith* (Ingolstadt(?), 1584).

Almain, Jacques, *Aurea clarissimi et acutissimi Doctoris theologi Magistri Jacobi Almain Senonensis opuscula* (Paris, 1518).

Annuario Pontificio (Vatican City: Tipografia Poliglotta Vaticana, 1947).

Arquillière, H. X., ed., *Le Plus Ancien Traité de l'église: Jacques de Viterbo De regimine christiano (1301–1302)* (Paris: G. Beauchesne, 1926).

Aubert, Roger, *Le Pontificat de Pie IX: 1846–1878* (Paris: Bloud & Gay, 1952), vol. xxi of *Histoire de l'Église*, ed. A. Fliche and V. Martin.

—— Beckmann, Johannes, Corish, Patrick J., and Lill, Rudolf, *The Church between Revolution and Restoration*, tr. Peter Becker (New York: Crossroad, 1980), vol. vii of *Handbook of Church History*, ed. H. Jedin and J. Dolan.

—— Beckmann, Johannes, Corish, Patrick J., and Lill, Rudolf, *The Church in the Age of Liberalism*, tr. Peter Becker (New York: Crossroad, 1981), vol. viii of *Handbook of Church History*, ed. H. Jedin and J. Dolan.

Augustine of Hippo, *Confessiones*. In *St Augustine's Confessions. With an English translation by William Watts 1631*, 2 vols. (London and New York: W. Heinemann, 1912).

Baluzius, Stephanus, *Vitae Paparum Avenionensium*, new edn., ed. G. Mollat, 4 vols. (Paris: Letourzey & Ané, 1914–27).

—— and Mansi, J. D., *Miscellanea*, 4 vols. (Lucca, 1761–4).

Baronius, C., Raynaldus, O., and Laderchius, J., *Annales ecclesiastici*, 37 vols. (Paris, 1864–83).

Barraclough, Geoffrey, *Papal Provisions* (Oxford: Basil Blackwell, 1935).

—— ed., *Mediaeval Germany, 911–1250: Essays by German Historians*, 2 vols. (Oxford: Basil Blackwell, 1948).

Barret, W., *Jus Regis, seu De absoluto et independenti secularium principum dominio et obsequio eis debito* (Basel, 1612).

Baumer, Franklin Le Van, *The Early Tudor Theory of Kingship* (New Haven and London: Yale University Press, 1939).

Bäumer, Remigius, *Nachwirkungen des konziliaren Gedankens in der Theologie und Kanonistik des frühen 16. Jahrhunderts* (Münster: Aschendorff, 1971).

—— ed., *Von Konstanz nach Trient: Beiträge zur Geschichte der Kirche von den Reformkonzilien bis zum Tridentinum* (Munich: F. Schöningh, 1972).

—— 'Um die Aufänge der papstichen Unfehlbarkeitslehre', *Theologische Revue*, 69 (1973), 441–50.

—— 'Antwort an Tierney', *Theologische Revue*, 70 (1974), 193–4.

Baumgartner, F. J., *Radical Reactionaries: The Political Thought of the French Catholic League* (Geneva: Droz, 1975).

Beal, John P., Coriden, James A., and Green, Thomas J., eds., *New Commentary on the Code of Canon Law* (New York: Paulist Press, 2000).

Beales, David, *Joseph II: In the Shadow of Maria Theresa*, 2 vols. (Cambridge: Cambridge University Press, 1987–9).

Beck, Hans-Georg, Fink, Karl August, Glazik, Josef, Iserloh, Erwin, and Walter, Hans, *From the High Middle Ages to the Eve of the Reformation*, tr. Anselm Biggs

(Freiburg and Montreal: Herder & Palm, 1970), vol. iv. of *Handbook of Church Hitory*, ed. H. Jedin and J. Dolan.

Becker, H.-J., *Die Appellation vom Papst an ein Allgemeines Konzil: Historische Entwicklung und Kanonistische Diskussion im späten Mittelalter und der frühen Neuzeit* (Cologne and Vienna: Böhlau, 1988).

Bellarmine, Robert, Cardinal, *Opera omnia*, 6 vols. (Naples: Joseph Giuliano, 1856–62).

—— *Risposta alle oppositioni di Fra Paolo Servita contra la scrittura de Cardinale Bellarmino* (Rome, 1606).

—— *Risposta del Card. Bellarmino a due libretti* (Rome, 1606).

—— *Risposta di Card. Bellarmino, ad un libretto intitulato Trattato, e resolutione, sopra la validità de la scommuniche di Gio. Gersono* (Rome, 1606).

—— *Risposta di Card. Bellarmino al Trattato de i sette Theologi di Venetia sopra l'interdetto della Santità di Nostro Signore Papa Paolo Quinto* (Rome, 1606).

Bellitto, Christopher M., *Nicholas de Clamanges: Spirituality, Personal Reform and Pastoral Renewal on the Eve of the Reformation* (Washington, DC: Catholic University Press, 2001).

Berington, Joseph, *The State and Behaviour of English Catholics from the Reformation to the Year 1781*, 2nd edn. (London, 1781).

—— *Reflections addressed to the Rev. John Hawkins* (London, 1785).

Berlin, Isaiah, *The Crooked Timber of Humanity*, ed. Henry Hardy (New York: Alfred A. Knopf, 1991).

Bermejo, Luis M., *Infallibility on Trial: Church, Conciliarity and Communion* (Westminster, Md.: Christian Classics, 1992).

Bianchi, Eugene C., and Ruether, Rosemary Radford, eds., *A Democratic Catholic Church: The Reconstruction of Roman Catholicism* (New York: Crossroad, 1992).

Bilson, Thomas, *The True Difference betweene Christian subjection and Unchristian Rebellion* (Oxford, 1585).

Black, A. J., *Monarchy and Community: Political Ideas in the Later Conciliar Controversy, 1430–1450* (Cambridge: Cambridge University Press, 1970).

—— 'The Realist Ecclesiology of Heimerich van de Velde', in Edmond J. M. van Eijl, ed., *Facultas S. Theologiae Lovanensis, 1432–1797: Bijdragen tot haar geschiedenis* (Louvain: Louvain University Press, 1977), 273–91.

—— *Council and Commune: The Conciliar Movement and the Fifteenth-Century Heritage* (London: Burns & Oates, 1979).

—— 'The Conciliar Movement', in J. H. Burns, ed., *The Cambridge History of Medieval Political Thought: c.350–c.1450* (Cambridge: Cambridge University Press, 1988), 573–87.

—— *Political Thought in Europe: 1250–1450* (Cambridge: Cambridge University Press, 1992).

Blackwell, G., *A large Examination taken at Lambeth . . . of M. George Blackwell made Archpriest of England by Pope Clement 8* (London, 1607).

Blythe, James M., *Ideal Government and the Mixed Constitution in the Middle Ages* (Princeton: Princeton University Press, 1992).

Bolton, Robert, *Two Sermons Preached at Northampton at Two Severall Assises There* (London, 1639).

Borde, Vivien de la, *Du témoignage de la verité dans l'Église* ([n.pl.]. 1714).

Bossuet, Jacques-Bénigne, *Œuvres complètes de Bossuet*, ed. F. Lachat, 31 vols. (Paris: L. Vives, 1863–7).

Bossy, John, 'Henry IV, the Appallants and the Jesuits', *Recusant History*, 8 (1965), 80–112.

—— *The English Catholic Community: 1570–1850* (New York: Oxford University Press, 1976).

Botte, B. *et al.*, *Le Concile et les conciles: Contribution à l'histoire de la vie de l'église* (Chevetogne and Paris: Éditions de Chevetogne, 1960).

Boucher, Jean, *De justa Henrici Tertii abdictione a Francorum regno* (Lyons, 1591).

Bouwsma, William J., *Venice and the Defense of Republican Liberty: Renaissance Values in the Age of Counter-Reformation* (Berkeley and Los Angeles: University of California Press, 1968).

Bramhall, John, *The Works of the Most Reverend Father in God, John Bramhall, D.D.*, ed. A.W.H. 5 vols. (Oxford: J. H. Parker, 1842–5).

Branca, Vittore, ed., *Storia della civiltà Veneziana*, 3 vols. (Florence: Sansoni, 1979).

Brandmüller, Walter, 'Besitzt des Konstanzer Dekret *Haec sancta* dogmatische Verbindichkeit?', *Römische Quartalschrift*, 62 (1967), 1–17.

—— *Das Konzil von Pavia–Siena: 1423–1424*, 2 vols. (Münster: Aschendorff, 1968–74).

—— 'Papst und Konzil auf dem Tridentinum', *Annuarium Historiae Conciliorum*, 5 (1973), 198–203.

—— *Das Konzil von Konstanz 1414–1418*, 2 vols. (Paderborn: F. Schöningh, 1991–9).

Bressolette, Claude, *L'Église et l'état: Cours de Sorbonne inédit, 1850–1851* (Paris: G. Beauchesne, 1979).

—— *Le Pouvoir dans la société et dans l'église: L'Écclésiologie politique du Monseigneur Maret* (Paris: Éditions du Cerf, 1984).

—— 'Ultramontanisme et gallicanisme engagent-ils deux visions de la société', *Freiburger Zeitschrift für Philosophie und Theologie*, 38 (1991), 3–25.

Bridge, William, *The Wounded Conscience Cured, the Weak One Strengthened and the Doubting Satisfied. By Way of Answer to Doctor Ferne* (London, 1642).

—— *The Truths of the Times Vindicated* (London, 1643).

Brosse, Olivier de la, *Le Pape et le Concile: La Comparaison de leurs pouvoirs à la veille de la Réforme* (Paris: Éditions du Cerf, 1945).

—— Lecler, J., Holstein, H., and Lefebvre, C., *Latran V et Trente*, vol. x of Gervais Dumeige (ed.), *Histoire des conciles oecuméniques* (Paris: Éditions de l'Orante, 1975).

Brutus, Junius [Philippe du Plessis Mornay], *Vindiciae contra tyrannos* (Basle, 1580).

——— *Vindiciae contra tyrannos . . . Being a Treatise Written in Latin and French by Junius Brutus and Translated out of Both into English* (London, 1689).

——— *A Defense of Liberty Against Tyrants: A Translation of the 'Vindiciae contra Tyrannos' by Junius Brutus*, ed. Harold Laski (London: B. Franklin, 1924).

Bubenheimer, Ulrich, Review of Remigius Bäumer, *Nachwirkungen des konziliaren Gedankens*, in *Zeitschrift der Savigny-Stiftung für Rechtsgeschichte*, 90 (1973), Kanonistische Abteilung, 59, 455–65.

Buchanan, George, *Opera omnia*, 2 vols. (Edinburgh, 1715).

Buckeridge, John, *De potestate papae in rebus temporalibus . . . adversus Robertum Cardinalem Bellarminum* (London, 1614).

Burns, J. H., 'John Ireland and "The Meroure of Wyssdome"', *Innes Review*, 6 (1955), 77–98.

——— *Scottish Churchmen and the Council of Basel* (Glasgow: J. S. Burns & Sons, 1962).

——— 'The Conciliarist Tradition in Scotland', *Scottish Historical Review*, 42 (1963), 89–104.

——— '*Politia regalis et optima*: The Political Ideas of John Mair', *History of Political Thought*, 2 (1981), 31–61.

——— '*Jus gladii* and *jurisdictio*: Jacques Almain and John Locke', *Historical Journal*, 26 (1982), 369–74.

——— *Lordship, Kingship, and Empire: The Idea of Empire, 1400–1525* (Oxford: Oxford University Press, 1992).

——— and Goldie, Mark, eds., *The Cambridge History of Political Thought: 1450–1700* (Cambridge: Cambridge University Press, 1991).

——— and Izbicki, Thomas M., eds., *Conciliarism and Papalism* (Cambridge: Cambridge University Press, 1997).

Butler, Charles, *The Historical Memoirs of the Church of France, in the reigns of Louis XIV, Louis XV, Louis XVI, and the French Revolution* (London: W. Clarke & Sons, 1817).

Cajetan, Thomas de Vio, Cardinal, *De comparatione auctoritatis papae et concilii, cum Apologia ejusdem Tractatus*, ed. V. M. Pollet (Rome, 1936).

Cappellari, Fra Mauro, *Il Trionfo della Santa Sede e della Chiesa contro gli assalti degli inovatori* (Venice: Giuseppe Baltaggia, 1832).

Carlyle, R. W. and A. J., *A History of Medieval Political Theory in the West*, 6 vols. (Edinburgh and London: William Blackwood & Sons, 1903–36).

Carter, Charles H., ed., *From the Renaissance to the Counter Reformation: Essays in Honour of Garrett Mattingly* (New York: Random House, 1965).

Chadwick, Owen, *The Popes and European Revolution* (Oxford: Clarendon Press, 1981).

——— *From Bossuet to Newman*, 2nd edn. (Cambridge: Cambridge University Press, 1987).

——— *A History of the Popes: 1830–1914* (Oxford: Clarendon Press, 1998).

Chinnici, Joseph P., *The English Catholic Enlightenment: John Lingard and the Cisalpine Movement, 1780–1850* (Shepardstown, WV: Patmos Press, 1980).

Christianson, Gerald, *Cesarini: The Conciliar Cardinal: The Basel Years, 1431–1438* (St Ottilien: EOS-Verlag, 1979).

——— and Izbicki, T. M., eds., *Nicholas of Cusa on Christ and the Church* (Leiden: E. J. Brill, 1996).

Clancy, Thomas C., *Papist Pamphleteers: The Allen–Persons Party and the Political Thought of the Counter-Reformation in England, 1572–1615* (Chicago: Loyola University Press, 1964).

Codex Juris Canonici (Rome: Typis Polyglottis Vaticanis, 1919).

Coffey, John, *Politics, Religion and the British Revolution: The Mind of Samuel Rutherford* (Cambridge: Cambridge University Press, 1997).

Coleman, Janet, *Ancient and Medieval Memories: Studies in the Reconstruction of the Past* (Cambridge: Cambridge University Press, 1992).

Collins, Paul, *Papal Power: A Proposal for Change in Catholicism's Third Millennium* (London: Fount, 1997).

Congar, Yves, 'Aspects ecclésiologiques de la querelle entre mendiants et séculiers dans la seconde moitié du XIIIe siècle et le début du XIVe', *Archives d'histoire doctrinale et littéraire du moyen âge*, 28 (1961), 35–151.

——— 'La "Reception" comme realité ecclésiologique', *Revue des sciences philosophiques et théologiques*, 56 (1972), 369–403.

——— 'Bulletin de théologie', *Revue des sciences philosophiques et théologiques*, 59 (1975), 465–531.

Coriden, James A., ed., *We, The People of God: A Study of Constitutional Government for the Church* (Huntington, Ind.: Canon Law Society of America, 1968).

Corpus juris canonici, ed. E. Friedberg, 2 vols. (Leipzig: B. Tauchnitz, 1879–81).

Costigan, Richard F., *Rohrbacher and the Ecclesiology of Ultramontanism* (Rome: Gregoriana, 1980).

——— 'Tradition and the Beginning of the Ultramontane Movement', *Irish Theological Quarterly*, 48 (1981), 27–45.

——— 'Bossuet and the Consensus of the Church', *Theological Studies*, 56 (1995), 652–72.

Cozzi, G., 'Fra Paolo Sarpi, l'Anglicanesimo e la "Historia del Concilio Tridentino"' *Rivista storica italiana*, 63 (1956), 556–619.

Crews, Clyde F., *English Catholic Modernism: Maude Petre's Way of the Faith* (Notre Dame, Ind.: University of Notre Dame Press, 1984).

Crowder, C. M. D., *Unity, Heresy and Reform: 1378–1460* (New York: St Martin's Press, 1977).

CSEL = *Corpus Christianorum Ecclesiasticorum Latinorum*, 95 vols. (Vienna: C. Geraldi Filium Bibliopolam Academiae, 1866–2001).

Cusa, Nicholas of, *Nicola de Cusa: Opera omnia*, ed. Gerhard Kallen, 14 vols. (Leipzig: F. Meiner, 1932–63).

—— *Nicholas of Cusa: The Catholic Concordance*, ed. and tr. Paul Sigmund (Cambridge: Cambridge University Press, 1991).

Decretum Gratiani, in *Corpus juris canonici*, ed. E. Friedberg, 2 vols. (Leipzig: Bernhard Tauchnitz, 1879–81).

Degart, A., *Histoire des seminaries français jusqu' à la Révolution*, 2 vols. (Paris, 1912).

Delaruelle, E., Labande, E.-R., and Ourliac, P., *L'Église au temps du Grand Schisme et de la crise conciliaire: 1379–1449*, 2 vols. (Paris: Bloud & Gay, 1962–4), vol. xiv of *Histoire de l'Église*, ed. A. Fliche and V. Martin.

Denzinger, H., and Schönmetzer, A., *Euchiridion definitionum et declarationum de rebus fidei et morum*, 23rd edn. (Rome: Herder, 1965).

Deutsche Reichstagsakten, Altere Reihe, ed. H. Weigel *et al.*, 17 vols. (Gotha and Stuttgart, 1898–1939).

Dictionnaire de droit canonique, ed. R. Naz, 7 vols. (Paris: Letourzey & Ané, 1935–65).

Dictionnaire de théologie catholique, 15 vols. (Paris: Letourzey & Ané, 1903–50).

Dietrich von Niem, *Dietrich von Niem: Dialog über Union und Reform der Kirche 1410*, ed. Heinrich Heimpel (Leipzig and Berlin: Teubner, 1933).

Döllinger, Ignaz von, *Kleinere Schriften*, ed. F. H. Rensch (Stuttgart, 1890).

—— See 'Janus'.

—— See 'Quirinus'.

Dominis, Marc Antonio de, *De republica ecclesiastica. Libri X* (London, 1617).

—— *Papatus Romanus: Liber de origine, progressu, atque extinctione ipsius* (London, 1617).

—— *De republica ecclesiastica. Pars secunda* (London, 1620).

Douglas, Mary, *How Institutions Think* (Syracuse, NY: Syracuse University Press, 1986).

Doussinague, José M., *Fernando el Católico y el cisma de Pisa* (Madrid: Espasa–Calpe, 1946).

Duchon, Robert, 'De Bossuet à Febronius', *Revue d'histoire ecclésiastique*, 65 (1970), 375–422.

Duffy, Eamon, 'Ecclesiastical Democracy Detected: 1 (1779–1787)', *Recusant History*, 10 (1970), 193–209.

—— 'Ecclesiastical Democracy Detected: 2 (1787–1799)', *Recusant History*, 10 (1970), 309–31.

—— *Saints and Sinners. A History of the Popes* (New Haven and London: Yale University Press, 1997).

Dulles, Avery, and Granfield, Patrick, *The Theology of the Church: A Bibliography* (New York: Papalist Press, 1999).

Dupin, Louis Ellies, *Traité de la puissance ecclésiastique et temporelle* (Paris, 1707).

—— *Histoire ecclésiastique du dix-septième siècle*, 4 vols. (Paris, 1714).

Ehler, S. Z., and Morrall, J. B., eds., *Church and State through the Centuries* (London: Burns & Oates, 1954).

Ehrle, Franz, ed., *Martin de Alpartils Chronica Actitatorum*, i. (Quellen und Forschungen aus dem Gebiete der Geschichte, 7, Paderborn: F. Schöningh, 1906).

Eliade, Mircea, ed., *The Encyclopedia of Religion*, 16 vols. (New York and London: Macmillan, 1987).

Ellis, John Tracy, *Catholics in Colonial America* (Baltimore and Dublin: Hellicon, 1965).

Enciclopedia cattolica, 12 vols. (Vatican City: Il libro cattolico, 1949–54).

Fasolt, Constantin, *Councils and Hierarchy: The Political Thought of William Durant the Younger* (Cambridge: Cambridge University Press, 1991).

Febronius, Justinus, *De Statu Ecclesiae et legitima potestate Romani Pontificis. Liber singularis, et reuniendos dissidente in religione christianos compositae* (Frankfurt, 1765).

Fentress, James, and Wickham, Chris, *Social Memory* (Oxford: Blackwell, 1992).

Ferne, Henry, *Conscience Satisfied: That There is no Warrant for the Arms now Taken up by Subjects* (Oxford, 1643).

—— *The Resolving of Conscience upon this Question: Whether upon such a Supposition or Case, as is Now Usually Made . . . Subjects may Take up Arms and Resist*, 2nd edn. (Oxford, 1643).

Figgis, John Neville, *Political Thought from Gerson to Grotius: Seven Studies* (New York: Harper, 1960).

Fink, K. A., 'Papsttum und Kirchenreform nach dem Grossen Schisma', *Theologische Quartalschrift*, 126 (1946), 110–22.

—— 'Zur Beurteilung des grossen abendländischen Schismas', *Zeitschrift für Kirchengeschichte*, 73 (1962), 335–43.

Finke, Heinrich, *Acta Concilii Constanciensis*, 4 vols. (Münster: Regensbergschen Buchhandlung, 1896–1928).

Fliche, A., and Martin, V., eds., *Histoire de l'Église depuis les origines jusqu'à nos jours*, 19 vols. in 21 (Paris: Bloud & Gay, 1946–64).

Fois, Mario, 'Il valore ecclesiologico del decreto "Haec Sancta" del Concilio di Costanza', *Civiltà cattolica*, 126/2 (1975), 138–52.

Foxe, John, *Actes and Monuments of these latter and perilous dayes, touching matters of the Church*, ed. St Reed Cattley, 8 vols. (London: R. B. Seeley & W. Burnside, 1837–41).

Franklin, Julian H., *John Locke and the Theory of Sovereignty: Mixed Monarchy and the Right of Resistance in the Political Thought of the English Revolution* (Cambridge: Cambridge University Press, 1978).

—— Review of Quentin Skinner, *Foundations of Political Thought, Political Theory*, 7 (1979), 552–8.

Franzen, August, 'The Council of Constance: Present State of the Problem', *Concilium*, 7 (1965), 29–68.

—— and Müller, Wolfgang, eds., *Das Konzil von Konstanz: Beiträge zu seiner Geschichte and Theologie* (Freiburg: Herder, 1964).

Frenken, A., 'Die Erforschung des Konstanzer Konzils (1414–1418) in den letzten 100 Jahren', *Annuarium Historiae Conciliorum*, 25 (1993), 1–509.

Ganzer, Klaus, 'Gallikanische und Römische Primatsauffassung im Widerstreit', *Historisches Jahrbuch*, 109 (1989), 109–63.

Garijo-Guembe, Miguel M., *Communion of the Saints: Foundation, Nature, and Structure of the Church*, tr. Patrick Madigan (Collegeville, Minn.: Liturgical Press, 1994).

Geary, Patrick J., *Phantoms of Remembrance: Memory and Oblivion at the End of the First Millennium* (Princeton: Princeton University Press, 1994).

Gerson, Jean le Charlier de, *Joannis Gersonii ... Opera*, ed. Edmond Richer, 2 vols. (Paris, 1606).

—— *Opera omnia*, ed. Louis Ellies Dupin, 5 vols. (Antwerp, 1706).

—— *Œuvres complètes*, ed. Palemon Glorieux, 10 vols. (Paris: Desdée, 1960–73).

Gerth, H. H., and Mills, C. Wright, eds., *From Max Weber: Essays in Sociology* (Oxford and New York: Oxford University Press, 1946).

Gettell, Raymond G., *History of Political Thought* (New York and London: Century Co., 1924).

Gewirth, Alan, *Marsilius of Padua: The Defender of Peace*, 2 vols. (New York: Columbia University Press, 1951).

Gierke, Otto, *Political Theories of the Middle Age*, ed. and tr. F. W. Maitland (Cambridge: Cambridge University Press, 1900).

Gignoux, C. I., *Joseph de Maistre: Prophète du passé, historien de l'avenir* (Paris: Nouvelles Éditions Latines, 1963).

Gill, Joseph, *The Council of Florence* (Cambridge: Cambridge University Press, 1959).

—— *Eugenius IV, Pope of Christian Union* (Westminster, Md.: Newman Press, 1961).

—— 'The Fifth Session of the Council of Constance', *Heythrop Journal*, 5 (1964), 131–43.

—— *Constance et Bâle-Florence* (Paris: Éditions de l'Orante, 1965). Vol. ix of Gervaise Dumeige, ed., *Histoire des conciles oecuméniques*.

—— 'Il decreto *Haec sancta synodus* del concilio di Costanza', *Rivista di storia della Chiesa in Italia*, 12 (1967), 123–30.

Glazier, Michael, and Hellwig, Monika K., eds., *The Modern Catholic Encyclopedia* (Collegeville, Minn.: Liturgical Press, 1994).

Gogan, B., *The Common Corps of Christendom: Ecclesiological Themes in the Writings of Sir Thomas More* (Leiden: E. J. Brill, 1982).

Goldast, Melchior, *Monarchia S. Romani Imperii*, 3 vols. (Frankfurt, 1611–14).

Goulart, Simon, ed., *Mémoires de l'Estat de France sous Charles IX*, 3 vols. (Meidelbourg, 1576).

Granfield, Patrick, *The Papacy in Transition* (Garden City, NY: Doubleday, 1980).

—— *The Limits of the Papacy: Authority and Autonomy in the Church* (New York: Crossroad, 1987).

Guilday, Peter, *The Life and Times of John Carroll Archbishop of Baltimore (1735–1815)* (New York: Encyclopedia Press, 1922).

Guillemain, B., *La Politique bénéficiale du pape Benoît XII* (Paris: H. Champion, 1952).

—— 'Punti di vista sul Papato avignonese', *Archivio storico italiano*, 111 (1953), 181–206.

—— *La Cour pontificale d'Avignon: 1300–1376* (Paris: Éditions E. de Boccard, 1962).

Guy, J. A., *Christopher St German on Chancery and Statute* (London: Selden Society, 1988).

Gwatkin, H. M., *et al.*, eds., *The Cambridge Medieval History*, 8 vols. (Cambridge: Cambridge University Press, 1911–36).

Haidacher, A., and Mayer, H. E., eds., *Festschrift Karl Pivec* (Innsbruck: Sprachwissenschaftliches Institut der Leopold-Franzens-Universität, 1966).

Halbwachs, Maurice, *The Collective Memory*, tr. Francis J. Ditter, jun., and Vida Yazdia Ditter (New York: Harper & Row, 1980).

Hallam, Henry, *View of the State of Europe in the Middle Ages*, 3 vols. (London, 1901; 1st publ. 1818).

Haller, Johannes, *Papsttum und Kirchenreform: Vier Kapital zur Geschichte des ausgehenden Mittelaters* (Berlin: Weidmann, 1903).

Hardt, H. von der, *Rerum concilii oecumenici Constantiensis*, 6 vols. (Leipzig, 1697–1700).

Harvey, Margaret, *England, Rome and the Papacy, 1417–1464: The Study of a Relationship* (Manchester and New York: Manchester University Press, 1993).

Headley, John, *The Emperor and his Chancellor: A Study of the Imperial Chancellory under Gattinara* (Cambridge: Cambridge University Press, 1983).

Hefele, C. J., *Histoire des conciles d'après les documents originaux*, tr. and ed. H. Leclercq, 11 vols. (Paris: Letourzey & Ané, 1907–51).

—— and Hergenröther, J., *Conciliengeschichte*, 9 vols. (Freiburg im Br.: Herder, 1855–90).

Heft, James, *John XXII and Papal Teaching Authority* (Lewiston, NY: Mellen, 1986).

Heimpel, Heinrich, *Dietrich von Niem* (Münster: Regensbergsche Verlagsbuch-handlung, 1932).

Hennesey, James, *American Catholics: A History of the Roman Catholic Community in the United States* (New York and Oxford: Oxford University Press, 1981).

Hild, Joseph, *Honoré Tournély und seine Stellung zum Jansenismus* (Freiburg: Herder, 1911).

Hobbes, Thomas, *Leviathan*, ed. Michael Oakeshott (Oxford: Basil Blackwell, 1946).

Hollnsteiner, Johannes, 'Das Konstanzer Konzil in der Geschichte der christlichen Kirche', *Mitteilungen des österreichischen Instituts für Geschichtsforschung*, 11 (1929), 395–420.

Holmes, Peter, *Resistance and Compromise: The Political Thought of the Elizabethan Catholics* (Cambridge: Cambridge University Press, 1982).

Hontheim, Johann Nikolaus von. *See* Febronius, Justinus.

Hooker, Richard, *Of the Laws of Ecclesiastical Polity*, ed. G. Edelin, W. Speed Hill, and P. G. Stanwood. *The Folger Library Edition of the Works of Richard Hooker*, i–iii. (Cambridge, Mass., and London: Belknap Press of Harvard University Press, 1977–81).

Hübler, Bernhard, *Die Constanzer Reformation und die Concordate von 1418* (Leipzig: B. Tauchnitz, 1867).

Hudson, W. S., *John Ponet (1516?–1556): Advocate of Limited Monarchy* (Chicago: University of Chicago Press, 1942).

Hutton, Patrick H., *History as an Art of Memory* (Hanover: University Press of New England, 1993).

Il Primato del Successore di Pietro: Atti del Simposio Teologico, Roma, dicembre 1996 (Vatican City: Libreria Editrice Vaticana, 1998).

Inglis, John, *Spheres of Philosophical Inquiry and the Historiography of Medieval Philosophy* (Leiden: E. J. Brill, 1998).

Iserloh, E., ed., *Reformata Reformanda: Festschrift Hubert Jedin*, 2 vols. (Münster: Aschendorff, 1965).

Izbicki, Thomas M., *Protector of the Faith: Cardinal Johannes de Turrecremata and the Defense of the Institutional Church* (Washington, DC: Catholic University Press, 1981).

—— 'Papalist Reaction to the Council of Constance: Juan de Torquemada to the Present', *Church History*, 55 (1986), 7–20.

—— 'Cajetan's Attack on Parallels between Church and State', *Cristianesimo nella Storia*, 20 (1999), 80–9.

—— and Bellitto, Christopher M., eds., *Reform and Renewal in the Middle Ages and Renaissance* (Leiden: E. J. Brill, 2000).

Jacob, E. F., *Essays in the Conciliar Epoch*, 2nd edn. (Manchester: Manchester University Press, 1953).

—— ed., *Italian Renaissance Studies* (London: Faber & Faber, 1960).

James I, King of England, *The Political Works of James I*, ed. C. H. McIlwain (Cambridge, Mass.: Harvard University Press, 1918).

'Janus' [Ignaz von Döllinger], *The Pope and the Council*. Authorized tr. from the German, 2nd edn. (London, 1869).

Jedin, Hubert, *Geschichte des Konzils von Trient*, 4 vols. in 5 (Freiburg: Herder, 1948–78).

—— *A History of the Council of Trent*, tr. Ernest Graf, 2 vols. (London: Thomas Nelson & Sons, 1952–61).

—— *Ecumenical Councils of the Catholic Church*, tr. Ernest Graf (London and New York: Herder & Herder, 1960).

—— *Bischöfliches Konzil oder Kirchenparlament: Ein Beitrag zur ekklesiologie der Konzilien von Konstanz und Basel*, 2nd edn. (Basle and Stuttgart: Helbing & Lichtenhahn, 1965).

—— *Kirche des Glaubens, Kirche der Geschichte: Aufsätze und Vorträge*, 2 vols. (Freiburg: Herder, 1966).

Jedin, Hubert, and Dolan, John, eds., *Handbook of Church History*, 7 vols. (Freiburg and Montreal: Herder & Palm, 1965–82).

Jewel, John, *The Works of John Jewel*, ed. J. Ayre, 4 vols. (Cambridge: Cambridge University Press, 1845–50).

—— *The Apology of the Church of England by John Jewel*, ed. J. E. Booty (Ithaca, NY: Cornell University Press, 1963).

John of Paris, *Johannes Quidort von Paris: Über königliche und päpstliche Gewalt*, ed. Fritz Bleienstein, Text kritische Edition mit deutscher Übersetzung (Stuttgart: Ernst Klett Verlag, 1969).

—— *On Royal and Papal Power*, tr. with an introd. by J. A. Watt (Toronto: PIMS, 1971).

Johnson, Robert C., Keeley, Mary Friar, Cole, Maija Jansson, and Bidwell, William B., eds., *Commons Debates 1628*, 6 vols. (New Haven and London: Yale University Press, 1972–83).

Kaminsky, Howard, 'The Politics of France's Subtraction of Obedience from Pope Benedict XIII, 27 July, 1398', *Proceedings of the American Philosophical Society*, 115/5 (1971), 366–97.

—— *Simon de Cramaud and the Great Schism* (New Brunswick, NJ: Rutgers University Press, 1983).

Kantorowicz, Ernst, *The King's Two Bodies: A Study of Medieval Political Theology* (Princeton: Princeton University Press, 1957).

Kasper, W., *Theology and Church* (New York: Crossroad, 1969).

Kelly, J. N. D., *The Oxford Dictionary of the Popes* (Oxford and New York: Oxford University Press, 1986).

Kilmartin, E., 'Reception in History: An Ecclesiological Phenomenon and its Significance', *Journal of Ecumenical Studies*, 21 (1984), 34–54.

Kley, Dale K. Van, 'The Estates General as Ecumenical Council: The Constitutionalism of Corporate Consensus and the *Parlement*'s Policy of September 25, 1788', *Journal of Modern History*, 61 (1989), 1–52.

—— *The Religious Origins of the French Revolution: From Calvin to the Civil Constitution 1560–1791* (New Haven and London: Yale University Press, 1996).

Klotzner, Josef, *Kardinal Domenikus Jacobazzi und sein Konzilswerk* (Rome: Apud Aedes Universitatis Gregorianae, 1948).

Klueting, Harm, Hinske, Norbert, and Hengst, Karl, eds., *Katholische Aufklärung: Aufklärung in katholischen Deutschland* (Hamburg: Meiner, 1993).

Knecht, R. J., 'The Concordat of 1516: A Reassessment', *Birmingham University Historical Journal*, 9 (1963), 16–32.

Konzil der Einheit: 550. Jahrfeier des Konzils zu Konstanz (Karlsruhe: Badenia Verlag, 1964).

Küng, Hans, *Strukturen der Kirche* (Freiburg: Herder, 1962), tr. Salvatore Attanasio, *Structures of the Church* (New York: Thomas Nelson & Sons, 1964).

—— *Unfehlbar? Eine Aufrage* (Zürich: Benzinger, 1970), tr. Edward Quinn, *Infallibility? An Inquiry* (New York: Doubleday & Co., 1971).

—— ed., *Papal Ministry in the Church* (Concilium, 64, New York: Herder & Herder, 1971).

Kurtz, Lester R., *The Politics of Heresy: The Modernist Crisis in Roman Catholicism* (Berkeley: University of California Press, 1986).

Küry, Urs, *Die Altkatholische Kirche: Ihre Geschichte, ihre Lehre, ihr Anliegen* (Stuttgart: Evangelisches Verlagwerk, 1966).

Lagarde, Georges de, *La Naissance de l'esprit laïque au déclin du moyen âge*, new edn., 5 vols. (Paris and Louvain: Éditions E. Nauwelaerts, 1956–70).

Lane, Frederick C.,*Venice: A Maritime Republic* (Baltimore and London: Johns Hopkins University Press, 1973).

Latreille, C., *Joseph de Maistre et la papauté* (Paris: Hachette, 1906).

Lawson, George, *Politia Sacra et Civilis*, ed. C. Condren (Cambridge: Cambridge University Press, 1992).

Le Bras, Gabriel, ed., *Histoire du droit et des institutions de l'église en Occident*, 18 vols. (Paris: Sirey, 1956–84).

Lebrun, Richard A., *Throne and Altar: The Political and Religious Thought of Joseph de Maistre* (Ottawa: University of Ottawa Press, 1965).

—— Introduction to Joseph de Maistre, *The Pope*, tr. Aeneas McD. Dawson (New York: Howard Fertig, 1975).

—— ed., *Joseph de Maistre's Life, Thought, and Influence: Selected Studies* (Montreal and Kingston: McGill-Queen's University Press, 2001).

Lecler, Joseph, *Vienne* (Paris: Éditions de l'Orante, 1964). Vol. viii of *Histoire des conciles oecuméniques*, ed. G. Dumeige.

Leclerc, G., *Zeger-Bernard van Espen (1646–1728) et l'autorité ecclésiastique. Contribution à l'histoire des théories gallicanes et du jansénism* (Zürich: Pas Verlag, 1964).

Le Concile et les conciles: Contribution à l'histoire de la vie conciliare de l'Église (Chevetogne and Paris: Éditions de Chevetogne, 1960).

Leflon, Jean, *La Crise révolutionnaire: 1789–1846*. Vol. xx of *Histoire de l'Église*, ed. A. Fliche and V. Martin (Paris: Bloud & Gay, 1951).

Le Gros, Nicholas, *De renversement des libertez de l'église gallicane dans l'affaire de la constitution Unigenitus*, rev. edn., 2 vols. ([n.pl.], 1717).

—— *Memoire sur les droits du second ordre du clergé avec la tradition qui preuve les droits du second ordre* ([En France], 1773).

Lehmann, Paul, *Erforschung des Mittelalters*, 2 vols. (Leipzig: Hiersemann, 1959).

Leibniz [Gottfried, Wilhelm], *Political Writings*, tr. and ed. Patrick Riley, 2nd edn. (Cambridge: Cambridge University Press, 1988).

Lentze, Hans, and Gampl, Inge, eds., *Speculum Juris et Ecclesiarum: Festschrift für Willibald M. Plöchl zum 60. Geburtstag* (Vienna: Herder, 1967).

Le Plat, J., ed., *Monumentorum ad historiam concilii Tridentini spectantium collectio*, 5 vols. (Löwen, 1781).

Letters and Papers Foreign and Domestic of the Reign of Henry VIII, ed. J. S. Brewer, 22 vols. (London: Longman, Green, 1862–1932).

Lexikon für Theologie und Kirche, 2nd edn., 10 vols. (Freiburg: Herder, 1957–65); 3rd edn., 11 vols. (Freiburg: Herder, 1993–2001).

Liere, Katherine Elliot van, 'Vitoria, Cajetan, and the Conciliarists', *Journal of the History of Ideas*, 58 (1997), 597–616.

Luard, Henry R., ed., *Matthaei parisiensis chronica majora*, Rolls Series, 57, 7 vols. (London: Longman & Co., 1872–83).

Lunt, William E., *Papal Revenues in the Middle Ages*, 2 vols. (New York: Columbia University Press, 1934).

—— *Financial Relations of the Papacy with England*, 2 vols. (Cambridge, Mass.: Mediaeval Academy of America, 1939–62).

McBrien, Richard P., ed., *The Harper Collins Encyclopedia of Catholicism* (San Francisco: Harper, 1995).

—— *Lives of the Popes* (San Francisco: Harper San Francisco, 1997).

Macek, Josef, 'Le Mouvement conciliaire, Louis XI et Georges Podebrady', *Historica*, 15 (1967), 5–63.

—— 'Der Konziliarismus in den böhmischen Reformation, besonders in der Politik Georgs von Podiebrad', *Zeitschrift für Kirchengeschichte*, 80 (1969), 312–30.

McGrade, Arthur Stephen, *Richard Hooker and the Construction of Christian Community* (Tempe, Ariz.: Medieval and Renaissance Texts and Studies, 1997).

McIlwain, Charles H., *The Growth of Political Thought in the West* (New York: Macmillan Co., 1932).

McKisack, Mary, *The Fourteenth Century: 1307–1399* (Oxford: Oxford University Press, 1959).

McManners, John, *Church and State in Eighteenth-Century France*, 2 vols. (Oxford: Clarendon Press, 1998).

Maistre, Joseph de, *L'Église Gallicane dans son rapport avec le saint-siège* (Lyons: Librairie Catholique E. Vitte, 1931).

—— *Du pape*, ed. Jacques Lovie and Joanner Chétail (Geneva: Librairie Droz, 1966).

Malament, Barbara C., ed., *After the Reformation: Essays in Honor of J. H. Hexter* (Philadelphia: University of Pennsylvania Press, 1980).

[Manning], Henry Edward, Archbishop of Westminister, *The Temporal Mission of the Holy Ghost or Reason and Revolution* (London, 1865).

Mansi, J., *Sacrorum conciliorum nova et amplissima collectio*, 53 vols. (Leipzig, 1759–1927; Florence, 1724–1937).

Maret, Henri, *Du concile général et de la paix religieuse*, 2 vols. (Paris: Henri Plon, 1869).

—— *Le Pape et les évèques: Defense du livre sur le concile général et la paix religieuse* (Paris: Henri Plon, 1869).

—— *L'Église et l'état: Cours de Sorbonne inédit 1850–1851*, ed. Claude Bressolette (Paris: G. Beauchesne, 1979).

Margull, Hans J., ed., *The Councils of the Church: History and Analysis*, tr. Walter F. Bense (Philadelphia: Fortress Press, 1966).

Mariana, Juan de, *De rege et regis institutione* (Mainz, 1605).

Marsilius of Padua, *Defensor pacis*, ed. C. W. Previté-Orton (Cambridge: Cambridge University Press, 1928).

Martène, E., and Durand, V., eds., *Thesaurus Novus Anecdotorum*, 5 vols. (Paris, 1717).

—— *Veterum Scriptorum et Monumentorum . . . amplissima collectio*, 9 vols. (Paris, 1724–33).

Martimort, Aimé-Georges, *Le Gallicanisme de Bossuet* (Paris: Éditions du Cerf, 1953).

—— *L'Établissement du texte de la Defensio Declarationis de Bossuet* (Paris: Éditions du Cerf, 1956).

—— *Le Gallicanisme* (Paris: Presses Universitaires de France, 1973).

Martin, Victor, *Les Origines du Gallicanisme*, 2 vols. (Paris: Bloud & Gay, 1939).

Maxwell, John, *Sacro-sancta Regum Majestas: Or, The Sacred and Royal Prerogatives of Christian Kings* (Oxford, 1646).

Maxwell-Stuart, P. G., *Chronicle of the Popes: The Reign-by-Reign Record of the Papacy from St. Peter to the Present* (New York: Thames & Hudson, 1997).

Mayer, T., ed., *Die Welt zur Zeit des Konstanzer Konzils* (Constance and Stuttgart, 1965).

Mayer, Thomas F., 'Marco Mantova, a Bronze-Age Conciliarist', *Annuarium Historiae Conciliorum*, 14 (1984), 385–408.

—— 'Thomas Starkey, an Unknown Conciliarist at the Court of Henry VIII', *Journal of the History of Ideas*, 49 (1988), 207–27.

—— *Thomas Starkey and the Commonweal: Humanist Politics and Religion in the reign of Henry VIII* (Cambridge: Cambridge University Press, 1989).

Méchoulan, Henry, ed., *L'État Baroque: Regards sur la pensée politique de la France du premier XVIIe siècle* (Paris: Librairie Philosophique J. Vrin, 1985).

Mercati, Angelo, 'The New List of Popes', *Mediaeval Studies*, 9 (1947), 71–80.

Mesnard, Pierre, *L'Essor de la philosophie politique au XVIe siècle* (Paris: Ancienne Librairie Furme, Boivin, 1936).

Meuthen, Erich, 'Das Basler Konzil in römisch-katholischer Sicht', *Theologische Zeitschrift*, 38 (1982), 274–308.

[Mey, Claude, and Maultrot, Gabriel-Nicolas], *Apologie des jugements rendus en France contre le schisme par les Tribunaux séculiers*, 3rd edn., 3 vols. ([En France], 1753).

[—— et al.], *Maximes du droit public François, tirées des capitularies, des ordonnances du royaume, et les autres monuments de l'histoire de France*, 2nd edn., 2 vols. (Amsterdam, 1775).

Meyer, Jean, *Bossuet* (Paris: Plon, 1993).

Milward, P., *Religious Controversies of the Jacobean Age: A Survey of Printed Sources* (Lincoln, Neb., and London: University of Nebraska Press, 1978).

Minnich, Nelson H., 'Concepts of Reform Proposed at the Fifth Lateran Council', *Archivum Historiae Pontificiae*, 7 (1969), 163–251.

—— 'The Healing of the Pisan Schism (1511–13)', *Annuarium Historiae Conciliorum*, 13 (1981), 59–192.

Minnich, Nelson H., *et al.*, *Studies in Catholic History in Honor of John Tracy Ellis* (Wilmington, Del.: Glazier, 1985).

Mittarelli, J. B., and Costadoni, A., eds., *Annales Camaldulensis*, 9 vols. (Venice: Apud Jo Baptistam Pasquali, 1755–73).

Molho, A., and Tedeschi, J. A., eds., *Renaissance Studies in Honor of Hans Baron* (Dekalb, Ill.: Northern Illinois University Press, 1971).

Mollat, G., 'Jean XXII et le parler de *l'Isle de France*', *Annales de St Louis des Français*, 8 (1903), 89–91.

—— *The Popes at Avignon (1305–1378)*, tr. Janet Love (New York: Harper Torchbooks, 1963).

More, Thomas, *The Correspondence of Sir Thomas More*, ed. E. F. Rogers (Princeton: Princeton University Press, 1947).

—— *The Complete Works of St Thomas More*, ed. Louis A. Schuster *et al.*, 20 vols. (New Haven: Yale University Press, 1963–87).

Morrall, John B., *Gerson and the Great Schism* (Manchester: Manchester University Press, 1960).

—— *Political Thought in Medieval Times* (New York: Harper Torchbooks, 1962).

Morris, Christopher, *Political Thought in England: Tyndale to Hooker* (London and New York: Oxford University Press, 1953).

Morrissey, Thomas E., 'The Decree "Haec Sancta" and Cardinal Zabarella: His Role in its Formulation and Interpretation', *Annuarium Historiae Conciliorum*, 10 (1978), 145–76.

—— 'After Six Hundred Years: The Great Schism, Conciliarism, and Constance', *Theological Studies*, 40 (1979), 495–509.

Morton, Thomas, *An Exact Discoverie of Romish Doctrine in the Case of Conspiracie and Rebellion* (London, 1605).

Moynihan, James M., *Papal Immunity and Liability in the Writings of the Medieval Canonists* (Rome: Gregorian University Press, 1961).

Müller, Wolfgang, *et al.*, *The Church in the Age of Absolutism and Enlightenment*, tr. Gunther J. Holst (New York: Crossroad, 1981), vol. vi of *Handbook of Church History/History of the Church*, ed. H. Jedin and J. Dolan.

Mundy, John Hine, and Woody, Kennerly M., *The Council of Constance and the Unification of the Church*, tr. Louis Ropes Loomis (New York and London: Columbia University Press, 1961).

Murphy, Francis X., and MacEoin, Gary, *Synod of '67: A New Sound in Rome* (Milwaukee, Wis.: Bruce, 1968).

Murray, John Courtney, 'St Robert Bellarmine on the Indirect Power', *Theological Studies*, 9 (1948), 491–535.

—— 'The Political Thought of Joseph de Maistre', *Review of Politics*, 11 (1949), 63–86.

Murray, R. H., *The History of Political Science*, 2nd edn. (New York: D. Appleton & Co., 1930).

Nederman, Cary J., 'Conciliarism and Constitutionalism: Jean Gerson and Medieval Political Thought', *History of European Ideas*, 12 (1990), 189–209.

—— 'Constitutionalism—Medieval and Modern: Against Neo-Figgisite Orthodoxy (Again)', *History of Political Thought*, 17 (1996), 179–94.

Nédoncelle, M. *et al.*, *L'Ecclésiologie au XIXe siècle* (Paris: Éditions du Cerf, 1960).

Newman, John Henry, Cardinal, *An Essay on the Development of Christian Doctrine* (1878 edn.; London: Longmans, Green & Co., 1885).

Norman, Edward, *Roman Catholicism in England from the Elizabethan Settlement to the Second Vatican Council* (Oxford: Oxford University Press, 1988).

Nörr, Knut W., *Kirche und Konzil bei Nicolaus de Tudeschis* (Cologne and Graz: Böhlau, 1964).

Oakley, Francis, 'On the Road from Constance to 1688: The Political Thought of John Major and George Buchanan', *Journal of British Studies*, 1 (1962), 1–31.

—— 'Pierre d'Ailly and Papal Infallibility', *Mediaeval Studies*, 26 (1964), 353–8.

—— *The Political Thought of Pierre d'Ailly: The Voluntarist Tradition* (New Haven and London: Yale University Press, 1964).

—— 'Almain and Major: Conciliar Theory on the Eve of the Reformation', *American Historical Review*, 70 (1965), 673–90.

—— *Council over Pope? Towards a Provisional Ecclesiology* (New York: Herder & Herder, 1969).

—— 'Figgis, Constance, and the Divines of Paris', *American Historical Review*, 75 (1969), 368–86.

—— 'The "New Conciliarism" and its Implications: A Problem in History and Hermeneutics', *Journal of Ecumenical Studies*, 8 (1971), 815–40.

—— 'Conciliarism at the Fifth Lateran Council?', *Church History*, 41 (1972), 452–63.

—— 'Celestial Hierarchies Revisited: Walter Ullmann's Vision of Medieval Politics', *Past and Present*, 60 (1973), 3–48.

—— 'Conciliarism in the Sixteenth Century: Jacques Almain Again'. *Archiv für Reformationsgeschichte*, 68 (1977), 111–32.

—— *The Western Church in the Later Middle Ages* (Ithaca, NY, and London: Cornell University Press, 1979).

—— 'Natural Law, the *Corpus Mysticum*, and Consent in Conciliar Thought from John of Paris to Matthias Ugonius', *Speculum*, 56 (1981), 786–810.

—— 'The "Tractatus de Fide et Ecclesia, Romano Pontifice et Concilio Generali" of Johannes Breviscoxe', *Annuarium Historiae Conciliorum*, 14 (1982), 99–130.

—— *Omnipotence, Covenant, and Order: An Excursion in the History of Ideas From Abelard to Leibniz* (Ithaca, NY, and London: Cornell University Press, 1984).

—— 'Constance, Basel and the Two Pisas: The Conciliar Legacy in Sixteenth- and Seventeenth-Century England', *Annuarium Historiae Conciliorum*, 26 (1994), 1–32.

—— 'Nederman, Gerson, Conciliar Theory and Constitutionalism: *Sed Contra*', *History of Political Thought*, 16 (1995), 1–19.

Oakley, Francis, '"Anxieties of Influence": Skinner, Figgis, Conciliarism and Early Modern Constitutionalism', *Past and Present*, 151 (1996), 60–110.

—— 'Complexities of Context: Gerson, Bellarmine, Sarpi, Richer and the Venetian Interdict of 1606–1607', *Catholic Historical Review*, 82 (1996), 1–28.

—— 'Bronze-Age Conciliarism: Edmond Richer's Encounters with Cajetan and Bellarmine', *History of Political Thought*, 20 (1999), 65–86.

—— *Politics and Eternity: Studies in the History of Medieval and Early-Modern Political Thought* (Leiden: E. J. Brill, 1999).

Oberman, Heiko, 'Et tibi dabo claves regni coelorum', *Nederlands Theologisch Tijdschrift*, 39 (1975), 97–118.

Ockham, Guillelmi de, *Opera politica*, ed. J. G. Sykes, R. F. Bennet, and H. S. Offler, 3 vols. (Manchester: Manchester University Press, 1940–56).

O'Connell, Marvin, *Critics on Trial: An Introduction to the Catholic Modernist Crisis* (Washington, DC: Catholic University of America Press, 1994).

Orcibal, Jean, *Louis XIV contre Innocent XI, les appels au futur concile de 1688 et l'opinion française* (Paris: J. Vrin, 1949).

Owen, David, *Herod and Pilate Reconciled* (London, 1610).

Palanque, Jean-Rémy, *Catholiques Libéraux et Gallicans en France face au Concile du Vatican: 1867–70* (Aix-en-Provence: Ophrys, 1962).

Pantin, W. A., *The English Church in the Fourteenth Century* (Cambridge: Cambridge University Press, 1955).

Parker, Robert, *De Politeia Ecclesiastica Christi* (Frankfurt, 1616).

Parsons, Robert [ps. Philopater], *Elizabethae Angliae Reginae Haeresim Calvinianam propagantis saevissimum in Catholicas sui regni Edictum* (Lyons, 1592).

—— *A Treatise tending to Mitigation towards Catholicke Subiectes in England* (St Omer, 1607).

Partner, Peter, *The Papal State under Martin V* (London: British School at Rome, 1958).

Pascoe, Louis B., *Jean Gerson's Principles of Church Reform* (Leiden: E. J. Brill, 1973).

—— 'Theological Dimensions of Pierre d'Ailly's Teaching on the Papal Plenitude of Power', *Annuarium Historiae Conciliorum*, 11 (1979), 357–66.

Patterson, W. B., *King James VI and I and the Reunion of Christendom* (Cambridge: Cambridge University Press, 1997).

Pennington, Kenneth, *Pope and Bishops: The Papal Monarchy in the Twelfth and Thirteenth Centuries* (Philadelphia: University of Pennsylvania Press, 1984).

—— *The Prince and the Law 1200–1600: Sovereignty and Rights in the Western Legal Tradition* (Berkeley: University of California Press, 1993).

Pereiro, James, *Cardinal Manning: An Intellectual Biography* (Oxford: Oxford University Press, 1998).

Perez, Juan Beneyto, *Historia de las doctrinas politicas*, 4th edn. (Madrid: Arguilar, 1964).

Perron, Jacques Davy, *An Oration made on the Part of the Lordes Spirituall in the Chamber of the Third Estate* (St Omer, 1616).

Piccolomini, Aeneas Sylvius, *De Gestis Concilii Basiliensis Commentariorum. Libri II*, ed. D. Hay and W. K. Smith (Oxford: Clarendon Press, 1967).

Pichler, I. H., *Die Verbindlichkeit der Konstanzer Dekrete* (Vienna: Herder, 1967).

Picotti, G., 'La pubblicazione e i primi effetti della "Execrabilis" di Pio II', *Archivio della R. Società Romana di Storia Patria*, 37 (1914), 5–56.

Pighius, Albertus, *Hierarchiae ecclesiasticae assertio* (Cologne, 1538).

Pitzer, V., *Justinus Febronius* (Göttingen: Vandenhoeck & Ruprecht, 1976).

PL = Patrologiae cursus completus... *Series Latina*, ed. J. P. Migne, 331 vols. (Paris: 1884–1904).

Pocock, N., ed., *Records of the Reformation: The Divorce 1527–1533*, 2 vols. (Oxford: Clarendon Press, 1870).

Pollet, Vincent-Marie, 'Le Doctrine de Cajetan sur l'Église', *Angelicum*, 11 (1934), 514–32, and 12 (1935), 223–44.

Ponet, John, *A Shorte Treatise of Politicke Power* (1556). Facsimile reprint in W. S. Hudson, *John Ponet (1516?–1556): Advocate of Limited Monarchy* (Chicago: University of Chicago Press, 1942).

Pons-Ludon, Joseph-Antoine des Hédouin de, *Lettre d'un patriote à son amis, aspirent à la députation des Etats-généraux* (Rheims, 1789).

Posthumus Meyjes, G. H. M., *Jean Gerson—Apostle of Unity: His Church Politics and Ecclesiology* (Leiden: E. J. Brill, 1999).

Pottmeyer, Hermann Josef, *Unfehlbarkeit und Souveränität: Der päpstliche Unfehlbarkeit im System der ultramontanen Ekklesiologie des 19. Jahrhunderts* (Mainz: Matthias-Grunewald-Verlag, 1975).

Pouvoirs: Revue française d'études constitutionelle et politiques, 17 (1981): whole issue devoted to *Le Pouvoir dans l'Église*.

Préclin, E., *Les Jansenistes du XVIIIe siècle et la Constitution Civile du Clergé: La Developpement du richérisme. Sa propagation dans le Bas Clergé 1713–1791* (Paris: Librairie Universitaire J. Gamber, 1929).

——— 'Edmond Richer (1559–1631): Sa vie, Son œuvre et le Richérisme', *Revue d'histoire moderne*, 51 (1930), 241–9, 321–36.

Přerovský, O., *L'elezione di Urbano VI e l'insorgere della scisma d'Occidente* (Rome: Pressa la Società alla Biblioteca Vallicelliana, 1960).

Prodi, Paolo, *The Papal Prince: One Body and Two Souls: The Papal Monarchy in Early Modern Europe*, tr. Susan Haskins (Cambridge and New York: Cambridge University Press, 1987).

——— *Il sacramento del potere: Il giuramento politico nella storia costituzionale dell' Occidente* (Bologna: Il Mulino, 1992).

Prynne, William, *The Soveraigne Power of Parliaments and Kingdoms* (London, 1643).

Puyol, Edmond, *Edmond Richer: Étude historique et critique sur la Rénovation du Gallicanisme au commencement du XVIIe siècle*, 2 vols. (Paris: Th. Olmer Librairie, 1876).

Quinn, John R., *The Reform of the Papacy: The Costly Call to Christian Unity* (New York: Crossroad, 1999).

'Quirinus' [Ignaz von Döllinger], *Letters from Rome on the Council*. Authorized tr. of the text reprinted from the *Allgemeine Zeitung*, 2 vols. (London, 1870).

Raab, Heribert, *Die Concordata Nationis Germanicae in der kanonistischen Diskussion des 17. bis 19. Jahrhunderts* (Wiesbaden: F. Steiner, 1956).

—— 'Georg Christophe Neller und Febronius', *Archiv für mittelrhenische Kirchengeschichte*, 11 (1957), 185–206.

Rahner, Karl, and Ratzinger, Joseph, *Episkopat und Primat* (Freiburg: Herder, 1961).

Rainolds, William [Rossaeus], *De justa reipublicae Christianae in reges impios et haereticos authoritate* (Paris, 1590).

Renouard, Yves, *The Avignon Papacy: 1305–1403*, tr. Denis Bethell (Hamden, Conn.: Archon Books, 1970).

Riccardi, A., *Neogallicanismo e cattolicismo borghese: Henri Maret e il Concilio Vaticano I* (Bologna: Il Mulino, 1976).

Richental, Ulrich, *Ulrich Richental, Chronik des Constanzer Concils*, ed. M. R. Buck (Tübingen: Literarische Verein in Stuttgart, 1882).

Richer, Edmond, *Apologia pro Ecclesiae et Concilii auctoritate adversus Joannis Gersonii doctoris christianissimi obtrectatores* ([n.pl.], 1607).

—— *Defensio libelli de ecclesiastica et politica potestate* (Cologne, 1701).

Rijkel, Denys van, *Opera omnia*, 42 vols. (Tournai, 1896–1935).

Robertson, Ritchie, and Beniston, Judith, eds., *Catholicism and Austrian Culture* (Austrian Studies, 10, Edinburgh: Edinburgh University Press, 1999).

Rohden, Peter R., *Joseph de Maistre als politischer Theoretiker: Ein Beitrag zur Geschichte des Konservatives Staatsgedankers in Frankreich* (Munich: Verlag der Münchner Drucke, 1929).

Rueger, Zofia, 'Gerson, the Conciliar Movement and the Right of Resistance 1642–1644', *Journal of the History of Ideas*, 25 (1964), 467–80.

—— 'Gerson's Concept of Equity and Christopher St. German', *History of Political Thought*, 3 (1982), 1–30.

Russell, Conrad, *Parliaments and English Politics: 1621–1629* (Oxford: Clarendon Press, 1979).

Rutherford, Samuel, *Lex, Rex: The Law and the Prince* (London, 1644).

—— *The Due Right of Presbyteries: or, A Peacable Plea for the Government of the Church of Scotland* (London, 1644).

Sabine, George H., *A History of Political Theory*, rev. edn. (New York: Henry Holt & Co., 1956.

Saige, Guillaume, *Catéchisme du citoyen ou éléments du droit public françois* ([En France] 1788: 1st publ. 1773).

[Saige, Guillaume], *Code National, ou Manuel François à l'usage des trois Ordres, et principalement des députés aux prochains états-généraux* ([En France], 1789).

St German, Christopher, *A Dyalogue shewing what we be bounde to byleve as thinges necessary to salvacion and what not*, MS, Public Records Office, London, State Papers, Henry VIII, 6/2 Theological Tracts, 89–168.

St. German's Doctor and Student, ed., T. F. T. Plunkett and J. L. Barton (Publications of the Seldon Society, 91; London: B. Quaritch, 1976).

Salmon, J. H. M., *Renaissance and Revolt: Essays in the Intellectual and Social History of Early Modern France* (Cambridge: Cambridge University Press, 1987).

Sandquist, T. A., and Powicke, Michael, eds., *Essays in Medieval History for Presentation to Bertie Wilkinson* (Toronto: University of Toronto Press, 1969).

Sarpi, Paolo, *An Apology or Apologeticall Answer, Made by Father Paule a Venetian unto the Exceptions and objections of Cardinall Bellarmine against certain Treatises and Resolutions of John Gerson* (London, 1607).

—— *History of the Council of Trent*, tr. Nathaniel Brent (London, 1676).

—— *Opere*, ed. M. D. Busnelli and Giovanni Gambarin, 9 vols. (Bari: Gius Laterza e Figli, 1931–65).

—— *Paolo Sarpi: Lettere ai Gallicani*, ed. Boris Ulianich (Wiesbaden: F. Steiner, 1961).

Sawada, D. A., 'The Abortive Council of Mantua and Henry VIII', *Academia*, 27 (Nanzan Gakkai Nagoya, Japan, 1960), 1–15.

—— 'Two Anonymous Tudor Treatises on the General Council', *Journal of Ecclesiastical History*, 12 (1961), 197–214.

Scarisbrick, J. J., *Henry VIII* (Berkeley and Los Angeles: University of California Press, 1963).

Schardius, Simon, *De jurisdictione, autoritate, et praeeminentia imperiali, ac potestate ecclesiastica . . .* (Basle, 1566).

Schatz, Klaus, *Vatikanum I: 1869–70*, 3 vols. (Paderborn: F. Schöningh, 1993–4).

—— *Papal Primacy: From its Origins to the Present*, tr. John A. Otto and Linda M. Maloney (Collegeville, Minn.: Liturgical Press, 1996).

Schneider, Hans, *Das Konziliarismus als Problem der neueren Katholischen Theologie* (Berlin and New York: de Gruyter, 1976).

Scholz, Richard, ed., *Die Publizistik zur Zeit Philipps des Schönen und Bonifaz VIII* (Stuttgart: F. Enke, 1903).

—— ed., *Unbekannte kirchenpolitische Streitschriften aus der Zeit Ludwigs des Bayern (1327–1354)*, 2 vols. (Rome: Loescher, 1911–14).

Schwaiger, George, ed., *Konzil und Papst: Historische Beiträge zur Frage der höchsten Gewalt in der Kirche* (Munich: F. Schöningh, 1975).

Seidlmayer, M., *Die Anfänge des grossen abendländischen Schismas* (Münster: Aschendorff, 1940).

Sheldon, R., *Certain General Reasons, Proving the Lawfulnesse of the Oaths of Allegiance* (London, 1611).

Sieben, Hermann Josef, *Die Konzilsidee des lateinischen Mittelalters* (Paderborn: F. Schöningh, 1984).

—— *Die Katholische Konzilsidee von der Reformation bis zur Aufklärung* (Paderborn: F. Schöningh, 1988).

Sieben, Hermann Josef, *Katholische Konzilsidee im 19. und 20. Jahrhundert* (Paderborn: F. Schöningh, 1993).

Sigmund, Paul, 'The Influence of Marsilius of Padua on XVth-Century Conciliarism', *Journal of the History of Ideas*, 23 (1962), 392–402.

—— *Nicholas of Cusa and Medieval Political Thought* (Cambridge, Mass.: Harvard University Press, 1963).

Skinner, Quentin, 'Meaning and Understanding in the History of Ideas', *History and Theory*, 8 (1969), 3–53.

—— *Foundations of Modern Political Thought*, 2 vols. (Cambridge: Cambridge University Press, 1978).

Sommerville, Johan, *Politics and Ideology in England: 1603–1640* (London: Longman, 1986).

Spiegel, Gabrielle M., *Romancing the Past: The Rise of Vernacular Historiography in Thirteenth-Century France* (Berkeley: University of California Press, 1993).

State Papers of the Reign of Henry VIII, 2 vols. (London, 1830–52).

Stickler, Alfons M., 'Papal Infallibility: A Thirteenth-Century Invention', *Catholic Historical Review*, 60 (1974), 427–41.

—— 'Rejoinder to Professor Tierney', *Catholic Historical Review*, 61 (1975), 274–7.

Stieber, Joachim W., *Pope Eugenius IV, the Council of Basel, and the Secular and Ecclesiastical Authorities in the Empire: The Conflict over Supreme Authority and Power in the Church* (Leiden: E. J. Brill, 1978).

Stump, Phillip H., *The Reforms of the Council of Constance (1414–1418)* (Leiden: E. J. Brill, 1994).

Sullivan, Francis A., *Magisterium: Teaching Authority in the Catholic Church* (New York: Paulist Press, 1983).

Sutcliffe, Matthew, *A New Challenge made to N.D.* (London, 1600).

—— *De conciliis, et eorum authoritate, adversus Robertum Bellarminum* (London, 1600).

—— *The Subversion of Robert Parsons* (London, 1606).

Swanson, R. N., *Universities, Academics and the Great Schism* (Cambridge: Cambridge University Press, 1979).

Swidler, Leonard, *Aufklärung Catholicism 1780–1850: Liturgical and Other Reforms in the Catholic Aufklärung* (Missoula, Montana: Scholars Press, 1978).

Tallon, Alain, *La France et le Concile de Trente (1518–1563)* (Rome: École Française de Rome, 1997).

Tanner, Norman P., *The Councils of the Church* (New York: Crossroad, 1999).

The Catholic Encyclopedia, 14 vols. (New York: Robert Appleton Co., 1907–14).

The Jurist, 36/1–2 (1976). [Whole issue devoted to *The Church as Communio.*]

The New Encyclopedia Britannica, 15th edn. 32 vols. (Chicago: Encyclopedia Britannica, 1991).

Thomas, Jules, *Le Concordat de 1516*, 3 vols. (Paris: A. Picard, 1919).

Thysman, Raymond, 'Le Gallicanisme de Mgr. Maret et l'influence de Bossuet', *Revue d'histoire ecclésiastique*, 52 (1957), 401–65.

Tierney, Brian, 'Ockham, the Conciliar Theory, and the Canonists', *Journal of the History of Ideas*, 15 (1954), 40–70.

—— *Foundations of the Conciliar Theory: The Contribution of the Medieval Canonists from Gratian to the Great Schism* (Cambridge: Cambridge University Press, 1955); rev. edn. with discussion of subsequent literature (Leiden: E. J. Brill, 1998).

—— 'Pope and Council: Some New Decretist Texts', *Mediaeval Studies*, 19 (1957), 197–218.

—— *Origins of Papal Infallibility: 1150–1350* (Leiden: E. J. Brill, 1972).

—— 'On the History of Papal Infallibility: A Discussion with Remigius Bäumer', *Theologische Revue*, 70 (1974), 185–93.

—— 'Infallibility and the Medieval Canonists: A Discussion with Alfons Stickler', *Catholic Historical Review*, 61 (1975), 265–73.

—— '"Divided Sovereignty" at Constance: A Problem of Medieval and Early Modern Political Theory', *Annuarium Historiae Conciliorum*, 7 (1979), 238–56.

—— *Religion, Law, and the Growth of Constitutional Thought: 1150–1650* (Cambridge: Cambridge University Press, 1982).

—— 'The Idea of Representation in the Medieval Councils of the West', *Concilium*, 19 (1983), 25–30.

Tillard, J. M. R., *The Bishop of Rome*, tr. John de Satgé (Wilmington, Del.: Michael Glazier, 1983).

—— *Church of Churches: The Ecclesiology of Communion*, tr. R. C. De Peaux (Collegeville, Minn.: Liturgical Press, 1992).

Torquemada, Juan de, *Summa de ecclesia* (Rome, 1489).

Tournély, Honoré, *Praelectiones Theologicae de Ecclesia Christi quas in Scholis Sorbonicis Habuit*, 2nd edn., 2 vols. (Paris, 1739).

Trexler, Richard, 'Rome on the Eve of the Great Schism', *Speculum*, 42 (1967), 480–509.

Ullmann, Walter, *The Origins of the Great Schism: A Study in Fourteenth-Century Ecclesiastical History* (London: Burns, Oates, & Washbourne, 1948).

—— *Medieval Papalism: The Political Theories of the Medieval Canonists* (London: Methuen, 1949).

—— *The Growth of Papal Government in the Middle Ages* (London: Methuen, 1955).

—— *Principles of Government and Politics in the Middle Ages* (London: Methuen, 1961).

—— *A History of Political Thought in the Middle Ages* (Harmondsworth: Penguin Books, 1965).

—— Review of Francis Oakley, *The Political Thought of Pierre d'Ailly*, *Renaissance News*, 18 (1965), 305–7.

Vallauri, Luigi L., and Dilcher, Gerhard, eds., *Cristianesimo, secolarizzazione, e diritto moderno*, 2 vols. (Baden-Baden and Milan: Nomos Verlagsgesellschaft, Giuffre, 1981).

Vansteenberghe, Edmond, *Le Cardinal Nicolas de Cues (1401–1464)* (Paris: H. Champion, 1920).

Vigener, F., 'Gallikanismus und episkopalistische Strömungen', *Historische Zeitschrift*, 111 (1913), 495–558.

Vincke, J., 'Acta Concilii Pisani', *Römische Quartalschrift*, 46 (1938), 81–331.

Villoslada, Ricardo Garcia, *La Universidad de Paris durante los estudios de Francisco de Vitoria, O. P.: 1507–1522* (Rome: Apud aedes Universitatis Gregorianae, 1938).

Viterbo, James of, *De regimine Christiano*, ed. H. X. Arquillière, *Le Plus Ancien Traité de l'église: Jacques de Viterbo, De regimine christiano 1301–1302* (Paris: Beauchesne, 1926).

Vitoria, Francisco de, *Francisco de Vitoria: Political Writings*, ed. Anthony Pagden and Jeremy Lawrence (Cambridge: Cambridge University Press, 1991).

Vooght, Paul de, 'Le Conciliarisme aux Conciles de Constance et de Bâle', in B. Botte *et al.*, *Le Concile et les conciles* (Paris: Éditions de Chevetogne, 1960), 143–81.

—— 'Le Concile oecuménique de Constance et le conciliarisme', *Istina*, 9 (1963), 57–86.

—— 'Le Conciliarisme aux conciles de Constance et de Bâle (Compléments et précisions)', *Irénikon*, 36 (1963), 61–75.

—— *Les Pouvoirs du concile et l'autorité du pape au concile de Constance* (Paris: Éditions du Cerf, 1965).

—— 'Les Controverses sur les pouvoirs du concile et l'autorité du pape au Concile de Constance', *Revue théologique de Louvain*, 1 (1970), 45–75.

Warmington, W., *A Moderate Defense of the Oath of Allegiance* ([n.pl.], 1612).

Watanabe, Morimichi, *The Political Ideas of Nicholas of Cusa, with Special Reference to his Concordantia Catholica* (Geneva: Droz, 1963).

—— *Concord and Reform: Nicholas of Cusa and Legal and Political Thought in the Fifteenth Century*, ed. Thomas M. Izbicki and Gerald Christianson (Aldershot: Ashgate/Variorum, 2001).

Watkin, E. I., *Roman Catholicism in England: From the Reformation to 1950* (New York: Oxford University Press, 1957).

Watt, John A., 'The Constitutional Law of the College of Cardinals: Hostiensis to Johannes Andreae', *Mediaeval Studies*, 33 (1971), 127–57.

Widdrington, R., *A Cleare, Sincere and Modest Confutation of the unsound, fraudulent and intemperate reply of . . . Mr. Thomas Fitzherbert* ([n.pl.], 1616).

Wilks, Michael J., *The Problem of Sovereignty in the Later Middle Ages* (Cambridge: Cambridge University Press, 1963).

Willaert, Léopold, *Après le concile de Trente: La Restauration catholique: 1563–1648*. Vol. xviii of *Histoire de l'Église*, ed. A. Fliche and V. Martin (Paris: Bloud & Gay, 1960).

Wright, A. D., 'Why the Venetian Interdict?', *English Historical Review*, 89 (1974), 536–50.

Zabarella, Francisco, *Acutissimi Jurisconsulti . . . Francisci Zabarellis Cardinalis Florentini . . . de ejus temporis Schismate Tractatus* (Strasbourg, 1609).

Zagano, Phyllis, and Tilley, Terrence W., eds., *The Exercise of the Primacy: Continuing the Dialogue* (New York: Crossroad, 1998).

Index

65150004R00176

Made in the USA
Middletown, DE
01 September 2019